Pavel Axelrod and the Development of Menshevism

Russian Research Center Studies, 70

Hoover Institution Publications 115

Pavel Axelrod and the

Abraham

The Hoover Institution
on War, Revolution and Peace

Development of Menshevism

Ascher

Harvard University Press
Cambridge, Massachusetts   1972

Printed in the United States of America

The Russian Research Center of Harvard University is supported by a grant from the Ford Foundation. The center carries out interdisciplinary study of Russian institutions and behavior and related subjects.

Hoover Institution Publications 115

Library of Congress Catalog Card Number 72-78423

SBN 674-65905-8

To Anna

Acknowledgments

I should like to express my appreciation to several institutions whose financial support made possible the research for this biography: the American Council of Learned Societies, the Hoover Institution on War, Revolution, and Peace, the Rockefeller Foundation, and the Russian Research Center at Harvard University. The Russian Research Center and the Hoover Institution, where I spent many months doing research and writing, were ideal settings for scholarly work. The staffs made every effort to facilitate my work.

I am also grateful to the International Institute for Social History in Amsterdam and the Verein für Geschichte der Arbeiterbewegung in Vienna for giving me access to their rich archival collections. The late Mr. Boris Nicolaevsky and Miss Anna Bourguina went out of their way to make available all pertinent material in the Nicolaevsky Collection on deposit at the Hoover Institution and in many other ways helped me to understand Russian Social Democracy and Menshevism. Professor Leopold Haimson and Mr. Ladis Kristof were equally helpful in allowing me to consult the holdings of the Inter-University Project on the History of the Menshevik Movement at Columbia University. I also wish to thank the late Professor Philip E. Mosely and Mr. Lev Magerovsky who gave me access to material in the Archive of Russian and East European History and Culture at Columbia University. Finally, I should like to express my gratitude to Mr. Alexandre Axelrod and Mr. George Garvy for providing me with documents from their private collections.

Several colleagues and friends read the manuscript, and each made valuable suggestions for its improvement: Abraham Eisenstadt, Julian Franklin, Solomon Goldstein, Guenter Lewy, Allen McConnell, Richard Pipes, and Marc Raeff. I owe more than I can express in words to my wife, Anna Schaffer Ascher, who has read the manuscript almost as frequently as I have, and whose recommendations for editorial and substantive changes contributed greatly to turning it into what I hope is a readable book. Needless to say, I alone am responsible for the book's defects.

Contents

Pavel Axelrod and the Development of Menshevism

Prologue

Few subjects in modern Russian history have been so intensively explored as the evolution of Marxism in the years from 1883 to 1917. Much of the literature is tendentious or unreliable, but a remarkably large proportion is of high scholarly quality. Even persons who do not know Russian now have access to an impressive list of ideological studies, party histories, and biographies, not to mention numerous monographs and articles on specialized problems. In view of this plethora of published works, it might be appropriate to explain why I chose to write a biography of Pavel Borisovich Axelrod.

I was drawn to Axelrod because I believed that a study of his intellectual and political career would enlarge our understanding of Menshevism, the movement within Russian Marxism that from 1903 to 1917 was the major rival of Bolshevism for labor support. Although in recent years Western historians have begun to study Menshevism in depth, they have, for understandable reasons, paid it much less attention than Leninism. In Russia the subject has been in official disfavor, and the source material has not been easily available. It seems to me, however, that in the history of politics the study of men who have failed can often be instructive, which is certainly true of the Mensheviks.

Lenin formulated many of his positions in direct response to challenges emanating from within the Marxist camp, most notably from the Mensheviks. Frequently his views on specific issues make little sense without reference to the arguments and policies of his adversaries. From 1903 to 1917 it was, moreover, by no means a foregone conclusion that he would emerge as the major figure in Russian Marxism, let alone as the ruler of Russia. On the contrary, there were occasions when it appeared that the Mensheviks would succeed in dominating the Social Democratic

1

party, and for much of 1917 they exercised far more influence over the working class and in the country at large than did the Bolsheviks. Indeed, it can be argued that Menshevik policies and blunders in 1917 contributed as much to the Bolshevik triumph as did the actions of the Leninists themselves.

No one played a more central role than Axelrod in shaping the political perceptions and tactics[1] that came to be the hallmark of Menshevism. On all the questions that separated the two factions—the organization and structure of the party, the nature of the revolution against the autocracy, the relationship between the working class and the bourgeoisie —Axelrod's views ultimately predominated among the Mensheviks, at least until Lenin's seizure of power. He was not the only spokesman for Menshevism; nor was he the party's main political leader. But he was the party's chief ideologist and tactician, and he established the theoretical underpinnings of many of its most important political positions. He contributed more than any other party member to the development of Menshevism into a distinct ideological, as against merely political, current within revolutionary Marxism.

Because Axelrod was concerned, above all, with tactics, an examination of his ideas and proposals brings into sharp relief the practical problems that arose from the attempt to introduce Marxism into Russia, a country meeting none of the economic, social, and political conditions that Marx had in mind when he devised his doctrines. Virtually everything Axelrod wrote from the 1880's until 1917 was designed to adapt a Western political strategy, which he had mastered during his long stay in Europe, to the peculiarities of the Russian situation. Though thoroughly inventive and sophisticated, the endeavor suffered from obvious defects and weaknesses. The very effort to create a democratic proletarian party in an autocratic police state was bound to be painful and problematical. It is not surprising that a number of Russian Marxists challenged Axelrod's conceptions (several of which were based on ideas first advanced by Georgii Plekhanov), and so provoked some of the most dramatic and

---

1. In this study the words "tactics" and "strategy" are used interchangeably. In the lexicon of early Russian Marxism no clear distinction was drawn between the two terms. Because the movement enjoyed so little opportunity to participate in the political process, leaders rarely felt the need to be concerned with day-to-day policies and actions, which are usually subsumed under the heading of tactics. Axelrod and other Russian Marxists of his time believed that in devising a political program for advancing the cause of socialism they were dealing with tactical questions.

momentous splits in the movement. In the attendant debates both Axelrod and his opponents were forced to clarify their positions, and analyses of these discussions illuminate the issues that were at stake and provide clues as to why Russian Marxism developed as it did.

Axelrod was acutely aware of the direct connection between tactics and ideology. This awareness led him to conclude, sooner than most Marxists, that Lenin's tactics, far from being merely minor and temporary innovations, implied a basic revision of doctrine. Thus, in 1906, by which time his tactical differences with Lenin encompassed several issues, he characterized Bolshevik policies as "a putschist-conspiratorial approach, as a mixture of anarchist and Blanquist tendencies, concealed under Marxist or Social Democratic phraseology"—a description that at the time seemed farfetched to some, but by 1917 turned out to have been remarkably prophetic.

An examination of Axelrod's political and intellectual career also illuminates several other radical currents in Russia. Active in revolutionary movements as early as the 1870's, he was initially a Bakuninist, then a *Chernoperedelets* (Black Partitionist), and in 1883 became a founder of Russian Marxism, whose organizational structure and tactics he helped determine during the following two decades. Such reevaluations of basic commitments and changes in political direction were common occurrences, especially during the 1870's and 1880's, and Axelrod's experiences of those years yield further insight into the political restlessness of the radical intelligentsia. But Axelrod's earliest involvement in political affairs deserves scrutiny for yet another reason.

There is a direct link between the political ideas that he adopted during the 1870's and the kind of Marxism to which he subscribed from 1883 until his death in 1928. It is therefore necessary to trace in some detail the steps by which he reached his final position. For several years he groped for a comprehensive political program and, like many of his colleagues, simultaneously held contradictory views. It was only gradually, as a result of long and sometimes tedious debates with comrades, that he was able to sort out his opinions and settle on a consistent program. Some of these polemical discussions seemed to revolve around minor points and, in fact, resemble talmudic exercises by a small number of individuals who were pathetically impotent and divorced from the realities of life in Russia. Yet it is important to keep in mind that these arguments engendered a set of ideas that within four decades inspired the most momentous revolution of the twentieth century. I am not, of course, suggesting that the revolution was caused by ideas alone, but they were a necessary prerequisite.

The radicals of the 1870's were agitated by several important questions, but the one that most troubled Axelrod was to haunt the revolutionary intelligentsia for decades to come: Given Russia's general backwardness (as compared to Western Europe), the lack of a strong and politically assertive middle class, the absence of civil liberties and political freedom, and the low cultural niveau of the people, how could a revolutionary party hope to be effective? Should it devote itself to mobilizing mass support and, if so, how? Or should it concentrate on training a radical elite that would somehow deal a deathblow to the archaic autocracy? The choice of one or the other alternative could not, as Axelrod realized, be made simply on the basis of the pragmatic criterion of effectiveness. The choice bore long-term implications: it would not only determine the nature of the revolutionary movement, but ultimately that of Russian society on the morrow of the revolution.

Axelrod's revolutionary impulse stemmed from his desire to help emancipate "the people" from their economic burdens as well as from their spiritual and moral bondage. The more he contemplated this goal during the 1870's the more he sensed that it could be achieved only if the masses were transformed into autonomous and conscious actors in the political arena. It was also this conviction that became the most distinctive feature of his Marxism and, in time, proved decisive in distinguishing his position from Lenin's elitism.

Aside from his ideological contributions, Axelrod is a particularly appealing personality, in many ways unique among leading revolutionaries of the late nineteenth and early twentieth centuries. Born into a poor family, he enjoyed none of the social or educational advantages that were the heritage of most eminent radicals. These origins no doubt made it easier for him than for his comrades fully to identify with "the people" who were the object of the radicals' concern. Axelrod was also somewhat unusual among Russian Marxist leaders in that he was less intolerant and contentious than most. Personal prestige and power were not of paramount concern to him. Yet he could be firm and even obstinate in his refusal to compromise his beliefs.

My biography of Axelrod was greatly facilitated by the availability of a rich repository of sources. Axelrod had the Marxist's keen sense of history and consequently took pains to preserve his private letters, manuscripts, and documents. But unlike most other Russian revolutionaries, he was rather sedentary. Except for a year, 1906–1907, and a few months in 1917, he lived in the West continuously from 1880 until 1928, generally in Switzerland. As a result, he was one of the few émigrés who did not lose much of his huge archive. And, fortunately for the historian, Axelrod was a diligent correspondent who maintained contact with many Russian as well as European socialists. In addition to yielding a fair amount of information about Axelrod's private life and his relations with friends, the archival sources are useful in providing evidence on the attitudes of foreign Marxists (mainly German) toward the Russian radicals, attitudes that on several occasions were decidedly important.

At all times I have focused on Axelrod himself—his personality, his evolution from Bakuninism to Menshevism, and his role in the revolutionary movement. But in order to render his ideas and actions intelligible and to demonstrate their significance, I have had to devote considerable attention to the positions and conduct of his adversaries and followers, more, in fact, than I had initially intended. My biography is therefore somewhat more than the story of one man's life. It encompasses the pertinent details about several groups of radicals, and in the sections dealing with the period after 1883, it is to a certain extent a study of the Marxist leadership, at least with respect to those issues that vitally concerned Axelrod. For the years after 1903, when he reached the pinnacle of his influence, I have found it necessary to give a brief account of the Menshevik party.

I have, of course, made extensive use of secondary sources for this background material, but at the same time I have tried to avoid detailed consideration of topics already treated by scholars. I have also tried to keep to a minimum discussions of the general history of Russia, which is easily available. Whenever I did deal at length with problems that have already been thoroughly discussed I did so because I believed that by exploring them from Axelrod's vantage point I could unravel some knotty issue or offer a new interpretation. Some overlap with other studies was therefore inescapable. Axelrod was involved in so many different movements and controversies that scholars working in various areas of Russian radicalism have already examined certain phases of his political career.

My purpose has been to describe and analyze the totality of his work: to locate the sources and nature of his radicalism, to distinguish between and account for the temporary and permanent aspects of his political outlook, and to assess his contributions to the revolutionary tradition and, in particular, to the development of Menshevism.

I | In Search of a Cause

Pavel Borisovich Axelrod was one of the few early leaders of Russian Marxism to come from the lower classes. His father, Baruch, was orphaned while young and seems to have had practically no formal education. Like most poor Jews in the Empire, Baruch was illiterate in Russian, but had mastered the rudiments of Yiddish, the language spoken in the Axelrod home. He also managed to read his Hebrew prayers, though he had little understanding of their meaning. Still, he was pious and observant, convinced that in the hereafter God would compensate all the Jewish poor for their deprivations and sufferings on earth.[1]

As a young man Baruch earned his livelihood by working as an unskilled laborer for a Jewish leaseholder. After marrying his employer's niece, he borrowed money from Jewish usurers to start his own business, a tavern, but his profits were meager, and he could barely support a family. His wife, also orphaned at an early age and illiterate, appears to have been a woman of considerable intelligence, initiative, and inner strength. She never complained about her lot and was quick to take advantage of every opportunity to make life easier for her children.

The Axelrods were obviously not the kind of people who kept records, and consequently Pavel Borisovich was never certain either of the place or date of his birth. He was reasonably sure that he had been born in 1849 or 1850 in a village not far from Pochep, a small town in the

---

1. The principal source for this chapter is Axelrod's autobiography, *Perezhitoe i peredumannoe* (Berlin, 1923). Written when Axelrod was in his seventies, the autobiography is hazy on certain events and probably inaccurate on some others. But like many old people, Axelrod vividly recalled numerous experiences in his childhood, and the reader cannot but be moved by the candor and humanity of the account. The volume ends with the year 1883.

Ukrainian province of Chernigov. His earliest and clearest recollection was that fear dominated the household. Pavel's father lived in perennial dread of the usurers, for he found it impossible to meet his payments. He also feared the police because he lacked the passport needed to live in the village. As soon as he heard that the district policeman was nearby he would go into hiding. Baruch's illegal situation made him particularly apprehensive about contact with the authorities. But all the villagers were awed by members of the privileged classes whom they considered "omnipotent." The sight of a well-dressed person or merely one who wore a cockade in his hat would cause them to take off their caps and bow down before him. The servility of the common people made a disagreeable impression on young Pavel, and during his adult life he frequently referred to it with aversion. The desire to encourage the people to shake off this deeply rooted trait became one of the wellsprings of his reformist zeal.

During the 1850's the Axelrod family was constantly on the move. When writing his memoirs Axelrod could no longer remember why: he supposed his father had failed to pay the rent or the landlord had found a tenant willing to pay more. On several occasions the hungry family of six was forced to roam the streets without knowing where to look for shelter. In those years "a glass of plain tea with a slice of a roll was an extremely unusual luxury, which the children enjoyed only on those occasions when they were recovering from a serious illness."[2] As the only Jews in the villages in which they settled, the Axelrods were completely cut off from the other inhabitants. Pavel was the firstborn, and for some time at least he must have been totally isolated. In his memoirs he says nothing about his relationship with his two younger brothers and sister. All that he mentions about his activities as a small child is that he spent most of his days in the family hut or on the dusty road outside.

The sole relief from this monotonous existence came on religious holidays, when his father would take him to a neighboring village to attend communal prayers. At the services there were new faces, people to talk to. But the conversation of the adults always centered on one subject: the miseries of human existence. There was constant speculation about the additional hardships the local landowner or district police

2. Quoted in Alexander Potresov, *P. B. Aksel'rod (sorok piat' let obshchestvennoi deiatel'nosti)* (St. Petersburg, 1914), p. 7. Potresov wrote the biographical sections mainly on the basis of information supplied by Axelrod.

officer might impose on the poor. Invariably the conversation ended with a general declaration, in which all concurred, that they must endure their suffering because the Lord had willed it.

In 1858 or 1859 the Axelrods moved to Shklov in the Mogilev province, where Baruch owned a one-room apartment, which he had apparently inherited. Pavel's parents made the 150-mile journey on foot, the children and belongings in a cart drawn by a lame horse they had bought from a gypsy. Though Shklov was a much larger and more interesting town than any in which the family had previously lived—it had a Jewish population of over 10,000—the move did not change the fortunes of the Axelrods. Quite the contrary. Soon after they arrived the apartment burned down, and all six were forced to live in a poorhouse run by the Jewish community. The father could not find steady work and from time to time accepted charity.

Pavel owed his secular education to an ironic combination of circumstances: his father's poverty and the tsarist regime's anti-Semitism. Normally, in mid-nineteenth-century Russia, a Jewish child was exposed to religious training only. He would be taught to read Hebrew, and if the family could afford it he might go on to study the various commentaries on the Bible and the Talmud. Few Jews attended secular schools: in 1840, out of 80,017 children in the country's primary and secondary schools, where there was a strong emphasis on "Christian teaching," only forty-eight were Jewish. In 1844, however, the government embarked on a program to increase Jewish exposure to secular learning by establishing secular schools in the Pale of Settlement,[3] to be limited to Jewish students and financed by special taxes imposed on Jews. Although the teachers could be Jewish, the principals could not, and instruction was to be in Russian. The purpose of the new institutions, as most Jews suspected, was to undermine the religious beliefs of young Jews and ultimately to "merge" them with the Christian population.

A good many such schools were created, but attendance was miniscule.[4] The supervisor of the new school in Shklov, however, was an ambitious

---

3. The Pale of Settlement, established in a series of decrees issued from 1773 to 1791, was the area in the western and southwestern provinces of the Empire in which Jews were allowed to reside. Travel to other parts of the Empire required a special permit.

4. Louis Greenberg, *The Jews in Russia* (New Haven, 1944), I, 32–33, 40–41.

official who insisted on enrolling a certain minimum number. The dignitaries of the Jewish community, anxious to protect their own offspring from spiritual contamination, therefore worked out a peculiar arrangement: a few children from poor families were chosen to meet the quota, and in return the well-to-do provided them with food and clothing. An offer was made to Pavel's mother to enroll her oldest son in the program. Fortunately for the future leader of Marxism, Baruch was away at the time, for he surely would have refused such a sacrilegious exchange which, among other things, involved the cutting of Pavel's "peis" (long sidelocks worn by religious Jews). But Pavel's mother could not resist the opportunity of providing her son with an adequate amount of food and clothing and, no less important to her, an education. Pavel received his new clothing and set out to study secular subjects. Some sixty-odd years later Axelrod declared that "Even now I can still remember quite vividly the pleasure I felt wearing the warm shabby fur coat and boots."[5]

The three years Pavel spent at the school were not spectacular in any way, but they did broaden his horizon somewhat. His life in the villages had been sheltered, and even in Shklov he had known only Jews. Jews and Gentiles lived in separate parts of the city and there was little contact between them. It was understandable that Pavel had assimilated the usual stereotypes about the unfriendly intentions of strangers. He was somewhat surprised to discover that among the "goyim" there were people who were "not only not hostile to Jews, not only not cruel, but even kind to Jews." The first person he met with these qualities was the principal of his school, who treated Pavel with great tenderness; in his old age Axelrod remembered him with "deep gratitude and fondness." In 1862 Axelrod was graduated with distinction and awarded a prize for his outstanding performance. At this time Pavel learned from a friend that in distant cities there were schools in which instructors were very learned people, known as professors, "who teach not from books, but from their own heads." This excited the boy who determined to enroll in one of these mysterious schools, but he soon found that first he would have to spend a few years at a gymnasium. Mogilev was the nearest city with a gymnasium, and so the twelve-year-old Pavel decided to go there to continue his studies, even though the only resident he knew was an uncle with whom his family does not seem to have had much contact.

5. Axelrod, *Perezhitoe*, pp. 23–24.

Once again his father had gone to another town to find work and thus could not shield Pavel from further exposure to secular influences. With thirty-five kopeks in his pocket the lad walked the fifteen miles from Shklov to Mogilev, his only fear being that he might encounter wolves in the woods through which he had to pass. Once in Mogilev he had to wait several weeks before taking the entrance examination for the gymnasium. He had no money to rent a room, but was so determined to pursue his studies that he stayed on, sleeping in wagons in the courtyards of inns and occasionally indoors on an empty bench. For a time his uncle provided him with shelter in a dark basement room. Finally, Pavel took the examination, passed, and was ready to begin study in the gymnasium. But he now came up against a new obstacle: he needed money to pay the school fees and to buy the full-dress coat traditionally worn by Russian students. By chance he met some comfortably situated Jews of liberal persuasion who came to his rescue by giving him the needed funds.

In his autobiography Axelrod does not discuss the reasons for the exceptional persistence, initiative, and independence he displayed as a youngster of twelve or thirteen. The evidence is so scanty that we can only speculate about the sources of these personal qualities. His passion for secular learning does not seem to have grown out of a conscious rebellion against his religion or cultural milieu. He did yearn, however, for contact with people who were somehow different from those with whom he normally associated, which suggests that he felt a certain dissatisfaction with the monotony of his limited experiences. This ennui may have been a compelling factor underlying his willingness to endure so many hardships for the sake of an education.

In addition to curiosity, young Pavel owed another character trait to his early upbringing, and that is what might be called the Jewish ethic: a stress on spiritual values and learning. In Shklov he had studied at the synagogue, where one teacher profoundly moved and excited him. This teacher was given to delivering philippics against new tendencies of any kind and denounced Jews who shortened their frock coats and adopted new hair styles; he attributed these innovations to an excessive concern with creature comforts and possessions. In his attacks on the deviants he emphasized the superiority of spiritual over material values, a doctrine with which Pavel found himself in accord, even though he did not fully understand the details of the teacher's denunciations. "In part," wrote

Axelrod, "the impressions that the first years of my life in the countryside had made on me psychologically prepared me to worship everything spiritual and to scorn everything that was purely material, superficial." Axelrod believed, quite correctly, that this notion of the superiority of the spiritual over the material—values he then regarded as mutually antagonistic—left a deep imprint on his personality and remained an integral part of his outlook throughout his life.

Later, of course, he radically changed the "content, character, and direction" of the principle expounded by the religious leader in Shklov.[6] But it may be that even the young boy who surmounted enormous difficulties to enroll in the gymnasium in Mogilev did not identify spiritual values merely with religious dogmas and a religious code of personal behavior. It would seem that he had already broadened the meaning of these values to include devotion to secular intellectual pursuits.

Pavel's stay in Mogilev marked a turning point in his intellectual development. It was not that the gymnasium was particularly stimulating. Rather, he found schoolwork somewhat boring. The teachers were not interested in their subjects, and the "entire system of instruction was penetrated by a spirit of deadening routine and bureaucratic formalism." There was, nevertheless, an occasional lively teacher who recommended books to him. He read N. M. Karamzin, V. G. Belinsky, and I. S. Turgenev, whose work introduced him to a world of culture he did not suspect existed. It was only then that he learned about such diverse things as the recently abolished institution of serfdom and the marvelous new invention, the railroad. He chanced upon a popular book on astronomy, whose contents led him to question certain of his religious beliefs. He was tormented and passionately prayed to God to restore his faith. But his call for divine intervention remained unanswered, and his religious commitment faltered, though for a time he continued to observe the Jewish laws.

Axelrod was an outstanding student; consequently his teachers recommended him as tutor to children of well-to-do Jews. Within a few months he was earning his room and board and living in greater comfort than he had ever known. He quickly became very popular among his pupils, especially because he engaged them in discussions about the "religion, national traditions, customs, and prejudices" of the Jewish people. He

6. *Ibid.*, p. 29.

enjoyed his work, and gradually came to conceive of himself as something of a missionary whose task was to introduce Russian culture to Jewish youngsters. Many of the students, already in rebellion against parental authority, welcomed Axelrod's "blasphemous talk" and began to look upon him as their intellectual mentor.

The Jewish community of Mogilev had been influenced by the enlightenment then flowering in Kiev and Odessa, and a number of the more progressive citizens were interested in secular Hebrew literature, science, and Russian and German culture. But they had not broken with traditional Judaism, and there was a point beyond which they would not tolerate heterodoxy. So alarmed were they by the proselytizing of the tutor that they charged him with misguiding the town's children and exercising a "pernicious influence" over them. He was said to encourage children to smoke on the Sabbath and advocate laxity in the relations between the sexes. Axelrod actually urged his pupils and friends not to be publicly defiant, in part because he feared that violations of rules and customs would harm the cause of Jewish enlightenment. When it was pointed out that Pavel himself did not flout public sensibilities or in any way behave like a "malicious heretic," the parents dismissed that evidence. The students who openly misbehaved, they contended, "are simply impudent fellows and idiots, but Axelrod is a real heretic and therefore much more dangerous for our children."

The hostility toward Axelrod reached its apex when it became known that a local boy had converted to Greek Orthodoxy. An uncle of the boy had visited Axelrod and urged him to use his influence to prevent the conversion. Axelrod did make an effort to dissuade the boy from carrying out his wishes, but his appeal went unheeded. Although Axelrod was in no way responsible for the conversion, the Jewish parents blamed him for contaminating their children and relieved him of his duties as their tutor. Stripped of his livelihood, he left Mogilev without completing his studies at the gymnasium.

He decided to move to a nearby town, Nezhin, where people were reputedly more receptive to advanced views. After some initial difficulties in obtaining work, he again began to tutor and prepare for the entrance examination to the lycée. Then a new crisis developed. A teacher in Mogilev, N. I. Khlebnikov, who had been well disposed toward Axelrod, wired that he would be drafted into the army if he did not immediately reenter the gymnasium. In a recruitment drive in

Shklov the community leaders had decided to surrender the heretical Axelrod rather than a worthy, pious Jew. The prospect of fifteen years in the Imperial Army did not appeal to Pavel who quickly moved on to Kiev, hoping to register at a school there. He naïvely showed the telegram to the principal of the gymnasium, who promptly questioned his patriotism. Pavel wasted no time in leaving Kiev and kept out of sight of the authorities until he heard that the recruitment drive had ended. He then learned that the Jews of Mogilev were, for some unknown reason, no longer so ill disposed toward him and were willing to tolerate his presence as "a necessary evil." He returned, began to tutor again, and resumed his studies.

By now, at the age of nineteen or twenty, Axelrod had become dedicated to the promotion of Jewish enlightenment. He was motivated by more than antipathy to superstition and narrow-mindedness and fascination with new intellectual currents. There was a strong romantic streak in him: he saw himself as a heroic figure battling mighty forces. He confessed that the realization that rich and powerful Jews in two cities had persecuted him "aroused in me a feeling of pride, gave me great moral satisfaction—and there flashed through my imagination figures from books, figures of martyrs for an idea, who had suffered in struggling for enlightenment, for truth and justice."[7]

During his second stay in Mogilev Axelrod set himself the grandiose task of "Europeanizing Jewry," the achievement of which required, as a first step, increasing their literacy in Russian. At this stage in his career as a reformer, Axelrod revealed his pragmatic bent of mind. He tried to realize his goal gradually, beginning with a modest change, and he succeeded. Aware that the reluctance of Jewish parents to allow their children to attend gymnasium had to do in large part with the fact that classes were held on the Sabbath, Axelrod asked the girls' gymnasium for a dispensation that had been extended to him some years earlier: the right to attend school on Saturdays without having to desecrate the day of rest by writing. After this request was granted, he went on to organize a free school for the Jewish poor, where youths from more comfortable families taught the rudiments of the Russian language. Axelrod housed the school in a ramshackle building and soon attracted a sizable student body. Word of the educational experiment reached the principal of the

7. *Ibid.*, p. 52.

gymnasium, who reprimanded Pavel and ordered him to close the school. It is not clear why the principal opposed the experiment, but he was probably motivated by the government's view that too much education for the lower classes was potentially dangerous.

Undaunted, Axelrod now appealed to the governor of Mogilev and to the son of the vice-governor to help him establish a library where Jewish youngsters would have the opportunity to read and discuss issues of common interest. Neither the governor nor any of the wealthy Jews whom he also approached was willing to finance the project. But Axelrod's appeal to them illustrates the rather limited nature of his reformist activities at this time. Not one of these projects, as he later admitted, was prompted by broad political purposes. Neither the dramatic trial of Sergei Nechaev[8] nor the Paris Commune made much of an impression on him or his group of friends. Even his brief involvement in 1870 in what he thought was a social conflict between the artisans and leaders of the Jewish community did not raise questions of a broad political nature in his mind.

He had heard that a controversy had broken out in Shklov over the election of a "village elder" of the *Kahal*,[9] a position of considerable local importance. The elections were usually a routine matter, completely under the control of wealthy Jews. In 1870, however, the artisans of the town put up their own candidate in the hope of breaking the power of the oligarchy. Though he knew few details, Axelrod was excited by the prospect of a struggle between "democracy" and the "patrician regime." He immediately set out for Shklov to participate in the conflict,

8. Sergei Nechaev, a follower of Mikhail Bakunin, formed a conspiratorial circle of five people in Moscow, which he claimed was only one cell in a vast network he had created. When one of the group, Ivan Ivanov, expressed doubts about the existence of the network, Nechaev accused him of being a police spy and persuaded the other members of the Moscow circle that the skeptic had to be killed. Nechaev then fled abroad, but his accomplices in the crime were caught by the police, and the story of the murder was widely publicized. During the trial the government circulated information about the *Revolutionary Catechism*, written by Nechaev and Bakunin. The *Catechism* states, among other things, that "everything that allows the triumph of the revolution is moral, everything that stands in its way is immoral." For details, see Franco Venturi, *Roots of Revolution: A History of the Populist and Socialist Movements in Nineteenth Century Russia*, tr. Francis Haskell (New York, 1960), pp. 354–388.

9. The Kahal (the Hebrew word for community) was the Jewish community organization that, prior to 1844, exercised wide jurisdiction over religious and economic matters and to a lesser extent in the judicial sphere. Thereafter it functioned as a fiscal agency of the imperial government.

only to discover that the candidate of the artisans also belonged to the Jewish "aristocracy." The man was simply using the "democratic opposition" for his own political gain. Axelrod's advice to the artisans seems to have had no effect on the conflict, and the wealthy Jews succeeded in getting their man elected. Axelrod then decided to publicize the event, hoping to procure relief for the poor of Shklov from higher authorities. He returned to Mogilev and, in his first publication, briefly described the decline of the Kahal from a democratic body into an oligarchic organization. Although the article, which was printed in a local paper, demonstrated Axelrod's antipathy to the wealthy, it did not contain any general political ideas or proposals for fundamental reform.[10]

Indeed, insofar as Axelrod did hold political views at this time, they were remarkably conventional. He was completely loyal to the Tsar, whom he regarded as the "benefactor of his citizens in general, and of Jews in particular, the protector of the weak against the strong and the guardian of justice." While he had now ceased to observe religious rituals, he occasionally felt a "sincere need" to attend synagogue in order to pray for the Tsar's well-being.[11]

Unconsciously, however, Axelrod seems to have been less devoted to the tsarist autocracy than his prayers would suggest. He expressed his lack of fervor unintentionally in an essay he wrote for his final examinations at the gymnasium in 1871 on the assigned theme "We reap as we have sown." Because he had always received the highest grades for his compositions, he was stunned when his teacher voiced disappointment and annoyance with his last literary effort at school. He was even more bewildered when the principal berated him for having acquired "the bad characteristics of Jewish writers" who always found fault with everything. It finally dawned on him that the teachers disapproved of the historical illustrations he had used. He had argued that monarchical absolutism in eighteenth-century France had caused the Revolution, and his examiner thought, mistakenly, that he was alluding to contemporary Russia. Axelrod wrote another essay, and the incident passed without further unpleasantness. But, as he had devoted insufficient time to phys-

10. Axelrod, *Perezhitoe*, pp. 62–64; Pavel Axelrod, "Padenie evreiskogo Kagala v Shklove," *Mogilevskie gubernskie vedomosti*, no. 59, July 29, 1870. There is a typed copy of this article in the Nicolaevsky Collection, on deposit at the Hoover Institution on War, Revolution, and Peace, Stanford University, Stanford, California.
11. Axelrod, *Perezhitoe*, p. 57.

ics, he failed that subject and therefore could not be graduated. He now understood, as he put it, the true meaning of the dictum on which he had written his ill-fated essay.

Unwilling to remain in the same class another year, Axelrod left for Nezhin, where he hoped to pass an examination in physics and then study at the lycée in preparation for entrance into the University of Kiev. He passed physics, but as he could not find any tutoring jobs in Nezhin he soon moved on to Konotop, where he secured a post teaching a young boy in the house of a Russified Jewish family. One of the attractions of his new home was its library stocked with a large number of Russian books, many of which he avidly read.

After a few months, late in 1871, Axelrod went through a deep personal crisis. He had reached a time in life when he had to decide on a career. Attendance at a university, his great ambition, proved to be financially unfeasible, and yet he had no training for either a profession or a trade. Following his previous interests, he thought of devoting himself to enlightening the Jewish masses by helping to root out prejudice among them and to procure for them the personal and civil rights enjoyed by Gentiles. He also considered the possibility of working for the improvement of the lot of all Russians. His social conscience was by now so highly aroused that public service was the only career that entered his mind, although he could not decide on its focus.

Several unexpected events and experiences during the winter of 1871 proved decisive in helping him resolve the uncertainties about his future. A close friend from Mogilev, Grisha Gurevich, brought him the unsettling news of the sudden death of a fifteen-year-old girl of whom Axelrod had been very fond. The girl had kept a diary (the contents of which are unknown), which he was permitted to read. As he did so, he became increasingly agitated and could not resist speculating about the doctrine of the immortality of the soul. He had, as we know, already had some vague doubts about his religious convictions. But whereas previously he had questioned the authenticity of the Bible and the usefulness of many religious rules, he now began to question the existence of God. By chance he came across Herbert Spencer's *Basic Principles* in his employer's library, a book he read with "a kind of aesthetic delight." Spencer's observation that the force that created the universe is perhaps as much beyond the grasp of human consciousness as is "the watchmaker beyond that of the watches he makes" provided Axelrod with "the real key for a way out of the labyrinth of questions and doubts that were agitating me."[12] But his gradual conversion to agnosticism, while it tended to lessen his enthusiasm for a life of service among Jews, did not help him define his professional goals.

Two other books in his employer's library gave direction to his musings and lifted him out of his despondent mood. Ferdinand Lassalle's *Speeches* and a novel by Karl Gutzkow, *The Knights of the Spirit,* persuaded him that he did not have the "right" to abandon himself to grief over a personal loss and thus to neglect the "interests, questions, and obligations of a higher order." Lassalle's call for freedom and equality for all, the creation of a new order based on the brotherhood of man, a civilization more lofty than the prevailing one made a "colossal impression" on Axelrod. To be sure, he did not understand everything he read and thought that when the German socialist used the term proletariat he had in mind simply the "poor, the wretched, the laborers, and all those oppressed by the rich and privileged strata in society." But the crucial point for Axelrod was Lassalle's vision of a new and beautiful social order; to dedicate himself to its realization now seemed far more important than to work in behalf of the Jewish people. Once the masses were liberated, he reasoned, the Jewish problem would automatically be solved. "And I decided to devote all my energy to working for the liberation of all the poor and oppressed in Russia."[13]

He now had acquired a purpose in life, but how should he go about realizing it? Gutzkow's book—a huge and rather tedious novel that deals, in part, with the revolutionary ferment in Germany in the 1840's—convinced him that Russia must undergo a revolution and that its preparation required the creation of a secret organization, which Axelrod set as his immediate task.

At the age of twenty-two, when Axelrod decided to become a revolutionary, his familiarity with the history and doctrines of radicalism was slight. The influence upon him of a number of books should probably be viewed as having contributed less to this decision than the deeply rooted predisposition to make his mark by working against retrograde institutions and beliefs. The writings of Lassalle and Gutzkow did not so much inspire him with a professional goal as show him how he might satisfy a personal need.

12. *Ibid.,* pp. 70–71.
13. *Ibid.,* pp. 72–73.

His first efforts at revolution making were not encouraging. In the conviction that the only way Russia could produce radical leaders as civilized and learned as Lassalle was through the organization of an all-Russian revolutionary movement among university students, he devised a plan for the formation of legal student groups at every university. Each was to be led by an underground nucleus, which, in turn, was to be linked to a national, central committee. The groups were to discuss social and political issues, develop a program, and gradually revolutionize an increasing number of nonstudents in their respective cities.

Axelrod, who was presumably still tutoring, traveled to Nezhin, Odessa, and Kiev to enlist support for his plan, but found most students more concerned with the cost of food than with the desirability of preparing a revolution. He eagerly looked forward to meeting with a particular student circle that intended to discuss the question of literacy, hoping to hear about concrete plans to educate the people and wage propaganda among them. Instead, to his chagrin, he had to listen to talk of the need for "religious and moral training for the people."[14] In Odessa he met Andrey Zheliabov, a young man who had already earned something of a reputation as a revolutionary and who nine years later was to achieve fame as a guiding spirit of the terrorist *Narodnaia volia* (The People's Will). Axelrod hoped to secure Zheliabov's support, but at that time the latter, in keeping with the mood prevalent among Russian revolutionaries in the early 1870's, opposed illegal organizational work. In his view, the only useful task was to educate the people. It became clear to Axelrod that the apathy of Russia's youth, heightened by the revelation in 1871 of the ghastly crime committed by Nechaev, made the realization of his plan impossible.

He then settled down in Kiev, where he found work as tutor in the house of Dr. I. Kaminer, a progressive with a reputation both as physician and Hebrew poet. Apparently Axelrod had now given up all thought of pursuing his education, for he spent much of his free time teaching workers to read and write. He would stop them in the street, inquire into their personal lives, and finally offer to come to their *artels* to teach them.[15] The workers nearly always accepted, and within a short

---

14. *Ibid.*, p. 85.
15. The artel was an artisans' cooperative. The members pooled their resources to buy equipment, usually produced manufactured goods separately, and then cooperated in marketing them.

time Axelrod and about nine of his friends had organized a series of classes in several artels.

Axelrod was the moving spirit of the group. In fact, according to Lev Deich, then a student in Kiev and later a revolutionary of some eminence, Axelrod was the dominant personality among all the city radicals. Deich remembered Axelrod as a young man of slight build with a "small, black beard and lively, intelligent eyes." Axelrod spoke rapidly and with great ardor and conviction, constantly gesticulating. He was indefatigable and would propagate his views from morning until late at night anywhere he could find an audience—in apartments, in the streets, and in the universities. He had the "passion of a fanatic," a quality that impressed many people. "Neither before nor since has there been anyone among the Jewish youngsters in Kiev who enjoyed such influence, affection, and respect as Pavel Axelrod." Even though he was only a few years older than the rest, the young radicals in the city regarded him as the most experienced and knowledgeable of the group.[16]

But Axelrod and his colleagues soon discovered that while the workers were receptive to education, they were less than enthusiastic about revolutionary propaganda, which was uppermost in the minds of their teachers. In most of the artels no subject concerning the Tsar could even be raised.[17] Dissatisfied with the results of their efforts with the workers, the students decided to prepare for more fruitful activity: propaganda in the countryside. Axelrod learned the trade of joiner (at which he apparently never became very proficient), and by the spring of 1874 he was ready to participate in the remarkable movement known as "Go-to-the-People." In the summer of that year hundreds of students and professional people, without any central direction or organization, went into the country to work, educate, and spread revolutionary propaganda. Even though they dressed as peasants and readily performed menial jobs, the police, often aided by peasants suspicious of the intruders, quickly discovered and arrested the vast majority of them.[18]

Axelrod had not, in fact, joined the idealists in the countryside because he first had undertaken a strange mission. He was searching for a robber in the Kiev province who was reputed to attack wealthy land-

16. Lev Deich, *Rol' evreev v russkom revoliutsionnom dvizhenii* (2nd ed., Moscow, 1925), p. 129.
17. Axelrod, *Perezhitoe*, pp. 96–98.
18. For details on this movement, see Venturi, *Roots of Revolution*, pp. 469–506.

owners and Jews and distribute the loot among the poor peasants. It was considered important to establish contact with the "virtuous robber." For many radicals, taking their cue from Bakunin's exaltation of the brigand as a rebel against society, believed that such a person might well become an inspiring and powerful revolutionary leader a la Stenka Razin or Emel'ian Pugachev. Axelrod never did find him and on his return to Kiev learned of the intensified police repression throughout Russia. Instead of "going to the people," he decided to flee the country and in September 1874 illegally entered Germany. He hesitated to abandon his homeland, but was consoled by the thought that finally he would meet some of the workers to whom Lassalle had addressed his "ardent speeches" and whom he had urged to create the new order, the "churches of the future."

At the time Axelrod left Russia he possessed solid credentials as a revolutionary activist, but his knowledge of radical doctrine was still elementary. When he went to Kiev he had only the vaguest ideas about the nature of contemporary society, social conflict, or the kind of new order he favored for Russia. He was essentially a utopian, and his political views, such as they were, derived fundamentally from certain ill-defined ethical and religious principles, the essence of which was the notion that the intelligentsia was obliged to commit itself to transforming society in order to repay its debt to the people. Axelrod recalled being tormented by the thought that he was enjoying advanced study while the people were illiterate.[19] This state of mind sufficed to sustain him in his propagandistic efforts among workers in Kiev, but it seemed inadequate as a basis for a lifelong career as a revolutionary. He came to feel that he needed more than the essentially "instinctive" and "idealistic" impulse that had led him to take up the cause of "the people." He began to search for a theory that would serve not only as the basis and rationale for his work but would also provide him with a clearer notion of social goals.

During his stay in Kiev, therefore, Axelrod began to read, in a rather unsystematic fashion, the works of some of the leading social philosophers. He read more Lassalle, some John Stuart Mill, and Marx's *Capital,* which he admitted to not having fully understood. Still, the

19. Axelrod, *Perezhitoe,* p. 89.

book made a strong impression on him. After reading it, he had the "feeling as though I had been transported out of the twilight into the full range of the sun, as though everything had become clear to me."[20] Here Axelrod, the veteran Marxist, seems to have ascribed to his youth a far greater admiration for *Capital* than he actually felt, for it was another decade before he converted to Marxism. In the early 1870's he was much more influenced by Petr Lavrov and Bakunin, whom he also studied.

It was apparently not until the ideological debates between exponents of the two dominant revolutionary currents, Lavrism and Bakuninism, in Kiev in 1874, that Axelrod began to identify with a specific political position grounded in theory. The discussion took place in a "commune" that met in the apartment of Katherine Breshko-Breshkovskaia, one of the first of a group of women who played an important role in the revolutionary movement. The debates centered on means rather than ends. For Lavrov and Bakunin shared a general outlook, one to which most socialist revolutionaries in the 1870's subscribed.[21] Both repudiated the autocratic regime and archaic social structure; both conceived of the peasant commune, supposedly organized in accordance with the principles of justice and equality, as the cornerstone of a new order—socialism —to be created in Russia. They also agreed that the commune demonstrated the instinctive propensity for socialism of the Russian masses and that this made it possible for Russia to avoid the horrors of capitalism. Finally, both men were anarchists; they scorned politics in all its forms. Universal suffrage, political and civil rights, and parliamentary government seemed to them irrelevant and futile, for they benefited only the privileged classes and could not produce a solution to society's evils: poverty, ignorance, and inequality. Only a revolution from below, staged by the oppressed themselves, could bring an end to man's wretchedness. But the two radicals differed decisively on the measures to be used to promote social transformation.

Lavrov assigned the major role in the coming revolution to the intelligentsia which, he contended, had to recognize its obligation and repay its debt to the people, a debt it had contracted because of its position as

20. *Ibid.*, p. 88.
21. To avoid the confusion surrounding the term *Narodnik* I shall refer to the radicals of the 1870's as socialist revolutionaries. For an analysis of the semantic problem, see Richard Pipes, "*Narodnichestvo:* A Semantic Inquiry," *Slavic Review,* XXIII (Sept. 1964), 441–458.

exploiter of the masses. But before the educated and privileged could perform any useful political service they must gain technical expertise in economics, the law, and military science. Then they must strive to prepare the masses for radical change through propaganda. "Knowledge," he declared, "is the fundamental power of the revolution which is under way and the force essential to carry it out."[22]

Axelrod respected Lavrov as a thinker and was much influenced by him, as is revealed by his propagandistic work of 1872 and 1873. But by 1874 Axelrod found Lavrov's gradualist approach abstract and lacking in that call for immediate action for which he then yearned. Nor did Lavrov's precepts, in Axelrod's view, call for sufficient self-sacrifice. "The demand," he wrote, "for serious theoretical preparation for propaganda left the radical with the possibility of very quietly enjoying all the good things of life—at a time when we had an inner moral need quickly to cut all ties with 'the world wallowing in depravity' and 'burn our bridges' behind us." Axelrod could not, moreover, accept Lavrov's contention that while ultimately the state must be destroyed, it would be necessary to maintain it during the period of transition to socialism. Axelrod favored the immediate and complete destruction of the state.[23]

It is not surprising that in this mood of militancy Axelrod found Bakunin's revolutionary anarchism more congenial. The latter's strident call for action appealed to his desire for self-sacrifice and to his romantic idealism. Bakuninism, he wrote, "won us over by its simplicity, straightforwardness, [and] by the fact that it radically resolved all questions. There is no doubt that Bakunin intoxicated us especially with his revolutionary phraseology and ardent eloquence."[24] In contrast to Lavrov, Bakunin scorned the value of education in preparing for the social upheaval. In his view, the people were always seething with discontent, and the slightest encouragement by intellectuals could rouse them to the fiercest outbursts of revolutionary violence. The very act of violence, moreover, was for him liberating and creative. And he was confident that once revolutionary violence had toppled the prevailing system, the people in their inherent goodness would know how to create a new and better life, free from the restraints of any political institution.[25]

22. Quoted in Venturi, *Roots of Revolution*, p. 458.
23. Axelrod, *Perezhitoe*, pp. 109–111.
24. *Ibid.*, p. 111.
25. For a good, brief account of Bakunin's ideas and activities, see James Joll, *The Anarchists* (London, 1964), pp. 84–114.

By the spring of 1874 Axelrod was sufficiently committed to Bakunin-ism that he undertook a mission to Odessa to convert a group of radicals to the creed. His success was minimal. It is not known why he failed, but it may be that his taste for violence was not as great as it should have been. In later years Axelrod prided himself on never having adopted all of the master's teachings. He belonged to the moderate wing of the movement. Thus, for example, he did not subscribe to the extremists' view that to teach the people to read and write was a mistake because such knowledge would surely expose them to the pernicious ideas and prejudices found in bourgeois writings.[26] Nor was he convinced that the peasants were naturally revolutionary and that all propaganda among them was therefore a waste of energy. Axelrod could not resist pointing out that occasionally an "ox protests by ramming its head against a wall and a dog 'rebels' when the master hits it hard with a cane, but in doing so [the dog] bites the stick, not the master."[27] Axelrod did believe in exploiting the disaffection of the peasants, but he also thought it neces-sary to guide their political development so as to provide the movement of protest with clear direction and meaningful goals.

Thus, by the age of twenty-four, when he paid his first visit to the West, he had embraced the cause of revolution and absorbed a recogniz-able set of political ideas: he saw the peasant commune as the foundation for a socialist system in Russia, he rejected the state as necessary or use-ful, and he had faith that the revolutionary fervor of the peasantry, once activated, would succeed in overthrowing the government. This was patently not a sophisticated political program. But in its primitive-ness and eclecticism it exemplified the political orientation of a large number of young revolutionaries in Russia during the 1870's.

26. Axelrod, *Perezhitoe*, p. 113.
27. *Ibid.*, p. 116.

II | A Bakuninist in Conflict

Among Russian radicals of the 1870's no one was as profoundly swayed by the ideas of German Social Democracy as Axelrod, and no one played as decisive a role as he in familiarizing other Russians with the doctrines and policies of that party. He was the first to observe how the German movement functioned, and his initial favorable reaction to it inspired him to study in depth its organization and tactics. As an anarchist he also found much to criticize, but in the long run his positive impressions far outweighed the negative ones. Moreover, within a few years he formed close friendships with several leaders of the party, and their impact on the evolution of his political thinking proved critical. In many ways the later fascination of Russian Marxists with German Social Democracy may be said to have originated in 1874 with Axelrod's brief stay in Berlin.

He arrived in September without money or passport. Fortunately for him, Grisha Gurevich, his old friend from Mogilev, was then studying in Berlin and generously shared with Axelrod the moderate allowance he received from his family. Axelrod also spent a few days at the home of Eduard Bernstein, then twenty-two years old, who did not hesitate to offer refuge to a fellow revolutionary hiding from the police.[1] Despite the difficulties of underground life and his ignorance of German, Axelrod had a number of new and exciting experiences in Berlin. He had never before visited a large cosmopolitan city—not even St. Petersburg or Moscow—and was therefore immensely impressed by the huge crowds in the streets, the endless rows of carts loaded with merchandise, the numerous shops. He was struck by the museums and art galleries,

1. Eduard Bernstein, "Pavel Aksel'rod, internatsionalist," *Sotsialisticheskii vestnik,* no. 15/16, Aug. 18, 1925, 23.

whose very existence surprised him. He was tempted to attend a theatrical performance, but was deterred by lack of money and a feeling that he should not indulge himself in such pleasures while his comrades in Russia were imprisoned or hiding from the authorities. Observing this display of affluence, Axelrod could not help but begin to understand the admiration of some economists for "bourgeois progress." But he quickly checked his own impulse to admire Western achievements by telling himself that those who did so failed to see the "reverse side of the coin."

Axelrod's favorite pastime in Berlin was attending workers' meetings, and aided by his knowledge of Yiddish he was soon able to follow the proceedings. He was startled by the mass character of the gatherings which were often attended by more than a thousand people. He found it even more astonishing that "genuine workers" were seated not only in the hall but also at the chairman's table and on the speakers' platform. Everyone spoke freely, expressing his opinion on the most complex subjects and criticizing the government. He was all the more impressed when he learned that policemen openly attended the meetings and took notes. Occasionally, the police would close a meeting and the audience would respond with protests and a spontaneous outburst of revolutionary songs.

Accustomed to meetings of small circles at which no one but intellectuals spoke and at which politics could often not be touched upon, Axelrod expressed enthusiastic admiration for the maturity, discipline, and sophistication of the German working class. At first he was puzzled by the failure of other radical Russian émigrés to share his enthusiasm. Then it occurred to him that the difference in reaction had to do with differences in social background. Nearly all the other émigrés came from noble or intellectual milieus and were accustomed to people with a sense of dignity and independence. Also, they lacked direct contact with the people. In the Kiev artels Axelrod had found a major feature of the workers' lives to be a "dull, gloomy ignorance." The very sight of a policeman caused laborers and peasants to tremble with fear. The entirely different spirit prevailing among the Berlin workers therefore affected him deeply.[2] He had discovered a model by which to gauge the progress of Russian workers, and it is no exaggeration to say that from this time

2. Pavel Axelrod, *Perezhitoe i peredumannoe* (Berlin, 1923), pp. 126–131.

Axelrod's radicalism took on a distinctly—and increasingly pronounced
—Western European tinge.

Within a few weeks Nadezhda Kaminer, his fiancée, joined him in
Berlin. Axelrod had met her while working as a tutor in her father's
house in Kiev, and although in his memoirs he said very little about
her personal qualities or their courtship, it is clear that in part he was
attracted to her because of her self-abnegation and devotion to the
cause. Raised in comfortable circumstances, she had nevertheless readily
agreed to having her dowry used to finance radical activities.[3] For a
while she had lived with a peasant family and helped with household
chores so as to gain the necessary experience "to go to the people." In
Berlin Nadezhda boarded with a working-class family in order to
familiarize herself with the wretched conditions of the poor. This style
of life was not easy for her. Yet she refused better quarters even though
she could then have afforded them. Her idealism and modesty were
personal qualities that were to serve her in good stead. For after she
married Axelrod in 1875 she had to endure poverty and material deprivation. She was never known to complain or to urge Axelrod to forsake
politics.

Toward the end of 1874, Dmitry Klements, a prominent member of
the Chaikovsky Circle[4] in St. Petersburg, came to Berlin and quickly
befriended Axelrod. Klements spent a considerable amount of time with
Axelrod, informing him of developments among the revolutionaries in
the capital. His appetite whetted, Axelrod in January 1875, moved on
to Switzerland to learn more about Russian radicalism. There he met
such revolutionary notables as Vera Figner, N. A. Sablin, S. M. Kravchinsky, and P. N. Tkachev, among others.

3. Actually, Nadezhda never received the dowry of three thousand rubles that her
father had promised her. Dr. Kaminer liked Axelrod and approved of his revolutionary work, but did not consider him a suitable husband for his daughter, or for
any woman. "A man such as Axelrod ought not to marry," he said. But fearful lest
his daughter elope with Axelrod, he agreed to the marriage. However, instead of
giving the newlyweds the three thousand rubles, which he did not think they would
spend on themselves, Dr. Kaminer suggested that they live in his house until Axelrod
had completed his university studies. But this was an empty gesture, as Axelrod had
no intention of pursuing his education or a career. *Ibid.*, pp. 122–123.

4. The Chaikovsky Circle, formed in 1869, was one of the more successful groups
propagating socialist ideas, and their work contributed much to the emergence of
the "Go-to-the-People" movement in 1874. For a detailed account of their activities
and views, see Franco Venturi, *Roots of Revolution: A History of the Populist and
Socialist Movements in Nineteenth Century Russia*, tr. Francis Haskell (New York,
1960), pp. 469–506.

Axelrod married Nadezhda in Geneva, and from then on he was almost always under severe financial pressure. Of course, he had never been well off and had had to earn his keep from the age of thirteen. But, obviously, as a family man—and soon a father—his needs became greater. Unlike many other Russian radicals he could count on no support from his parents. And it never occurred to him to become the permanent charge of others, either living off personal loans or subsidies from the movement for which he worked, practices that were not rare among Russian revolutionaries. He was nearly always engaged in some kind of work, often the most menial, so as to provide for his family. Only when he was in his seventies and too ill to work did he depend on the generosity of friends for financial support. In a sense, then, he was not a professional revolutionary as that word came to be defined in the twentieth century, that is, a person who devotes all his time and energy to the cause. The cause was his major concern, but he never allowed it to be his only concern.

In his first job he polished banisters for eleven hours a day at fifteen francs a month, not enough to support two people at even a minimum level of subsistence. Fortunately, the Russian community in Geneva was generous in extending help to those who were hungry, and, no less important, the local store allowed the Axelrods to buy food on credit whenever they were out of cash. In addition to paying badly, his new occupation soon presented him with a minor *crise de conscience*. In 1875 there was extensive agitation in Switzerland for a reduction of the working day to ten hours. As a Bakuninist, Axelrod should have opposed such a "picayune improvement" for fear that even a small concession might dampen the revolutionary ardor of the laboring class, but as a worker himself he could not help but hope for a lightening of the burden, if only by an hour a day. Publicly, however, he remained true to his beliefs and was careful to conceal his sympathy for the proposal.[5]

In the summer of 1875 Axelrod's career as handrail polisher abruptly came to an end, not for reasons of incompetence but because the émigrés decided to send him to Russia on an important mission. They had received reports of civil disorder in two regions of Eastern Europe, and both seemed to call for speedy action. In Herzegovina several groups of Slavs had staged an uprising against the Turkish overlords. The Baku-

5. Axelrod, *Perezhitoe*, p. 143.

ninists hoped that, by taking part in the struggle, they might introduce socialist tendencies into what was essentially a nationalist uprising. They felt, moreover, that participation in the rebellion would provide invaluable military experience for the future; Axelrod's first task was, therefore, to encourage Russian Bakuninists to volunteer for service in Herzegovina.

His second task was quite bizarre and served as introduction to one of the most dramatic and irresponsible chapters in the annals of the Russian revolutionary movement. Word had reached Geneva that there were serious disorders in the Ukrainian region of Chigirin and that the rebellious peasants were confident that the Tsar, their father, supported them. Ya. V. Stefanovich, Lev Deich, and I. V. Bokhanovsky conceived of a plan, which they carried out a year later with disastrous consequences, to rally more peasants against the landlords by issuing an "imperial" proclamation calling for rebellion in the name of the Tsar. Axelrod and his moderate Bakuninist colleagues urged a "more responsible" tactic, which was adopted. They favored an appeal to the peasants that would point out the futility of relying on the Tsar because he always sided with the landlords and local authorities. But, in order to maximize the impact of their call to rebellion, they had it printed in golden letters in the style of imperial documents. In this form it would presumably attract the attention of the ignorant peasants, and at least assure a hearing for its antitsarist message. Five hundred copies were printed in Ukrainian for Axelrod to take to Russia, where he was to find comrades to distribute them in the locale of the disturbance.[6] This harebrained scheme was not uncharacteristic of the 1870's, a period that Adam Ulam has aptly described as one in which the revolution was "in search of the masses."[7]

Axelrod was also asked to establish contact with a group of Georgian revolutionaries led by G. F. Zdanovich and to arrange through them for regular delivery to Russia of the Bakuninist periodical *Rabotnik*. The editors of *Rabotnik* supplied Axelrod with some money for the trip, but as he had no passport he would need to enter Russia illegally.

Axelrod attempted to enter the Chigirin region through Romania, where he had been told there were several comrades adept at smuggling

6. *Ibid.*, pp. 145–147.
7. Adam Ulam, *The Bolsheviks. The Intellectual and Political History of the Triumph of Communism in Russia* (New York, 1965), p. 74.

revolutionaries across the border. He reached the town of Jassa, but found no one ready to help him. At last he secured the address of a frontier Jew who agreed to get him into Russia, but not if Axelrod insisted on taking along his five hundred appeals to the peasants. And so he left them in Jassa, intending to arrange for their subsequent shipment. He then dressed up as an "Old Testament Galician Jew" and with ticket in hand crossed the border without incident. The frontier guards did not even have to be bribed. It did not occur to them that revolutionaries would don the garb of a pious Jew.

Getting into Russia turned out to be much easier than performing the tasks assigned to him. Wherever he went—Kishinev, Nikolaev, Kherson, Odessa, Moscow, St. Petersburg—Axelrod discovered that the recent wave of government arrests had made a shambles of the revolutionary movement. In those cities where he met radicals who had survived the suppression, the demoralization was so great that he could not evoke a positive response to his various schemes. He and his colleagues in Geneva, far removed from the state of affairs in Russia, had devised plans that were totally unrealistic.

Still, the trip was not a complete waste, for in St. Petersburg Axelrod met some of the leading figures in the revolutionary movement: Sofiia Perovskaia, Mark Natanson, and German Lopatin. He was impressed by the fact that unlike so many radicals they did not spend their time discussing the nature of their obligations to the people. They had already resolved this question. Their only concern was to reassemble and revitalize the revolutionary forces.[8]

Also, in St. Petersburg Axelrod for the first time met Georgii Valentinovich Plekhanov, who was to become one of his closest collaborators and friends, and who for two decades was to exercise a major influence on his political outlook. There are two brief accounts of the meeting, one by Axelrod and one by O. V. Aptekman, who was an intimate of both men in the late 1870's and early 1880's. Aptekman based his account on information supplied him by Plekhanov, though it is not clear exactly how much time had passed when he received it. The principal difference between the two versions is that Aptekman placed greater emphasis on the influence Axelrod exerted on the young Plekha-

8. On Axelrod's trip to Russia, see Axelrod, *Perezhitoe*, pp. 148–159.

nov in encouraging him to commit himself fully to the revolution. The point is of some interest in clarifying the nature of the subsequent relationship between them. In the 1880's and 1890's Plekhanov was generally regarded as the dominant personality and Axelrod as incapable of following an independent line. In fact, however, the relationship was never quite as one-sided as it appeared, and Aptekman's account of the initial encounter suggests that at first Plekhanov looked to Axelrod as the more knowledgeable and experienced.

Axelrod was, after all, six years older and had already devoted several years to revolutionary work when he arrived in St. Petersburg. Plekhanov, then a nineteen-year-old student at the Mining Institute, had a room considered safe from the police, and it was there that Axelrod's contacts arranged for him to stay. In his version Axelrod recalls that he took an immediate liking to the young man, who "spoke well, in a businesslike, simple yet very literary style. I sensed that he had great curiosity, and the habit of reading, thinking and working." But Axelrod was disappointed to hear that Plekhanov intended to study chemistry abroad after completing his courses at the institute. "That is a luxury!" the elder said, with obvious reproach. "If you take so long to perfect yourself in chemistry, when will you begin to work for the revolution?" Axelrod subsequently told his friends about the mining student and urged them to try to bring him into the revolutionary movement.[9]

As Aptekman tells it, at the time of the meeting Plekhanov was so preoccupied with his studies that he had no interest in radical activities. Axelrod, however, impressed him deeply "with his selfless devotion to the revolution," introduced him to several revolutionaries, and spoke to Natanson about that "very talented youngster, who ought to be drawn into the cause." Within a year Plekhanov abandoned his studies and became a full-time revolutionary.[10]

Aptekman probably exaggerated Axelrod's influence on Plekhanov. It is questionable whether a young man would have been prepared to risk giving shelter to a person living underground if he had not already been at least sympathetic to radicalism. There is evidence, moreover, that Plekhanov had already attended some clandestine meetings. Yet, it was only in early 1876, shortly after Axelrod shared his room, that

9. *Ibid.*, pp. 156–157.
10. O. V. Aptekman, "Chernyi peredel," in *Chernyi peredel* (Moscow, 1923), p. 98.

Plekhanov's interest in the revolutionary movement seems to have become a total preoccupation.[11] It would appear reasonable to conclude, therefore, that although Axelrod's was probably not the sole influence on Plekhanov, it nevertheless gave considerable impetus to his evolution from chemist to revolutionary.

Plans called for Axelrod's return to Geneva by early 1876, when his wife was expected to give birth to their first child. There was no reason to prolong his stay in Russia, as not much could be accomplished anyway. A smuggler managed to get him across the border, and he reached Switzerland shortly before his daughter was born. Now under greater financial pressure than ever before, he decided to become a typesetter, a trade at which it was theoretically possible to earn a fairly decent wage. Paid on a piecework basis, he could have made up to five francs a day, but even though he put in ten to eleven hours he was too slow to earn more than three. This was not enough to live on. There were times when the Axelrods could barely afford to buy milk for their baby. Their own nourishment, aside from bread, often consisted of no more than snails that they picked off the bushes along the streets of the city and soaked in vinegar before eating. This extreme deprivation lasted for several years, but Axelrod did not recall the period as having been particularly unhappy. They seem to have been too preoccupied with the lively political debates within the Russian émigré colony to worry excessively about material comforts.

In 1876 the radical Russian exiles in Geneva were divided into two major groups, the Bakuninists and the followers of Tkachev, who published a journal called *Nabat* (The Tocsin). Tkachev was the leading exponent of Russian Jacobinism (or Blanquism), which held that in view of the political apathy of the masses the intellectual elite was obliged to create a tightly centralized, conspiratorial organization for the violent overthrow of the existing order. Axelrod, despite his disappointing experiences in Russia, remained loyal to the Bakuninists, who far outnumbered their rivals. But he also attended meetings of various Social Democratic groups, with the avowed purpose of converting them to anarchism. Far from sharing his interest in Social Democracy, his

11. Samuel H. Baron, *Plekhanov: The Father of Russian Marxism* (Stanford, 1963), p. 16.

comrades held it in contempt. This did not deter Axelrod from playing a leading role in attempting to bring about a reconciliation between
anarchists and Social Democrats in the fall of 1876, after Bakunin's death
appeared to have removed the major obstacle to collaboration. In a
written appeal Axelrod argued that the tactical differences between the
movements were merely a reflection of the different conditions under
which they operated. He subsequently realized that he had vastly over-
simplified the issue, but at the time several people, including N. I.
Zhukovsky and Z. K. Ralli from *Rabotnik*, were taken in by his argument. A congress was convened to effect a reconciliation.

But the meeting had the opposite results from those intended. Very
few representatives from foreign countries showed up, and because of
the "improvised character" of the Russian Bakuninist group, Axelrod,
one of the more enthusiastic advocates of reconciliation, did not have
voting status. The small contingent that did participate in the deliberations acted in accordance with what appears to be the iron law of radical
congresses: no one was prepared to make any concessions whatsoever,
and consequently the two camps parted company more convinced than
before that an unbridgeable gulf separated them.[12]

After the failure of the congress the Russian Bakuninists in Geneva
were relatively inactive for about a year and a half. In 1876 they stopped
publishing *Rabotnik* and were temporarily unable to disseminate their
program. But a series of developments soon prompted them to resume
their propaganda and agitation. For one thing, they seem to have felt
called upon to answer Tkachev, who continued to publish *Nabat* and
to develop with increasing detail and stridency his Jacobin views. Fearful that a delay in starting the revolution would permit capitalism to
entrench itself further and thus render impossible the realization of
the socialist ideal, Tkachev argued for an immediate seizure of power
by those few individuals whose education and moral training enabled
them to appreciate the true interests of the nation. Tkachev had no
use for the anarchists, whose plan to destroy the state, he maintained,
would achieve nothing more than chaos. Axelrod remembered an exchange he had in the 1870's with one of Tkachev's followers: "Do you
really believe it is right for a minority forcefully to make the people

12. Axelrod, *Perezhitoe*, pp. 170–182.

happy?" asked Axelrod. "Of course. If the masses do not understand what is good for them, then it is necessary to impose it upon them by force."[13]

But more important than the Jacobinist threat in activating the Bakuninists was the news of a revival of the revolutionary movement in Russia. In 1876 there was formed the second *Zemlia i volia* (Land and Liberty), which has been called the first genuinely revolutionary party in Russia. A year later the long "Trial of the fifty" and the "Trial of the one hundred and ninety-three," designed by the government to frighten the people by exposing the "red peril," aroused sympathy and admiration for the radicals.[14] It was against this background that the Geneva Bakuninists, together with several Chaikovsists, decided to found a new periodical, *Obshchina*, which was to pay more attention to theoretical and tactical problems than its predecessor, *Rabotnik*. Axelrod, Klements, Ralli, and N. I. Zhukovsky served as its editors, and although only nine issues were published, all of them in 1878, it was soon considered one of the best informed and penetrating of the publications put out by Russian revolutionaries.[15]

For Axelrod personally, participation in the editorial work marked his emergence as a ranking revolutionary. His first important writings appeared in *Obshchina*, and from this time it is possible to recount and analyze his social and political views without relying wholly on personal recollections.

Obshchina's editorial position accurately reflected the new mood of a fairly sizable number of revolutionaries in Russia. In large measure this was the case because the émigrés deliberately tried to expound a broad program that could elicit maximum support. They stressed the fundamental importance of the commune for the creation of socialism in Russia, insisted on the necessity of violent revolution to overthrow the tsarist regime, and called for a federation of autonomous communes in place of the existing state structure. They also agreed with many of their colleagues in Russia that the participants in the "Go-to-the-People" movement had blundered in attempting to convert the peasants to alien socialist doctrines. Instead, revolutionaries should develop a social-

13. *Ibid.*, p. 198.
14. Venturi, *Roots of Revolution*, pp. 558, 586–587.
15. Alphons Thun, *Geschichte der Revolutionären Bewegung in Russland* (Leipzig, 1883), p. 164.

ist program more closely attuned to the views, traditions, and customs of the Russian people. In a clear renunciation of Tkachev's Jacobinism, the editors proclaimed as one of their guiding principles the Marxist dictum, inscribed in the Statutes of the First International, that "the emancipation of the working classes must be accomplished by the working classes themselves."

Despite the wide area of agreement between the *Obshchina* group and many revolutionaries in Russia, there were also important differences between them. The émigrés were unwilling to make as sharp a break with the Western socialist heritage as were some of their comrades at home. "We believed," according to Axelrod, "that it went without saying that the aim and content of the Russian Revolution must not in any essential respect differ from the aims and content of the socialist revolution in the West." The editors contended that intensive study of peasant life would affect only the "pedagogical side of the questions concerning propaganda and agitation among the masses" by enabling the revolutionaries to improve their methods of appealing to the masses.[16]

Even among the editors there were differences of emphasis on this issue. Axelrod assumed the most pronounced Western stance, which is indicated by the very subjects he chose to write about. His longest contribution to the journal, an article appearing in five installments, dealt with German Social Democracy.[17] At first glance it appears to be nothing more than a savage critique of the German party from an anarchist standpoint, for Axelrod dwelt on the defects and dangers of a movement expounding "state socialism." But a careful reading reveals that he also took pains to point out the significant achievement of the German radicals: creation of the first mass party. Indeed, it had caught his attention precisely because it had evolved into the strongest socialist party in the world and was already exercising considerable influence on the other socialist movements.[18] By contrast—and this too could not fail to impress the reader—the anarchist groups were everywhere so weak that he found little purpose in examining either their doctrines or organizations.

16. Axelrod, *Perezhitoe*, pp. 209–210.
17. Pavel Axelrod, "Itogi sotsial'no-demokraticheskoi partii v Germanii," *Obshchina*, no. 1 (1878), 26–30; no. 2 (1878), 22–25; no. 3/4 (1878), 35–44; no. 6/7 (1878), 33–41; no. 8/9 (1878), 40–49.
18. Axelrod, *Perezhitoe*, pp. 219–221.

In its format and style the article reveals several characteristics that came to typify Axelrod's writings: thorough research, mastery of historical detail, and simplicity of expression. But it is far less mature in its conclusions than his later works.

He believed that the critical weakness in the thinking of the German Social Democrats was their failure to realize that no state could establish an egalitarian order. What guarantee would there be that the new socialist state would not mistreat workers? Even if August Bebel and Wilhelm Liebknecht occupied Bismarck's place, no one would be safe from government arbitrariness. Axelrod recalled that Cromwell and Robespierre had subscribed to the loftiest ideals, but this did not prevent them from turning into despots. History showed, he declared, that any "state or centralized social order always and everywhere has been and is at one and the same time the fulcrum and cause of inequality and antagonisms within society." If anything, the new kind of state favored by the German socialists would be more dangerous than any other because it would have more power.

Axelrod's critique of German Social Democracy is of interest because it plainly demonstrates the strength of his attachment to anarchism and, following from this, his uncompromising hostility to political action. It also contributes to an understanding of the evolution of his outlook. However unfavorable his assessment of the German party, his close study of its history influenced his thinking. In his memoirs Axelrod admitted "that already in the course of my work for that article I became contaminated by the Social Democratic heresy without being aware of it . . ."[19] He did not articulate the heresy in 1878, but there is no doubt that the knowledge he acquired then served him in good stead when he began to shed his anarchist beliefs.

In his second article for *Obshchina* Axelrod addressed himself to a major problem of the Russian revolutionary movement: its growing disarray. To be sure, the movement had never been firmly united either ideologically or organizationally, but in the early 1870's the two major groups, the Lavrists and the Bakuninists, did have in common a romantic faith in "the people" and the conviction that the people themselves must accomplish the regeneration of Russia. In reaction to the fiasco of 1874 and the subsequent wave of government repression, however,

19. *Ibid.*, p. 263.

several new tendencies emerged in Russia, and for about four years the condition of the revolutionary movement can only be described as highly confused.

Some socialist revolutionaries continued to be propagandists or Lavrists in the traditional sense. Others stressed the importance of replacing itinerant propagandists with persons who would settle more or less permanently in the countryside. More important, there was a growing shift of emphasis from socialist propaganda to political action, which Russian radicals had traditionally scorned. But here, too, there were differences: some advocated a coup d'etat; some proposed collaboration with liberals or pressure for a constitution; and, finally, some advocated terror against government officials. By 1878 the last group gained the most publicity, if not the largest number of adherents. But even the terrorists were not united in purpose or motivation. Several believed that their "propaganda through deeds" would activate the masses and unleash the popular revolution, thus realizing the people's deepest aspirations. Others thought that by means of terror the government could be so disrupted and weakened that the revolutionaries would be able to seize power. Yet another group expected that terror would force the government into making political concessions, that is, granting a constitution and civil liberties. A few favored it simply as a weapon of revenge. And, finally, there were apparently some who were drawn to it "from a natural inclination towards the sensational." In the period 1874–1878 none of these positions can be said to have constituted a carefully worked out program, based on a consistent set of doctrines. Nor should it be assumed that individuals stressing one particular tactic found it impossible to collaborate with people emphasizing a different one. And to confound the confusion, revolutionaries often abandoned one tactic for another or sympathized with several mutually contradictory ones.[20]

This ideological chaos was the general background to Axelrod's analysis. But the specific event that stimulated him to write the article was receipt by *Obshchina* of a letter from Yakov Stefanovich that deviated in yet another way from traditional beliefs. Although Stefanovich asserted that he was writing only in the name of a small group of revo-

---

20. Thun, *Geschichte der Revolutionären Bewegung*, pp. 115–190; David Footman, *Red Prelude: A Life of A. I. Zhelyabov* (2nd ed., London, 1968), *passim*, but esp. p. 104.

lutionaries then working in the Ukraine, to Axelrod and his colleagues in Geneva it seemed that the letter articulated the views of a number of radicals. Stefanovich argued that so far revolutionaries had failed to secure a large following because they had relied on ideals and modes of struggle borrowed from European socialists. As a result, Russian radicals had neglected to take into account certain "prejudices" to which the peasants were so firmly tied that they could not be persuaded to abandon them. They could not, for example, be shaken in their conviction that the Tsar was their "father" and genuinely wanted to improve their lot. Nor could they be induced to alter their authoritarian family structure or the custom of beating their wives. "We are convinced . . ." Stefanovich contended, "that at present the Russian people do not represent a basis for . . . a rapid and thorough implementation of the socialist idea. There exists a basis for the realization of only those aspects of . . . ideals which are shared by the people."[21] In short, Stefanovich suggested that Russian radicals develop a program calculated to appeal to the peasants' prejudices and desire to own all the arable land.

The strategy Stefanovich proposed was not new; it had been debated for about two years. But its boldness made it one of the more extreme formulations of the anti-Western position. It shocked Axelrod because his reformist zeal had always been impelled by the desire to purge the masses of their ignorance, superstition, and barbaric customs. If Stefanovich's proposal were adopted the elite would no longer strive to enlighten and educate the masses; it would, rather, be wholly guided in its propaganda and agitation by the people's immediate needs and aspirations.

Stefanovich's thesis, taken together with other reports he had received about reassessments of revolutionary practices, underlined Axelrod's feeling that the movement had lost its bearings. He therefore decided to examine all the new tendencies and to map a course of action to unify and revitalize radicalism. As he saw it, the revolutionary movement was in a transitional stage and could move into one of two directions: under favorable conditions it might "develop toward a full, coherent and extensive program of federalist socialism, capable of adapting itself to specific conditions of Russian life"; or it might be-

21. Ia. Stefanovich, "Nashi zadachi v sele," *Obshchina*, no. 8/9 (1878), 33–38.

come part Jacobinist and part constitutionalist. His concern was to find a way to avoid the second and realize the first. In doing so, he intended to promote the formation of a single "popular party."[22]

Axelrod traced the confusion in the movement to several miscalculations made in 1873 and 1874, at the time the radicals went "to the people." He granted that their aims had been sound and lauded their decision to attack the prevailing order on every front, political, economic, and religious. Most important, as far as he was concerned, the activists of 1873–1874 did not regard the masses as "cannon fodder, but as a force summoned to the great cause of *conscious destruction* of the existing order and at the same time *conscious creation* of a new order on entirely new principles." To prepare the masses for active participation in the struggle was an aim on which Axelrod placed the highest priority. Hence his acute aversion to the emerging group of Jacobins, who "offer the people happiness and prosperity under the leadership of a wise authority and say that the consciousness of the masses is, if not entirely superfluous, then at least of secondary importance."[23]

Why, Axelrod asked, were so many revolutionaries abandoning their position of 1873? He explained the shift as the consequence of deep disappointment with tactics that had been based on erroneous assumptions. In expecting quick and brilliant results from their work the radicals had from the beginning been unrealistic. "We treated the matter of organizing the popular masses for the social revolution so lightly and superficially that we supposed (at least the majority among us) that a few years of active propaganda would suffice for the realization of our ideals."[24]

According to Axelrod, from this "childish" conception there flowed several mistakes, the most notable of which was the notion that one method of propaganda was suitable for every region of the Empire; the radicals did not realize that there were vast differences in the traditions and aspirations of the Russian peasantry in different parts of the country. Nor was it understood that preparation of the social revolution might require people to engage in tasks other than propaganda in the countryside. "The dominant view recognized as a *real revolutionary*

22. Pavel Axelrod, "Perekhodnyi moment nashei partii," *Obshchina*, no. 8/9 (1878), 21.
23. *Ibid.*, pp. 22–23.
24. *Ibid.*, p. 24.

only the person who dressed himself in peasant clothing." This concentration on the countryside, derived from the "narrow" conviction that the "peasants were the only real people," prevented the activists from paying as much attention as they should to urban laborers. In the cities it would have been much easier than in the villages for the radicals to have familiarized themselves with the conditions of the oppressed, and they would have realized that industrial workers also constituted an important reservoir for the revolutionary movement. Axelrod's interest in the urban workers at this early period of his career is noteworthy because of his later profession of Marxism, but it should be pointed out that he was not the first socialist revolutionary to advocate propaganda among the proletariat.[25]

Axelrod concluded the article with a set of proposals broad enough, he hoped, to serve as a rallying point for the formation of a single party. In the first place, he called on his Russian comrades to give up the notion that they could realize their ideals with "one brief act." They must come to accept the painful truth that success would only result from a series of long, difficult, and diverse efforts, beginning with theoretical propaganda and ending with a period of "active struggle" in the ranks of the people. Some would work among the privileged classes, others among the proletariat, and still others among the peasants; it would also be necessary for a few to avoid all practical work and concentrate on literary enterprises.

The last point derived directly from another of Axelrod's major proposals: the creation of a socialist press that would print leaflets, journals, brochures, and books. A permanent press would make it possible to publicize the tactics of foreign socialist movements, from whose mistakes and successes Russians could learn much. From a purely practical standpoint, a press was needed to inform people of developments elsewhere in the country, advise party members of local conditions, and, in general, provide guidance to the activists in the field. In view of the censorship and repression in Russia, he recommended that the press be located in Western Europe.

Finally, Axelrod proposed that all revolutionary activity be localized, by which he meant that workers in the field should settle more or less permanently where they were waging propaganda. Only by proceeding

25. *Ibid.*, pp. 24–25; see also Venturi, *Roots of Revolution*, pp. 507–557.

in this manner would it be possible to create strong local organizations that would be capable of refining tactics to fit local conditions and, in keeping with anarchist principles, would be in a position to create from below a federation of local units based on a "recognition by them of a solidarity of interests" of the people in the area. "And a general popular uprising can lead to serious consequences only if the people, or at least a certain part of them, having destroyed the state, are capable of forming a federated organization in the name of entirely concrete economic benefits." But here again he sounded a warning, clearly directed at the thesis advanced by Stefanovich: revolutionaries must not yield to the temptation of shaping their policies solely in accordance with the wishes of the people, for that could involve catering to the masses' prejudices, which were often reactionary. Radicals must not repudiate basic principles for the sake of immediate tactical advantages.[26]

Axelrod's diagnosis of the malaise of the revolutionary movement was remarkably acute: he understood the nature of the dissatisfactions with past practices; he had a sound grasp of the various ideological currents, some of which were still inchoate; he correctly perceived the psychology of those who were searching for new approaches; and subsequent developments proved him right in most of his predictions about the consequences of the emerging tendencies. It should be noted, moreover, that his colleagues in Geneva generally shared his apprehensions, so that in expressing them he was voicing the sentiments of a larger group.[27]

Because the analysis dealt with questions basic to the entire movement, the article enjoyed "great success in Russia." According to Aptekman, who was then in St. Petersburg, it was read with "keen interest" by the "leading groups within the revolutionary party and among the intellectual youth." Aptekman also thought that had the article appeared two years earlier it probably would have influenced the movement decisively by steering it away from the policy of terror. But by 1878 the advocates of a direct violent struggle against the government had become too powerful.[28]

26. Axelrod, "Perekhodnyi," pp. 28–32.
27. Axelrod, *Perezhitoe*, pp. 297–298.
28. *Pavel Borisovich Aksel'rod: Ego zhizn', literaturnaia i prakticheskaia deiatel'nost'* (n. d.), on deposit at the Archive of Russian and East European History and Culture, Columbia University, pp. 57–58, 68–69 [hereafter cited as Russian Archives]. The author of this biography chose not to reveal his identity, but there is much evidence to

Today, Axelrod's comprehensive program appears to belabor the obvious. It must be remembered, however, that in the 1870's the radicals were more adept at expounding lofty ideals than at developing concrete and sensible plans to realize them. By emphasizing propaganda, moreover, Axelrod refused in effect to sanction a disposition of many socialist revolutionaries, that of glorifying the revolutionary instincts of the masses. In time, after the failure of the policy of terror became evident, most of his proposals were adopted by one or another revolutionary party. His plan for the publication, outside of Russia, of a whole range of radical literature bears a striking resemblance to the course of action followed by Russian Marxists some two decades later.

All of his proposals required patience, hard work, and an acknowledgment that the revolution should not be unleashed until the masses had been won over to socialism; they were unacceptable, consequently, to an increasing number of activists who despaired of ever gaining mass support, or at least of doing so before the spread of capitalism and government repression destroyed their chances of success. Here was a difference directly related to the crucial question of the relationship between revolutionaries and the masses, which was to become the single most troublesome issue for Russian radicalism throughout its history. With some modifications, Axelrod always upheld the position he took in 1878, and this endowed his political outlook with remarkable consistency.

Shortly after the appearance of his article, Axelrod was given an unexpected opportunity to return to Russia. In the summer or fall of 1878 Viktor Obnorsky, an experienced organizer of industrial workers, asked Axelrod to become one of the editors of a newspaper to be published in St. Petersburg by the recently created Northern Union of Russian Workers. Word had reached the capital of Axelrod's interest in the Western labor movement; he therefore seemed a logical choice for the

suggest that O. V. Aptekman wrote it shortly before the First World War. In the Axelrod Archive, on deposit at the International Institute for Social History, Amsterdam [hereafter cited as I.I.S.H.], there are several letters by Aptekman requesting personal information from Axelrod. Furthermore, Mr. Boris Nicolaevsky confirmed that Aptekman had written a biography of Axelrod and that this is the one at the Russian Archive. Conversations with Mr. Nicolaevsky, summer, 1965, at the Hoover Institution.

post.[29] He accepted with alacrity, as he was eager to return to Russia. Obnorsky provided him with funds, and in February 1879 he set off with his wife and three-year-old daughter, again without documents.

They traveled to Vienna, where some Polish comrades with "connections" were to procure some sort of passports and arrange for their crossing into Russia. But by the time the family reached Vienna there had been several arrests of revolutionaries in the Polish regions of the Empire, and this had cut one of the essential links in the underground chain from St. Petersburg to the Austro-Hungarian capital. On the theory that the closer he was to Russia the better his chances of getting in, Axelrod moved on to Cracow. There he met a profiteer who exacted a handsome fee for a family pass that permitted them to cross into Russia for a one-day visit. Axelrod seized the opportunity, even though this meant that they would lack documents for the duration of their stay.

On the train to the Chernigov province, where mother and daughter were to stay with his wife's parents, there were some unsettling moments. Two policemen occupied the same compartment as the Axelrods and engaged little Vera in conversation. The child was very responsive and began to talk about life in Geneva. She alarmed her parents by mentioning their friends "Uncle Dragomanov" and "Uncle Kropotkin." Fortunately, she mispronounced the names, and the unsuspecting officers did not associate Geneva with revolutionary activity. "This saved us," declared Axelrod. As planned, he left his wife and daughter and went to Moscow.[30]

There he immediately looked for a certain engineer, Tveritinov, who

29. Axelrod had published a long article on English trade unions in the legal periodical, *Slovo*, which had created something of a sensation among students in St. Petersburg and was avidly read in workers' circles. The article—based largely on Lujo Brentano's *Zur Geschichte der englischen Gewerkvereine* (Leipzig, 1871) and *Zur Kritik der englischen Gewerkvereine* (Leipzig, 1872)—is a detailed account of the history, organizational structure, aims, and tactics of the English unions. Axelrod criticized them for not opposing the capitalist system and stressed what he believed to be their limited achievements. Still, the article aroused interest because it was one of the few publications from which people in Russia could secure information about a relatively powerful labor movement whose successes, despite Axelrod's deprecations, seemed rather substantial to activists who had not even managed to found a permanent and effective workers' organization. See N. D. [Axelrod], "Angliiskie tred-iuniony," *Slovo*, nos. 1 and 2 (Jan.–Feb. 1879), 1–38, 57–92. On the reaction of readers in Russia to Axelrod's article, see *Pavel Borisovich Aksel'rod*, pp. 50–51.

30. Axelrod, *Perezhitoe*, pp. 299–301.

was to introduce him to other revolutionaries. But Tveritinov had recently been arrested, and as Axelrod had no other names of comrades he moved on to St. Petersburg. At the editorial office of *Slovo* he was given the address of a lawyer named Korsh, whom he had never met or heard of. When he arrived at Korsh's apartment and indicated his wish to meet other members of the movement, the lawyer became very agitated because there was no way he could be sure that Axelrod was not a police spy.

Fortunately, the door suddenly opened, and from another room there emerged Nikolai Morozov, Aaron Zundelevich, Alexander Mikhailov, Lev Tikhomirov, and a few others, all members of the Central Committee of Zemlia i volia. They had just concluded a business meeting, and the expressions on their faces showed that they were in a grim mood. Zundelevich, pointing to his colleagues, said to Axelrod: "That is all that is left of us . . . And you still ask for an intensification of propaganda!" (This was a reference to Axelrod's proposals in the *Obshchina* article.) "There are so few of you," answered Axelrod, "because you abandoned propaganda. You spent the available capital without paying sufficient attention to renewing it."

A general discussion of tactics ensued, and Axelrod was asked his opinion of a plan to assassinate the Tsar. "Once a terroristic struggle against the agents of authority has been started," he replied, "logic requires that it be carried to its conclusion. You cannot allow to go unpunished the person who is mainly responsible for all that is happening."[31] Axelrod's answer evaded the basic issue: should terror be the policy of the movement? Apparently he was loath at this point to get involved in an argument that could lead to an unpleasant rupture.

The *Zemlevoltsi* warned Axelrod that it would be extremely dangerous for him to remain in St. Petersburg. As a Jew, he needed a special passport permitting him to live in the capital, and there was no way of obtaining one. Moreover, they predicted that because of "certain events" police repression would soon be intensified. What they had in mind was Alexander Soloviev's impending attempt to assassinate the Tsar, which actually took place on April 2, 1879, and produced a new wave of arrests. The police succeeded in crushing the Northern Union of

31. *Ibid.*, p. 302.

Russian Workers and seized its printing press. Axelrod lost his job even before he started to work.

Axelrod had lived underground for several weeks, constantly moving from one apartment to another, but now it was plain that he could accomplish nothing in St. Petersburg. His comrades at last found a document for him, the passport of a British subject, which was hardly appropriate, as Axelrod did not speak English, but "it was better than nothing." For the next few weeks he was on the road and on several occasions barely missed being apprehended by the police. He visited Kovno, Kiev, and Odessa, but without the proper documents he could not spend long periods of time in any of these cities. Finally, after several more adventures at the border, he reached Romania, where he looked up Z. K. Ralli, a Bakuninist with whom he had been friendly in Geneva. Through Ralli, who had wide contacts, Axelrod obtained a Romanian passport. Passing as the Romanian subject Professor Libikh, in the summer of 1879 he returned to Odessa, where he spent several months organizing workers.[32]

He was immediately struck by the profound changes that had taken place in the revolutionary movement since his previous stay in Odessa four years earlier. The local organizations had assumed a "purely military character," and their activities were conspiratorial and centralized. The activists, though "hardened, brave fighters, experienced in revolutionary work," were a contentious lot.[33] Axelrod complained that in Odessa the practice was for three to five like-minded people to form a circle and immediately to become hostile toward every other group. Axelrod visited many of these organizations, and everywhere he heard of the same projects and plans. He could not tell anyone that similar plans were being made by various groups, for he was not supposed to reveal the "secrets" he learned at the meetings. As he did not know the local people well, he thought it presumptuous to try to unite them into one organization. Gently he pointed out the danger and wastefulness of splintering the movement, but no one paid any attention to him.[34]

It is not surprising that the radicals of Odessa showed no enthusiasm

32. *Ibid.*, pp. 304–315.
33. *Ibid.*, p. 316.
34. *Revoliutsionnoe narodnichestvo 70-kh godov XIX veka*, ed. S. S. Volk (Moscow, 1965), II, 163–164.

for Axelrod's plan to concentrate on propaganda. They treated with scorn his assurance that the workers would be willing to risk several years' imprisonment just for the pleasure of reading brochures smuggled in from the West. Axelrod persisted, however, and fared much better than expected. Workers did show up for his meetings, and within a few weeks he created the Southern Union of Russian Workers, named after the group that had existed in Odessa four years earlier.

In keeping with his federalist outlook, he conceived of the union as the first of a series of regional organizations that would ultimately unite into one national federation. Axelrod devised a program for the new organization that was highly eclectic and demonstrated beyond any doubt the degree to which he was beginning to strike out on his own ideologically. He posited as the ultimate goal of the union the transformation of the social order in accordance with anarchist principles. He called for the confiscation of all the nobles' land and its allotment to the peasants. He also stressed the mutuality of interest between peasants and workers, both of whom, he said, stood to benefit from an agrarian revolution. Up to this point the program was orthodox. But then Axelrod appended a series of immediate demands: universal, equal, direct, and secret suffrage; freedom of association and the press; reduction in hours of work. These last demands were mainly political and were similar to the minimum program of the German Social Democratic party, which, of course, made them heretical from the standpoint of the Bakuninists.[35]

Indeed, a striking feature of Axelrod's thinking and activities in Russia throughout much of 1879 was their lack of consistency. Caught in a crosscurrent of conflicting revolutionary tendencies, he avoided unequivocal endorsement of any one. Instead, he tried to reconcile different positions, and thus he argued that terror and propaganda were compatible techniques, both of which could be employed by one organization. In part, his failure to take a firm stand in favor of one point of view resulted from his ignorance of the details of the controversy raging within revolutionary ranks.[36] Not having attended the Voronezh Congress of June 1879, he does not seem to have appreciated the depth of the differences that were emerging between the two major factions. It was some time before he heard that Plekhanov had split with the terrorists, who had declared their intention of fighting for a constitution. Nor did

35. Axelrod, *Perezhitoe*, pp. 327–331.
36. *Ibid.*, pp. 320–321.

he immediately know that at the congress Zheliabov had shocked Plekhanov by proposing abandonment of the "class struggle" and sanction-
ing an accommodation with the liberals in order to strive for political
liberty.[37]

But toward the end of the year, even though he was not directly involved in the ideological conflict at Voronezh, Axelrod on his own became uneasy about the stress on terror. From his conversations with its
proponents and his observation of the work of revolutionary circles, he
concluded that the preoccupation with terror was absorbing more and
more of the energies of the movement at the expense of propaganda and
agitation among the people. By concentrating on the more dramatic
"blow from above," the terrorists perforce had to neglect the attempt to
prepare the masses for a "blow from below." Not only were the two
forms of activity—terror and propaganda—psychologically incompati-
ble: the movement had neither the financial resources nor the manpower
to engage vigorously in both with any hope of success. There seemed to
be no way to harmonize them, as he had wished. Hence, in October
1879, when Zemlia i volia formally split into two groups, Narodnaia
volia and *Chernyi peredel* (The Black Partition), Axelrod promptly
joined the latter. Broadly stated, the differences between the parties may
be summed up as follows: Narodnaia volia placed primary emphasis on
terror and political action in general, whereas Chernyi peredel wanted
to concentrate on agitation in the countryside for an agrarian revolution.
The crucial point for Axelrod, he recalled in his memoirs, was that the
latter group was determined to devote "all its energy and resources to the
development of the independent revolutionary activism of the masses in
order to prepare them for the socialist revolution." But even then he was
not nearly as decisive in opposing terror as, for example, Plekhanov.
Axelrod admitted, in fact, that one reason he joined Chernyi peredel so
quickly was that two of his close friends, Deich and Stefanovich, had
gone over to it.[38]

Actually, Axelrod was not altogether happy with the general ideological direction of the new party. For instance, he felt uncomfortable about
the "medieval smell" of the name Chernyi peredel, a term that harked

37. On the Voronezh Congress, see the thorough account in Baron, *Plekhanov*, pp.
38–42.
38. Axelrod, *Perezhitoe*, p. 333. Although Axelrod had previously criticized Stefanovich, the two men had remained friends.

back to the age-old demand of peasants for the transfer of all the land to them.[39] He thought it a mistake to adopt nomenclature that tended to dramatize Russia's isolation from the West and pleaded with his colleagues to abandon not only the title Chernyi peredel but also the term *Narodnik* (Russian Populist). If they would refer to themselves as "socialist-federalists," the term would immediately make clear their allegiance to the international labor movement. Axelrod's friends did not abandon the title, but they did try to placate him somewhat. As subtitle for their newspaper, also named *Chernyi peredel,* they adopted "Organ of the Socialist-Federalists." They also formally announced that their organization subscribed to the principles of scientific socialism, which at that time meant not Marxism, but the entire Western corpus of socialist doctrine, a rather general body of thought. Axelrod's insistence on a European orientation for the new movement caused him to be nicknamed *Zapadnik,* or Westernizer, a sobriquet that became more appropriate with each passing year.[40]

For a few weeks after the collapse of Zemlia i volia Axelrod devoted most of his time to work among the Odessa proletariat. Then, late in the fall of 1879, he received a request to move to St. Petersburg to replace Plekhanov, who was about to leave for the West, as one of the editors of *Chernyi peredel.* Although not eager to desert his organization in Odessa, Axelrod felt he ought to accede to the wishes of his comrades. He was also aware that a move to the capital and an editorial position on the party paper would place him at the center of the movement, thus enabling him to exert greater influence on its policies.[41]

The St. Petersburg *Chernoperedel'tsy* were a gifted group of revolutionaries. First, there was Plekhanov, the "intellectual leader and soul" of the party, the man most responsible for its formation. Although only twenty-three years old, he had already acquired a reputation as a courageous revolutionary and an incisive disputant in ideological debate.[42] In addition to some lesser figures, Aptekman and Vera Zasulich were there, soon to be joined by Stefanovich and Deich. But it was a tiny circle without much influence and no match for the more activist and better organized Narodnaia volia. In January 1880 the ranks of Chernyi peredel

39. *Ibid.,* pp. 341–343.
40. O. V. Aptekman, "Zapiski semidesiatnika," *Sovremennyi mir,* no. 5/6 (1916), 226.
41. Axelrod, *Perezhitoe,* p. 338.
42. Baron, *Plekhanov,* Chap. 3.

were greatly depleted by the departure of Plekhanov, Deich, Zasulich, and Stefanovich. They left primarily to avoid arrest, but another major consideration for Plekhanov was his desire to study and prepare himself for what he believed would be a more effective role in the movement. Had the chances for a revolution in the near future looked brighter, the four would have stayed in Russia.[43]

For about six months Axelrod tried to breathe life into Chernyi peredel, but his efforts were not rewarding. For one thing, he found it impossible to hold on to the party's following. Several groups, including the Southern Union of Russian Workers he had founded in Odessa, went over to the rival organization, which promised quicker and more dramatic results. Even more distressing, in January 1880 the party was betrayed to the police, who confiscated the printing press and arrested several Chernoperedel'tsy, including Aptekman.[44] Axelrod was now the only prominent *Chernoperedelets* still free in Russia.

As soon as the immediate danger passed, he resumed work and succeeded in forming a small circle of young revolutionaries, who called themselves the "party of Socialist-Federalists," though they remained part of Chernyi peredel. In outlining a program for the group Axelrod ran into some difficulties. The main plank was unexceptionable: it called for the transfer of all land to the peasants, who were to exercise communal ownership over it. He did not, however, justify the demand with the traditional contention of Russian revolutionaries that the peasant commune must be the foundation of a socialist system on a national scale. Axelrod argued instead that a socialist revolution was imminent in Western Europe and that continued existence of bourgeois Russia was as inconceivable as had been the preservation of serfdom alongside a bourgeois Europe. He did concede the importance of the commune, but only because it facilitated collectivist propaganda among the masses. This argument was designed as a response to the fear of some younger revolutionaries that the communes would eventually disintegrate and leave the country without a basis for the introduction of socialism.

Axelrod included two more "heretical" ideas in the program. First, he indicated that the anarchist ideal could be realized only some time after the socialist revolution, that is, only after the people had learned to perform a variety of functions necessary for running a modern society. He

43. *Ibid.*, p. 47; Axelrod, *Perezhitoe*, p. 347.
44. Axelrod, *Perezhitoe*, pp. 348–349.

had been influenced to modify his views along these lines by some conversations he had had a year earlier in Bern with a Professor Nikolay Ziber, formerly of the University of Kiev, who had been one of the first to expound Marxist economic doctrines in the Russian legal press. Second, he added a set of immediate demands for political and economic rights identical to those he had written into the program of the Southern Union of Russian Workers.[45]

Axelrod had no difficulty in obtaining the agreement to his program of small groups of younger people in St. Petersburg and Moscow, but he thought it necessary to sound out the émigré Chernoperedel'tsy. A delegate sent to Geneva returned with the message that the program was totally unacceptable to the foreign comrades. "This is not Populism, but Social Democracy," they charged, not without justification. They objected most strenuously to the "immediate demands," which signified too much of an interest in politics. Axelrod and his followers were not ready to relinquish their program, and yet they were reluctant to break with their colleagues in Geneva. It was decided that Axelrod himself should go abroad for further negotiations. Because of some matters he had to arrange in St. Petersburg and Moscow, he delayed his departure until June 1880. Had he postponed his trip any longer, he would have been arrested. The police came for him a few days after he had left.[46]

Although as leader of the Chernoperedel'tsy in Russia Axelrod concentrated on organizing a group clearly distinguishable in outlook from the Narodovol'tsy, it must be emphasized that relations between the two factions were far from hostile. Their members often helped each other, trading loans of money and warnings about suspicious police activities. On occasion the Chernoperedel'tsy even rendered material aid for terroristic enterprises. For example, when Axelrod went to Kharkov late in 1879 he took along revolvers and cartridges for some Narodovol'tsy. In the minds of many radicals in Russia the distinctions between the two groups were still vague and fluid, seeming to revolve more around questions of emphasis than principle. Indeed, Axelrod later recalled that at the time he himself was "psychologically" drawn to Narodnaia volia because among its members were many "choice revolutionaries, people hardened in struggle, possessing a great deal of revolutionary experience." He even entered into negotiations with Lev Tikhomirov for a

45. *Ibid.*, pp. 351–355.
46. *Ibid.*, pp. 356–357.

possible reunification of the parties, but in the end the discussions proved futile. Axelrod departed for Geneva still representing a fully independent group.[47]

To his surprise, agreement on his program with the émigré Cherno-peredel'tsy was easier to obtain than he had anticipated. But apparently he had some stormy exchanges with Plekhanov, who at that time was more "orthodox" on the question of the mir than Axelrod. Actually, Plekhanov was already beginning to have certain doubts about the durability of the commune, but according to one account he pressed Axelrod to state categorically whether or not he believed that the commune was an institution on the basis of which Russia could become socialist without a socialist revolution taking place in Europe. At first Axelrod refused to commit himself, but when Plekhanov insisted on an answer, he asked: "Are you sincere in formulating the question in this way?" Offended, Plekhanov replied: "If you doubt my sincerity, then there is nothing that I can do," and stalked out of the room. Plekhanov's wife urged Axelrod to apologize, but he refused. Within a few days, however, the two men settled their differences and through a series of mutual concessions decided on a common program.[48]

Axelrod's section on immediate demands was replaced by a general statement that recognized that urban laborers were not primarily concerned with the land question and attributed to the demands for higher wages and a shorter working day "a specially important significance." Although no demands of a specifically political nature were listed, the projected program did stipulate that in the event of the establishment of a constitutional system in Russia, Chernoperedel'tsy could participate in the elections and even put up their own candidates. In the electoral campaign, however, the main function of the party's candidates should be to "weaken the people's faith in the significance of peaceful, legal reforms." It also recognized the necessity of a direct struggle against the government by means of "political terror." The program did not contain an explicit statement on the question over which the two men had quarreled, though the final version was much closer to Plekhanov's thinking than to Axelrod's. In view of the "preservation of the landed

47. *Ibid.*, pp. 334, 360, 364–367; for a favorable assessment of the Narodovol'tsy written by Axelrod in 1880, see his "Russland," *Jahrbuch für Sozialwissenschaft und Sozialpolitik*, II (1880), 304–305.

48. On this incident, see Boris Nicolaevsky's lecture at Harvard University, Mar. 17, 1960, typescript on deposit at the Russian Research Center, Harvard University.

communes . . . it would be very important for the people to make the expected agrarian revolution as quickly as possible, [and this would be] . . . a step toward the complete reorganization of society on socialist principles." All in all the new draft program was as diversified in its ideological underpinnings as the first.[49]

His mission accomplished, Axelrod began his return journey to St. Petersburg. He decided to stop off in Jassa in order to settle his family there and to arrange for the regular transportation of revolutionary literature across the Romanian border into Russia. In consequence of a variety of mishaps, however, he had to stay in Jassa much longer than the two months he had anticipated. At first his departure was delayed because he did not receive the money his colleagues in Geneva had sent him for his work. By some strange and unexplained set of circumstances, it turned up in North Africa before reaching Jassa.

When the money finally arrived, he was in jail. Shortly after the assassination of Alexander II in March 1881, the Romanian police, under pressure from the Russian government, rounded up several foreign socialists, Axelrod among them. The police questioned him about possible connections with the terrorists. His statement that he had been in Romania for six months and therefore could not have participated in the assassination satisfied the interrogators, though they were stunned by his audacious expression of sympathy with the deed. Within a week he was freed and was ordered to leave the country. In the meantime, his colleagues in Geneva had urged him not to push on to Russia, as the police were known to be looking for him. He crossed the border into Turkey, where he boarded a French ship and after several adventures reached Geneva some time in the summer of 1881.[50]

It was only then that he learned of the crushing blow the Russian government had dealt the revolutionary movement. Thousands had been arrested, and it was doubtful whether any groups capable of effective work still existed in the country. Under the circumstances, the émigrés abandoned hope of returning to Russia in the near future. The immediate response of the Chernoperedel'tsy—with the exception of Plekhanov—was to entertain the idea of outright support for terror and

49. Axelrod, *Perezhitoe*, pp. 367–369. The program agreed upon by the two men was published in *Chernyi peredel*, no. 2 (Sept. 1880).
50. Axelrod, *Perezhitoe*, pp. 371–380.

political work. They made a new attempt to reunite with Narodnaia volia and sent Stefanovich to Russia to negotiate. But soon after he arrived in St. Petersburg he went over to the rival party, and several others followed him. According to Axelrod, he and his colleagues were not greatly disturbed by the defections because they were confident that Narodnaia volia was about to make concessions to their point of view. They even accepted with equanimity the likelihood that Chernyi peredel would soon be dissolved.[51] Actually the party remained intact, but it consisted of little more than a group of generals without an army.

Plekhanov, Zasulich, Deich, and a few other Chernoperedel'tsy lived in or near Geneva and often met to discuss the latest developments in Russia and theoretical questions. Axelrod maintained close contact with them and tended to share their views, but late in the summer of 1881 he moved to Zurich, which made meetings with his colleagues difficult. The move was prompted by an offer from M. P. Dragomanov to become a regular contributor to a new journal, *Vol'noe slovo*. Axelrod had met Dragomanov, a somewhat enigmatic figure among Russian émigrés, in 1876 and had been impressed by his erudition and devotion to the cause of Ukrainian nationalism. Formerly a professor at the University of Kiev, Dragomanov apparently went to the West to publicize his program, which called for autonomy for the nationalities in the Russian Empire and the introduction of a democratic form of government. Because he also expressed vague sympathy for socialism, he was in a position to be on good terms with people representing a broad ideological spectrum, liberals, socialists, and anarchists. In 1881 Dragomanov became editor of *Vol'noe slovo*—no one seems to have known the source of his funds for the enterprise—and on the recommendation of Lavrov he asked Axelrod to take charge of a section of the paper devoted to the Western European labor movement. The subject fascinated Axelrod, and he jumped at the opportunity to earn his living as a journalist. Lavrov's interest seemed a sufficient guarantee of the "probity" of the undertaking. Although the political sympathies of the paper would be liberal democratic, Axelrod saw no reason to refuse the offer, as he had been promised complete freedom to express his views.[52]

It was difficult for Axelrod to collect material for his columns in

51. *Ibid.*, pp. 381–389.
52. *Ibid.*, pp. 391–392.

Geneva, a city without either a strong working-class movement or active socialist groups outside of a few Russians. By contrast, Zurich was the center of both the country's national political life and the fairly large proletarian movement of German Switzerland. It was the city to which several leading German Social Democrats, among them Karl Kautsky, Eduard Bernstein, and Georg von Vollmar, had emigrated after the anti-socialist laws of 1878. It was also the home of the German party's newspaper, *Sozialdemokrat.* August Bebel and Wilhelm Liebknecht frequently visited Zurich for discussions of party affairs. Much as Axelrod regretted leaving his compatriots in Geneva, once he had settled in Zurich and become acquainted with the socialist circles he found life there very agreeable. He formed some friendships, particularly with Kautsky and Bernstein, that he retained for the rest of his life. No less important, he found the "atmosphere" in Zurich conducive to his work for *Vol'noe slovo* and "very favorable for my development along Social Democratic lines."[53]

In the six years since he had first set foot in the West, Axelrod matured considerably as a political thinker. It is true that in 1881 he still did not subscribe to a comprehensive and uniform body of ideas: his commitments were somewhat tenuous, and he tended to borrow his views freely from various sources. Thus, he continued to regard himself as a Bakuninist and repudiated the state as well as Western parliamentarism. At the same time, however, he repeatedly endorsed certain political demands, most notably those calling for universal suffrage and civil liberties. Similarly, although he believed that the revolutionary movement should concern itself primarily with socialist propaganda and agitation, he did not flatly reject political terror as a potentially useful tactic. Despite this lack of consistency, his political outlook had gained in sophistication. He had mastered a wide range of radical currents and tactical positions, both Western and Russian, and he had cultivated and refined his critical powers. He was now capable of developing an elaborate and largely realistic series of tactics as the basis for the formation of a united revolutionary party. The premise underlying his proposals was one he would never forsake: that a revolution could genuinely liberate the masses only if the latter participated in its execution. He had, more-

53. *Ibid.*, p. 392.

over, gained sufficient self-confidence so that he did not hesitate publicly to declare his reservations about Bakuninism. Although in 1881 no one would have predicted that he would continue to move along a new direction, in retrospect it seems obvious that he had not yet reached the final stage of his evolution as a revolutionary.

III | The Turn to Marxism

Axelrod's first two years in Zurich, from 1881 to 1883, encompassed the single most important change in the evolution of his political position. Gradually he turned from Bakuninism to Marxism, applying concepts from the latter while continuing to profess the former. It is impossible to explain his conversion as the consequence of any one specific occurrence, although his final change can be attributed to two parallel developments, both of them somewhat accidental. First, the research for his writings on European labor and his personal closeness to Kautsky and Bernstein exposed him, more than ever before, to Marxist thought. At the same time he became embroiled, quite unintentionally and unexpectedly, in sharp polemics with the Narodovol'tsy, and the public airing of differences that ensued disclosed that on some fundamental questions he had deeper misgivings about the terrorists' ideological outlook than he had suspected. But it was certainly not accidental that he became aware of the profundity of his differences with the Narodovol'tsy at a time when he was more and more drawn to Social Democratic ideas. Axelrod's rift with one group and attraction to another should be viewed as related aspects of his effort to define his political position.

The dispute with Narodnaia volia resulted from a speech he delivered at the International Socialist Congress at Chur, Switzerland, early in October 1881. At the suggestion of Eduard Bernstein, the local organizational committee of the congress invited Axelrod to participate in the meetings. He thought it presumptuous to accept without being formally designated a delegate and therefore approached his colleagues in Geneva, who suggested to the Chernoperedel'tsy in St. Petersburg that they choose a representative. They could not see any practical significance to the suggestion, but were prepared to empower Axelrod to represent them if he considered it useful. In view of this lack of enthusiasm, he refused. Still, he agreed to attend the congress as a guest. To conceal his identity from the police he appeared under the name of G. Alexandrovich. He was then prevailed upon to give a report on the Russian movement, though he warned his listeners at the outset that he would only speak in an unofficial capacity and that because of his fifteen-month absence from Russia his information might be obsolete.[1]

Axelrod sought to convince the congress that the absence of a representative from his country was not a snub but rather the consequence of a lack of "practical, tangible points of contact between the revolutionary movement in Russia on the one hand and that in Western Europe on the other." In the West there already raged an "organized class struggle," whereas in Russia two relatively small groups, a revolutionary minority and the government, were locked in conflict. Neither of the latter camps derived its support exclusively or primarily from one social class. The tsarist government leaned on the "mass of bureaucrats and soldiers, representing a band of robbers who sap the vital juices of the country and mercilessly suppress all opposition, no matter from what social class it comes." At the same time the forces hostile to the existing order, in particular the party that was best known in Europe, Narodnaia volia, received direct or indirect support from dissatisfied individuals in all classes.

Additionally, the sweeping and intense repression in Russia had impelled revolutionaries—again he had in mind primarily the Narodovol'tsy—to concentrate on the creation of small, illegal organizations committed to the elimination of "barbaric arbitrariness." But Axelrod hastened to assure the delegates that the Narodovol'tsy had neither lost interest in socialism nor in maintaining close relations with Western comrades. Nearly all of the Russian activists, with the possible exception of Zheliabov and a few others, wanted "to get rid of absolutism" only to make possible the more agreeable and important job of agitating among the people for socialism. He was certain that "the tactic and program of . . . [Narodnaia volia] did not arise in accordance with a formulated plan or principle, but gradually, almost involuntarily, under the influ-

1. Pavel Axelrod, *Perezhitoe i peredumannoe* (Berlin, 1923), p. 293; "Rech' G. Aleksandrovicha [Axelrod] na sotsialisticheskom kongresse v Khure," *Vol'noe slovo*, no. 13 (1881), 5.

ence of frightful government repression and extreme difficulties [that were encountered] in [trying] to form our party."

Axelrod admitted that his group, the Chernoperedel'tsy, had a somewhat different orientation, but he considered the disagreements not so significant as to preclude collaboration. He felt that both groups were abandoning extreme positions and that they "will probably soon unite into one organization," a development that he himself would welcome in view of the achievements, experience, and organizational skill of the Narodovol'tsy.[2]

Axelrod's judicious and conciliatory speech made a favorable impression, and in a subsequent intervention in the debates of the congress he succeeded in persuading the delegates to pass a resolution praising the Russian revolutionaries. The American delegate had introduced a general motion that called on socialists not to engage in the preparation of a "violent revolution, but only in the organization of the masses for the resistance against the bourgeoisie." Axelrod protested, pointing out that adoption of the motion would preclude a rapprochement between Russian revolutionaries and Western socialists, for in Russia there was no alternative to violence. The delegates thereupon passed a different resolution, formulated by the French representative, which hailed the efforts of the Russian revolutionaries who, "in a situation where they have to defend themselves, answer force with force, terror with terror." It also exhorted all "free peoples" to express sympathy for those who were "struggling, suffering and dying for freedom and social justice under the yoke of Muscovite tyranny." This was the first "brotherly greeting" sent to Russian revolutionaries by foreign socialists, and, according to Aptekman, it was of "great moral significance" to the beleaguered movement.[3]

The Narodovol'tsy were not pleased, however, by Axelrod's performance at the congress. In a lead article in *Narodnaia volia*, Tikhomirov, the chief theorist of the organization, subjected Axelrod's speech to a stinging attack. He acknowledged his party's "sincere gratitude" for the "moral support" afforded by the resolution of the congress and its appreciation to Axelrod for having tried to explain the status of the Russian revolutionary movement. But to his "sorrow" he had to voice his

2. "Rech' G. Aleksandrovicha," pp. 5–8.
3. *Pavel Borisovich Aksel'rod: Ego zhizn', literaturnaia i prakticheskaia deiatel'nost'* (n. d.), on deposit at Russian Archives. The resolution is reproduced in *Narodnaia volia*, no. 7, Dec. 23, 1881.

"regret" that the congress had not been able to find a person "better informed on this subject. The characterization by the 'Russian guest' of our point of view is distinguished by extreme inaccuracy and is at variance with the real state of affairs."

When Tikhomirov actually presented his objections to Axelrod's speech, the differences seemed to be primarily matters of emphasis. But as so often happens in ideological disputes, what appear to be different emphases conceal divergencies of far deeper significance than the disputants themselves initially recognize.

Tikhomirov was particularly vexed by Axelrod's assertion that Narodnaia volia had no central doctrine, that its tactical positions had emerged "empirically." No charge could more deeply wound the nineteenth-century radical, nourished as he was on the notion of the overriding importance of "theory." Tikhomirov insisted that the basis of his movement was the principle of *Narodnichestvo*, which had clearly distinguishable doctrines. Narodnichestvo had provided the party with "its orientation toward the state, its assessment both of popular forces and of the elements hostile to the people. By logically extending the principle of Narodnichestvo into practice, Narodnaia volia creates in the theoretical sphere not only a doctrine, but an entire world outlook." Tikhomirov did not, unfortunately, spell out in further detail the meaning of this rather general statement, but it seems to imply that Narodnaia volia's turn to politics and neglect of propaganda among the peasants were not merely tactical maneuvers but policies dictated by a new political creed. And if this is what he intended to say, then the differences between Tikhomirov's and Axelrod's positions were rather substantial.

Yet, in the very same article Tikhomirov made several other assertions that belie this interpretation. He took Axelrod to task for analyzing the Russian revolutionary movement on the basis of European political categories, a charge that missed the point of the speech. Accusing Axelrod of having made a false distinction between "political radicals" and "socialists," Tikhomirov explained that his comrades had concluded that in a country without political freedom such a separation was impossible. They must be both political radicals and socialists because no economic reform was possible until there had first been fundamental changes in the political structure. At the same time, there could be no genuine popular self-government without "economic liberation." Axelrod had therefore been completely wrong, according to Tikhomirov, in stating that Narodnaia volia had even temporarily ignored the "popular masses." On the contrary, the Narodovol'tsy were "imbued with a consciousness of the importance of the masses and with esteem for them," but they had no use for individuals who simply "talk" about "the people." They were eager to do something for them. Specifically, they intended to overthrow the government at the earliest possible moment and hand over power to the people. This last comment seemed to suggest that the Narodovol'tsy's desire to eliminate tsarism was a tactic designed to give the people the opportunity to create a new social order, and this was precisely what Axelrod had said.

Finally, Tikhomirov accused Axelrod of having misrepresented the facts by asserting that Zheliabov did not subscribe fully to the movement's program. The Narodovol'tsy were at one on all fundamentals, claimed Tikhomirov.[4]

Axelrod was stunned and hurt by the attack. He thought he had been eminently fair to the Narodovol'tsy. Bernstein felt, in fact, that his report amounted to an "apology or semiapology" for them. He went so far as to suggest that after hearing the speech he was not sure to which party Axelrod himself belonged.[5] At first Axelrod planned to reply to Tikhomirov's criticisms, but after studying them he simply could not understand the nature of the objections. In an effort at conciliation, he offered to publish, as an appendix to a brochure containing the talk, a letter by the Narodovol'tsy explaining their position.[6] For reasons not known the brochure never appeared.

The episode planted serious doubts in Plekhanov's mind about the feasibility of collaborating with the Narodovol'tsy. The other Chernoperedel'tsy in Geneva were also puzzled by the attack and came to Axelrod's defense. They indicated their intention of publishing a reply to Tikhomirov in *Narodnaia volia*.[7]

The Executive Committee of Narodnaia volia, however, did not relent. Early in February 1882 it sent a long confidential letter to "foreign comrades," also composed by Tikhomirov, in which it delivered another

4. *Narodnaia volia*, no. 7, Dec. 23, 1881 (unsigned lead article on pp. 1–3).
5. Axelrod, *Perezhitoe*, pp. 394, 399.
6. Axelrod to Deich, winter, 1881, *Gruppa 'Osvobozhdenie truda,'* ed. L. Deich (Moscow, 1924–1928), IV, 148–150.
7. Deich to Axelrod, Apr. 21, 1882, *ibid.*, I, 159; L. Deich, "O sblizhenii i razryve s narodovol'tsami," *Proletarskaia revoliutsiia*, no. 8 (1923), 9–10.

assault on Axelrod's speech. The letter basically reiterated the points already made. But it is significant that the tone and thrust were much more explicitly Jacobinist. Tikhomirov now referred to the seizure of power as the major aim of the party, to which "all else"—"program, tactics, all interests, all questions"—had been subordinated. "This you must understand in the most profound way," he told the Chernoperedel'tsy, "if you wish to be with us."[8]

Axelrod's dispute with the Narodovol'tsy continued to bewilder and anger him and surely helped loosen his ideological bonds to many of his Russian comrades. But as a discussion of issues it was not productive. In his attempt to be conciliatory, he papered over those differences he knew existed. And, at least initially, the members of the Executive Committee stated their position ambiguously and in certain respects even falsely because they did not want to alienate potential support. In fact, a year and a half after the polemical attack Tikhomirov admitted that at Chur Axelrod had accurately described Zheliabov's position.[9] The irrational and indignant response of the Narodovol'tsy to Axelrod's speech seems fundamentally to have been caused by their fear that he had somehow exposed them and thus damaged their image. But if at first the Tikhomirov affair only suggested the existence of basic disagreements, an exchange of views between Axelrod and another *Narodovolets* at the same time brought the issue into much sharper focus.

Late in September 1881 Ivan Prisetskii, a Narodovolets of some importance, published a letter in *Vol'noe slovo* calling for unification of the two factions of the revolutionary movement. He contended that the parties had too much in common to maintain separate organizations. But unfortunately the Narodniks, as Prisetskii called the Chernoperedel'tsy, clung to the belief that "illegal propaganda" among the "backward, downtrodden, illiterate peasants" could yield results. They did not realize that even in Western Europe, which enjoyed freedom of speech, press, and assembly, socialists had encountered enormous difficulties in trying to mobilize the indifferent masses. All the more so in Russia only a relatively small number of people could be expected to

8. Executive Committee of Narodnaia volia to foreign comrades, beginning of Feb. 1882, *Gruppa*, ed. Deich, III, 143–151.
9. Axelrod, *Perezhitoe*, p. 402.

appreciate the importance of fighting for a constitutional order, a truth that Narodnaia volia had come to recognize.

Prisetskii admitted that this attitude toward the people violated an important principle cherished by the Chernoperedel'tsy: "Everything for the people by means of the people." But he insisted that the creation of a constitutional order would benefit all the people, not only because the freedoms they would be granted were of intrinsic value but also because the new form of government would allow for overt socialist agitation. Still, since the people could not be made to understand this, Prisetskii suggested that the Chernoperedel'tsy's canon be changed to read: "Everything for the nation and the entire cause by means of that part of the nation which is most interested in the cause." He defined "part of the nation" as the intelligentsia, which was the social stratum most eager to establish a constitutional system and the major source of Narodnaia volia's support. Once the autocracy was overthrown, the Narodovol'tsy would, according to Prisetskii, dedicate themselves to their "earlier cause," socialism.[10]

Narodnaia volia's preoccupation with political terror at the expense of propaganda among the peasants had always implied a Jacobinist bent. The party had never relied on the active support of more than a few dozen people for its terrorist activities. But its avowed intention had been to unleash a *popular* revolution. When Narodnaia volia was first formed the leaders tried to stress their continuing interest in mobilizing the masses by assigning one-third of the available funds to terror and two-thirds to propaganda. This was a piece of gross self-delusion, but it did indicate a reluctance on the part of the Narodovol'tsy to acknowledge, even to themselves, that they were a minuscule group acting in the name of the people. Prisetskii's letter is arresting because it seems to be the first time a Narodovolets publicly and unequivocally asserted that the political revolution had to be the work of a minority of the population. More important, he honored his proposed tactic with a doctrinal rationale—albeit not one of impressive theoretical sophistication—namely, that it would be impossible to impart the proper degree of political education to the masses.

Much as he sympathized with Narodnaia volia's immediate goal and

10. Letter by I. P. [Ivan Prisetskii], *Vol'noe slovo,* no. 10 (1881), 6–8.

tactics, Axelrod found Prisetskii's thesis too dangerous to go unchallenged. In a lengthy article, in which he formulated in embryonic form many of the ideas that were to become an integral part of his political outlook in later years, Axelrod sought to refute the central premise of the Narodovolets. He rejected the notion that the "organized intelligentsia," after overthrowing the absolutist regime, could be relied upon to create a political system that would benefit everyone. He had too little faith in human altruism to accept the Tkachevian idea that a minority could be trusted to further the interests of the entire community.

Admittedly a sizable number of individuals within the intelligentsia were genuinely democratic, and they probably constituted a larger group in Russia than anywhere else. But as a whole the Russian intelligentsia came from the privileged, well-to-do classes, to whom it was tied "by upbringing, habit [and] by its intellectual and material interests." Should it alone succeed in eliminating the old order, it would behave as its British and French counterparts had several decades earlier, securing political rights for itself and establishing a system that would serve its interests. The laboring masses, again as in Western Europe, would have to stage another revolution to gain freedom for themselves. They could avoid this prospect only by playing a major role in the initial struggle for "constitutional guarantees" and thus earning for themselves a position to secure rights for all the people once the autocracy had fallen.

Axelrod also contested Prisetskii's belief that the people could not be mobilized to campaign for a constitutional regime. If revolutionaries would only agitate on the basis of the genuine aspirations of the masses, their interest could be aroused. Such issues as taxes, military service, Russification, and the right of association could easily be used to persuade the people that substantial reform was possible only after basic political changes were made. Instead of leading to desirable changes, Prisetskii's tactic would only further weaken the movement's ties to the people.[11] Thus, although Axelrod had for long been a warm advocate of unity within the revolutionary ranks, he could not but repudiate Prisetskii's conditions.

11. Pavel Axelrod, "Vse dlia naroda i posredstvom naroda (Otvet na pis'mo I. P.)," *Vol'noe slovo*, no. 19 (1881), 11–17.

During the months that Axelrod was engaged in dispute with the Narodovol'tsy and becoming increasingly disenchanted with their Jacobinism, he spent most of his time writing articles for *Vol'noe slovo*. From August 1881 until March 1882 he contributed some fifteen "Letters on the Labor Movement" and twelve "Chronicles of the Labor Movement." The salient feature of these writings is that they illustrate the degree to which he was absorbing Marxist ideas.

It is noteworthy that the socialist ideas of both Axelrod and Plekhanov were in the process of being Westernized at about the same time. It is significant, though, that the two men who did more than any others to introduce Social Democratic thought into Russia traveled quite different intellectual routes before arriving at Marxism. As Boris Nicolaevsky has suggested, Plekhanov may be regarded as the last great Russian Westernizer in the tradition of Belinsky, Alexander Herzen, and Nikolay Chernyshevsky. He was an *intelligent* in the full and best sense of the word. He came to his new *Weltanschauung* by way of intensive study of Western philosophy, economics, history, and, in particular, the major works of socialism. He made considerable contributions in the areas of philosophy and sociology. A talented writer, Plekhanov became without question the most eminent exponent of Russian Marxism. But as is often characteristic of people gifted at broad generalization and sweeping theoretical analyses, he did not "understand that in the . . . pursuit of lofty goals even petty, everyday details have enormous significance."[12] Nor did he ever truly perceive either the life-style or the aspirations of the social class so central to all his writings, the proletariat. These shortcomings are evident in Plekhanov's work, which was marked by abstractness and dogmatism.

Axelrod's conversion to Marxism had different roots. It resulted essentially from his knowledge of the practices of Western Social Democracy, acquired both at workers' meetings in Berlin in 1874 and from studying the contemporary European working-class organizations for his articles in *Vol'noe slovo*. Even though he had dipped into the writings of Marx and Lassalle, it is no exaggeration to suggest that he first became a Social Democrat and then a Marxist. That is to say, he understood and appreciated the practices of the European labor movement before he had thoroughly assimilated its theory. And it is therefore no accident that

12. B. N—skii [B. Nicolaevsky], "P. B. Aksel'rod (Osnovnye cherty politicheskoi biografii)," *Sotsialisticheskii vestnik*, no. 15/16, Aug. 18, 1925, 10.

his Marxism was at all times Social Democratic in its contents; in other words, he valued democracy as much as socialism. Nor is it fortuitous that his chief interest and contributions were in the sphere of strategy, tactics, and organization. What concerned him, above all, was to discover a way to apply Western methods of political struggle to Russian conditions. If Plekhanov may be regarded as the "last great representative of the old and glorious galaxy of Russian intelligentsia-Westernizers, then Axelrod must be called the first pioneer of a new school of Westernizers —worker-Westernizers."[13]

There was yet another difference in the two men's approaches to Marxism. Because of his theoretical and scholarly bent of mind, Plekhanov tended to stress the objective laws of history that he believed would lead to man's emancipation. Axelrod had personally experienced the degradation of poverty and therefore awarded to the proletariat a direct role in achieving its liberation. Much more than Plekhanov, he viewed Marxism as a movement that would free man from servility by entrusting him with an important function in shaping the historical process. Leopold Haimson perceptively summed up this difference between the two men when he wrote "that while Plekhanov's confidence in the proletariat grew out of a faith in the determining forces of history, Axelrod's confidence in these determining forces was born out of a faith in the proletariat."[14]

It is not at all clear that in the gradual process of conversion Axelrod himself was conscious that he was making statements that were inconsistent with his avowed beliefs. Some forty years later he admitted as much: "By examining and elucidating the phenomena, events, and problems of the proletarian liberation movement in the West from the Social Democratic standpoint, I acquired the habit, imperceptively to myself, as it were, of also applying the Marxist point of view to questions relating to the Russian revolutionary movement. Thus, the work for *Vol'noe slovo* became for me a school from which I emerged a fully conscious Social Democrat not only 'for the West' but also for Russia."[15]

Actually, as early as October 1880, before he had begun writing on European labor, he betrayed a predilection to use certain Marxist argu-

13. *Ibid.*
14. Leopold Haimson, *The Russian Marxists and the Origins of Bolshevism* (Cambridge, Mass., 1955), p. 48.
15. Axelrod, *Perezhitoe*, pp. 405–406.

ments.[16] It is true, however, that he did so most distinctly and unequivocally in his contributions to *Vol'noe slovo*. These writings were supposed to have been reportorial, and to a considerable extent Axelrod confined himself to factual accounts of developments in the various European labor movements and on one occasion even that of the United States. He worked hard collecting material for the articles, which are impressive for the information they contain. But he had no qualms about expressing his opinions, which reveal his growing admiration for Social Democratic principles and policies.

Thus, for example, he pointed out that the French proletariat had found it impossible to make substantial gains by simply waging an economic struggle against capitalists, who could always rely for support on the state's instruments of coercion. It therefore became evident to the workers that they must democratize the state and then use it to emancipate themselves. To Axelrod this strategy seemed sound.[17] In an analysis of the 1881 election in Germany he did not so much as suggest that the socialist party was engaging in a futile gesture by campaigning vigorously for votes. On the contrary, he argued that only police repression had prevented the German Marxists from electing more *Reichstag* deputies than they had. His implied conclusion was not that workers should cease to participate in politics, but rather that they should strive to end government interference in the electoral process.[18]

Equally important, Axelrod categorically acknowledged the preeminence of industrial workers in the revolutionary struggle: "At the present time the proletariat in the industrial centers are the most conscious and the most ardent pioneers of the high ideals common to all mankind. That is why they are at the head of the liberation movement of the laboring masses of Western Europe and America, and are the focus on which are concentrated all the revolutionary aspirations of our epoch. Thus, the labor movement is in its aggregate the embodiment, as it were, of the conscious aspirations and efforts of our epoch in the transition to a higher stage of civilization."[19]

---

16. Pavel Axelrod, "Russland," *Jahrbuch für Sozialwissenschaft und Sozialpolitik,* II (1880), 267–268.

17. [Pavel Axelrod,] "Pis'ma o rabochem dvizhenii," *Vol'noe slovo,* no. 5 (1881), 6–8.

18. [Pavel Axelrod,] "Pis'ma o rabochem dvizhenii," *Vol'noe slovo,* no. 16 (1881), 7–8; see also [Pavel Axelrod,] "Pis'ma o rabochem dvizhenii," *Vol'noe slovo,* no. 13 (1881), 9–10.

19. [Pavel Axelrod,] "Pis'ma o rabochem dvizhenii," *Vol'noe slovo,* no. 4 (1881), 7.

In an article commemorating the Paris Commune, he lauded the French workers for demonstrating the ability to run a complicated governmental machinery. "The working class," he wrote, "had matured [sufficiently] for its mission of transforming the contemporary social and political order; it had sufficient intellectual forces so that it could dare take upon itself this task. Let the proletariat succeed, by revolutionary means, in eliminating the ruling class from their role as legislators and rulers even if only for one year—and it will show in practice what organizational strength it has accumulated." The Paris Commune was glorious because it had destroyed the illusion that "the proletariat, on the morrow of its victory, would nevertheless need the intelligentsia of the vanquished bourgeoisie."[20]

Marxist influences were no less evident in Axelrod's general statements about Europe's social and political system. He contended on one occasion that the economically dominant class had developed a "system of political institutions" and a "system of religious, moral, and philosophical ideas" conforming to their class interests and cultural traditions and having as their purpose the subordination of the "exploited classes." As a result the proletariat had concluded that they must concentrate their struggle for emancipation on three goals: undermining the foundations of the existing forms of civilization; disseminating the positive ideals of the new social order; and organizing their forces as well as educating and training themselves to acquire the habits of self-help and self-government.[21] One might question the theoretical sophistication of Axelrod's formulation, but there can be no doubt that it bore the imprint of Marx's concept of historical materialism.

Aside from theoretical remarks, Axelrod's articles in *Vol'noe slovo* contained a reservoir of information that he would only draw upon years later. One of the chief features of his reports was the detailed account of the organizational structure and tactics of the various labor movements. This knowledge provided him with what may appear to be an obvious perspective, but it was one that Russian Marxists often disregarded. He came to have an appreciation of the importance of applying divergent tactics under varying conditions, without, however, abandoning what he regarded as the most fundamental principle, that a

20. [Pavel Axelrod,] "Pis'ma o rabochem dvizhenii," *Vol'noe slovo*, no. 34 (1882), 8.
21. [Pavel Axelrod,] "Pis'ma o rabochem dvizhenii," *Vol'noe slovo*, no. 4 (1881), 7.

socialist movement must strive to activate the largest possible number of workers.

Axelrod derived considerable satisfaction from his work for *Vol'noe slovo*. In addition to providing him with an income, it enabled him to follow intellectual pursuits that had long interested him. He even had enough time to read at greater leisure than ever before the theoretical works of leading socialist writers, which further deepened his understanding of Marxism. But the period of contentment soon ended.

After the first issue of *Vol'noe slovo* appeared, the story began to circulate among émigrés that the journal was being financed by the Ministry of the Interior and that A. P. Malshinsky, the publisher, was an agent of the Third Section. Neither Dragomanov nor Axelrod put any stock in these rumors, but after a few weeks Vera Zasulich received evidence to support them. It is still not possible to make a definitive statement on the matter, but the circumstantial evidence suggests that the charges may have had merit.[22]

It is understandable that the rumors discomfited Axelrod. Then several incidents occurred that made it difficult for him to continue as an employee of *Vol'noe slovo*. The first was a sharp attack by Dragomanov on Narodnaia volia's terroristic campaign. He warned that it would have a deleterious effect on the entire revolutionary movement and that if the Narodovol'tsy were to succeed in toppling the autocracy, a regime similar to that created in "Jacobin France" might be the consequence.[23]

The Chernoperedel'tsy in Geneva took offense, not merely, one suspects, at what Dragomanov said, but because a liberal had said it. They felt constrained to come to the defense of their fellow revolutionaries, all the more so because they had not yet given up hope of reuniting with them. Axelrod drafted a letter protesting Dragomanov's attack on the Narodovol'tsy, but his colleagues were divided on the advisability of merely registering dissent. Nearly all of them urged him to resign. Sergei Kravchinsky (Stepniak), whose credentials as a proponent of terror were impeccable, took issue with the majority view on the ground that even a protest by Axelrod would constitute an attempt to interfere

---

22. For additional details, see *Iz arkhiva P. B. Aksel'roda, 1881–1896*, ed. W. S. Woytinsky, B. I. Nicolaevsky, and L. O. Tsederbaum-Dan (Berlin, 1924), pp. 46–47.

23. M. Dragomanov, "Obaiatel'nost' energii" (The Fascination of Energy), *Vol'noe slovo*, no. 34 (1882), 1–3.

with Dragomanov's freedom to express his views. "I attach such great importance," he wrote Axelrod, "to the rights of free thought and free criticism that I believe that to a significant degree the future of the party depends on them."[24] He advised Axelrod to withdraw his protest and continue writing for *Vol'noe slovo*.

Axelrod seems to have been moved by this argument. He hesitated in tendering his resignation, but in the end he felt impelled to yield to the relentless pressure of his comrades in Geneva.[25] In any case, at this time Malshinsky took certain actions that left him no alternative. The publisher arbitrarily cut one of Axelrod's articles and then appended a statement to another expressing the "editor's disagreement," a highly irregular procedure that the young journalist did not appreciate.[26] In May 1882 the paper announced that Axelrod's column would no longer appear. The Geneva Chernoperedel'tsy were much relieved and did not hide their displeasure at his delay in breaking with Dragomanov. "I tell you openly," Deich wrote to Axelrod from Geneva, "that neither I nor Vera [Zasulich], none of us, expected such disreputable conduct as you displayed during the entire history of your participation in this . . ." In an effort to appear understanding, Deich indicated that he assumed Axelrod had not been able to resign earlier because of financial pressures.[27]

The strain in the relations between Axelrod and his colleagues, so evident in the tone of Deich's letter, was not merely the result of their differences over his work for *Vol'noe slovo*. A more serious disagreement arose as a consequence of the anti-Jewish pogroms that spread through parts of Russia immediately after the assassination of Alexander II in March 1881. Although Axelrod had given up interest in specifically Jewish affairs in 1872, at this time a variety of circumstances led him to reconsider his earlier decision. His friends, however, were not persuaded

24. Kravchinsky to Axelrod, Apr. 1882, *Iz arkhiva Aksel'roda,* ed. Woytinsky, Nicolaevsky, and Tsederbaum-Dan, pp. 64–69.

25. Axelrod, *Perezhitoe,* p. 419.

26. *Iz arkhiva Aksel'roda,* ed. Woytinsky, Nicolaevsky, and Tsederbaum-Dan, pp. 51–54; see also [M. Dragomanov,] "Ot redaktsii" (From the Editorial Board), *Vol'noe slovo,* no. 35 (1882), 8. We do not know exactly what the publisher deleted from Axelrod's article. Apparently it was a section in which Axelrod did not, in Dragomanov's view, emphasize sufficiently that political freedom had to prevail in Russia before socialism could be established.

27. Deich to Axelrod, Apr. 7, 1882, Axelrod Archive, I.I.S.H.

that it was wise for him to take a public stand on the matter. The subsequent clash reveals much about the attitudes and tactics of many Russian revolutionaries as well as the way Axelrod handled a problem that he would frequently face later in life: a conflict between his convictions and his sense of loyalty to close comrades.

The pogroms of the 1880's were a turning point for many Jewish revolutionaries, not so much because of the unprecedented intensity and duration of the disorders, but because substantial numbers among the enlightened and progressive elements of society were indifferent to them or even approved of them. Indeed, it is ironic that at least during the early stages the government of Alexander III opposed the pogroms while a significant number of revolutionaries welcomed them. Their reasoning was identical: both believed that the pogroms might well set off the general social revolution. Thus, while Tsar Alexander ordered the provincial governors to suppress the violence and protect the Jews, all the major socialist papers in Russia except one carried articles hailing the pogroms as the first sign that the masses were bestirring themselves.[28]

One Narodovolets, for example, reporting on the disorders in Odessa, assured his readers that the slogan of the *pogromshchiki* was "Let us finish off the Jews, and then we will revolt against the Russians." He urged the revolutionary movement not to stand aside but to strive to lead the forces of rebellion. A Chernoperedelets did not doubt that the peasants had turned against the Jews first only because they considered exploitation by them more odious than by their own countrymen. In the lead article of a leaflet a Narodovolets acknowledged that the violence had not been initiated by an organized group, but nevertheless claimed with satisfaction that it was an "echo" of revolutionary agitation. Elsewhere in the same leaflet the Jews were accused of sharpening the general hostility to them by appealing for help to the authorities.[29] The most extreme statement was made in the Ukraine on August 30, 1881, by the Executive Committee of Narodnaia volia who, in a procla-

---

28. R. Kantor, "Aleksandr III o evreiskikh pogromakh," *Evreiskaia letopis'*, I (1923), 149–158. The only revolutionary paper to speak out against the pogroms at this time was *Zerno*, a publication of Chernyi peredel intended primarily for urban laborers. My discussions of Axelrod and the Jewish question draw heavily on my article "Pavel Axelrod: A Conflict between Jewish Loyalty and Revolutionary Dedication," *Russian Review*, XXIV (July 1965), 249–265.

29. "Vnutrennee obozrenie" (Domestic Review), *Narodnaia volia*, no. 6 (Oct. 23, 1881), 8–14; "Pis'ma s iuga," *Chernyi peredel*, no. 4 (Sept. 1881); "Iz derevni," *Listok narodnoi voli*, July 22, 1881.

mation, encouraged the people to smite the Jews, allegedly the greatest exploiters of the peasants. The man who apparently inspired the document, G. Romanenko, was undoubtedly an anti-Semite, but most of the other revolutionaries who welcomed the pogroms were not.[30] They were simply so convinced of the revolutionary potential of the peasants and so desperate to see it manifest itself that they were prepared to clutch at straws.

A number of young Jewish radicals, thoroughly dismayed and disillusioned by this turn of events, left Russia and began to reappraise their political commitments. Several settled in Zurich and formed a circle to study the Jewish question in Russia. One of the more active members of the group was Gregory Gurevich, who had for some time been living with the Axelrods and frequently discussed political issues with his host, many of whose views he shared. But unlike Axelrod, Gurevich had never severed his ties with Jewish politics and was among the first to advocate agitation in Yiddish among Jewish workers. At a social gathering one evening—probably early in 1882—Gurevich reproached Axelrod, then the most prominent Jewish revolutionary, for not speaking out against the pogroms. Axelrod defended himself by saying that he lacked sufficient information about them. "I objected to this," Gurevich relates, "by saying that for a declaration of one's attitude toward the outrageous pogroms it was not necessary to engage in scholarly research or to be acquainted with the literature on the question . . . " All that was necessary, as far as Gurevich was concerned, was to register a protest.[31]

But for Axelrod the matter was not quite so simple. And his plea of ignorance was not the whole story: he had already thought about the pogroms, and his assessment had not been as radically different from that of the revolutionaries quoted above as Gurevich seems to have supposed. Late in 1881 Axelrod publicly contended that had the organized socialist groups expended sufficient effort, the anti-Jewish disorders could have constituted "the beginning of a socialist *class* movement in the name of 'land and freedom' for the laboring masses. It was only neces-

30. See S. Valk, "G. G. Romanenko: iz istorii 'narodnoi voli,'" *Katorga i ssylka*, no. 48 (1928), 36–59. The proclamation is reproduced in this article. It should be noted that by 1884 the editors of *Narodnaia volia* changed their minds about the pogroms. They acknowledged that morally and tactically it had been a mistake to welcome them. See *Narodnaia volia*, no. 10 (Sept. 1884), esp. p. 10.

31. G. Gurevich, "Sredi revoliutsionerov v Tsiurikhe," *Evreiskaia letopis'*, IV (1926), 98–103.

sary, in Kiev for example, to direct the crowd to the quarter of the Jewish capitalists, to the banks, where the capital of the upper classes of all nationalities is concentrated. Of course, if the 'disorder' had received this sort of direction the further course of the movement would inevitably have been such as to lead the rebellious masses into direct clashes with the wealthy elements in general and with their natural ally, the government." But to the shame of the socialists, Axelrod held, they had permitted the disorders to develop into a general campaign against an entire nation, during which tens of thousands of proletarians and small shopkeepers had been ruined.[32]

In Axelrod's view, then, the pogroms had degenerated into senseless rioting only because the socialists had botched a fine opportunity to bring about the long-awaited social upheaval. He could not conceive of the possibility that the peasant, in his fury, might be inspired as much —or more—by religious prejudice as by revolutionary idealism. Clearly, he had not completely abandoned Bakuninism, for his faith in the peasant's innate propensity for revolutionary activism was not yet fully undermined. He still believed that an outburst of violence, no matter what its immediate cause or aim, might be the spark to set off the revolution for which he yearned.

But the continuing pressure of the Jewish colony in Zurich, coupled with letters from Jewish *intelligenty* in Russia telling of the anti-Semitism they were encountering and of their disillusionment with the revolutionary movement, had their impact on Axelrod. In February 1882 he discussed with Plekhanov, Lavrov, Deich, and Kravchinsky the advisability of putting out a brochure protesting the pogroms and their favorable reception by the revolutionary press. They all agreed that such a brochure would be desirable and thought that a Gentile among them should write it. But Plekhanov, who privately expressed strong disapproval of the Narodovol'tsy's call for anti-Semitic action, was too busy with other work, and neither Lavrov nor Kravchinsky felt equipped to write on the subject. Vexed that his colleagues seemed to consider the question of the pogroms less important than others, Axelrod decided to write the brochure himself in the hope that it would be published by the Executive Committee of Narodnaia volia. When requested to make a commitment, the committee apparently indicated lack of interest in the

32. Axelrod, "Vse dlia naroda," pp. 16–17.

undertaking. Plekhanov then promised to issue the brochure, after it had been approved by him and his colleagues, in the name of a "Group of Social Revolutionaries." It was to be signed by Lavrov, Plekhanov, Zasulich, Kravchinsky, Deich, and Axelrod, so as to demonstrate that several eminent socialists—not just one man—were appalled by the events in Russia.[33]

Axelrod did not complete the brochure, and the draft that is available is sketchy and somewhat disjointed. He merely mentions some of his more important points without elaborating them. Still, the general trend of his thought is plainly revealed.

Axelrod addressed himself primarily to Jewish radicals in an effort to clarify their future political tasks. He assured them that he understood and sympathized with their despair at discovering that their attempts to assimilate themselves into Russian culture and politics had been rebuffed by the "truly disgraceful spectacle" of anti-Semitism. He appreciated their being disheartened by the revelation that many Russians still regarded them as members of an alien and despised national group. He argued, nevertheless, that it would be erroneous to regard the pogroms only as the manifestation of deep-seated national and religious prejudice. He contended that their major cause derived from the economic structure of the country and the position occupied by the Jews in that structure.

Because of their long history of persecution and exclusion from what he termed "productive work," and especially from agriculture, an inordinately large number of Jews served as middlemen, as traders, shopkeepers, and usurers. Most of them were far from wealthy, as he could well recall from his childhood. In fact, in all but function many could be classified as proletarians. The peasants, however, looked upon the Jews as parasites, exploiters, people who did not earn their livelihood by the sweat of their brows. The Gentile petty bourgeoisie and capitalists despised Jews because they saw in them their fiercest competitors. And many professional people were antagonistic to them because they feared the rivalry of Jews attempting in increasing numbers to enter the universities. "In Russia, therefore," Axelrod concluded, "the Jews are an economic force that in the struggle for existence and wealth comes into

33. Lev Deich, *Rol' evreev v russkom revoliutsionnom dvizhenii* (2nd ed., Moscow, 1925), p. 5; Deich to Axelrod, Mar. 27, 1882, *Gruppa*, ed. Deich, I, 153–154; Deich to Axelrod, Apr. 3, 1882, *ibid.*, pp. 155–156; Deich, "O sblizhenii," p. 10.

conflict with the most varied strata of the population." This explained the solidarity of the Gentile population in its hostility to the Jews. And the government, as well as the Gentile capitalists, was prepared to exploit the hostility in order to provide an outlet for the widespread unrest.

Axelrod's analysis, which has been refined and modified but not discarded by recent historians of the pogroms, constituted an acknowledgment that the Jewish problem in Russia was far more complicated than he had previously thought. For if anti-Semitic feelings were not simply a prejudice of misguided individuals, but deeply ingrained in all social strata of Russia, was it a realistic option for Jewish intelligenty to dedicate themselves wholly to the general revolutionary cause and abandon their people until the new and just order had been established? Were not the Jews suffering from a special form of oppression that might not be altered—at least in the foreseeable future—by the revolutionary programs then being advocated? Axelrod dealt with this problem in the last part of his draft, unfortunately the sketchiest section of the manuscript. He raised several possibilities, but did not work out any of them in detail. While drafting the brochure he was in touch both with the Jewish colony in Zurich and his political colleagues in Geneva; one senses that he was laboring under conflicting pressures and inner uncertainties.

He conceded that it was legitimate for Jewish socialists to concern themselves primarily with the plight of the Jewish lower classes, though not for the purpose of achieving a "national renaissance of Judaism" or the establishment of a Jewish state. Axelrod stressed several times that this interest in strictly Jewish affairs must go no further than concern for the well-being of poor Jews. But in one place he said that, as soon as the persecution of his coreligionists ended, "Jewish socialists must be entirely indifferent to the fate of their own capitalists," who, he asserted, had shown far more interest in their pocketbooks than in the "Jewish nation" during the disorders. The implication here—and it is no more than an implication—is that until the disappearance of religious animosities Jewish socialists should concern themselves with the persecution of all Jews, regardless of class.

For Axelrod the most radical and desirable solution of the Jewish question required a twofold development: first, conversion of the Jewish masses into a genuine proletariat engaged in physical labor; second, their "fusion" or "amalgamation" with the "corresponding strata of the 'native' population." Here Axelrod was extremely vague. He used the word *sliianie,* but did not specify what he meant. From the context it would appear that at the very least he had in mind that Jews adopt the Russian language, immerse themselves in Russian culture, live among non-Jews, and join nonsectarian political organizations.

Axelrod conceded that it would be extremely difficult to realize the two goals. Even if "external circumstances" were favorable (by which he probably meant a cessation of anti-Semitic outbursts and legislation) and the Jewish masses made every attempt to take up "productive work," it would take at least fifteen years for a new generation of Jewish laborers to emerge—a rather optimistic estimate. Moreover, the Jewish masses in Russia had attained a higher intellectual and political niveau than their Gentile counterpart, which ruled out the possibility of an immediate amalgamation. It would be feasible only after further reforms had raised the intellectual and political sophistication of the Russian lower classes. Ultimately, Axelrod believed, the solutions he was proposing could be achieved only if the autocratic regime was replaced by political institutions allowing the people a maximum of freedom and participation in the government. The Jews would then be granted the right to settle in any part of the Empire, and the necessary reforms would be effected.

Axelrod felt that, in the meantime, Jewish socialists ought to collaborate with Gentile socialists in educating cadres of dedicated revolutionaries within the Jewish community and in explaining the main causes of the pogroms to the Jews. Jewish radicals should also strive to make the Jewish masses aware that they had much more in common with lower-class Christians than with their wealthy coreligionists. Christian revolutionaries ought to campaign simultaneously against the wholesale attacks on the Jewish community. In the event of further pogroms, they should direct the crowd, as Axelrod had previously suggested, "if not against the exploiters in general, then against the rich Jewish quarter only and primarily against such wealthy people as Brodsky, Poliakov, Ginsburg, etc."[34]

While working on the article he considered another possibility then being discussed by Gurevich and his friends: that Russian Jews be encouraged to emigrate to Palestine and take up farming. This plan should not be confused with Theodor Herzl's subsequent program, for the aim

34. Axelrod's manuscript was published in *Iz arkhiva Aksel'roda,* ed. Woytinsky, Nicolaevsky, and Tsederbaum-Dan, pp. 217–227.

was not to establish a Jewish state but simply to provide an escape from persecution. Axelrod consulted the noted geographer and Bakuninist, K. E. Reclus, who found the proposal impracticable. He admitted that the upper Galilee could be cultivated, but only after a considerable amount of irrigation. In addition, most of the land was in private hands, and the Russian consul there, who was very influential, would do his utmost to prevent its being sold to Jews for fear they would clash with the sizable Russian colony. Reclus therefore predicted that should Jews settle in Palestine they would once again become traders and exploit the local population. Deich also urged Axelrod to give up the Palestinian project on the ground that socialists should not advocate measures that would in any way recognize the Jews as a separate national group. Deich feared, moreover, that in Palestine the Jews would only "stagnate in their own prejudices." If emigration was to be encouraged, then it should be to America, where the Jews would be able to "amalgamate with the local population." These arguments apparently persuaded Axelrod, for he did not mention the Palestinian project in his manuscript.[35]

In tone and content Axelrod's draft of the brochure was moderate. Indeed, it was not so much a protest against the pogroms as an attempt to understand them and chart a course of action for Jewish radicals. The proposals in it implied only a temporary deviation from the position on the Jewish question to which he had previously subscribed. Nevertheless, his friends were beginning to have second thoughts about the advisability of publishing anything at all on the pogroms and their aftermath. On April 14, 1882, Lavrov, who cannot be accused of harboring anti-Semitic prejudice, wrote Axelrod that it was tactically unwise for a Russian revolutionary party publicly to oppose the anti-Jewish outbreaks. "Theoretically," said Lavrov, "it is very easy to solve . . . [the Jewish question] on paper, but in view of popular passions and the need of Russian socialists to have the people on their side whenever possible, it becomes an entirely different matter." In a postscript to the letter, Deich, himself a Jew, voiced unqualified agreement with Lavrov, though he confessed to being pained at having to take such a stand. He explained that the revolutionary movement confronted a dilemma that was not of its own mak-

35. Deich to Axelrod, Mar. 27, 1882, *Gruppa*, ed. Deich, I, 153–154; Deich to Axelrod, Apr. 21, 1882, *ibid.*, p. 160.

ing and that it could handle in no other way. And, he added, " . . . I shall always remain a member of the *Russian* revolutionary movement and will not separate myself from it even for one day . . . "[36]

Despite the obvious cogency of this argument for a man who ten years earlier had decided that he could contribute most to solving the Jewish question by working for the triumph of the Russian socialist movement, Axelrod at first persisted in his intention to publish the manuscript. Conviction aside, he feared that the Jewish colony would conclude that the Chernoperedel'tsy had promised to speak up without really intending to do so. If his colleagues could or would not sign the brochure, then he would publish it under his name alone. He pointed out to his friends that the German Social Democratic party, despite its insistence on maintaining a united stand on basic issues, did not prevent an individual from expressing his personal views.

Deich, speaking for the Chernoperedel'tsy in Geneva, rejected Axelrod's argument. The example of the German party did not seem applicable to the small group of Russians operating under extremely difficult conditions. The Chernoperedel'tsy were few in number, and if they were to accomplish anything, they would have to be "firmly united and act in complete solidarity." Their cause would surely be harmed if it came to light that one person had views different from the others on the Jewish question. "We are all very sorry," he wrote Axelrod on May 26, 1882, "that you persist in your decision with respect to the Jewish brochure." Still, he indicated that the group would publish it if Axelrod insisted.[37]

The pressure proved to be too much. Not the type of person who could easily strike out on his own in defiance of his colleagues, Axelrod must have found it especially difficult to ignore their advice at a time when he was already at odds with them over his continuing collaboration with Dragomanov. After all, he did share their basic revolutionary creed and probably thought it unwise to risk a split over an issue on which he himself had not formed an unambiguous position. To be sure, the circumstances surrounding the pogroms had engendered doubts in his mind about the viability of the solution to the Jewish question he had hoped

36. Lavrov to Axelrod, Apr. 14, 1882, *Iz arkhiva Aksel'roda,* ed. Woytinsky, Nicolaevsky, and Tsederbaum-Dan, pp. 30–31.

37. Deich to Axelrod, Apr. 21, 1882, *Gruppa,* ed. Deich, I, 159–161; Axelrod to Deich, May 22, 1882, *ibid.,* V, 81–82; *Iz arkhiva Aksel'roda,* ed. Woytinsky, Nicolaevsky, and Tsederbaum-Dan, p. 217.

for in 1872, but he was far from having found an alternative that fully satisfied him. As a consequence, he left the manuscript, unfinished, in his drawer.

There is evidence to suggest that Axelrod later regretted his silence of 1882. In his autobiography, the published part of which ends with the year 1883, Axelrod did not mention the pogroms of 1881 or his unfinished manuscript, though he could hardly have forgotten the episode. He still had the manuscript in his personal archive, and in his memoirs he related many incidents from an earlier period that were often much less significant. Yet the only reference to Jews, aside from the account of his early childhood and adolescence, appears in his discussion of the meeting in 1880 during which he opposed the name Chernyi peredel for the new revolutionary party then being founded.[38] Several comrades objected to his suggestion that the term "socialist-federalist" be adopted on the ground that Axelrod's title implied that after the revolution the Russian Empire should be broken up into separate political entities, an idea that might not find favor with the people at large. Axelrod then quotes—forty years after the event—his own reply: "And if the people want to beat up Jews? I answered. What if the people forcefully want to oppose Poland's separation from Russia? No! As socialists, we cannot confine our goals exclusively to suit the wishes of the people at a given moment, if those wishes are dictated by prejudice."[39]

We cannot, of course, be sure that Axelrod quoted himself correctly. But that is far less important than the fact that he made this particular reference to Jews in his autobiography, written in the 1920's. For when in 1882 he gave up his intention to speak out against the pogroms, he betrayed the very principle of not bowing to the dictates of popular prejudice. It is altogether possible that it was too painful for Axelrod to mention the unpublished manuscript and the events associated with it and that his insertion of the statement just quoted was his way, perhaps unconsciously, of expressing remorse for his silence in 1882 on the type of moral issue on which he now considered silence by a political leader impermissible.[40]

38. See Chap. II, above.
39. Axelrod, *Perezhitoe*, pp. 341–343.
40. For other indications that Axelrod changed his position on the Jewish question, see Chap. IX, below.

Once Axelrod had abandoned the article on the pogroms, he and the Geneva Chernoperedel'tsy were again in full agreement on basic issues. During the early months of 1882 they were all rapidly moving toward formal adoption of Marxism. In late spring or early summer of that year Axelrod began to consider himself an unqualified Social Democrat. It is not clear precisely what prompted him to take the final step. All we know is that some time in the middle of 1882 he visited Plekhanov and was gratified to discover that his comrade had also been fully converted, as had Zasulich and Deich. Both Axelrod and Plekhanov had fallen under the spell of Marx's Preface to *A Contribution to the Critique of Political Economy*. They were particularly moved by Marx's comment that with the disappearance of capitalism the prehistorical period would end and man would begin, as Axelrod put it, his "fully conscious and truly historical existence." Axelrod recalled the substance of his remarks to his colleague: "What grandiose perspectives face contemporary humanity if all its past, splendid, great scientific discoveries and technical inventions, cultural and spiritual achievements are only the preliminary phase and prehistorical stage to the historical epoch of its existence!"[41] Axelrod had persuaded himself that he was adopting a scientific theory of historical development, but it seems evident that in large measure he was attracted by its utopian vision of the future. At bottom he was still very much the romantic.

For a whole year the turn to Marxism by the four émigrés did not lead to the formation of a new organization. The former Chernoperedel'tsy, and most of all Plekhanov, still hoped for reunification with Narodnaia volia, which at least offered the semblance of an organization and some financial resources. Involved negotiations took place, and at times it looked as though a merger might be possible. After being promised the right to vent his views freely, Plekhanov even agreed to become an editor of a projected journal of Narodnaia volia, *Vestnik narodnoi voli*. Both he and Axelrod contributed articles of an unmistakably Marxist bent.[42] The negotiations were snarled, however, by the insistence of the Marxists that they be permitted to enter the party as a faction. At first the Naro-

41. Axelrod, *Perezhitoe*, p. 421.
42. Axelrod's first major publication completely free from any traces of Bakuninism was his "Sotsializm i melkaia burzhuaziia," *Vestnik narodnoi voli*, I (1884), 159–185; II (1884), 203–214.

dovol'tsy were willing to entertain the possibility, but they soon recognized the danger of allowing an organized faction into their movement. They then stipulated that only individuals could join, a procedure the Marxists rejected. By September 1883 the negotiations collapsed, and the circle around Plekhanov decided to form its own organization. Plekhanov proposed that the group refer to itself as Social Democratic, but his colleagues refused for fear that too open an identification with the Germans would repel other Russians. They then settled on the name *Gruppa osvobozhdenie truda* (Group for the Emancipation of Labor [GEL]).[43]

Actually, the protracted negotiations, during which both sides frequently engaged in intrigue, were doomed to fail from the start. As Deich correctly pointed out to Axelrod in July 1883, the ideological gap between them was too wide. Moreover, the major purpose of the Marxists had been not to collaborate with Narodnaia volia but to convert the party to their new beliefs.[44] For their part, most Narodovol'tsy were not inclined to make the change. It is inconceivable that had the two groups somehow merged the party would have had a long life.[45]

For the next two decades Axelrod's public life was inseparably linked to the GEL: all his efforts as a revolutionary were now focused either on strengthening the organization or propagating its doctrines. His period of ideological vacillation and uncertainty was over. It is true that with changing circumstances he found it necessary to modify his views on specific issues or to adapt Marxist doctrines to new situations, but he never consciously deviated from the creed. In none of Axelrod's writings did there ever again appear the suggestion that he looked with favor on anarchism, terror, or "agrarian socialism." By 1883 his political conception had become completely Westernized; thereafter he considered it one of his major duties to help Westernize Russian socialism.

It is noteworthy that Axelrod's conversion to Marxism involved more than a change of ideology. According to V. I. Sukhomlin, the two years in Switzerland had transformed him into a thorough Westerner both in attitudes and style of life. They had first met in 1879, in Odessa, when

43. Axelrod, *Perezhitoe*, pp. 438–439.
44. Deich to Axelrod, July 1883, *Gruppa*, ed. Deich, I, 176.
45. For a detailed account of the negotiations, see Samuel H. Baron, *Plekhanov: The Father of Russian Marxism* (Stanford, 1963), pp. 78–88.

Axelrod spent two weeks in Sukhomlin's home. They became good friends, and Axelrod, the older and more experienced activist, exerted a strong influence on Sukhomlin. In 1883, Sukhomlin, following his friend's earlier advice to travel and thus broaden his knowledge of European socialism, went to the West. He visited Axelrod in Zurich and barely recognized him, "so much had he changed in his outward appearance." Sukhomlin recalled that in 1879 Axelrod had looked like an "emaciated intelligent," always slovenly dressed and disheveled. Awkward at public and social gatherings, he gave the impression of being a high-strung person constantly in rapid motion.

Now, in 1883, Sukhomlin found Axelrod much more relaxed and settled. He had developed into a "European in the full sense of the word: quite plump, properly dressed, his hair combed and with a neatly trimmed beard." At first Sukhomlin thought that the change in Axelrod's appearance was the result of his wife's influence, but after closer observation he concluded that the decisive influence had been the "tranquillity and order" characteristic of Switzerland.

During the conversation Axelrod made no denial of his "Western European orientation." He joked good-naturedly about "our Russian Narodnik utopianism" and wondered how he himself had ever been able to live illegally in Russia. Not "for the love of money" could he endure such an ordeal again. He scoffed at the conspiratorial activities of Russian revolutionaries and compared them, unfavorably, to the mass organizations of the European proletariat. These were hardly sentiments calculated to appeal to Sukhomlin, a dedicated Narodovolets. But Axelrod's gift of charming even people with whom he disagreed made it possible for him to express his views in a way that did not offend. After spending "several agreeable hours with this attractive, friendly family," Sukhomlin moved on to another country without any feelings of ill will toward his friend and former political comrade.[46]

46. V. Sukhomlin, "Iz epokhi upadka partii 'Nar. volia'," *Katorga i ssylka*, no. 25 (1926), 39–42.

IV | The Solitary Years

The period 1883–1894 was marked by intense personal hardship and political frustration for Axelrod. When he gave up his post with *Vol'noe slovo* he also relinquished his only source of steady income, and over the years his expenses had increased substantially. In 1879 his wife had given birth to a boy, Alexander, and in 1881, to another girl, Sophie. There were now five mouths to feed, but he could find no satisfying work, as he lacked training in a trade or profession. All the Russian journals in which he might have placed occasional articles for pay had been closed by the government. He considered once again taking up some sort of unskilled work, but realized that he was not suited for it, either physically or psychologically. It was entirely by chance that he found a way out of his predicament.

In 1884 Axelrod took sick, probably as a result of mental depression over his personal situation. The nature of his ailment seems never to have been determined, but there is no doubt about its seriousness. He was practically incapacitated, unable to concentrate on work of any kind. No remedy prescribed by his doctor helped. In a mood of despair, Axelrod's wife accepted the advice of Plekhanov's sister that she treat Pavel with a homemade cure-all, kefir, a kind of fermented milk. Plekhanov's sister claimed to have cured herself and her husband of a variety of illnesses with the remarkable beverage and asserted that in Russia several noted professors of medicine strongly advocated its use. Nadezhda Axelrod had nothing to lose, and since the drink was unknown in Switzerland she began to make it herself. Whether or not kefir was responsible, once Axelrod started to consume it regularly, his health improved.

The episode inspired the Axelrods with an idea for solving their financial problems. Before Pavel's illness Nadezhda had thought of opening a restaurant in the hope thereby of freeing her husband for revolutionary work. Now it occurred to them to set up a kefir shop instead. Toward the end of 1884 they began to produce the drink in a primitive way in their fourth-floor apartment. Axelrod calculated that if he could sell between thirty and sixty bottles a day, he would be assured of a modest income.

Axelrod's first task was to publicize his product. He visited several professors at the university clinic, and they agreed to try it out on their patients. It seemed to work, though Axelrod later admitted to not being sure whether it was kefir itself that cured the patients or the rest, fresh air, and nourishing food that they were getting at the same time. Whatever the reason, people convinced themselves that kefir helped. Moreover, they liked its taste, and that was probably more important than its curative value.

Axelrod's business began to enjoy a modest success. But then a certain Professor Vis, director of the local children's clinic, advised Axelrod that people were reluctant to climb the four stories to his dingy apartment to purchase kefir despite its beneficial qualities. In addition, the apartment made such a bad impression that many found it unsuitable for dispensing medicine. Axelrod either had to find a larger and more appealing establishment or he would be forced out of business. The latter was unthinkable, not only because he needed the income but also because he had gone into debt in order to open the shop.

Kautsky and Bernstein came to his rescue. By this time the two Germans had become close friends of Axelrod, and, according to Kautsky, the three "formed a closely united three-leaf clover [Trifolium] that was as cheerful as it was thirsty for knowledge." They spent many hours discussing politics and the European labor movement, and it was at this time that Axelrod stimulated Kautsky's interest in Russian affairs, which he then followed carefully for the rest of his life.[1] When his friends heard of Axelrod's plight, they went to great lengths to help. They managed to secure a loan of five hundred francs for him, and this enabled him to move into a larger apartment on the first floor of his house and to rent part of the cellar for a workshop.

1. Karl Kautsky, "Was Axelrod uns gab," *Die Gesellschaft*, II (1925), 117. My discussions of Axelrod's relations with Kautsky—here and in subsequent chapters—draw heavily on my article "Axelrod and Kautsky," *Slavic Review*, XXVI (Mar. 1967), 94–112.

Kautsky and Bernstein also tried to publicize Axelrod's product and thought of some schemes that were rather farfetched but not without humor. Kautsky, at heart the didactic professor, went to the trouble of writing a learned article on kefir's beneficial effects on the human body. Axelrod did the research, supplying translations of whole passages from Russian books on kefir. Kautsky wrote the piece in the hope of publishing it in the *Sozialdemokrat*, then being printed in Zurich and smuggled into Germany. But it soon occurred to the three that even Kautsky's profound treatise would not induce German Social Democrats to travel to Zurich just to buy kefir. In an attempt to create a market in Zurich they then tried to have the article published in a local newspaper, but were refused on the ground that the subject was too "specialized."

Undaunted, Bernstein and Kautsky came up with another proposal that demonstrated a flair for advertising techniques altogether out of keeping with their disdain for capitalistic practices. They suggested that posters be distributed in Zurich displaying a portrait of Kautsky, drawn and emaciated, at the top, with the caption: "Before the kefir treatment." Below would appear Bernstein, a model of health and vigor, and the caption: "After the kefir treatment." This was not a serious proposal, and fortunately Axelrod did not have to go that far to promote his product. More and more people heard about it, and sales increased steadily, so much so in fact that Axelrod began to dream of profits high enough to enable him to finance all the publications of the GEL. The enterprise never actually came close to yielding that kind of return, but it did provide Axelrod and his family with a means of subsistence, much of the time at a not very comfortable level. There were, for example, days when horse meat was a luxury.

The work was demanding and time-consuming. As the Axelrods had no machinery and little experience, every phase in the process was physically taxing. They would begin work at five in the morning and quit after six in the evening. During the night they took turns resetting and moving the bottles every two hours. They had learned from several Russian "medical books" that in order to make the finest kefir the milk had to be shaken at regular intervals. Only after he had been in the business for ten years did Axelrod discover that the frequent shaking was unnecessary. In the meantime he had subjected himself to a grueling schedule in order to eke out a living. By the end of the working day he was often completely exhausted. The first time Alexander Helphand (Parvus) visited him (apparently in 1887) and observed him in his shop, he exclaimed: "Pavel Borisovich, you will extract 'surplus value' from yourself."

The kefir enterprise not only tired Axelrod physically; it caused him much anxiety as well. He got along satisfactorily for a few months, but then suddenly business dropped sharply. He thought he faced bankruptcy. "Day and night," he wrote, "I was weary to death by worries and anxieties troubling my mind: where would I find the money to pay for the labels, advertisements, and prospectuses?" He was also perturbed lest bankruptcy lead to his expulsion from Zurich and to his compromising the Russian émigrés in the eyes of the Swiss authorities. Soon it became evident that the slack was only seasonal. Early in 1886 business picked up again, and he managed to meet his bills. For the next few years the months from June to December always saw a decline in the sales of kefir, and each time Axelrod feared that his enterprise would collapse.

Only in the 1890's was the firm solidly enough established so that he no longer needed to worry about its survival. By this time he could count on a sizable number of steady customers; also, several doctors regularly recommended kefir to their patients. Indeed, in the medical profession his reputation soared: both professors and ordinary practitioners sought his advice on the effectiveness of kefir in treating certain diseases or the dosage to be prescribed in specific cases. On occasion people even came to him from abroad to learn how to produce the beverage. Still, he was far from prosperous. Only rarely could he afford to attend theatrical performances or concerts.

Quite aside from the financial pressures, Axelrod was not happy in his role as businessman, and his letters are filled with disparaging remarks about "that damned kefir." As late as 1898 he complained that "The accursed necessity to struggle through life with kefir has often caused me moral torment. For it is truly moral agony never to be in a position to satisfy the indispensable needs without having to borrow—and at the same time to appear to be a capitalist."[2] He had a pronounced

2. Axelrod to Karpeles, July 22, 1898, Kleine Korrespondenz, I.I.S.H.

prejudice against trade and business, which he traced to a lifelong disdain for all "purely worldly and material interests." No doubt his Marxist convictions added to his dislike for any activity whose main purpose was to yield a profit. "I personally experienced," he recalled, "directly and tangibly the abomination and stupidity of the capitalist system and the extremely difficult and unstable, often really disastrous, condition of the petty bourgeoisie." Axelrod was so uncomfortable in his role that he made an unusual proposal to an official of the Zurich Canton, who frequently came to the shop to buy kefir. Axelrod offered to hand over his establishment to the canton or city in return for a salaried position as its manager. Much to his regret, the official dismissed the proposal as unfeasible, probably not even believing it had been made in all seriousness.

What most distressed Axelrod about his business was that it required so much time and energy that for several years he found it difficult to devote himself to his most "vital task," party work. Before long his health gave way. He himself appreciated the irony of his situation: "Precisely at that time," he wrote in the 1920's, "amidst all those salutary bottles of kefir, I contracted neurasthenia and insomnia, which paralyzed my capacity for literary work and from which I have suffered since." For over two and a half decades he was forced to do much of his reading and writing in the cellar whenever he could pull himself away from his work on kefir.[3] In large measure, Axelrod's relatively small literary output—as compared to that of the other leading Russian Marxists—can be attributed to his preoccupation with business affairs.

Despite his many complaints about his line of work, he derived satisfaction from earning his livelihood. It was, as he told a colleague in 1896, a matter of principle for him to do hard physical labor in order to provide for his family.[4] Nor did he ever become morbid about his lot. He had a sharp and well-developed sense of humor and the habit of laughing about his fate. Nowhere is this trait more evident than in his letters to Kautsky, who in 1885 moved to London. For the next forty-three years the two men engaged in a lively correspondence, in

3. This section on Axelrod's kefir business is based on the unpublished portion of his memoirs, on deposit in the Axelrod Archive, I.I.S.H. [hereafter cited as "Unpublished Memoir"].

4. See V. D. Bonch-Bruevich, *Izbrannye sochineniia* (Moscow, 1959–1961), II, 209.

which, using the informal *Du*, they took up a wide range of theoretical, political, and personal matters. Like all of Kautsky's friends, Axelrod referred to him as "Baron," probably in recognition of his theoretical preeminence. Late in 1886 Axelrod turned to Kautsky for help in carrying out a peculiar plan. "Your Excellency, Baron of Jauchzer,"[5] he wrote, "will probably remember that in Zurich there lives a certain P. Axelrod, Jew, manufacturer, nihilist (also Governor of Palestine). He even had the honor and good fortune to become your friend. Since I have respectfully reminded you of all this, I take the liberty, highly honored Herr Baron, of turning to you on the following matter."

He then revealed that he and Plekhanov were "dreaming" of a visit to London to spend some time near the "Marxist sun [Engels]" and allow "its rays to penetrate our heads. But the damned money!"[6] In order to prepare Kautsky for his plan, Axelrod had already sent him a small package containing a prospectus of his business and several testimonials by professors to the effectiveness of kefir. "Don't think," Axelrod assured his friend, "that kefir has made me completely crazy . . . But in order that my kefir-diplomatic plans will not appear as 'fantasies of fever' (see Dühring on Hegel) in your baronial eyes, I will tell you the following." Axelrod related the story of a Russian émigré who had spent half a year in his workshop and had then gone to Leipzig, where he had helped a local businessman set up a kefir shop in return for 2,000 francs. He had just returned to Zurich a "small capitalist" with a "clear profit" of 1,000 francs.

Axelrod's plan was to enter into a similar arrangement with a well-to-do person in London, and he appealed to his friend to locate an enterprising Englishman. He was certain that the undertaking would earn a "handsome profit," enough for a trip to London by him and Plekhanov and a bonus for Kautsky for his efforts.[7] But Kautsky did not think it would be easy to promote an unknown product in London without incurring large expenditures. "Since you cannot expect to have the opportunity of curing with kefir the Princess of Wales or any other highly honored creature, you will have to make a stir with money,"

5. Apparently this was a play on the German word *jauchzen*, to exalt, to shout with joy.
6. Axelrod to Kautsky, Nov. 24, 1886, Kautsky Archive, I.I.S.H.
7. Axelrod to Kautsky, Dec. 3, 1886, *ibid.*

at least two or three thousand pounds. He considered it unlikely that anyone would be willing to invest so large a sum in kefir.[8] Kautsky's words led Axelrod to give up his project and to postpone visiting Engels for three years.

If Axelrod's personal situation during the 1880's was trying, he found no solace in the progress made by the GEL. The initial circle of five (Plekhanov, Zasulich, Deich, V. I. Ignatov, and Axelrod) found it extraordinarily difficult to attract support. They appealed to Lavrov for help, but he responded by criticizing them for failing to collaborate with other revolutionary groups. This was a serious blow, as Lavrov enjoyed great esteem among radical youth. In general the émigré community in the West sympathized with Narodnaia volia and reproached the former Chernoperedel'tsy for not joining the terrorist organization. Some actually ridiculed the Marxists; the most contemptuous comment was made by the prominent Bakuninist N. I. Zhukovsky, who charged that they were "not revolutionaries, but students of sociology."[9]

The GEL did not achieve greater success in Russia. Those who were favorably inclined to the revolutionary cause seem not to have been aware of the weakness of Narodnaia volia and continued to believe that its tactics of terror would prove successful in overthrowing the autocracy. In 1883 and 1884 the GEL could not claim a single active supporter in St. Petersburg.[10] Late in November 1883 Deich, the chief organizer and fund raiser of the GEL, acknowledged that there were probably no more than eight or ten people in all of Russia who took an interest in its work. He was thoroughly pessimistic and feared that the organization was destined for a brief existence.[11]

The GEL had set rather modest aims for itself. According to Axelrod, the founders did not intend to organize a political party; they considered themselves "only a *literary* group, that is, a group of Marxist writers, united by a common world outlook and [by a desire] to propagandize orally and in writing this outlook among Russian revolutionaries, hoping in this way to further the revival and reinforcement of

8. Kautsky to Axelrod, Dec. 10, 1886, Axelrod Archive, I.I.S.H.
9. L. Deich, "Pervye shagi gruppy 'Osvobozhdenie truda'" (The First Steps of the Group "Emancipation of Labor"), *Gruppa "Osvobozhdenie truda,"* ed. L. Deich (Moscow, 1924–1928), I, 11.
10. *Ibid.*, pp. 9–12.
11. Deich to Axelrod, Nov. 27, 1883, *Gruppa,* ed. Deich, I, 191.

the party Narodnaia volia." In other words, initially they still intended to convert the Narodovol'tsy to Marxism and made no great effort to enlarge the group. But they desperately longed for ties with revolutionary circles in Russia that could provide them with moral and financial support.[12] The latter was particularly necessary because the activities the GEL planned required large sums of money. They intended, specifically, to translate the more important relevant Marxist works into Russian as well as write their own critiques of the traditional views of the revolutionary intelligentsia, analyzing the social and economic problems of Russia from a Marxist standpoint.

The resources of the GEL were pitiful. Ignatov was a man of moderate means, and he launched the organization in its endeavors with a donation of 500 rubles, hardly an imposing sum. The need to pay for printing and the lack of resources of the other members, who had to borrow just to meet living expenses, made it necessary to appeal once more to Ignatov. This time he sent 1,500 francs, which enabled the GEL to purchase a printing press. Even so, there was far too little money in the treasury. Deich believed that only by sending people to Russia to organize sympathetic circles that would regularly send contributions could the financial crisis be solved. But at the time there was no one with a sufficiently "revolutionary past" who could be sent with confidence. Either he or Axelrod could have accomplished such a mission, but it would have been "unthinkable" for them to go, probably because both would have been arrested immediately. The GEL finally dispatched a few emissaries, but their efforts were unavailing.[13]

To make matters worse, in March 1884 Deich was arrested in Freiburg for trying to smuggle literature into Russia. The German authorities handed him over to the Russians who exiled him to Siberia, where he remained until 1900. Deich had been exceptionally energetic and competent in administering the GEL; in fact, no other member could discharge his functions as well. When asked to take on the administrative burden, Axelrod accepted although he was not temperamentally suited for the task. For the next two decades he devoted considerable time to running the affairs of the organization: his correspondence increased

12. Axelrod, "Unpublished Memoir"; Pavel Axelrod, "Gruppa 'Osvobozhdenie truda,'" *Letopisi marksizma*, VI (1928), 98–99.
13. Deich, "Pervye shagi," pp. 14–15, 18–19; Deich to Axelrod, Nov. 27, 1883, *Gruppa*, ed. Deich, I, 191.

enormously; he found himself more and more at the center of negotiations with various revolutionary organizations; and he was constantly pressed to solicit contributions. In 1885 the GEL suffered another loss. Ignatov, ill with tuberculosis, died in Egypt, where he had gone to recuperate. Aside from being a deep personal blow to the group, his death put an end to an important source of income.[14]

In view of the meager financial resources and the series of adversities, it is a remarkable testimony to the energy and doggedness of its members that the GEL accomplished anything at all. Actually, only two were active, and one of them was preoccupied with private affairs. Zasulich, though gifted and held in high esteem, could not be of much help. She was frequently ill, a slow writer, and depressed by the arrest of Deich, who had been her common-law husband. Nearly all the work therefore fell on Plekhanov and Axelrod.

They made a concerted effort to gain the support of the rather large colony of Russian students enrolled at Swiss universities, most of whom were apolitical. The members of the GEL would attend their meetings and lectures to talk to them about politics. Plekhanov, a talented speaker and polemicist, soon succeeded in attracting large audiences throughout the country. Axelrod was not an effective orator, but he possessed other gifts that enabled him to make a strong impact on small groups of people. He already had something of a reputation among young Russians in Zurich and so was able to locate potential converts with relative ease. When facing a small audience he succeeded, according to Deich, in reaching his listeners by dint of the "conviction, sincerity, [and] uprightness with which he expressed his views. That which he recognized as true and useful for another person to know, he was always able to transmit in such a simple, lively, interesting, and yet profound manner that he rarely encountered any opponents, any serious adversaries. In this respect, as a propagandist, Axelrod was always an invaluable person; his role therefore in our—and in part also in the Western European—socialist movement was very important." He was instrumental in forming a particularly helpful circle of supporters in Zurich, consisting at first only of students but in time also of older émigrés. Soon similar circles appeared in other Swiss cities. They

14. Axelrod, "Gruppa 'Osvobozhdenie truda,'" pp. 96–98.

studied Marxism and on occasion collected small sums of money for the GEL.[15]

Without doubt, the GEL's major achievement during this early period was to formulate the basic principles of Russian Marxism. Unlike revolutionaries in the West, the Russians could not simply proclaim themselves Marxists and then proceed to organize a labor party. The situation in their country differed so fundamentally from that in Western Europe that their first priority was to demonstrate the relevance of Marxism to Russia, an agricultural country with a minuscule proletariat. The scant guidance in Marx's writings complicated this task.

Marx passionately hated the tsarist autocracy, which he considered the strongest bastion of reaction in Europe, and he was therefore prepared to support any revolutionary group that seemed to be waging an effective fight against it. In the early 1880's he (as well as Engels) greatly admired the Narodovol'tsy, by far the strongest and boldest opponents of the autocracy. At the same time, he was cool toward the Russians who were gradually adopting his ideas because they had been Bakuninists. There was probably no radical whom Marx detested more vehemently than the Russian anarchist.

Aside from these personal and political factors, a formidable theoretical problem presented itself: must Russia undergo an economic development similar to that of Western Europe? Was the agrarian commune doomed to extinction, and was Russia destined to pass through an industrial, capitalist phase? Or could the country move directly from an agrarian society based on the mir into socialism? Put succinctly, Marx's answer amounted to the not very helpful conclusion that Russia might or might not be able to avoid capitalism.[16]

Such an evasive assessment could not, obviously, support the theoretical framework for a Marxist movement in Russia. Plekhanov undertook to repair this deficiency. In two important works, *Socialism and*

15. *Ibid.*, p. 103; Deich, "Pervye shagi," pp. 27–30.

16. On the question of Marx's and Engels' attitude toward Russia's economic and political development, see the following, which is only a portion of the literature on the subject: *K. Marks, F. Engel's i revoliutsionnaia Rossiia* (Moscow, 1967), pp. 77–79, 89, 443–444; Solomon Bloom, *The World of Nations: A Study of the National Implications in the Works of Karl Marx* (New York, Columbia University Press, 1941), pp. 151–169; Boris Nicolaevsky, "Marx und das russische Problem," *Die Gesellschaft*, I (1924), 359–366; Richard Pipes, "Russian Marxism and Its Populist Background: The Late Nineteenth Century," *Russian Review*, XIX (Oct. 1960), 323–325.

Political Struggle (1883) and *Our Differences* (1885), he sought to demonstrate beyond any doubt the applicability of Marxism to his country and to show how the political conception of his circle differed from that of other Russian revolutionaries. In the first place, he denied the possibility of a unique economic, social, and political development for Russia. Persuaded that "in Russian history, there is no essential difference from the history of Western Europe," he proceeded to apply Marxian categories of analysis to the Russian situation, claiming that the pattern of development Marx had discovered for Europe would inevitably hold true for Russia. An examination of the agrarian situation in his country had convinced Plekhanov that the commune was doomed. Ever since the emancipation of the serfs in 1861 the institution had been disintegrating, and everywhere capitalism was making inroads into the economy. He therefore dismissed as utopian the expectation that the commune could serve as the basis for the establishment of socialism. It was only a matter of time before capitalism would dominate the economy.

Second, as a historical materialist he argued that the emergence of new economic relationships would lead to the transformation of the social and political order. Just as in the West at an earlier period, so now in Russia the feudal, autocratic system of rule would be replaced by a bourgeois form of parliamentary government under which the citizens would be granted political as well as civil rights. Plekhanov viewed the achievement of bourgeois democracy as an important step forward, and, on the basis of the advice Marx and Engels had given the German workers in 1848, he urged the Russian proletariat to join together and assist the bourgeoisie in its struggle against the autocracy. During the era of bourgeois domination the industrial workers were to seize every opportunity to heighten their class consciousness and organize themselves into a force capable of staging the second revolution, for the achievement of socialism.

Third, Plekhanov repudiated anarchism and the distinction he and the Bakuninists had drawn between economics and politics. He now held that the two were inextricably intertwined. Every attempt to achieve economic improvement was essentially a political effort. Thus, he now saw the fight for socialism as fundamentally a political struggle for power. The masses could only realize their aspirations by gaining control over the state machinery. Henceforth, when developing strategy for Russian Marxists, Plekhanov accorded primacy to political questions.

Finally, he no longer attributed a central role in the movement to the peasantry but to the proletariat, the only class firmly committed to the abolition of private ownership of the means of production. He foresaw a more or less extended period of capitalist development, during which the workers would evolve into a class-conscious force constituting a majority of the population. The primary tasks of the Marxist intelligentsia were to imbue the proletariat with class consciousness, enlighten them about the nature of capitalist society, clarify and articulate their aspirations, organize them into a political movement: in short, prepare them for their historically ordained mission, the realization of socialism.

At first glance, Plekhanov's Marxism had about it an appealing simplicity and persuasiveness. His claim that it was a scientific doctrine lent it an aura of sanctity, for how could one refute laws of social development? Moreover, the progress of industrialization after the early 1880's, the growth in the size and militancy of the working class in the 1890's, the rise of an urban bourgeoisie—all these trends seemed to confirm the basic thrust of Plekhanov's assertions. Yet it soon became evident that his schematic outline of Russia's future course raised a series of theoretical, political, and psychological problems, some endemic to every deterministic philosophy and some peculiar to the Russian situation. Plekhanov attempted to resolve the problems, but in virtually no case did he arrive at answers acceptable even to all who considered themselves Marxists. This was, in large part, because he vacillated between conflicting positions. But some of the problems were, at least from the Marxist point of view, simply intractable.

To begin with, Plekhanov's application of the doctrine of stages to Russia immediately gave rise to some baffling questions. For the middle class, as he admitted, was too weak to overthrow the autocracy. Who, then, was to create the bourgeois order? Plekhanov's response that the working class would play a major role in the first revolution only confused the issue. Would the proletariat be prepared to spill its blood for the sake of its class enemy? Moreover, if the masses were needed to put the bourgeoisie into power, might they not also be needed to help keep them in power? Perhaps even more vexing was the issue of the duration of bourgeois domination. Plekhanov's scheme implied a rather long period of maturation for capitalism before the start of the struggle for socialism; indeed, he was often explicit in predicting a protracted era of middle-class control over Russia. But a political program based on such a forecast could easily engender fatalism among the masses, especially since the ultimate triumph of the ideal was said to be foreordained by the ineluctable laws of the historical process. No mass political movement can be organized on the basis of such remote rewards, as Plekhanov himself fully realized. He therefore tried to reconcile his determinism with the widespread yearning for immediate results by arguing that because the workers in Russia were being organized into a class-conscious force before the triumph of capitalism, the era of middle-class domination would be briefer than in the West. "Our capitalism," he wrote in 1885 in *Our Differences*, "will fade without having fully flowered." Plekhanov failed, unfortunately, to clarify this arresting statement. Did he intend to suggest that the proletariat would seize power before it constituted a majority of the population? If so, the notion would seem to imply an acceptance of Jacobinism, precisely the doctrine Marxists had repudiated in their criticisms of the Narodovol'tsy.

Plekhanov's Marxism left yet another unanswered question. Although he considered the urban laborers the motive force in the drive for socialism, he did not believe they could attain socialist consciousness on their own. The Marxist intelligentsia would have to prepare the proletariat for its predestined role. Since he held that the doctrines of scientific socialism were based on observation of working-class life, Plekhanov did not foresee any difficulty in persuading the masses to accept them. But what if the workers proved recalcitrant? What if they came to reject the Marxist interpretation of their interests and advanced their own views on how best to improve their lot?

Eventually, it turned out that the working class did not measure up to Plekhanov's image of it. Many workers were either unresponsive to socialist teachings or otherwise acted contrary to Marxist expectations, which baffled Plekhanov and his comrades. The trouble was that the theorists spent most of their time speculating about the proletariat; because they failed to familiarize themselves with the workers' real state of mind their political views assumed an abstractness that was bound to hinder the development of an effective proletarian organization.

It should be emphasized that most of these questions and problems did not become paramount immediately after the publication of Plekhanov's works. But in time, as the number of the GEL's adherents grew and as a labor movement emerged in Russia, they led to interminable debates, controversies, and, ultimately, splits. Specific strategic and tactical issues arose, all of them impinging on the broader theoretical scheme developed by Plekhanov. Only then did Axelrod become involved in the discussions, directing his efforts at adapting the tactics of Western Marxists to the unique conditions in Russia. During the GEL's early years he subscribed to Plekhanov's formulations and, like its other members, recognized him as the outstanding authority among them on philosophy in general and on Marxist theory.[17]

At this time Axelrod made no attempt to write weighty or original works. His major written contribution was a short volume, *The Workers' Movement and Social Democracy* (1885), designed to serve as a handbook for "workers' intelligentsia." It was understood that Plekhanov's writings were far too difficult for ordinary workers, many of whom the GEL hoped to reach. In the preface, which they wrote together, Axelrod and Plekhanov warned that the proletariat could avoid "trailing after the tail" of the "intelligentsia circles" only if they produced their own intelligentsia, who in turn must create an *"independent labor* association or *labor party* in the full sense of that word." They predicted that the more vigorously this aim was pursued, the easier it would be, as it had been in Germany, to attract support of the traditional intelligentsia for the labor movement.[18] The significant point here is the group's disavowal of any intention to assume the initiative in founding a labor party; that task was to be left to individuals belonging to the proletariat.

Axelrod found the writing of the work difficult and uncongenial, and, to his chagrin, two of his drafts were rejected by his colleagues.

17. See G. V. Plekhanov, *Sotsializm i politicheskaia bor'ba* and *Nashi raznoglasiia* in his *Sochineniia*, ed. D. Riazanov (2nd ed., Moscow, 1923–1927), II; for a detailed exposition and analysis of Plekhanov's views, see Samuel H. Baron, *Plekhanov: The Father of Russian Marxism* (Stanford, 1963), pp. 89–116; the "problems" in Plekhanov's Marxism are also incisively explored by J. L. H. Keep, *The Rise of Social Democracy in Russia* (Oxford, 1963), pp. 19–24, and Jonathan Frankel, "The Polarization of Russian Marxism (1883–1903): Plekhanov, Lenin and Akimov," in *Vladimir Akimov on the Dilemmas of Russian Marxism 1895–1903*, ed. Jonathan Frankel (Cambridge, Eng., 1969), pp. 7–17.

18. Pavel Axelrod, *Rabochee dvizhenie i sotsial'naia demokratiia* (Geneva, 1885), pp. xiv–xv.

His first effort was not so much a "popular brochure for workers," Deich complained, as an "explanatory glossary of certain foreign words, expressions, and formulas." After Axelrod had thoroughly revised the manuscript his colleagues were delighted and could "not praise it enough."[19] In truth, the final product turned out to be a masterful pedagogical exercise, though it is doubtful whether large numbers of Russian workers actually took the trouble to read some 150 pages on Marxist theory. Axelrod illustrated every point with concrete examples, repeated complicated ideas several times in different forms, and used the simplest possible language. Though the volume did not break any new ground in doctrine, it was useful as a succinct summary of the GEL's beliefs.

Most of Axelrod's political efforts at this time were devoted to his administrative work for the GEL, which yielded disappointing results. Because the burden was too much for him, he enlisted the help of Saul Greenfest, a former Chernoperedelets who had joined the Marxists in 1883. That year Greenfest went to Russia and tried unsuccessfully to organize circles for the GEL. Few active revolutionaries remained, and Greenfest did not manage to establish firm links with those he encountered. When he returned to Switzerland, he expected automatically to be co-opted into the GEL, but as the organization insisted on retaining its identity as a small literary circle it refused to accept him. Apparently he had no literary gifts, but the exclusion quite naturally distressed him. Plekhanov and Axelrod looked upon their group as something special: they wanted supporters to form a "periphery" giving material and moral aid to the parent organization without direct membership in it. The only new person enrolled into the GEL was Sergei Ingerman (born in 1868), a medical student in Zurich who later emigrated to the United States, where he organized the Russian Social Democratic Society and regularly collected money for the GEL. This exclusiveness was bound to arouse resentment and in no small measure contributed to the tension that eventually emerged between the GEL and its periphery.

The precariousness of the operation is exemplified by the kind of contributions on which the GEL relied. In 1884 and 1885 the group's treasury received the following sums: seventy rubles from Russia, fifty

19. Deich, "Pervye shagi," p. 36; Deich to Axelrod, Jan. 17, 1884, *Gruppa,* ed. Deich, I, 197; Deich to Axelrod, Feb. 10, 1884, *ibid.,* p. 199.

marks from a student in Germany, five marks from a certain Ivan, seventeen and a half francs from the United States, and a few "large" donations of one hundred francs.[20] In the summer of 1884, to speed up the completion of some of their projects, Greenfest proposed that Plekhanov and Axelrod devote themselves full time to literary work and be paid a monthly salary of 150 francs. He immediately realized the impracticability of the scheme, however, as the GEL did not have the requisite funds. It is ironic that they were forced even to exploit the man who worked their printing press: a printer of Slavic material was normally paid 250 to 300 francs a month; the GEL paid 75 to 80, if the money was available.[21]

What disturbed Axelrod and his colleagues even more than their financial and organizational difficulties was their failure to win the approval of Western Marxist leaders. The GEL evoked a sympathetic response only among those socialists with whom they had close personal relations: Jules Guesde, whom Plekhanov knew well, and Kautsky and Bernstein. Most of the other leaders avoided them. The full extent of their isolation seems to have dawned on the group only in January 1885, when Engels made it clear to Zasulich that he favored the approach of the Narodovol'tsy, who, he was sure, would soon succeed in overthrowing the autocracy. In Engels' view, Russia was in a position similar to that of France in 1789, and he did not find it important which "faction" gave the "signal" for the start of the revolution. He recalled Hegel's concept of the "irony of history": "Look at Bismarck— a revolutionary against his will, and Gladstone, who ended with a disagreement with the ruler whom he adored." In a similar way, the Narodovol'tsy could be counted on to deliver the first blow against the old regime, the collapse of which would then have consequences they neither anticipated nor willed. If the revolution turned out to be merely the work of a "court conspiracy, it will be swept away in a day." From his analysis of conditions in Russia, however, Engels believed that the terrorists' strike against the Tsar would produce another "1789," and, if he was right, then "1793 cannot be far behind." For the rest, he expressed pride, in a somewhat condescending manner, "that there exists among the Russian youth a party that accepts without hesitation

20. *Iz arkhiva Aksel'roda, 1881–1896*, ed. W. S. Woytinsky, B. I. Nicolaevsky, and L. O. Tsederbaum-Dan (Berlin, 1924), p. 106.
21. *Ibid.*, pp. 86–89; Deich "Pervye shagi," p. 39.

and reservation the great economic and historical theories of Marx and that has decisively broken with the anarchist and rather Slavophile traditions of its predecessors."[22]

Even in the 1920's Axelrod could not refrain from bitterness in explaining Engels' reaction to the Russian Marxists. Western socialists would gladly have "greeted the devil," Axelrod sneered, if he had promised to "rid the civilized world of this stronghold of reaction [tsarism]."[23] Axelrod had obviously not taken Marx's earlier statements about Russia seriously, for Engels was really only echoing ideas both he and Marx had previously voiced.

During these "solitary years," as Axelrod referred to the 1880's, it seemed as though the GEL's efforts would come to naught. For a short period in 1885 the group had reason to rejoice. It learned that a circle in St. Petersburg, led by Dmitri Blagoev, considered itself Social Democratic and wished to establish contact with the Marxists in Switzerland. But within a year the Russian police liquidated the circle through arrests and the expulsion of Blagoev to his native Bulgaria.[24] Thereafter, Axelrod would occasionally receive requests from groups in Odessa, Warsaw, or Moscow for information and advice, and he would respond with long missives explaining the views of the GEL.[25] Somehow, the contacts were always short-lived, usually because of police action. Not until the mid-1890's did Axelrod and his comrades establish permanent connections with sympathizers in Russia. In the meantime they could only guess how widely their literature was being distributed in Russia and its impact on their readers.

Axelrod's proselytizing in Zurich proved to be more rewarding. By 1888 young people frequently gathered in his apartment to discuss politics. When visitors appeared, Axelrod was "always good-natured, always smiling, even merry . . . Pavel Borisovich was generous, hospitable in a comradely way, and no one could depart [from his home]

22. *Gruppa*, ed. Deich, III, 24–27.
23. Axelrod, "Gruppa 'Osvobozhdenie truda,' " p. 91.
24. For a good, brief discussion of the contacts between the Blagoev circle and the GEL, see Baron, *Plekhanov*, pp. 126–128. For Axelrod's reaction to the news of the existence of the circle, see his "Gruppa 'Osvobozhdenie truda,' " pp. 102–103.
25. Some of these letters are reproduced in *Iz arkhiva Aksel'roda*, ed. Woytinsky, Nicolaevsky, and Tsederbaum-Dan, pp. 231–240.

until he had been treated to coffee or tea."[26] Aptekman, who visited him at this time, commented—as did many other observers—on his winning ways with students. Axelrod, though twice as old as his guests, did not address them as a "tribune," but talked to them directly "face to face, selecting one or another individual, one or another group: in the [exercise] of direct, personal influence, his power was irresistible." Aptekman did not exaggerate much when he said that in Axelrod's apartment "were formed the first cadres of the [future Social Democratic] party."[27]

The list of Russian Marxists who by the twentieth century were to regard Axelrod as their political teacher is quite impressive. Among them was Vladimir Bonch-Bruevich, who regularly saw Axelrod in the 1890's. Anatoly Lunacharsky, even after he turned to Bolshevism, spoke of him in the warmest terms: "Axelrod and his family received me with delightful hospitality [in 1893] . . . I am very much indebted to Axelrod for my education in socialism and, however far apart he and I may have moved subsequently, I look upon him with gratitude as one of my most influential teachers." Leon Trotsky became Axelrod's most prominent "student." In 1904 Trotsky dedicated a book to "My dear teacher Pavel Axelrod," in which he referred with great respect to Axelrod's views. Axelrod felt affection for his disciples and kept in touch with them. Only after 1917 did he publicly repudiate Trotsky, and even then he did so with a heavy heart.[28]

Important as such supporters were, what Axelrod wanted most of all during its early years was to infuse new talent into the GEL. He was eager to attract revolutionaries of some repute who were also gifted writers. With this in mind in 1888 he appealed to Lavrov to join the GEL. Though sympathetic to Marxist ideas, Lavrov had previously re-

---

26. Bonch-Bruevich, *Izbrannye sochineniia*, II, 209.

27. O. V. Aptekman, "Zapiski semidesiatnika," *Sovremennyi mir*, no. 5/6 (1916), 227.

28. Anatoly Lunacharsky, *Revolutionary silhouettes*, tr. Michael Glenny (London, 1967), p. 85; N. Trotsky, *Nashi politicheskie zadachi* (Geneva, 1904); Pavel Axelrod, "Die Persönlichkeit Trotzkis," in *Die Tragödie Trotzki*, ed. Grigori Dimitrioff (Berlin, 1925), pp. 76–78; Bonch-Bruevich, *Izbrannye sochineniia*, I, 323–324; II, 209–212, 227–230, 289. Bonch-Bruevich, who became an important official in Lenin's government, claimed that although he was always warmly received by Axelrod he soon tired of the older man, whom he found insufficiently militant. Bonch-Bruevich also had doubts about Axelrod's usefulness to the cause because the latter was ill so much of the time. "I knew," Bonch-Bruevich wrote in the late 1950's, "that only in a healthy body can there be a healthy spirit." (*Ibid.*, p. 209.)

fused such an invitation, but now Axelrod felt a new effort had to be made. He was stunned by the defection from the revolutionary camp of Tikhomirov and feared that a reactionary mood might be growing. In the belief that a united effort by revolutionaries was called for, he invited Lavrov to become an editor of the *Library of Contemporary Socialism,* put out by the GEL, or to collaborate with it on a socialist journal.[29]

Lavrov declined, explaining his position in a lengthy letter that reveals much about his approach to politics and about the rather unfavorable reputation of the GEL as a contentious lot. Lavrov neither denied the usefulness of unity among revolutionaries nor the practicality of working with persons of slightly different theoretical persuasions. He objected to the idea of trying to unite only some revolutionaries when there were several other social revolutionary groups, all of whom shared a common goal and common enemies. A broad coalition had so far not been formed because the various groups had refused to discuss the differences between them in a "comradely spirit." And he made it clear that he looked upon the Marxists as the worst offenders. "Why," he asked, "do the organizers of the workers' party without fail insult . . . [the Narodovol'tsy] with mockery, regard them with contempt; in a word, do not recognize them as *comrades?*" He would consider collaborating with the GEL only when its members changed the tone in which they discussed ideas they disputed.[30]

The Marxists soon confirmed all of Lavrov's charges against them. Somehow, by the summer of 1889, the GEL and the Narodovol'tsy agreed to work together on a journal, to be entitled *Sotsialist,* which was sponsored by several revolutionary groups. Lavrov served as one of the editors. All the participants were fully aware that there were important differences of opinion among them, but they decided to hide their "socialism in their pockets" for the time being and concentrate on promoting the idea of an alliance with the liberals against absolutism. The central purpose of the journal was to appeal to people regardless of class affiliation, social interest, or ideological predisposition.

Plekhanov, however, submitted an article in which he criticized the program of Narodnaia volia and asserted that only the working class

29. Axelrod to Lavrov, Aug. 16, 1888, *Iz arkhiva Aksel'roda,* ed. Woytinsky, Nicolaevsky, and Tsederbaum-Dan, pp. 34–35.
30. Lavrov to Axelrod, Sept. 7, 1888, *ibid.,* pp. 36–41.

could create a genuine socialist movement.[31] He made it clear privately that he had little respect for the revolutionaries, led by Charles Rappoport, who were putting out the journal. He also indicated that he did not intend to abide by the agreement. Still, Plekhanov thought the collaboration valuable because it might be possible to exert a wholesome influence on Rappoport. "If we see that these gentlemen begin to talk nonsense, then we can always quit . . . We will either gradually correct [their views] . . . or part with them."[32] Needless to say, neither Lavrov nor the Narodovol'tsy took kindly to the sentiment in Plekhanov's article or to the breach of agreement. Thereafter the Narodovol'tsy refused to have any dealings with the Marxists, and only one issue of *Sotsialist* appeared.[33]

Axelrod also contributed an article to the journal, but he managed to stay within the agreed upon ideological confines. Although he concentrated on certain organizational issues relevant mainly to industrial workers, he went out of his way to indicate that his concern also extended to the peasantry. The question he raised was one he had briefly touched on in 1881 and 1885: how could the Russian masses be mobilized to fight for a constitutional form of government, which must be their "immediate goal"? As he saw it, the Russian proletariat was no less capable of being politicized than the Western European proletariat. The real problem was how to go about it.

Axelrod proposed that workers' resistance to politics be overcome by means of a new stratum, the "workers' intelligentsia" (also known as "advanced workers"). In elaborating this idea he developed, for the first time, the outline of his conception of a labor party, which in later years led him to become so staunch an opponent of Lenin's organizational views. Axelrod conceived of the workers' intelligentsia as a group of people who worked with their hands and at the same time were sufficiently educated to understand radical doctrines. To help form such groups he urged the publication of journals and newspapers that could appeal to workers, acquaint them with the history and conditions of labor movements in other, more advanced countries, and explain to them their tasks

31. See Plekhanov, *Sochineniia*, III, 83–95.
32. Plekhanov to Axelrod, Apr.–May 1889, *Perepiska G. V. Plekhanova i P. B. Aksel'roda*, ed. B. I. Nicolaevsky, P. A. Berlin, and W. S. Woytinsky (Moscow, 1925), I, 63.
33. Axelrod, "Unpublished Memoir."

and obligations. It was in the preparation of such material that the existing intelligentsia would be of most help to the labor movement. The actual waging of propaganda among the mass of laborers would then devolve upon the advanced workers.

Axelrod was mindful of the difficulties the workers' intelligentsia would encounter, but because of their "position, occupations, and interests" they would be much better placed than anyone else to establish direct and immediate contact with the "popular masses" and to "exert direct influence on them." Among the tasks Axelrod assigned to the workers' intelligentsia was one that bore some interesting resemblances to a technique just beginning to be applied in Russian Poland and that came to be known as "agitation." Axelrod did not use this term, but he obviously had in mind a method of work quite different from traditional propaganda, which involved attempts by intellectuals to educate people— generally small groups—in socialist doctrine. Because the advanced workers would be familiar with the proletariat's specific grievances, they would be able to exploit concrete discontents and thus demonstrate the impossibility of economic improvements without political freedom. "Every strike and every clash between workers and employers can very easily serve as graphic proof of the importance for the workers to elect their representatives to various public positions, and especially as deputies to an all-state assembly (parliament or *Zemskii sobor*), summoned to pass laws and to supervise the actions of the government."

Although Axelrod considered the peasants too scattered and too far removed from urban and educational centers to be readily organized or enlightened in the need for political change, he did not ignore them. He pointed out that sizable numbers of peasants worked in the cities for a few months every year, and, if properly indoctrinated, they could disseminate the political program he had outlined when they returned to the countryside. Once the revolutionary movement took root in the industrial centers, moreover, it would "gradually cross over" to the agrarian regions. Though secondary, the role Axelrod assigned to the peasants was not unimportant.[34]

This article in *Sotsialist* marks the first time Axelrod struck out on his own as a Marxist writer. The ideas in it were neither profound nor entirely original. But, in emphasizing that the workers' intelligentsia

34. Pavel Axelrod, "Zadachi rabochei intelligentsii v Rossii," *Sotsialist*, no. 1 (1889).

was to play the leading role in the revolutionary movement, he became the chief spokesman of a specific tendency within Russian Marxism. He declared, in effect, that the situation existing at the time of his writing, when the movement was dominated by intellectuals, should be no more than temporary. In the late 1880's his words did not seem particularly momentous because there was no mass movement. Still, there are hints that even at this early period Axelrod and Plekhanov differed over the nature of the organization Marxists should create.

One such hint can be found in a letter Plekhanov wrote to Axelrod in 1888: "And my Jacobinism? It is necessary that you restrain me; you have every right to restrain my centralistic and Jacobin tendencies. For it is true that I have sinned on that score. And what is more, for little reason."[35] In later years Plekhanov from time to time not only articulated elitist views, but in important party matters acted in accordance with such views. Axelrod, however, placed ever greater emphasis on the need to lessen the influence of intellectuals in the movement and to broaden its composition. More than anything else, this emphasis on a mass movement was ultimately responsible for his assuming the ideological leadership of an entire wing of the Russian Marxist party.

This is not to suggest that fundamental differences had emerged between Axelrod and Plekhanov during this early period. On the contrary, a close and warm, though not uncomplicated, relationship had evolved between them. They corresponded regularly, and the letters reveal strong mutual admiration. They discussed general political questions, their work, and, not infrequently, personal matters. Plekhanov, whose financial situation was even more precarious than Axelrod's, would occasionally appeal to his friend for help. If Axelrod ever refused, it was only because he himself had no money. At times Plekhanov could not afford to buy stamps for his letters, and so Axelrod paid for the postage in Zurich.

Plekhanov was clearly the dominant partner in the relationship. Axelrod looked up to him as a philosopher and a man of far greater originality than he, in short, as his intellectual superior. He sought Plekhanov's advice on books to read and, above all, depended on his friend for critical comments on his writings. Yet it seems that Axelrod occasionally resented what he believed to be Plekhanov's insistence that

35. Plekhanov to Axelrod, [May 1888], *Perepiska*, ed. Nicolaevsky, Berlin, and Woytinsky, I, 44.

his "authority" (that is, superiority) be openly acknowledged by the other members of the GEL.[36]

Axelrod also played a subordinate role in his other close friendship of the 1880's and 1890's. Kautsky, too, had a more theoretical mind than Axelrod and was immensely productive as well. There is no doubt that Axelrod suffered acutely from his failure to make a major contribution to the development of Marxist thought, a failure brought into sharp relief by the growing fame of his two most intimate colleagues. His sense of inadequacy manifested itself in diverse ways. Thus, in a letter to Plekhanov he once wrote that "My opinion does not have the same significance for you, as does yours of my work [for me]."[37] He expressed his need for approbation and encouragement more explicitly in a letter to Kautsky, written in a later period, which accurately describes his feelings on the subject from the mid-1880's on. "You can hardly imagine," he said, "the decisive importance for me of your assessment of my work. There are several circumstances that produce in me a need for moral encouragement in order to engage in literary work . . . The assessments [rendered by] you [and] Plekhanov . . . are therefore impulses of the strongest kind for me."[38] And when they praised Axelrod for his work, his friends had to reassure him that they were not merely being kind. For example, after Kautsky accepted one of Axelrod's manuscripts for *Die Neue Zeit,* he explained that he had often rejected articles submitted by friends and would certainly have turned down his had it not been of high quality.[39]

It is not that Axelrod lacked ideas for articles or books: his letters are filled with plans for writings, most of which he never completed. His failure to carry out so many of his projects resulted in large measure from his preoccupation with the kefir business and his persistent illnesses. But there was something else that held him back—a gnawing fear that he had nothing new and important to say. "I make no claim to originality," he wrote Kautsky, "but I have a deep inner aversion to chewing over someone else's work . . . It is not simple vanity, but a, so to speak, theoretical-artistic need that makes it odious for me to produce a work repeating another's ideas."[40] He was troubled by this apprehen-

36. Plekhanov to Axelrod, [April 1888], *ibid.,* p. 37.
37. Axelrod to Plekhanov, [Sept.–Oct. 1891], *ibid.,* p. 69.
38. Axelrod to Kautsky, Mar. 17, 1898, Kautsky Archive, I.I.S.H.
39. Kautsky to Axelrod, Nov. 19, 1892, Axelrod Archive, I.I.S.H.
40. Axelrod to Kautsky, May 23, 1895, Kautsky Archive, I.I.S.H.

sion for the rest of his life, and it may well have been a factor in causing some of his ailments, which seem to have been the type generally associated with psychological anguish: acute insomnia, constant fatigue, headaches, and writer's cramp. The upshot was his frequent inability to complete articles on time or at all, and every time this happened he endured something of a personal crisis. He worried endlessly lest his friends consider him a "lazy or frivolous fellow."[41] Occasionally he became so despondent that he would question his usefulness to the movement.

The first such crisis occurred in 1888. Plekhanov and Axelrod were planning to publish a new journal, *Sotsial-demokrat,* and Axelrod agreed to write the lead article for the first issue, an essay on "Political Freedom." He wrote a section of it, which he sent to Plekhanov for criticism. Plekhanov raised some substantive questions in a perfectly polite manner and then urged Axelrod to write in a "more lively and more pungent style." Because of illness Axelrod never completed the article and in a fit of depression resigned from the journal, stating that he had "played the 'celebrated role' of a fictitious editor" and had been of no use at all. Plekhanov responded with a warm note in which he apologized for having tormented him in "a very cruel way" by pressing him to finish the article when he should have realized that illness prevented him from doing so. He categorically refused to accept Axelrod's resignation on the ground that it was not for him to decide on his usefulness to the movement. "For me your editorial collaboration is very useful. I know that if you approve of a certain work written by me, then it is really good." He would, of course, continue to consult Axelrod even if he did resign, but he feared that such a step would give rise to "rumors and gossip." Moreover, some day Axelrod might have to assume sole editorial responsibility for the GEL's publications, and it was therefore important that the public be accustomed to thinking of him as an editor. It was at this point, in order to emphasize Axelrod's usefulness, that Plekhanov recalled that he had restrained him from giving vent to Jacobinist views. He pleaded with him to forget about the article and invited him to join him for a vacation. "I embrace you heartily, my dear Pavel," he concluded.[42]

Axelrod was mollified and continued to serve as editor. Possibly he was

41. Axelrod to Kautsky, Feb. 3, 1895, *ibid.*
42. Plekhanov to Axelrod, probably May 1888, *Perepiska,* ed. Nicolaevsky, Berlin, and Woytinsky, I, 43–44.

encouraged to resume his position by a windfall that enabled the GEL to publish the journal in a rather handsome format similar to that used by major literary periodicals. By chance, Plekhanov and Axelrod had met a retired wealthy Russian doctor visiting Switzerland. This Dr. Gur'ev had no particular views on politics, but by family tradition he considered himself a radical and was flattered to be in the company of "real revolutionaries." Also, in the 1870's his brother-in-law had helped Peter Kropotkin escape from a prison hospital, and to honor his relative's memory the doctor gave the GEL a generous sum of money, which was used for the new journal.[43] Chance events of this kind often determined the scope of the activities of the Russian Marxists.

Four volumes of *Sotsial-demokrat* appeared between 1888 and 1892, and once Axelrod recovered from his illness and depression he participated in the editorial work. He even managed to write two long articles. He returned to his favorite subject, European—and especially German— Social Democracy, and once again analyzed the tactics that had proven so successful in the previous two decades. It was particularly satisfying to him that Kautsky proposed to publish in *Die Neue Zeit* some of the sections dealing with the German party. "Substantially," Kautsky wrote to his friend, "I do not have a single objection. I am amazed at how accurately you have managed to understand the situation. For a non-German this is an extraordinary achievement with which you ought to be very pleased."[44]

By this time, 1890, Axelrod considered the experience and tactics of the German party more relevant to Russian Marxists than ever before. Among his countrymen it was still fashionable to believe that the party's primary and immediate aim was a "communist transformation of society . . . conceived of as one single revolutionary act by which private property and private production will all at once be completely abolished." According to Axelrod, the socialists' immediate goal was far more political than economic and social: "it is not bourgeois democracy, but the workers' party that serves as the focus of the democratic aspirations of the nation." The middle-class parties had neither the "ability . . . [nor] the will seriously to strive for democratization of the state." Precisely because the labor movement had placed the achievement of political rights so high on its agenda it had managed to make impressive showings

43. Axelrod, "Gruppa 'Osvobozhdenie truda,'" p. 111.
44. Kautsky to Axelrod, Nov. 13, 1892, Axelrod Archive, I.I.S.H.

at elections and to develop into a powerful political force.[45] Axelrod's analysis was basically sound, even if somewhat overdrawn. Bismarck's success in forging a strong national state and pressure from the working class for economic and social change had dampened the enthusiasm of certain middle-class groups for liberalism and democracy. There were signs, which were to increase during the 1890's, that some members of the bourgeoisie who were committed to democracy actually voted for the Marxist party because of its emphasis on political rights. To Axelrod it seemed likely that this strategy could be applied to Russia, where the middle classes as a group also could not be relied upon to lead the fight for democracy.

After writing the article on the German party Axelrod was presented with his first opportunity to make practical use of the tactical lessons he had learned. Russian "society" had suddenly awakened as a result of the famine of 1891 and the subsequent cholera epidemic, which killed hundreds of thousands of people. Natural disasters had befallen the country before, but the glaring feature of the catastrophe of 1891 was the government's total inability—and even unwillingness—to cope with it. Eventually, late in 1891, the authorities were forced to allow voluntary associations and the *zemstvos* to take up the work of caring for the needy and sick. Recognition of the autocracy's incompetence and contact with the wretchedness of the people combined to produce a new wave of social concern and oppositional sentiment among the intelligentsia. Thus the period of quiescence that had set in after the assassination of Alexander II in 1881 came to an end.

In 1891 the Marxists in Switzerland were especially gratified by the news of a May 1 celebration in St. Petersburg. Late that year a comrade named Gavrilo Gliko appeared in Geneva with barely legible copies of the speeches delivered at the illegal meeting. At the time Axelrod was staying with Plekhanov, and both were exhilarated by the report. "It is difficult," Axelrod wrote many years after the event, "for me to convey the joyful excitement that seized us. This was for us one of those rare, festive occasions, which remains in one's memory for life." It turned out that the entire proceedings had been arranged by workers, and all the

45. Pavel Axelrod, "Die politische Rolle und die Taktik der deutschen Sozialde-mokratie," *Die Neue Zeit,* XI, pt. 1 (1893), 492–502, 524–533; this was a section of his article "Politicheskaia rol' sotsial'noi demokratii i poslednie vybory v germanskii reikh-stag," *Sotsial-demokrat,* II (1890), 1–42; III (1890), 23–40; IV (1892), 3–45; see also his "Rabochee dvizhenie v nachale shestidesiatykh godov i teper', " *ibid.,* I (1888), 132–188.

speeches had been "imbued with a fully, distinct Social Democratic consciousness. The worker-orators were not only familiar with the contemporary labor movement in the West (especially with German Social
Democracy) but were fully aware of the necessity and inevitability of the
development of a Social Democratic movement in Russia as well." In
language clearly borrowed from Social Democrats, the speakers called for
civil liberties and universal suffrage. The writings of the GEL, so it
seemed, had made an impact after all. Axelrod and Plekhanov sensed
that at last their period of isolation was drawing to a close.[46]

The news from Russia encouraged Axelrod to try out a plan he had
been contemplating for several weeks: the formation of a nonparty organization that would exploit the widespread dissatisfaction caused by
the famine. He considered it an "unpardonable mistake, more, a crime
against one's banner" for a revolutionary not to take advantage of the
crisis "in the interest of stimulating constitutional-democratic agitation
—in society and [among] the popular masses." He therefore called on
radicals of all persuasions to found a Society for the Struggle against the
Famine, whose purpose would be to mount a campaign against the
autocracy, the "primary cause of the famine." Although Axelrod assumed
that Marxists would constitute the spearhead of the society, he expected
all members to put aside their differences for the time being. They were
to rally around two demands: a constitution and convocation of a
Zemskii sobor (national assembly). He realized that radicals might scoff
at his proposal because it was moderate. But in his view such a posture
missed the point of his strategy, for the premise underlying it was that
the "democratic stage" was "one of the most important" for Russia "in
the process of preparing the socialist revolution." Support for his program did not, therefore, compel socialists to violate their principles.[47]

Axelrod called on Russian émigrés all over Europe to form local
groups, which were to help determine the policies of a central organization that would coordinate the activities of the movement as a whole.
They were also to collect money for the publication and transportation
into Russia of a newspaper, Zemskii sobor, and various other writings

46. Axelrod, "Unpublished Memoir"; Pavel Axelrod, "Das politische Erwachen der russischen Arbeiter und ihre Maifeier von 1891," *Die Neue Zeit*, X, pt. 2 (1892), 36–45, 78–84, 109–116.

47. *Iz arkhiva Aksel'roda*, ed. Woytinsky, Nicolaevsky, and Tsederbaum-Dan, pp. 117–123.

on the famine. On the local level some progress was made. Axelrod succeeded in forming an "interparty" circle in Zurich composed of Marxists and Narodovol'tsy, the secretary of which was J. Kalmanson, a Social Democrat and Axelrod's brother-in-law, and Plekhanov agreed to write a pamphlet on the famine, which was to be rushed into Russia.

The success of the plan depended ultimately on gaining the support of important non-Marxist revolutionaries. To Axelrod's disappointment, neither Lavrov nor Kravchinsky would fully participate in the campaign for a constitution. Lavrov expressed sympathy with the aims of the new society, but disapproved of its emphasis on bourgeois democracy: "just at this time when so many Russian revolutionaries are prepared to hide the red flag in their pockets, I consider it necessary to emphasize that our political demands flow from our *socialist* convictions." Still, in order to help the cause he was willing to collaborate with other socialists in the society, but not with Kravchinsky.[48] Two months later, however, when asked to serve on the Central Committee of the society, Lavrov claimed that "neither his age, nor his health, nor his work" permitted him to accept so demanding a post. His refusal to work with Kravchinsky was superfluous because the latter also would not serve on the Central Committee. Kravchinsky opposed on principle any plan of political action that assigned leadership to émigrés. In his view, revolutionaries in exile should serve only one purpose: to produce radical literature dealing with theoretical questions.[49]

Despite these obstacles, sometime in the winter or early spring of 1892 Plekhanov traveled to Paris to discuss the possibility of forming the society with representatives from other Russian revolutionary movements. But the negotiations did not get far. The other delegates pressed Plekhanov to state publicly that the GEL did not consider the Narodovol'tsy to be anarchists. His refusal brought to an end the efforts to unite the revolutionaries in a common cause.[50]

The principal achievement of the endeavors seems to have been Ple-

48. Lavrov refused to collaborate with Kravchinsky because *Free Russia,* published by Kravchinsky and F. V. Volkhovsky in London, failed to defend the assassination of a Russian general in France. Kravchinsky considered it improper for Russian terrorists to carry out assassinations in a free country giving asylum to political refugees.

49. *Iz arkhiva Aksel'roda,* ed. Woytinsky, Nicolaevsky, and Tsederbaum-Dan, pp. 122, 129, 130.

50. *Perepiska,* ed. Nicolaevsky, Berlin, and Woytinsky, I, 241–243.

khanov's two works on the famine, in which he urged socialists to take advantage of the internal crisis by agitating among the masses on the basis of immediate political and economic demands.

Although the failure disappointed him, Axelrod was nevertheless heartened by the political ferment engendered by the famine. Eager to demonstrate to his European colleagues that Russian labor was following a path similar to that of its Western counterpart, he immediately wrote an article on the May 1 celebration for *Die Neue Zeit;* thereafter he made a practice of reporting on Russian developments in the German press. This was partially an effort to win the esteem of the German Marxists, who still did not appear to look favorably upon the Russians.

In fact, early in 1891 the collective ego of Axelrod and his comrades had suffered a severe blow: in transforming the *Vorwärts* into the German party's central organ, Wilhelm Liebknecht had ignored the Marxists and asked Lavrov to serve as official contributor on Russian affairs.[51] Clara Zetkin, already something of a stormy petrel in the German party, was outraged by Liebknecht's conduct. The arrangement had been kept secret, but somehow she managed to discover the identity of the author of several articles on Russia. She then begged for "forgiveness" from the Russian Marxists for Lavrov's "shameful articles" which, she said, completely "misrepresented conditions," and she urged Plekhanov to expose the errors. When he begged off for lack of time, she declared that "the good Axelrod will have to sacrifice himself and write." Aware that divulging this information about *Vorwärts* was in violation of party discipline, she pleaded with him *"to keep all this strictly secret."*[52]

How much Zetkin's entreaty to write influenced Axelrod is not known, but he made a point of stressing the similarity in the strategies followed by Russian and Western workers in his article. The "elite of the Russian proletariat already thinks and feels precisely as do the advanced workers of Germany, Austria, and France; . . . in a word, on the whole [it] accepts the principles of international Social Democracy." The demonstration of May 1, 1891, opened a "new epoch in the social-political life of Russia." At last there had emerged a genuine workers' intelligentsia, which was "closely and organically linked with its class, [and was] fully conscious of its obligation toward the oppressed masses." Axelrod

51. B. N—skii [Nicolaevsky], "K istorii 'Partii russkikh sotsialdemokratov' 1884–1886 g.," *Katorga i ssylka,* no. 54 (1929), 49.
52. Zetkin to Axelrod, sometime in first half of 1891, Axelrod Archive, I.I.S.H.

thought that the proletariat's involvement in the political struggle might now "set in motion all other oppositional forces in Russia."[53] This marked the first occasion on which he explicitly suggested that the Russian proletariat might play an instigative role in the bourgeois revolution; it was an idea to which he returned some five years later and which thereafter caused considerable discussion in Marxist circles.

One of the ironies of the history of the Group for the Emancipation of Labor is that although the GEL desperately sought to enlarge its sphere of influence, as soon as it found supporters fierce conflicts erupted between the veterans and the converts. It is no less ironic that often one of the principal sources of dissension among these enemies of capitalism was money. This is not all that surprising, for the GEL could accomplish nothing without money, and it was always in short supply. It was expensive to publish books, newspapers, and leaflets, and their transportation into Russia often meant bribing officials. Moreover, once the Russian Marxists decided to organize a party, it was necessary to pay a salary to full-time functionaries. Consequently, Russian revolutionaries would make prodigious efforts in order to lay their hands on a few thousand rubles. Persuasion and intrigue were the normal techniques, but less honorable methods were not shunned. This frantic scramble for money, occasionally producing scandals of dramatic proportions, began in 1892 and did not end until 1917, when the Bolsheviks received funds from the German High Command. (One could probably write a fascinating account of Russian Marxism using the conflicts over money as a framework.)

Axelrod was directly involved in many of the financial disputes, but the first one caused him the greatest anguish. It resulted from his close relationship with Leo Jogiches (also known as Grozovskii and Tyshko), who went to Zurich in 1890 at the age of twenty-three. Their friendship—and the ensuing contacts between Jogiches and the GEL from 1890 to 1893—became entangled in the first serious attempt to create a formal arrangement between the veterans and a group of younger Marxists. The attempt failed and produced resentments that profoundly affected all future efforts at reaching an understanding between the "fathers" and the "sons."

53. Axelrod, "Das politische Erwachen," p. 115.

There is, unfortunately, a paucity of source material on the first meetings between Jogiches and Axelrod. We therefore have to rely heavily on Axelrod's unpublished memoirs, which are clearly biased, not only because every personal document is one-sided but also because he came to dislike Jogiches intensely. Although Axelrod detested any sort of personal altercation and found it painful to break with people who had been his friends, his anguish became particularly acute at this time because late in 1892 rumors were circulated by his adversaries about his "bourgeois style of life." He was alleged to be making huge profits from the kefir shop, which was, of course, patently untrue. It unnerved him, nevertheless, and did much to color his attitude toward the younger supporters of the GEL in subsequent years.[54]

Axelrod's comments on Jogiches, despite their acerbity, do not appear to be overly unjust. From all accounts of his later activities in the German and Polish Social Democratic parties and his role as confidant and intimate of Rosa Luxemburg, it is evident that Jogiches was indeed an arrogant, overbearing, and unscrupulous man.[55] He made quite a different impression on Axelrod at their first meeting: he seemed to be a "very practical, experienced [and] energetic" person. He had just come from Vilno, where he had acquired a reputation as a Marxist propagandist and effective organizer of Jewish workers. "This was for me important and happy news," Axelrod wrote, "which involuntarily disposed me favorably toward the young man . . ." Axelrod was delighted that he had immediately approached the GEL, as nothing pleased the group more than to make contact with a burgeoning Social Democratic movement in Russia. To be sure, the young man displayed certain "tendentious manners," but under the circumstances Axelrod dismissed that as unimportant. Jogiches soon visited him almost every day, and a warm friendship developed between them.

Jogiches gradually began to become increasingly self-confident and unduly familiar. He boasted of his exploits, claiming to have escaped from a Russian prison. Axelrod had no reason to suspect the truth, which was that Jogiches had run away from Poland in order to escape military service. When he offered to return to Russia to establish connections between the GEL and local groups, Axelrod naturally was elated and

54. *Perepiska*, ed. Nicolaevsky, Berlin, and Woytinsky, I, 82.
55. There does not exist a biography of Jogiches. The best discussion of his work and personality may be found in J. P. Nettl, *Rosa Luxemburg* (London, 1966), *passim*, but esp. I, 65–69.

somehow managed to procure a passport for him. Axelrod's suspicion was apparently aroused by Jogiches' frequent delays of his departure, but he was not yet disenchanted. In fact, late in 1891 he sponsored him for membership in the GEL, a recommendation approved by Plekhanov and Zasulich. Axelrod was certain that Jogiches would be honored by the offer and was surprised when the young man said: "Yes, but what will my rights be in your group?" Axelrod explained that this question had never been discussed, that every decision was reached by common understanding, and that Jogiches would enjoy the same rights as the older members. But Jogiches insisted on having his prerogatives spelled out, which infuriated Axelrod. He pointed out that the GEL had functioned harmoniously for almost a decade and could continue to do so. If it ever became much larger, rules would have to be drawn up, and then Jogiches would know precisely what his rights were. The young man still refused to join.

The crux of the problem, as Axelrod began to suspect, was that Jogiches wanted a dominant position in the organization so as to be able to "subordinate it to his iron discipline." He thought he could achieve his purpose with a commodity that Plekhanov and Axelrod needed—money. He came from a rather wealthy family, which kept him well supplied with funds. Sometime in 1892 he told Axelrod that he had just received 40,000 rubles, which he could dispose of as he saw fit. Axelrod recalled that Jogiches carefully watched the expression on his face as he mentioned the huge figure. Only later did he realize that Jogiches was waiting for him to specify then and there the rights pursuant to membership in the GEL. The 40,000 rubles were to serve as an inducement. When this tactic failed to produce the desired response, Jogiches abruptly threatened to join the Polish Social Democratic movement.

But he preferred the GEL, which had gained much more of a reputation than the Polish Marxist group. He therefore tried a second approach, surpassing all others in crudity. He contrived to run into Axelrod and Zasulich at a railway station, joined them on the train, and pulled out his wallet. "Here it is," he said, "here . . . the money," as he held it under their noses. Any lingering doubts about Jogiches' intentions now disappeared: "For 40,000 rubles we should recognize his dictatorship over the group and in the future dance to his tune."[56]

In the meantime, Jogiches had managed to annoy Plekhanov in an-

56. This section is based on Axelrod's "Unpublished Memoir."

other way. He had contributed to the financing of *Sotsial-demokrat* and a pamphlet on Ludwig Feuerbach. He suddenly demanded a careful accounting of his money and complained that he had not received the 300-odd copies of the pamphlet promised him. Plekhanov responded indignantly that the GEL had always lumped together all donations, making it impossible to provide a precise breakdown of how particular contributions had been spent. It had never dawned on any of them to suspect a comrade of dishonesty. Plekhanov assured Jogiches that his donation had been spent as originally specified by the GEL and that if he required further explanations it might be necessary to convoke a "revolutionary court of arbitration" to settle the dispute.[57] On this matter Jogiches also did not receive satisfaction from Axelrod, who in August 1892 announced that in view of the young man's conduct he did not care to meet him to discuss the issue. In October 1892 the three finally reached an agreement on the outstanding issues, but relations between the GEL and Jogiches were permanently severed.[58]

The conflict with Jogiches was unpleasant enough, but still more unpleasant was his pernicious influence on other young people sympathetic to the GEL. He apparently managed to persuade Rosa Luxemburg to stop visiting Axelrod, who had befriended her. Then a few people began to criticize the GEL, contending that it was too preoccupied with theoretical works, ignored agitation among the people, and failed to utilize the talents of young émigrés. Some also claimed that the tactics adopted during the famine were at variance with the views expounded in *Our Differences*. Marxists were supposed to organize the proletariat, but instead they had stressed agitation for a constitution, which should be the work of bourgeois liberals. It was also alleged that the veterans had favored restoration of the peasantry ravaged by the famine, which would impede the growth of the proletariat.

Axelrod was convinced that Jogiches was the Svengali behind the discontent. Jogiches' influence had been especially noticeable at a conference the GEL had called in 1893 to form a periphery around the group. Axelrod had proposed the new organization, not in order to satisfy what he considered to be the baseless charges of the young people, but rather to provide some formal structure to the group's sympathizers, whose

---

57. "Perepiska G. V. Plekhanova, P. B. Aksel'roda i V. I. Zasulich s L. Iogikhesom (Grozovskim, Tyshkoi), 1891–1892," *Proletarskaia revoliutsiia*, no. 11/12 (1928), 270–271.
58. *Ibid.*, pp. 272–274, 285.

number had grown substantially in the previous two years. At the meetings, attended by some twenty people from various cities, a young man named Boris Krichevsky led a group of critics of the old guard. The atmosphere, Axelrod recalled, was "unhealthy and insincere." People seemed afraid to speak their minds freely. Krichevsky was especially sullen, a mood Axelrod explained as having been caused by the GEL's recent rejection of an article by him.

During a break between sessions Axelrod and Plekhanov saw Krichevsky and Jogiches (who had not been invited) talking in the street. Axelrod was sure that Jogiches was "pumping his interlocutor full [of advice], inspiring him to hold firm to the end."[59] Nevertheless, Axelrod and Plekhanov created a Union of Russian Social Democrats to which the younger people could belong. Not much is known about its activities, and apparently it existed for only a few months.

Whatever Jogiches' vices, and they were many, the GEL was not blameless in its relations with the young supporters. Part of the problem was that the group refused to yield any of its prerogatives and regarded itself as the sole guardian of orthodoxy. As early as 1887 and 1888, when a few youthful Russians were dissatisfied because of the exclusiveness of the GEL, Axelrod opposed their acceptance into the select inner circle. He felt that since they had "still not been through the revolutionary school, it would suit us to utilize these forces in this manner [that is, in a union] rather than formally accept them into the group."[60] In his unpublished memoirs Axelrod also confessed that he had always questioned the dedication of the young comrades who expressed their sympathy for Marxism; they seemed more interested in getting their diplomas at the university than in sacrificing themselves for the revolutionary cause.

In 1893 Zasulich insisted that the newly created union be completely independent of the GEL: "none of us must enter into the administration of the union." She feared that the organization might come under the influence of people who were not "sufficiently orthodox."[61] The young radicals could not but sense these condescending attitudes; it is not surprising that they were offended, for they wanted to share in the responsibilities as well as in the work. Denied the opportunity for full

---

59. Axelrod, "Unpublished Memoir."
60. Axelrod to Plekhanov, late 1887 or early 1888, *Perepiska*, ed. Nicolaevsky, Berlin, and Woytinsky, I, 27.
61. Zasulich to Axelrod, Apr. 13, 1893, Axelrod Archive, I.I.S.H.

participation in the GEL's activities, they increasingly found fault with the work of their elders. The veterans, in turn, did not accept criticism gracefully. After all, in less than a decade a group of three people, with extremely limited financial resources, had published more than twenty books and brochures (including journals). The GEL had not, admittedly, produced much popular literature, but there were good reasons for this: no regular means of transporting illegal literature into Russia existed; no one knew how much of a demand there was for it; and for the development of a Social Democratic movement in Russia Axelrod and Plekhanov believed the first essential step was to effect an "intellectual revolution" among the radical intelligentsia.[62] Both sides sustained a strong case, an ideal situation for a collision.

The controversy between Jogiches and the GEL should really be viewed within the broader context of distrust and suspicion that surrounded the organization. Without the potential for open antagonism, it is unlikely that Jogiches, despite the power of his personality, would have been able to muster support for his campaign of criticism.

Axelrod and Plekhanov seem never to have forgotten the unpleasantness of 1892, and the memory of Jogiches discouraged flexibility on their part. Nor, to their discredit, did they take to heart the substantive criticisms of the newcomers to the movement, which, however vaguely expressed, deserved consideration. In many ways the altercation between the GEL and Jogiches foretold things to come. But the later conflicts were for higher stakes, and their consequences were therefore farther reaching.

62. Axelrod, "Unpublished Memoir."

V | Expansion and Turbulence

In the mid-1890's Russian Marxism entered a new phase. It ceased to be the preserve of a handful of individuals living abroad and instead became a movement with a variety of organizations and adherents in Russia and the West. Although it would be an exaggeration to characterize these diverse groups as amounting to a mass movement of major proportions, their existence was very much in evidence. Labor unrest increased, and connections were established between active working-class organizations and Marxist propagandists. By the late 1890's, moreover, Marxist doctrines had been adopted by a remarkably large number of students, publicists, and even academics, who legally published their views in Russia. It is paradoxical that at the same time the dramatic expansion in the influence of Marxism inspired a sense of satisfaction in the members of the GEL it caused unexpected turbulence within the Marxist camp as a whole.

The conditions of exile life seemed to stimulate a penchant for contentiousness. Because of their distance from Russia, the Marxist émigrés were unable effectively to participate in the direction of the nascent labor movement. Nor were they in a position to affect the general course of political developments in their country. Thus, virtually free from concern about the practical implications of their actions and pronouncements, during the 1890's the Marxists in exile did not feel the need for constraint or compromise.

There were also less subjective sources of conflict. In the first place, the corpus of doctrines handed down by Marx and Engels was ambiguous on many issues. As the number of people writing on theoretical questions grew, disputes on points of interpretation were bound to multiply. More important, as the proletarian movement materialized, the tasks of

Russian Marxists inevitably changed, and here again there was fertile soil for disagreement. Plekhanov had laid the theoretical bases of Russian Marxism by 1885, but now attention had to be focused on specific organizational and tactical questions for which no clear-cut course of action had been prescribed. If to these developments is added the impact on Russian Marxist circles of the controversy over Revisionism in the German Social Democratic party, it is easy to understand why the new era in the history of the GEL was characterized by ideological, organizational, and personal conflict of the most intense sort.

It did not take long for new adherents of Russian Marxism to articulate their discontent with the work of the founders. In criticizing Plekhanov and Axelrod for publishing too little material for the average worker, the new converts were echoing complaints that the "opposition" around Krichevsky had lodged in 1892 and 1893. But there was an important additional factor: the critics of 1895 had just arrived from Russia, they represented genuine workers' organizations, and they were often experienced revolutionaries; thus, they held out the promise of lasting links between the GEL and active circles of Social Democrats in Russia. They could not be easily ignored by Plekhanov and Axelrod.

Among the earliest to arrive in Switzerland were two young militants, who appeared in the spring of 1895. The first was E. J. Sponti, whom Plekhanov dubbed the "teacher of life." A former army officer, Sponti in 1894 and 1895 had been one of the more prominent activists in the Moscow Union of Workers. He went to the West to urge the GEL to publish popular literature and took 400 rubles with him as a contribution toward defraying the cost of the undertaking.

Axelrod's description of his meetings with Sponti, written in the early 1920's, reveals both warmth and admiration as well as slight condescension toward the emissary. Axelrod remembered him as a kind of "Social Democratic Narodnik: in him there were combined Social Democratic convictions with that emotional idealism and revolutionary temperament which was so [characteristic] of Narodnichestvo of the 70's." Sponti stayed in Zurich over a week and visited Axelrod once or twice a day. He always brought up the same subject: that Marxist leaders—not only the GEL but Marx and Liebknecht as well—had concentrated on "scientific, philosophical theories" and ignored the task of writing works that could be understood by the masses. He even went so far as to accuse the GEL of being opposed to agitation among the workers, an opinion that proved unshakable.

Axelrod found Sponti's single-mindedness naïve and even primitive. He tried to reassure him that the GEL had long recognized the importance of agitation among workers and would be more than happy to write popular literature. But it was hopelessly difficult to do so from abroad because in order to be effective one had to be familiar with local conditions in the various Russian cities. Axelrod promised that as soon as the émigrés established regular contact with revolutionaries active among workers and thus acquired a source of information they would direct writings to the proletariat. These assurances always appeased Sponti—until the next time he saw Axelrod, and then he would raise the subject again. Had these encounters taken place with anyone else, Axelrod "would long ago have lost [his] temper." Only once did he express slight annoyance, when Sponti repeated a charge made earlier by Jogiches—whom Sponti met in Zurich—that Plekhanov's brochure on the famine was worthless. But the "teacher of life" was not offended and gave Axelrod the 400 rubles which they agreed would be used to publish popular literature.[1]

No sooner had Sponti gone than another young Russian appeared at Axelrod's house. The new visitor was the twenty-five-year-old Vladimir Ulianov, who had just spent a few days with Plekhanov in Geneva. Ulianov immediately gave Axelrod a bulky collection of articles entitled *Materials on the Question of the Economic Development of Russia,* which had recently been published in Russia and was being confiscated by the authorities. Ulianov did not detain his host, but promised to return the next day, if Axelrod agreed, in order to talk with him.

Axelrod spent the day and evening reading the volume. He was particularly impressed by K. Tulin's long article, which subjected some of Peter Struve's ideas to critical analysis, though Axelrod did harbor reservations.[2] When Ulianov arrived the next morning he promptly asked his host whether he had read the essays. Axelrod told him that he had been especially taken by Tulin's article. "That is my pseudonym," answered the guest, who is now known as Lenin.

1. *Perepiska G. V. Plekhanova i P. B. Aksel'roda,* ed. B. I. Nicolaevsky, P. A. Berlin, and W. S. Woytinsky (Moscow, 1925), I, 265–269.
2. For an analysis of this article, see Richard Pipes, *Struve. Liberal on the Left, 1870–1905* (Cambridge, Mass., 1970), pp. 137–139.

Axelrod proceeded to explain the nature of his disagreement with the article, arguing that Lenin made the mistake of identifying "our attitude toward the liberals with the socialists' attitude toward the liberals in the West." In his own uncompleted article for the volume, Axelrod had contended that "at the present historical moment the immediate interests of the proletariat in Russia coincide with the basic interests of the other progressive elements in society," for both of whom the overthrow of absolutism was the most urgent task. Smiling, Lenin answered: "You know, Plekhanov made exactly the same comment on my article. He expressed his view graphically: 'You . . . turn your back to the liberals, but we—our face.' "

This difference notwithstanding, Lenin made a good impression on Axelrod. He gave no evidence of conceit, not even mentioning that he had already acquired a considerable amount of influence in revolutionary circles in St. Petersburg. "He conducted himself in a businesslike, serious, and at the same time modest manner." They arranged to go to the country together for a few days so that they would have ample opportunity to discuss politics free from interruption. It was May, and the weather was beautiful—ideal for the long walks during which they exchanged views. "And I must say," Axelrod wrote, "that these conversations with Ulianov were for me a genuinely festive occasion. Even now I think of them as one of the most joyful, [and] brightest moments in the life of the Group for the Emancipation of Labor."

Lenin made every effort to appear sensible and reasonable. He listened carefully to whatever Axelrod said and did not hesitate to change his mind on important issues. For instance, he acknowledged that he had to accept the "correctness of the point of view of the group" on the attitude Russian Social Democrats should assume toward liberals. He also did not object to Axelrod's conception of the relationship between the GEL and emerging Marxist circles in Russia. Axelrod predicted that with the growth of the Russian Marxist movement there were bound to develop "centrifugal forces, disagreement, conflict of tendencies." It seemed to him important, therefore, to preserve the group "as an independent cell, which would stand guard over the revolutionary traditions and theoretical stability of the movement." He elaborated this point by comparing the GEL to a "small detachment of an army that finds itself on a high mountain, in a safe place, at a time when the battle is continuing in the valley." The detachment follows the fighting and from its advantageous position can easily observe the entire field of battle and assess the general situation, even though it may overlook some details. "These details can be mastered only by our comrades who are directly engaged in the battle. In the interest of the cause it is necessary that there be a very close link and reciprocal control between the army and its detachment abandoned on the top of the mountain." Such a relationship, Axelrod continued, should prevail only during periods when the movement was in decline. Revolutionaries forced to emigrate would then take "refuge" in the GEL and would find it possible to carry on the struggle. During periods of heightened revolutionary activity, however, the guiding center of the movement should be in Russia. Lenin, Axelrod remembered, "agreed with me" on this matter. It therefore came as a complete surprise when, eight years later, he discovered that Lenin had suggested a rather different "relationship between the foreign center and the Russian party." At that later date Lenin insisted on the unquestioned primacy of the "foreign center."

The two men parted company on the best of terms. Axelrod was gratified, for "with the appearance of Ulianov on our horizon we finally established more or less regular relations with Russia."[3] Lenin, for his part, was pleased with his introduction to the group and, according to his sister, "spoke of Axelrod with great warmth" on his return to St. Petersburg.[4] The two began to correspond and managed to stay in touch even after Lenin's arrest late in 1895 and his subsequent exile.[5]

Shortly after the departure of Sponti and Lenin the GEL began to publish works geared to the immediate interests of Russian workers. The popular literature was to appear under the imprimatur of the Union of Russian Social Democrats Abroad, a new organization composed of younger Marxists and the GEL, but the editorial work was to be controlled by the GEL. Specifically, the union supplied funds and supervised the transportation of the works, while the group determined their content. Sometime in 1895 Plekhanov and Axelrod agreed to bring out a periodical, *Rabotnik,* with Axelrod as chief editor. Within the movement it was generally understood that Plekhanov would devote himself to more theoretical matters.

3. *Perepiska,* ed. Nicolaevsky, Berlin, and Woytinsky, I, 269–275.
4. A. I. Elizarova, "Kak ne sleduet pisat' istorii" (How One Should not Write History), *Izvestiia,* no. 72, Mar. 29, 1925.
5. Lenin to Axelrod, beginning of Nov. 1895, V. I. Lenin, *Sochineniia* (3rd ed., Leningrad, 1926–1937), XVIII, 7–8; Lenin to Axelrod, Aug. 16, 1897, *ibid.,* XXVIII, 17.

From 1896 until 1899 Axelrod supervised the publication of three volumes of articles and ten leaflets, which, according to a Soviet historian writing in 1964, "played an important role in the propagation of Marxism, in educating the working class to adopt an irreconcilable attitude toward the exploiting class and a spirit of brotherly solidarity toward the workers of foreign countries." Although he criticizes the editors for having slighted the revolutionary potential of the peasants, this historian cites *Rabotnik* as "an important phenomenon in the history of the Marxist press."[6]

Axelrod intended to use the pages of *Rabotnik* for a purpose he had long advocated: to familiarize Russian workers with the tactics and techniques of Western labor movements. In his own writings for the journal Axelrod drew extensively on the experience of those movements to drive home some simple lessons. In one article, for instance, he described in detail how the railway workers in Switzerland in the spring of 1896 had succeeded in exacting improvements in their conditions. The point he tried to convey was that before they even thought of going out on strike they waged a long and intensive campaign to impress their grievances on the population at large. As a result, the strike was unnecessary. The employers, sensing the strength and determination of the workers as well as the widespread popular sympathy for them, yielded to most of the union's demands.[7]

All told, *Rabotnik* carried over thirty articles, most of which dealt with practical questions. Even those that treated theoretical problems were devoted more to tactics than to philosophical issues. The journal was a demonstrable achievement for which Axelrod deserves most of the credit, especially since in 1896 he formally became its sole editor. Whatever satisfaction he derived from the work, however, was more than outweighed by the anguish it caused him. During his three-year editorship the "youngsters"[8] in the union constantly kept a sharp eye on the GEL's

6. N. A. Fenster, "V. I. Lenin i marksistskii sbornik 'Rabotnik,'" *Istoriia SSSR*, no. 2 (1964), 112.

7. Pavel Axelrod, "Bor'ba zheleznodorozhnykh rabochikh v Shveitsarii s ikh ekspluatatorami," *Rabotnik*, no. 3/4 (1897), 17–46.

8. The leading "youngsters" were Boris Krichevsky, Pavel Sibiriak-Teplov, Timofei Grishin-Kopel'zon, I. M. Somov-Peskin, Ekaterina Kuskova, Sergei Prokopovich, Vladimir Ivanshin, and, after 1900, Vladimir Akimov-Makhnovets. The youngsters had all been active in the illegal movement in Russia, and when they arrived in the West (most of them after 1895) they were eager to engage in political work that would be of immediate, direct, and practical help to their comrades in Russia. They tended to be impatient with the GEL's preoccupation with theoretical questions.

activities. It was a situation rife with tension; hardly a month passed without a quarrel.

The initial source of conflict was, once again, money. Early in 1896, I. Gukovskii, treasurer of the union, sent Axelrod a statement of financial support the organization had rendered the GEL since 1894 and asked for a detailed account of the group's expenses during the previous two years. Axelrod was beside himself with anger. He could not possibly provide such a reckoning, as the GEL had continued to lump together the contributions it received and had not kept a detailed record of its expenses. He suspected the union of wanting to embarrass the veterans, of being up to some "swinish trick."[9] The request also deeply offended Plekhanov, who thought he was being accused of profiteering from his work for the revolutionary cause. In short, both men felt that their integrity was being questioned.

Somehow this particular issue seems to have been resolved, but there was no abatement in hard feelings between the union and the GEL. The GEL's sloppy handling of finances continued to be a source of irritation to the youngsters. As long as there were only a few active Marxists in the West, there had been no need to maintain careful accounts. But now there were several dozen living in different cities, and it was only natural that they should want to know how their money was being spent. The problem was compounded by the fact that when the union was founded the statutes were imprecisely written. Although the union was to handle the financial aspect of the publications, apparently nothing was said about contributions the GEL continued to receive on its own. The GEL assumed that it could keep that money to finance publications other than those sponsored by the union, but the youngsters thought of their treasury as the repository for *all* funds used for the publication of works by anyone belonging to the union. As far as is known, the two groups never formally reached an agreement on this point.

The controversy over money could probably have been resolved had other issues not emerged. The youngsters on occasion made so much fuss over relatively small sums that there is reason to suspect them of using this issue to force the GEL to make concessions on other matters. They had a whole series of complaints. Perhaps most of all they objected

9. Axelrod to Plekhanov, n. d., *Perepiska,* ed. Nicolaevsky, Berlin, and Woytinsky, I, 122–123.

to the provision in the union's statutes that required unanimous approval of every candidate applying for membership. This gave the GEL veto power, which it often used arbitrarily to exclude people it distrusted. The youngsters were also distressed because the GEL was too slow in publishing popular literature—after the decision had been reached to put out *Rabotnik* it took six months for the first issue to appear—and because the veterans frequently rejected their literary contributions. Finally, the union felt entitled to having one of its members on the editorial committee.[10]

The legitimacy of these complaints was not acknowledged by Axelrod and Plekhanov. Axelrod denounced privately the youngsters' "formalism [and] doctrinairism" in financial affairs. It was possible, he conceded, that their behavior was simply the result of "coarseness and naïveté. But, nevertheless, I personally cannot but rebuff them." He claimed that because of the frequent controversies "complete anarchy" had prevailed during the preparation of the first issue of *Rabotnik*. Under the circumstances, he thought it best to sever his connection with the journal. The "restoration of formal autocracy" in all editorial affairs could induce him to remain in his post, but only because he felt duty-bound not to abandon the work.[11]

There is no reason to assume that Axelrod was disingenuous in offering to resign. He, too, had legitimate grounds for complaint. The manuscripts submitted by the youngsters were often so poorly written and organized that they needed extensive rewriting, which he did not enjoy. Sometimes articles had to be completely reworked. Several people who during the early 1920's examined *Rabotnik*'s archive testified that on occasion no more than the author's name and title remained of the original manuscript after it had been published.[12] Needless to say, the young members of the union did not take kindly to these editorial practices.

The quarrels with the union so demoralized Axelrod that he considered going to London for six months. "The moral and intellectual at-

---

10. *Vladimir Akimov on the Dilemma of Russian Marxism, 1895–1903*, ed. Jonathan Frankel (Cambridge, Eng., 1969), pp. 348–349. For a brief history of the various controversies from the union's standpoint, see *Otvet redaktsii "Rabochago dela" na "pis'mo" Aksel'roda i "Vademecum" G. Plekhanova* (Geneva, 1900), pp. 70–80.

11. Axelrod to Plekhanov, beginning of Apr. 1896, *Perepiska*, ed. Nicolaevsky, Berlin, and Woytinsky, I, 131–134.

12. Axelrod to Plekhanov, beginning of Apr. 1896, *ibid.*, pp. 133–135; see also Axelrod to Plekhanov, end of Feb. 1896, *ibid.*, pp. 115–117.

mosphere," he complained, "is killing me." He even seriously thought of temporarily dropping all conspiratorial and literary work and breaking off relations with the union.[13] But he remained in his post. Apparently, Plekhanov and Zasulich intervened, for late in the summer of 1896 Axelrod was named sole editor of *Rabotnik*.

The promotion may have strengthened Axelrod's hand, but it did nothing to improve his relations with the youngsters. On the contrary, a new issue arose, one that added an ideological dimension to the conflict. Sometime in mid-1896 the union obtained a copy of a manuscript entitled *Ob agitatsii* (On Agitation), which had already been distributed in hectographed form in Russia and which the younger people were eager to publish in the West. Because they disagreed with the contents of the work, the members of the GEL demurred. It took a year and a half of pressure from the union to get the veterans to publish the manuscript, and when they finally did they made sure to add an epilogue by Axelrod criticizing the ideas in it.

The publication of *Ob agitatsii* in the middle of 1897 marked the beginning of an incredibly complicated and bitter controversy. Scholars in the West still do not agree in their interpretations of the dispute. That is not particularly unusual, but it is astonishing that Western writers still differ over whether Economism, the phenomenon that many Marxists in the late 1890's and early twentieth century accused of dividing and destroying the movement, ever really existed. Thus, one historian has written that Economism seems to have been "any idea that challenged the tenets of the 'old guard.' For the term was their invention; and like most such labels it did as much to obscure the real questions at issue as to clarify them."[14] Another has contended that the Economist controversy should not be viewed as basically a dispute over ideology. Rather, "at the root of the conflict . . . was the question of whether 'junior' and 'untrustworthy' members of the party were to have the right to express their views or whether criticism was to result in immediate expulsion."[15] These interpretations, supported by an impressive array of factual data and closely reasoned arguments, challenge the

13. Axelrod to Zasulich, end of Aug. 1896, *ibid.*, pp. 153–155; Axelrod to Plekhanov, beginning of Sept. 1896, *ibid.*, p. 159.

14. J. L. H. Keep, *The Rise of Social Democracy in Russia* (Oxford, 1963), p. 58.

15. Jonathan Frankel, "Economism: A Heresy Exploited," *Slavic Review*, XXII (June 1963), 284. For another such interpretation of Economism, see Leonard Schapiro, *The Communist Party of the Soviet Union* (London, 1960), pp. 33–35.

traditional view of Economism as a theory that did in fact have a clearly definable content, an "emphasis on economic struggle, rather than political struggle against the Tsar."[16]

The most telling point made by the "revisionist historians" is that at the time the sharpest attacks were leveled against Economism—by Plekhanov and Lenin—it no longer could claim many adherents. There can be no question, moreover, that Plekhanov and Lenin used the campaign against the Economist "heresy" in order to discredit anyone who did not fully agree with them even on issues unrelated to Economism. If we examine the entire controversy, however, it appears that at one time at least there was a definite ideological issue in dispute. It would perhaps be helpful to speak of two phases in the Economist conflict, one from 1897 to 1899, the other from late 1899 to 1903. During the first period Axelrod was the main defender of orthodoxy, and there is no evidence to suggest that he had anything in mind other than combating what he considered a harmful ideological tendency. The waters have been muddied by his involvement in organizational and personal conflict with his adversaries at the same time. The two sets of differences inevitably became interlaced and impinged on each other, but the substance of each is sufficiently clear to deserve separate discussion.

Economism emerged as an ideological tendency because of widespread dissatisfaction with propaganda as a technique for activating the laboring class. At best, propagandists succeeded in enlightening small circles of workers in Marxist theory, but they proved incapable of training cadres that could spread the socialist gospel among the masses. As early as 1889 some socialists in the Polish part of the Empire began to urge a new approach, agitation, according to which the working class was to be encouraged to act on the basis of immediate economic interests.

The agitational method was successfully applied. Russian Poland experienced a period of labor unrest culminating in a series of major strikes in 1892. Within a few years interest in the new technique spread to Russia proper. Late in 1895 several circles in St. Petersburg, in some of which Lenin and Iulii Martov had been active, formed the Union of Struggle for the Emancipation of the Working Class, an organization

16. Bertram D. Wolfe, *Three Who Made a Revolution. A Biographical History* (New York, 1948), p. 144; see also Donald W. Treadgold, *Lenin and His Rivals. The Struggle for Russia's Future, 1898–1906* (New York, 1955), p. 85.

committed to agitation. In May 1896 a major strike took place in textile factories in the capital. Although the work stoppage began spontaneously, and did not achieve its aims, it was a momentous event. To Social Democrats it seemed further evidence that Russian labor had come of age, that it was following a path similar to that of its Western counterpart. More important, the strike proved to be a powerful stimulus to workers in the rest of the country, particularly when the government, yielding to pressure from below, early in 1897 introduced a law limiting the working day to eleven and a half hours. Labor unrest spread during the remainder of the 1890's, though it should be noted that only a small percentage of the total work force participated. Nor was there a steady increase in the number of strikes; a recession in 1897 and 1898 led to a temporary decline. Still, there can be no question that for the first time labor unrest became a matter of serious concern to the autocracy.[17]

The events in Russia gratified the members of the GEL, but they soon became uneasy about a central feature of labor's nascent activism. Although the avowed purpose of "agitation" was to prepare the factory workers for political action, once they entered into a struggle for economic gains they tended to concentrate on concrete, immediate matters at the expense of politics. In other words, they behaved more like trade unionists than Social Democrats. This mistrust of agitation accounts for the veterans' reluctance to publish *Ob agitatsii*, which had been written in 1894 by Arkady Kremer, one of the leading exponents of the new technique in Russian Poland. Kremer's manuscript, edited by Martov, was designed to persuade the hesitant workers of Vilno to adopt agitation. Within short order, *Ob agitatsii* became something of a handbook for Social Democratic action in Russia.

In the pamphlet Kremer and Martov explicitly challenged the principles on propaganda and agitation that had been set forth by the founders of Russian Marxism. Their experience in trying to mobilize Russian workers had led them to conclude "that the first steps of Russian Social Democrats were wrong and that in the interests of the cause

17. On the background to Economism, see Richard Pipes, *Social Democracy and the St. Petersburg Labor Movement, 1885–1897* (Cambridge, Mass., 1963), pp. 57–116. On the strike movement from 1895 to 1900, see *Khronika revoliutsionnogo rabochego dvizheniia v Peterburge*, ed. E. Korolchuk and E. Sokolova (Leningrad, 1940), I, 178–279.

their tactics must be changed."[18] The Russian theorists were led astray, Kremer and Martov held, because they had maintained so little contact with the masses that they did not understand their needs and aspirations. There was, therefore, danger of a split between the theorists and the "practicals," those working among the laborers and trying to organize them. They hoped that their pamphlet would contribute to restoring unity between practice and theory, between agitation and propaganda.

The central point of *Ob agitatsii* was that the Russian worker would come to appreciate the importance of political struggle only at that point "when the economic struggle demonstrates to him clearly that it is impossible for him to improve his lot under existing political conditions."[19] In support of their thesis, Kremer and Martov contended that the labor movements in other countries, particularly Great Britain, had gone through a phase of economic agitation before developing into influential political organizations.

The tactics they proposed for Russia involved a progression through several stages. Russian Social Democrats should first agitate among factory workers "on the basis of existing small needs and demands" for economic improvement. Some successes were likely to be scored, and this would increase the workers' courage and self-confidence. Then Social Democratic agitators should apply pressure for ever more important economic concessions, which, the workers would soon realize, could only be extracted if they united into a large organization. At that point the employers would resist and the government would come to their aid, bringing home to the proletariat two basic facts: that the entire bourgeoisie is ranged against the working class, and that the state apparatus serves the interests of the bourgeoisie. Now the masses would have no choice but to organize politically. The intelligentsia should contribute to this process by producing agitational literature "adapted to the conditions of life of a given field of production or a given industrial center, literature that would speak to the worker about his needs and would serve as an appropriate supplement to oral agitation." Although theorists should try to broaden the workers' horizons, Kremer and Martov warned against trying to "tear them away from concrete

18. [A. Kremer and Iu. Martov,] *Ob agitatsii* (Geneva, 1896), p. 3. Although the date of publication is 1896, the pamphlet actually appeared late in 1897.
19. *Ibid.*, p. 7.

ground into a region of completely abstract scientific propositions."[20]

The epilogue in which Axelrod repudiated the views of Kremer and Martov is almost as long as *Ob agitatsii* itself. Obviously stung by the authors' criticisms, Axelrod responded by pointing out that their charges resembled those leveled by Bakuninists against other revolutionaries in the 1870's. At that time the Bakuninists (especially Stefanovich) also accused radicals of ignoring local conditions and the immediate interests of the peasants. But subsequent developments demonstrated the "primitiveness" of Stefanovich's approach, which had inspired a few strikes and demonstrations in the Chigirin region but had provided no lasting benefits for the people. The chief defect of the tactics—as of those advocated in *Ob agitatsii*—was that they were "too narrow and one-sided."

Like their Bakuninist predecessors, Kremer and Martov made the mistake of basing their tactics on the notion that in Russia there existed antagonisms between two social classes only. The Bakuninists had conceived of the conflict as between peasants and landlords, Kremer and Martov as between the proletariat and the capitalists (identified with the bourgeoisie as a whole). But Axelrod held that this was an erroneous view of the situation in Russia, and consequently the aim of Social Democrats ought not to be *restricted* to increasing the number of their adherents among the working class and organizing them into a political instrument. Russian Marxists must also try to exploit the antagonisms between other classes in order to strengthen the opposition to the autocratic regime. "From this point of view, one of the most important tasks of Russian Social Democracy is to acquire for the proletariat allies and sympathy among those strata of the population and their ideological representatives that suffer from the social-political system in contemporary Russia" and are interested in its transformation. Neglect of this task could lead "if not to the exhaustion of the forces of the [Social Democratic] movement, then to an extreme retardation of its growth and development." By ignoring broader political issues the labor movement would isolate itself, and this would reduce the proletariat to a negligible force within the country.[21]

Axelrod emphasized that neither he nor his colleagues opposed agitating on the basis of concrete demands. On the contrary, Plekhanov had

20. *Ibid.,* p. 23.
21. *Ibid.,* p. 43.

always acknowledged the centrality of agitation in Social Democratic tactics and had maintained that there was a "reciprocal relationship" between agitation and propaganda. Axelrod himself had made the same point to Lenin a year and a half earlier. He objected to *Ob agitatsii* because its authors contended that economic agitation would automatically lead to political action by the workers. In his view such an outcome could be assured only if activists stressed politics at each stage of the agitational process.[22]

Axelrod's critique of *Ob agitatsii* was quite mild and completely free of polemical attacks. It would be a mistake, however, to deduce from this that he and his colleagues were not distressed by the Economist tendency. By temperament Axelrod was inclined to operate on a low key. Only rarely, when he was severely provoked, would he resort to the kind of *ad hominem* assaults for which Russian Marxists have become renowned. He gave a considerable amount of thought to his reply to *Ob agitatsii* and before publication showed it to Plekhanov, who expressed full agreement with its content. In fact, Plekhanov heaped praise on his friend for the piece: it "once again revealed you to me in that form in which I have always thought of you: as a man who is extremely sensible and has a subtle understanding of the implications of political events that are taking place before his eyes . . . [who] possibly surpasses all of us in the depth of his understanding."[23] Thus, Axelrod was fully justified in claiming in the epilogue that he was speaking not only for himself but for comrades as well.

Aside from the differences over the publication of *Ob agitatsii*, there is other evidence to suggest that by 1896 the conflict between Axelrod and the youngsters had taken on an ideological dimension. As editor of *Rabotnik*, he was also supposed to supervise the publication of leaflets, the purpose of which was frankly agitational. He had no taste for the work, preferring to devote himself to more theoretical writings. He confided to Plekhanov that the union could publish "such literary caricatures as the 'leaflets' " without his help.[24] The youngsters, who constantly prodded him to work on the leaflets, must have realized that his procrastination was not merely a consequence of his slow and deliberate working habits but also of his unwillingness to lend support to

22. *Perepiska,* ed. Nicolaevsky, Berlin, and Woytinsky, I, 272–273.
23. Plekhanov to Axelrod, July 20, 1896, *ibid.,* pp. 137–138.
24. Axelrod to Plekhanov, probably early in 1897, *ibid.,* p. 167.

activities he deemed potentially harmful.[25] Then, in the fall of 1897 Axelrod's apprehensions about the spread of Economism intensified. In St. Petersburg a small group of workers began to publish *Rabochaia mysl'*, the first issue of which was openly hostile to the revolutionary intelligentsia and urged workers to concern themselves primarily with bread-and-butter issues.

For the next few years almost everything Axelrod wrote was composed with an eye to the Economists. His two major works of 1897 and 1898 —*The Historical Situation and the Reciprocal Relations between Liberals and Social Democrats in Russia* and *On the Question of the Contemporary Tasks and Tactics of Russian Social Democrats*—were, in fact, inspired by the conviction that a detailed and concrete alternative to the views of the "opposition" must be presented. He published the first in *Die Neue Zeit* in large measure because he felt that "whatever appears in the *German* language makes a greater impression." When Kautsky delayed its appearance Axelrod became impatient. He told his friend that the essay "deals with current questions that are extremely important and vital for Russian Social Democracy and that are at the moment in the foreground [of our concerns]." He begged Kautsky to print it immediately.[26] He hoped that "these letters [which constitute the contents of the pamphlet] will clear away the misunderstandings that the epilogue [to *Ob agitatsii*] has provoked in certain Social Democratic circles."[27] There can be no question that in 1897 and 1898 Axelrod took Economism very seriously.

The two works were Axelrod's first significant contributions to Russian Marxism. For five years, from 1898 to 1903, the tactical views outlined in them were generally accepted as the hallmark of orthodoxy. Some supporters of the GEL harbored reservations about his proposals,

25. V. A. Bukhgolts to Axelrod, Nov. 14, 1896, Axelrod Archive, I.I.S.H. From Bukhgolts' letter it is evident that Axelrod did not hide his distaste for the work on leaflets even from people not very close to him.

26. Axelrod to Kautsky, Jan. 31, [1898,] Kautsky Archive, I.I.S.H.; Axelrod to Karl and Luise Kautsky, Mar. 6, 1898, *ibid.*

27. Pavel Axelrod, *K voprosu o sovremennykh zadachakh i taktike russkikh sotsial-demokratov* (Geneva, 1898), p. 1. This pamphlet actually consists of two letters that Axelrod had written late in 1897, one to be published in New York and the other in *Rabochaia gazeta*. The New York volume in which the letter was to appear was for some unexplained reason never published, and when Axelrod's second letter reached the editors of *Rabochaia gazeta*, the issue for which it was intended was already in press. Axelrod therefore published both missives in *Rabotnik*, no. 5/6 (1899), 3–34, and also as a separate pamphlet.

as we shall see, but they were not serious enough to lead to a rift. In fact, the lead article of the first issue of *Iskra*, founded by the orthodox in 1900, quoted Axelrod to the effect that the central task of Social Democrats must be "to extend the framework and broaden the content of our propagandistic-agitational and organizational activities."[28]

To a considerable degree Axelrod's tactics of 1897 and 1898 represented a retreat from those advocated in his earlier Marxist writings, in which he had stressed the applicability of Western methods to Russian conditions. He was probably led to reconsider his previous stand because the Economists justified their position by claiming that the technique they proposed had been effective in the West. Whatever the reason, Axelrod warned against simple imitation of sister parties.[29] This is not to say that he ceased to admire the European labor movement or that he considered its experience irrelevant for Russian Marxists. But he now felt that the traditional methods should be adapted and modified to fit conditions in his country. All in all, Axelrod's political conception had gained in refinement and subtlety.

It should be noted that he did not repudiate Plekhanov's general position of the 1880's. Rather, in 1898 he extended and elaborated his colleague's earlier line of reasoning, repeating several of the basic arguments used by Plekhanov in the draft program of the GEL.

Axelrod's key point was that class alignments in the West differed markedly from those in Russia. He traced this divergence to the fact that in revolutionary France and early nineteenth-century Germany the opposition to the old regime had emerged "on the basis of a *common struggle* of the popular masses, intelligentsia, and commercial-industrial classes, against the privileged classes."[30] Later, capitalism had fully developed, and the bourgeoisie had become entrenched in positions of political power. It was only after the triumph of the bourgeoisie over the monarchy that Social Democratic movements had appeared in these countries. The German and French proletariat could therefore legitimately regard the middle class as "one reactionary mass" and engage in a merciless fight against it.

28. Axelrod, *K voprosu o sovremennykh zadachakh*, p. 28.
29. *Ibid.*, p. 26.
30. Pavel Axelrod, *Istoricheskoe polozhenie i vzaimnoe otnoshenie liberal'noi i sotsialisticheskoi demokratii v Rossii* (Geneva, 1898), p. 8. This pamphlet first appeared in German as "Die historische Berechtigung der russischen Sozialdemokratie," *Die Neue Zeit*, XVI, pt. 2 (1898), 100–111, 140–149. It also appeared in *Rabotnik*, no. 5/6 (1899), 38–71.

Axelrod admitted privately that in his eagerness to make a point he had presented a somewhat misleading analysis of conditions in Germany and in the West generally. He told Kautsky that he had not intended to suggest that the older Marxist parties "had a special interest only in the decline of bourgeois society and none in its *development*, in its further extension." What he had meant to indicate was that because the West was far along in the process of industrialization the socialist movements could draw fairly clear-cut distinctions between their interests and those of the middle class.[31] In Russia, however, Social Democracy faced a far more complicated and precarious situation. It had emerged before the country had passed through the initial phase of capitalism, that of "primary accumulation," and before the "barbaric" tsarist regime had been overthrown. Consequently, the Russian proletariat, unlike its Western counterpart, was forced "to begin its historical career in the clutches of bureaucratic absolutism and under the great pressure of the *forceful* expropriation and differentiation of the peasantry, perpetrated by the joint forces of the state and commercial-usurious capital,"[32] which is to say that the Russian laborer faced two enemies at the same time: the autocratic state and the bourgeoisie. Axelrod's central thesis was that under prevailing conditions Social Democracy, though conscious of its antagonism to both, had to assign priority to one or the other.

If it chose to proceed against the bourgeoisie by concentrating on economic conflicts between workers and entrepreneurs, the movement would surely neglect political action. The fight for political freedom would then devolve upon bourgeois elements, and the proletariat would not play an "independent revolutionary role," though it might well follow the middle class in its assault on the autocracy (as had the French and German workers several decades earlier).

A second alternative open to Social Democrats was to attempt to organize the masses into "an independent political party fighting for freedom, *in part side by side and in alliance with* the bourgeois revolutionary factions (insofar as such exist) and in part by drawing directly into its ranks or carrying with it those elements from the intelligentsia that are the most revolutionary and the most democratic [literally: people-loving]." Axelrod conceded that this course required a high "level of political consciousness and initiative [*samodeiatel'nost'*]"[33] on the part

31. Axelrod to Kautsky, Jan. 31, 1898, Kautsky Archive, I.I.S.H.
32. Axelrod, *K voprosu o sovremennykh zadachakh*, p. 6.
33. The word *samodeiatel'nost'* appears regularly in Axelrod's writings and speeches

of the workers; it would not be easy for the proletariat to develop these qualities. But if the masses could not play an independent and leading role in the struggle against the autocracy, then Russian Social Democracy had "no historical right to exist. In that case, it is deprived of all viability and its existence would be an obstacle to the growth of the revolutionary movement, rather than an aid to it."[34]

In this rather dogmatic formulation of the alternatives facing Russian Social Democracy, Axelrod expressed two important tactical ideas: he called for greater emphasis on political rather than economic concerns, and he announced that the proletariat might play a "leading role" in the campaign against the Tsar. This latter notion, which had already been suggested some years earlier by Plekhanov, soon came to be known as the "doctrine of the hegemony of the proletariat" and was considered a cornerstone of Social Democratic tactics. But its meaning was not always clear. In 1900, for example, one writer defined the doctrine as recognition by the middle class of the labor movement's "preeminent political significance in contemporary Russia," a formulation that hardly clarified the issue.[35] Plekhanov used the term "hegemony" for the first time in the spring of 1901. To him it meant that "our party will become the liberator *par excellence,* a center toward which all democratic sympathies will gravitate and where all the greatest revolutionary protests will originate."[36] It was Lenin who gave the doctrine its sharpest and narrowest definition. He argued that Social Democrats must become the undisputed masters of all the forces interested in overthrowing the autocracy and advocated that Marxists "utilize" for their own purposes the bourgeois opposition to the existing order.[37]

Lenin's views constituted a significant modification of Axelrod's idea, though it must be said that in 1898 Axelrod was not as precise or specific as he might have been. His statements on the subject and the gen-

and sums up, better than any other term, the ultimate goal of his political activities. Literally translated, *samodeiatel'nost'* means "self-activity." In the revolutionary lexicon it came to signify the ability of the masses to act independently, or to assume the initiative without outside direction, in the political arena.

34. Axelrod, *K voprosu o sovremennykh zadachakh,* pp. 19–20.

35. "Burnyi mesiats" (A Stormy Month), *Iskra,* no. 3, Apr. 1901; see also A. Potresov, "Evoliutsiia obshchestvenno-politicheskoi mysli v predrevoliutsionnuiu epokhu," in *Obshchestvennoe dvizhenie v Rossii v nachale XX-go veka,* ed. Iu. Martov, S. Maslov, and A. Potresov (St. Petersburg, 1909–1914), I, 613–615.

36. G. V. Plekhanov, *Sochineniia,* ed. D. Riazanov (2nd ed., Moscow, 1923–1927), XII, 101–102.

37. See Chaps. VI and VII for details.

eral thrust of his political conception reveal, nonetheless, much about the meaning he assigned to the "doctrine of the hegemony of the proletariat." In point of fact, Axelrod used the word "hegemony" only once, and then in a private letter.[38] He tended to speak of the party's "leading role," which implies a less rigid attitude. He definitely did not recommend that the proletariat direct or command other social classes opposed to the autocratic regime. On the contrary, he always insisted that the classes must maintain independent political parties no matter how close the collaboration between them. Nor did he suggest that the Russian proletariat strive for a seizure of power during the bourgeois revolution or in the period immediately following it. "Our war under the banner of democracy," he declared, "leads directly not to domination by the proletariat, but to such a system in which it will only be possible to begin the struggle for its domination."[39]

Axelrod assigned the proletariat a limited, but twofold part in the first revolution. First, its "historical mission" was consciously "to serve as a lever pushing all the enemies of absolutism into an organized attack against it." Social Democrats should attempt to transform every minor skirmish between bourgeois elements and the autocracy into a "general revolutionary campaign against tsarist autocracy." Axelrod did not publicly elaborate this tactic until 1904, but in 1898 he indicated that it was not to be carried out by intervening in the affairs of other parties.

The second aspect of the proletariat's role during the period of the first revolution appeared more important to Axelrod in 1898. He reasoned that if Social Democracy devoted itself to the "all-national" goal of a constitutional regime, other classes—the peasants as well as progressive liberals—would come to see that the proletariat constituted the strongest and most determined force opposing the autocracy. This in itself would accord the labor movement a position of prestige and influence. "The task of acquiring adherents for Social Democracy, and direct and indirect allies for it among nonproletarian classes will be resolved first of all and for the most part by the character of the agitational and

38. Axelrod to Struve, n. d., but late in 1900. Even in this letter Axelrod emphasized that in a coalition between liberals and Social Democrats each group was to maintain an independent organization and distinct program. *Perepiska*, ed. Nicolaevsky, Berlin, and Woytinsky, II, 141–142.

39. Axelrod, *Istoricheskoe polozhenie*, p. 26.

propagandistic activities among the proletariat itself."[40] This formulation testifies to the impact that his studies of the German party had made on Axelrod's thinking. In 1890 he had concluded, correctly, that a principal reason for the German party's growing influence had been its concentration on agitation for democracy. Now he believed that the Russian movement could travel a similar route in fashioning a powerful political organization.

In the final analysis, the basis of Axelrod's doctrine of proletarian hegemony was as much psychological and moral as political. For he contended that Social Democracy's example of commitment to democracy would affect other social classes disposed against the old order by strengthening their determination and goading them into ever more militant action.

Yet, he understood that his tactical conception was vulnerable in one important respect. It could be argued that in urging the labor movement to fight for a constitutional system he was really asking it to engage in forms of political activity that presupposed the existence of a constitutional state. For without civil liberties no labor organization could even be created, let alone function effectively.[41] Axelrod saw two ways of getting around the paradox. In the first place, once the proletariat had made clear that its intention was political change, groups within the middle classes who already enjoyed certain freedoms would use their influence to have at least some of those freedoms extended to the working class.[42] In the second place, Axelrod maintained—and he considered this more significant—that, because the bourgeoisie in Russia was not a unified class, there were opportunities for Social Democrats to exert influence in the political arena. They could take advantage of the tensions in the middle classes, which had resulted from certain policies followed by the government. By means of high tariffs on manufactured goods and repression of the working class, the autocracy had succeeded in taming the industrialists politically. Axelrod was sure that the latter's political passivity would be only temporary, but for the time being the industrialists could not be counted upon to help in the struggle against the autocracy.

By contrast, the intelligentsia, whom Axelrod identified with the lib-

40. Axelrod, *K voprosu o sovremennykh zadachakh,* pp. 16–17.
41. Axelrod, *Istoricheskoe polozhenie,* p. 2.
42. Axelrod, *K voprosu o sovremennykh zadachakh,* pp. 17–18.

eral professions, already constituted a potent oppositional force. In his view, lawyers, doctors, scholars, writers, teachers, educated technicians, and students suffered from so many disabilities that they were naturally attracted to movements hostile to the government. Not only did the absence of personal and civil rights hamper the intelligentsia in its work, but the economic backwardness of the country had led to a surplus of certain professionals. For example, there were doctors who found it impossible to earn a living, not because there was no need for their services but rather because many people could not afford them. In addition, many professionals were idealistically motivated to promote the cause of social and political justice.

Yet, no matter how vigorously the intelligentsia supported progressive causes, the government could not crush it as a group. On the contrary, the authorities had to allow it a "relatively wide" latitude in the "social sphere" because the intelligentsia had become an "indispensable factor" in a modern state: "It fills all the pores in the upper reaches of society, it forces itself into [every institution] and—oh, irony of history!—the organs of the state and bureaucracy themselves cannot dispense with it." During periods of crisis the government's need for the intelligentsia is especially acute, as was shown during the famine of 1891 and the subsequent epidemic. As a result, the oppositional movement could count on support from people in high and influential positions.[43]

Axelrod also expected the educated landowners to support Russian liberalism, for they suffered economically as a result of the favors bestowed on the industrialists. The domestic market for agricultural goods was weak, and because of the backwardness of farming methods Russians found it difficult to compete on the world market. According to Axelrod, many landowners favored more rapid industrialization because it would broaden the internal market for their products and facilitate the mechanization of agriculture, which in turn would place them in a more competitive position. They understood that the autocracy had impeded industrialization by its failure to educate the people, its economic policies, and its insistence on maintaining a bureaucratic structure.[44]

As Axelrod saw it, the lack of harmony within the Russian bourgeoisie was precisely the element that precluded mechanical application of Western Marxist tactics. Because those hostile to the old order were too

43. Axelrod, *Istoricheskoe polozhenie*, p. 6.
44. *Ibid.*, p. 8.

weak to overthrow it, or to take the initiative against it, there devolved upon the proletariat a complicated and delicate role in the first revolution. It had to work temporarily with the progressive strata of the middle classes despite the latter's hostility to the proletariat's ultimate aims. Collaboration was possible because in the "feudal-absolutistic order" the two had a common immediate enemy. Even more delicate was the need for the Social Democrats to assume "leadership" over the democratic camp in the sense of pushing the progressive bourgeoisie into implementing a genuine constitutional system. But such a tactic could be successfully followed only if Russian Marxists avoided concentrating on purely economic demands, which would only alienate the bourgeoisie and isolate the proletariat.[45]

Axelrod pointed to yet another weakness in the tactics advocated by the Economists. In claiming that concentration on economic struggle had been effective in the West they failed to appreciate that in the industrialized countries there existed a relatively sophisticated working class, which had benefited from long contact with bourgeois culture and constitutionalism. "In Russia, however, where the working class is still very young, where it is only in the process of separating itself from the masses who for centuries have vegetated in barbaric ignorance and slavery, the vast majority are still on too low a cultural level to be able to emerge—within the chains of absolutism—as a conscious revolutionary force without the direct and indirect help of the bourgeoisie." To ignore this factor would lead to the advocacy of tactics both "utopian" and "reactionary": utopian because they did not take into account the necessity for the proletariat to absorb bourgeois cultural values and the political training that results only from the exercise of political rights; reactionary because they would preclude "direct intellectual interaction between the educated strata and the popular masses." To him, such interaction would have "enormous progressive significance, for even the most insipid liberalism of any intellectual still towers over the uncultured attitudes of the masses."[46]

The question of the relationship between the proletariat and the bourgeoisie was to absorb Russian Social Democrats for the next two decades. No Marxist could avoid it, for it went to the heart of the problems labor faced in tsarist Russia. In time, alternatives other than those

45. *Ibid.,* p. 24.
46. *Ibid.,* p. 27.

proposed by the Economists and Axelrod (and the GEL) were to be set forth and adopted, thus determining the fate not only of the labor movement but of Russia itself, but in 1898 the choice seemed to be between these two, both of which projected a democratic phase for Russia. It is significant that Axelrod never strayed from the tactical position he developed that year.

He had tried, essentially, to uphold the Marxist stress on the primacy of political action and yet at the same time provide an appealing alternative to the Economists' tactic of economic struggle. Almost fifteen years had passed since Plekhanov had predicted a bourgeois revolution without any appreciable increase in the amount of political ferment among the middle classes. It was natural, therefore, for a growing number of younger Marxists and workers to be swayed by the arguments in favor of economic agitation. A strike against an employer involved immediate action against the class enemy and often led to concrete benefits. To counteract this enticing prospect, Axelrod called attention—with considerable justification, as the next few years would show—to the divisions within the Russian bourgeoisie and the likelihood of active opposition to the autocracy in the near future. And by stressing the proletariat's "leading role" in the bourgeois revolution, he held out the hope of major achievements by the working class, again in the not too distant future.

In his reasoning he had impressively adapted Marxist doctrine to Russian conditions. He remained faithful to Plekhanov's conception of the 1880's and yet took into account certain complexities that only visibly emerged in the 1890's. Nevertheless, Axelrod did not really resolve the problems inherent in his comrades' theoretical framework, but rather slightly shifted the basis of the discussion. He seems, in fact, to have been aware that he had left some loose ends. In March 1898 he told Kautsky that the writings described his tactical views "only in general terms" and that he planned to write a "larger work" on the subject.[47] Unfortunately, the larger work never materialized, and so it is not clear which problems he intended to explicate.

Of these problems, the most serious was one that he never satisfactorily resolved: was it reasonable to expect the Russian workers to subscribe to a program that on the one hand proclaimed the evils of capitalism

47. Axelrod to Karl and Luise Kautsky, Mar. 6, 1898, Kautsky Archive, I.I.S.H.; Axelrod to Kautsky, Mar. 17, 1898, *ibid.*

and the middle classes and yet called for the further development of capitalism and alliances with the middle classes? Axelrod partially answered by stressing that Social Democrats should not neglect their advocacy of socialist ideals even while supporting the bourgeoisie against tsarism and that they should continue to provoke industrial strife.[48] But in the heat of conflict the workers would probably come to look upon the employer—and his whole class—as their bitter enemy. Would it not have required extraordinary self-control for them to collaborate politically with that enemy? It is also surprising that in view of his low opinion of the cultural niveau of Russian workers Axelrod should have thought it possible to persuade them to understand and adopt so complicated and sophisticated a tactic as he proposed. Axelrod's plan seemed feasible theoretically, but in practice, as events would show, he was asking too much.

During the first phase (1897–1899) of the Economist controversy the youngsters as a group failed to engage Axelrod in an open, direct, and frank debate. The main reason for their reticence was probably that they did not have a publication of their own. This makes it extremely difficult to describe their political position in detail, especially since there seem to have been differences of emphasis among them. But there is little doubt that they tended to be sympathetic to the ideas in *Ob agitatsii*. When they acquired their own journal early in 1899 a rational discussion of disagreements between them and the veterans might have been expected. Instead, the youngsters initiated an altogether peculiar debate with the GEL.

The exchange was occasioned by a preface Axelrod composed in the summer of 1898 for a pamphlet by Lenin. Axelrod praised it lavishly for stressing the importance of political agitation and for pointing to an inseparable link between the socialist and democratic aspects of Social Democratic work. He suspected that, unfortunately, not many activists in Russia shared Lenin's outlook. And he was certain that most young comrades in the West were "still quite far from those practical views . . . [expounded] by the author of this brochure . . . In general, so it seems, our movement is still only striving for that degree of development which fully corresponds to the tactical views of the author [Lenin]."[49]

48. Axelrod, *K voprosu o sovremennykh zadachakh,* p. 26.
49. [V. I. Lenin,] *Zadachi russkikh sotsialdemokratov. S predisloviem P. Aksel'roda* (Geneva, 1898), pp. 3–4.

The first issue of *Rabochee delo*, the journal edited by the younger members of the union, carried a review by Boris Krichevsky of Lenin's brochure. Apparently speaking for the youngsters, he declared that "we do not know which young comrades Axelrod was speaking about" when he referred to Social Democrats who did not subscribe to Lenin's ideas. Then he asserted that neither he nor his colleagues believed "for one minute" that it was permissible for "Russian Social Democracy to think of the possibility of only an economic struggle."[50] There is a considerable amount of evidence to suggest that several youngsters had undergone a change on the question of agitation, but it is inconceivable that Krichevsky did not know whom Axelrod had had in mind.[51]

Indeed, Boris Nicolaevsky, who in the 1920's examined the personal correspondence of the editors of *Rabochee delo*, concluded that "the members of the editorial board knew that their assertion did not correspond to reality, and . . . only in a purely casuistic manner did they persuade themselves of the *formal* truth of the declaration." In a private letter, probably written in December 1899, Krichevsky admitted that the editors' denial was "a diplomatic repulse of Axelrod's attack," which they felt justified in making because in November 1898 certain younger comrades had accepted the program of *Rabochee delo* and therefore "for *us* they ceased to exist as a special tendency." But then Krichevsky confessed that "you know that essentially Axelrod is right inasmuch as there really *were*, and perhaps—or even most likely—there still are up to this time . . . [some] 'younger [comrades]' " who adhere to views different from those of the majority of the union. Krichevsky further revealed that one of the dissidents, V. P. Ivanshin, distressed that his position was not receiving sufficient attention in *Rabochee delo*, was thinking of resigning from the editorial board. Finally, Krichevsky admitted that even "If the facts cited by Axelrod are groundless, then *objectively* there exist *other* facts that speak in Axelrod's favor."[52] Axelrod was not aware of this avowal of distortion, of course, but he knew the youngsters well enough to dismiss their plea of ignorance and innocence as sophistry.

Consequently, in a long letter to the editors of *Rabochee delo* he replied to the accusation of having exaggerated the influence of Economism by citing a number of comments recently made to him in private

50. *Rabochee delo*, no. 1 (Apr. 1899), 139–142.
51. See esp. "Ot redaktsii" (From the Editorial Board), *Rabochee delo*, no. 1 (Apr. 1899), p. 3.
52. B. N. [Nicolaevsky,] "Iz epokhi 'Iskri' i 'Zari,' " *Katorga i ssylka*, VI (1927), 20–21.

letters, without, however, identifying his youthful correspondents by name. One youngster had written that the struggle to destroy capitalism and autocracy and replace it with socialism was "foolish and a waste of time," for Russian workers were interested only in immediate, bread-and-butter issues. Another averred that propaganda aimed at overthrowing the tsar constituted a call for revolution, a prospect that would subject the people to the greatest danger. A third had sent Axelrod a manuscript devoted to refuting the main arguments in his writings on tactics. If all this information was inaccurate or no longer correctly described the outlook of the youngsters, Axelrod declared, he could only rejoice. "I am sincerely happy with this favorable change of mind and mood on the part of these comrades."[53]

That he did not believe it is evidenced by his continuing to rebut the opposition. He was particularly distressed by the claim of one youngster that the intelligentsia could make only a negligible contribution toward arousing the political consciousness of the masses and that the workers would spontaneously enter the phase of political action. Axelrod's views in 1899 on spontaneity are especially noteworthy because within a few years this question was to become paramount and lead to divisions far deeper than those caused by the Economist controversy.

He granted that famines, epidemics, economic crises, and foreign wars were often crucial in stimulating the masses to deliver the final blow against oppression. A spontaneous outburst on their part could be instrumental in producing a shift in power. But the real question—and he had frequently raised it—was how the masses would utilize the power that might fall into their hands. Only if they had become organized and politically conscious would they know how to press for meaningful institutional change, that is, a constitutional order.[54]

Much as he favored the exercise of political initiative by the masses, Axelrod stressed repeatedly the corollary notion that workers unschooled in politics and social thought could not be expected to act in the political realm with foresight and judiciousness. Instead of relying on spontaneity, therefore, he proposed the exercise of patience and deter-

---

53. Pavel Axelrod, *Pis'mo v redaktsiiu "Rabochago dela"* (Geneva, 1899), pp. 6, 7–8. The last reference is to a manuscript submitted by Sergei Prokopovich, which will be discussed below. The material that Axelrod cited was later published in G. V. Plekhanov's *Vademecum dlia redaktsii "Rabochago dela," sbornik materialov* (Geneva, 1900).

54. Axelrod, *Pis'mo v redaktsiiu*, p. 12.

mination. He called for prolonged and intensive political training for the masses: "Such a program cannot be mastered by hundreds of thousands of backward, semiliterate workers in a year or even a few years."[55] Nor could the proletariat do without the services of the revolutionary intelligentsia, the only persons capable of imparting the necessary knowledge to it.

One of the more puzzling features of the first phase of the Economist controversy is Plekhanov's failure to take a public stand. He was certainly not coy about entering a polemical fray; nor did he disagree with the substance of Axelrod's argument. Before publishing *On the Question of the Contemporary Tasks* Axelrod showed the manuscript to Plekhanov, who was unstinting in his praise. "I liked it very, very much," he wrote. "I agree with every word of it and positively insist that it be printed immediately as a separate brochure." And then, in order to encourage his comrade, always so full of doubts about his abilities, Plekhanov expressed particular pleasure that he had written this piece. "If you are able to write such things, then there is no reason for you to give way to despair and to think that you are incapable of literary work. Quite the contrary!"[56] There are several possible reasons for Plekhanov's silence. At first he may have felt that the disagreements were not of fundamental importance. The problems raised by *Ob agitatsii* were, moreover, basically tactical, outside his area of major interest. Probably the main reason was that by early 1898 he had immersed himself in another issue, Eduard Bernstein's Revisionism, and devoted his polemical talents to counteracting the new tendency, which left him little time for the affairs of the Russian movement.

Throughout 1898, and much of 1899, the GEL was actually engaged in two campaigns, one against Revisionism and one against Economism. Although the controversies developed along different lines, they intersected at certain points. There seems to have been a natural division of labor within the GEL, Plekhanov's fire being directed against Revisionism and Axelrod's against Economism. It is interesting that each urged moderation on the other.

55. *Ibid.*, p. 17.
56. Plekhanov to Axelrod, Feb. 28, 1898, *Perepiska*, ed. Nicolaevsky, Berlin, and Woytinsky, I, 200–201.

Bernstein's critique went to the roots of Marxism. He repudiated the theory of catastrophe, which postulated the inevitable collapse of capitalism as a result of economic crises of mounting severity. Careful analysis of statistical data had persuaded him that there was no basis to the Marxist claim that there existed a tendency for the means of production to come under the ownership of an ever smaller group of capitalists. Contrary to Marx's prediction, the middle class was not only not disappearing but increasing. Nor did Bernstein discover evidence in support of the theory of the pauperization of the masses. He described the dialectical method as "an excrescence which must be eliminated from Socialist theory." He did not look upon socialism as a historically preordained order; rather, he considered it desirable on moral grounds. It would be achieved not by means of some cataclysmic event, but gradually, through working-class participation in the parliamentary democracy emerging in Germany. Socialism and democracy were "two final values" for him, and he was not prepared to compromise either one.[57] Bernstein continued to call himself a Marxist, yet even this brief account indicates the extent to which he had discarded vital tenets of the master's teachings.

Plekhanov was shocked by Bernstein's heretical views. He immediately wrote Axelrod that Bernstein's attacks on orthodoxy had almost made him ill. He was especially chagrined because Bernstein was partly right, for instance, in asserting that one could not count on the realization of socialism in the near future. "But the truth may be employed for different ends . . . " He begged Axelrod to write quickly because "this question torments me ruthlessly."[58]

Axelrod's reply was one of the strangest and most perplexing letters he ever wrote. He began by indicating that he sympathized with Plekhanov's position on Revisionism, but immediately added that "I must nevertheless confess to you that it grieved and agitated me only fleetingly, and then not very greatly." Axelrod proceeded to explain his ambivalent reaction:

I remember how in the early '70's, at the dawn of our revolutionary movement "love of humanity," "love of the people," in a word, a celebrated altruism

57. Peter Gay, *The Dilemma of Democratic Socialism: Eduard Bernstein's Challenge to Marx* (New York, 1952), pp. 143, 244.
58. Plekhanov to Axelrod, Feb. 2, 1898, *Perepiska*, ed. Nicolaevsky, Berlin, and Woytinsky, I, 189.

was on everyone's lips and, perhaps, in the heart of each of our revolutionaries who loved the people. I was then very distressed that I did not experience such feelings, that I only felt compassion for the popular masses, but by no means love. But compassion alone did not take me far. In a chance conversation . . . in the spring of 1874 I defined my inner revolutionary impulse in this way: "I have come to the revolution not out of love, but out of hatred for the ugliness of the contemporary system and out of love for the future system, which I picture as an ideal; I hate the present form of human existence and love the future." Now, however, after having convinced myself of the nasty meanness not only of the forms of society but also of the very nature of the *bête humaine,* I would formulate my view differently. The inner motivation of my idealism, all my social activity served and serves the idea of infinite (of course, in a relative sense) progress of the human race—I say, infinite but not uninterrupted— this is an essential difference. And strange to say: the more unappealing contemporary human nature appears to me, the more passionately I dream of its perfection in the future—in a thousand years. One would think that this would be for me such a hazy, infinitely far-off future! And yet, I must say that this infinitely far-off perspective, with its *Uebermenschen* [superhuman beings] is for me the impulse, the source, or as one might say, the inspiration (if I were an artist or an important thinker or writer). It seems to me that the psychological root of this [strange feeling] . . . lies in a kind of religious feeling, which I cannot characterize in any other way except with these words: worship of thought, consciousness, spirit reaches within me the point of fanaticism or enthusiasm. It has not been easy for me to write these words because in my everyday life I have not revealed . . . [this outlook] and very likely you will be very astonished by such *Anmassung* [presumption] on my part. And nevertheless, I can say with confidence, at least to my own conscience: in me this enthusiasm is infinitely greater than among those youngsters who devour hundreds of volumes containing all sorts of wisdom and discuss [issues] in entirely philosophical terms and language. If there is no God who has created the universe . . . then we are preparing for the appearance on earth of divine men, possessed of the essence of all-powerful reason and will, appealing to consciousness and self-consciousness, capable through wisdom of comprehending and changing the world . . .—there is the psychological basis of all my spiritual and social strivings, ideas, and actions . . . In the early '70's I drew spiritual nourishment (and I still do draw it now, sinner that I am) for this kind of "faith" in Darwinism. It seems to me that Belinsky, whom I read in the fourth class in gymnasium, understanding a fifth to a tenth, had such a fascinating effect on me because his work is imbued with a deep, passionate enthusiasm for progress, for the idea of the ultimate triumph of the spirit over crass matter, of consciousness over the domination of the dismal, dark unconsciousness.

And here, during recent years, the very idea of the relatively infinite perfectibility of the earthly creatures, in the form of humanity, is beginning to become the subject of supercilious irony on the part of decadents and blasé people, not only among bourgeois intelligentsia but among our own . . . I look upon Bernstein's articles as one of the manifestations and logical or psychological consequences of this *manque de foi* in the progressive movement of humanity, more correctly, as a complete lack of faith in it. If you can imagine the depressing effect on me of this pessimism that has manifested itself in such a variety of ways, then you will understand why the last of Bernstein's articles could not shake me to the roots of my being. I now have one *idée fixe*—by the summer I want to free myself from all party and worldly affairs, worries, agitation, etc. and try to read the necessary books and reduce to the same denominator the uncoordinated, undeveloped ideas running through my head—all this from the standpoint of the *profession de foi* that I have set forth above. Possibly I will come to the same conclusion . . . long ago reached by *geistreiche Leute* [ingenious people] or, on the contrary, my position will become firmer. In any case, I will feel that I am on more or less firm philosophical ground, and now I feel as though I am half-stupid and that others say in a mocking way with a smile and a barely hidden scornful condescension: "The light which you seem to see in the distance is in essence a mirage, or more accurately, the darkness which surrounds us but only in another shade." And until such time as I am myself clear on all this, Bernstein's tendencies will not make that impression which they ought to. In my view, they have no less right to exist than the ultrarevolutionary: it all comes down to a question of temperament. And if one already takes the point of view that relegates humanity to the eternal condition of cattle, not admitting its elevation to the state of full rationality, then the philistine-tortoise movement recommended by Bernstein has a certain superiority over the methods of *Sturm und Drang:* at least less blood will flow and there will be less reason for entire nations to give themselves airs to the same degree as has been attempted by the French. No doubt it will be a boring road, but only for some individuals. Eventually it will lead to what more revolutionary methods might bring. A boring perspective and a boring path, and that's all. I derive a kind of *Schadenfreude* [malicious joy] from the appearance of Bernstein's articles.[59]

Basing his opinion largely on this letter and on Plekhanov's earlier missive, Samuel Baron has argued that "Bernstein's attack had a traumatic effect [on Plekhanov and Axelrod] . . . because, in their view, it robbed socialism of its heroic and idealistic character."[60] There is much to be said for this interpretation, but in the case of Axelrod there are other factors that must be considered. When he heard of the German socialist's apostasy, he was in a pessimistic mood and, as the letter itself indicates, in the throes of an intellectual crisis. An examination of the source of this crisis helps explain the nature of his reaction to Bernstein's articles and also reveals that he was groping for an approach to politics intrinsically different from that of his colleagues in the Russian movement. He did not publicly articulate that approach until he had

---

59. Axelrod to Plekhanov, Feb. 5, [1898,] *ibid.*, pp. 192–195.
60. Samuel H. Baron, *Plekhanov: The Father of Russian Marxism* (Stanford, 1963), p. 174.

experienced further—and more agonizing—crises, but there can be no doubt that in 1898 he was already moving in a new direction.

For several months early in 1898 Axelrod was overcome with emotion by the trial of Émile Zola, who was charged with slander for having accused several officers in the French army of improper conduct in procuring the condemnation of Alfred Dreyfus. Axelrod could concentrate on nothing but the newspaper reports from France, which absorbed his "head, heart, and entire being." The Dreyfus Affair had moved him because it appeared to be "an index, a symptom of the moral and political degradation of an entire nation, the manifestation of the atrophy of the *elemental* sense of justice and of wild, tribal, shameful chauvinism." But during the trial of Zola his sense of outrage became "ten times" greater. He could not understand how the French people could allow a "great writer" and "great citizen" to be vilified. He was especially baffled by the indifference of the French working class. "And this is the result of four revolutions! In my mind, this corruption, this decay of political sense and consciousness is somehow wretchedly associated with these revolutions." The failure of the French proletariat to demonstrate against the distressing events had convinced him that "one-half or four-fifths of the Paris working-class population were degenerate fools and cretins." He feared that the events in France signified the "beginning of the complete downfall, the ruin of the nation." And if this was true, then Axelrod thought it might be best for the people to perish and make room "for a less degenerate, historically more viable nation. The most diverse feelings and thoughts are crowded and mixed in my chest and head."[61]

While in this distraught mood Axelrod received Plekhanov's letter on Bernstein's repudiation of orthodoxy, which accounted for his initial openness to at least a consideration of the new tendency. For the events in France had prompted Axelrod to question many of his most cherished beliefs. His comments about the Paris proletariat show that he had come to doubt that a laborer was necessarily, or even potentially, the embodiment of virtue. His romantic view of the proletariat as the only possible savior of mankind had been severely undermined, a shattering experi-

---

61. Axelrod to Plekhanov, n. d., but early in 1898, *Perepiska*, ed. Nicolaevsky, Berlin, and Woytinsky, I, 184–185.

ence that led him to profoundly pessimistic conclusions about mankind in general.

It is significant that Axelrod did not assess the French crisis from a Marxist point of view. He did not even raise the question of whether the proletariat stood to gain or lose from the situation; nor did he discuss the political beliefs of those who took sides during the affair. He viewed the matter from an entirely different perspective, as a moral issue, a case involving, above all else, elemental justice. It seemed to him that a political movement dedicated to a lofty ideal but that nevertheless exhibited blindness to such moral issues—as French Marxist labor had done—suffered from serious defects.

Plekhanov's reaction to the developments in France only deepened Axelrod's pessimism and exacerbated his anger. Plekhanov seems initially to have avoided the issue altogether, which prompted Axelrod to express himself with some sarcasm: "I cannot believe that you have followed all the troubles of Zola's trial dispassionately, with Olympian indifference. Truly, you must be very absorbed in some kind of work." Axelrod suggested that the Russian colonies in Zurich and Geneva write Zola a letter of sympathy and support in order "morally to reward him for the loathsome attitude toward him of his countrymen."[62] Plekhanov's reply reveals, perhaps as much as anything, the profound difference in character and outlook between the two founders of the Russian Marxist movement. He accused Axelrod of being too severe in his condemnation of France and the French workers. After all, miscarriages of justice occur everywhere, for example the sentence imposed on Oscar Wilde in 1897 for an alleged violation of the moral code. At least in France a protest movement had arisen in response to the trials of Dreyfus and Zola. Then Plekhanov indicated that although he himself was convinced of Dreyfus' innocence—without being sure why—he still could not be too censorious of the workers for refusing to get involved in a "bourgeois affair." To be sure, the workers' attitude was wrong: "an innocent person must be defended even if he is a bourgeois, but if you keep in mind how badly and spitefully the French bourgeoisie has treated the workers, then you yourself will agree that this wrong behavior is pardonable." He was willing, nevertheless, to send a letter of

62. *Ibid.*, pp. 185–186.

support to Zola, although the "sympathy of socialists is hardly of value to him."[63]

It was in reply to this letter that Axelrod indulged in such extensive soul-searching. That Plekhanov's opinion of the Dreyfus Affair was very much on Axelrod's mind is clear from the fact that after describing his intellectual crisis he returned to the subject of the events in France. He found it "strange" that Plekhanov should have drawn a comparison between the cases of Wilde and Zola. In the former, a country "steeped in prejudice" was supposedly attempting to protect its moral standards. The salient point for Axelrod was that England did not contradict its historical traditions, though he plainly did not approve of the treatment accorded Wilde. France, however, the "vanguard of humanity," had betrayed its "whole revolutionary past" by not preventing the blatant infringement of justice. Although he had now calmed down somewhat, he still regretted that the Russians had not sent Zola a letter of sympathy.[64]

We cannot be sure whether Plekhanov's halfhearted approval of the idea was a factor in the failure to send the letter, but there is no question that his attitude displeased Axelrod. This displeasure may have caused, in part, the *Schadenfreude* he mentioned. It may have derived even more from a sense that Bernstein's challenge conformed to and buttressed his own doubts about some of the dogmas to which he had subscribed for fifteen years. He had become conscious of a moral dimension to politics, and in this there was an obvious philosophical correspondence between his views and those of Bernstein. Despite its depth, Axelrod's crisis seems to have been short-lived, and there is no evidence that for the next few years he was again troubled by the thoughts he had expressed to Plekhanov.

Because of his involvement in other conflicts Axelrod did not participate in the public debate on Revisionism. For much of 1898 and 1899, as he confided to Kautsky, he was in a "dreadful psychological state" caused by the endless feuds with the Economists and by the Dreyfus Affair.[65] He therefore restricted himself to urging restraint on Ple-

63. Plekhanov to Axelrod, Feb. 12, 1898, *ibid.*, p. 188. After Plekhanov's death, sometime in the early 1920's, his wife claimed that he had been far more agitated over the Dreyfus Affair than this letter suggests. *Ibid.*, pp. 190–191.
64. Axelrod to Plekhanov, early in 1898, *ibid.*, pp. 196–197.
65. Axelrod to Kautsky, Mar. 18, 1900, uncatalogued, I.I.S.H.

khanov, whose polemics he feared would alienate important persons in the German Social Democratic party. He also warned his friend that there were few Marxists who could follow the fine philosophical points in his attacks on the Revisionists.[66]

But Axelrod's attempt to remain personally aloof from the controversy did not succeed. Late in 1898 he received a letter from Kautsky informing him that Bernstein had "triumphantly" declared that Plekhanov had been forced to give up the editorship of the union's publications because his "point of view was too revolutionary." More disturbing to Kautsky was Bernstein's claim that "in your heart you [that is, Axelrod] side with him and that it was only out of old friendship that you did not want to separate yourself from Plekhanov. I would be very pleased to receive authentic information about this from you."[67] On the basis of this claim as well as Axelrod's initial statements about Revisionism, it has been argued that he was really sympathetic to the new ideas.[68]

Actually, once he had overcome his intellectual crisis, Axelrod remained squarely in the orthodox camp. It turned out, as he was eager to explain, that Bernstein had mistaken hospitality for political agreement. Axelrod wrote Kautsky that Bernstein and his wife had recently visited him, and as host to a man of whom he was extremely fond he had been loath to initiate a "passionate debate." Gentle by nature and inclined to avoid conflict whenever possible, Axelrod had been reserved and guarded in his statements. In short, he had gone out of his way "not to spoil the pleasure" of reunification with an old friend. In any case, he considered himself incapable of a "cold-blooded debate conducted with fine dialectical arguments." When Bernstein complained about Plekhanov's attacks on him, Axelrod answered approximately as follows: "I do not speak from special personal motives and sympathies for Plekhanov; *personally,* you and Karl [Kautsky] are possibly closer to me than Plekhanov, but *nevertheless* I must say that Plekhanov is right; I

---

66. Axelrod to R. M. Plekhanova, Sept. 1, [1898,] *Perepiska,* ed. Nicolaevsky, Berlin, and Woytinsky, II, 54–58; Axelrod to Plekhanov, spring, 1899, *ibid.,* pp. 74–75; for a detailed analysis of Plekhanov's criticism of Revisionism, see Baron, *Plekhanov,* pp. 164–185, and Dietrich Geyer, *Lenin in der russischen Sozialdemokratie. Die Arbeiterbewegung im Zarenreich als Organisationsproblem der revolutionären Intelligenz 1890–1903* (Cologne, 1962), pp. 139–155.

67. Kautsky to Axelrod, late in 1898, Axelrod Archive, I.I.S.H.

68. Keep, *Rise of Social Democracy,* p. 65.

make this judgment against you not from prejudice against you and for him." Bernstein, Axelrod continued, must have interpreted his failure to argue with him as agreement with his views. "That Ede [Bernstein] could so deceive himself is evidence of an inner recognition of the weakness of his position."[69]

Bernstein eventually realized that he had misinterpreted Axelrod's position. In 1925 he recalled that at the International Socialist Congress of 1904 Axelrod supported the opponents of Revisionism on every issue. Bernstein now avoided personal contact with his friend for fear that a meeting would provoke a quarrel.[70]

However much anguish Plekhanov endured as a result of his campaign against Bernstein, Axelrod suffered even more during his conflict with the youngsters. Plekhanov could confine himself to polemical sallies, but Axelrod, in addition to engaging in ideological dispute, had to contend with challenges related to organizational and financial matters, and, because these challenges came from members of his own movement, he often found himself at close quarters with his antagonists. It is not surprising that differences over political questions quickly became enmeshed with personal feuds, and it is not always possible to ascertain whether the dramatis personae acted from conviction or from pique. In his letters Axelrod gave the impression of being surrounded by enemies perennially intriguing against him. Justified or not, this feeling was bound to affect his behavior toward the youngsters.

It is not necessary to describe all the conflicts; several were petty and some hopelessly confusing. The main ones will serve to illustrate the atmosphere of recrimination and distrust in which the controversy over Economism unfolded. But in order to reproduce that atmosphere we must retrace our steps and consider certain events that took place during the period when Axelrod was formulating his tactical ideas and Plekhanov was criticizing Revisionism.

In the winter of 1897–1898 the Berlin section of the union (composed, in part, of Timofei Grishin-Kopel'zon, the official representative of the Jewish Bund, V. A. Bukhgolts, S. N. Prokopovich, E. D. Kuskova, and I. M. Somov-Peskin) tried to oust the secretary of the organization, D.

69. Axelrod to Kautsky, Dec. 6, 12, 1898, Kautsky Archive, I.I.S.H.
70. Eduard Bernstein, "Pavel Aksel'rod, internatsionalist," *Sotsialisticheskii vestnik*, no. 15/16, Aug. 18, 1925, 24.

Kol'tsov, who was ideologically close to Plekhanov. The section charged Kol'tsov with tactlessness, arbitrariness, and running an anarchic administration. Two of their number, Grishin and Somov, threatened to resign if the secretary was not removed from office. Believing that the "union could not accept such ultimatums" and that the two were determined to break with the organization anyway, Plekhanov urged that nothing be done to stop them.[71]

Before receiving this advice, however, Axelrod and Zasulich had engineered a "revolution" within the union that they thought would placate the youngsters. They had secured Kol'tsov's promise to resign, but before he had a chance to step down another conflict arose, and thereafter all attempts at reconciliation were doomed.[72]

The new crisis was caused by a letter written by S. N. Prokopovich, a young economist with whom the veterans had thought they would be able to collaborate. When Prokopovich submitted a manuscript noticeably similar to *Ob agitatsii* in content, Plekhanov urged its publication on the ground that "it is essential to encourage 'the young talents.'" Axelrod agreed because he felt "that it would not be difficult to reach an understanding" with Prokopovich, whom he considered more reasonable and trustworthy than the other youngsters.[73]

But the GEL quickly became disenchanted with Prokopovich. Late in November 1897 Zasulich spoke of his monumental conceit: he had persuaded himself that he had "taken a new step in the elaboration of [Marx's] theory," indeed, that he had made a "complete revolution" in the ideological realm. He showed scant respect for the works of the "little old men" of the GEL, as he referred to them, and cavalierly dismissed Axelrod's criticisms of his writings. Zasulich claimed that many youngsters accepted his teachings and that he might well raise "the banner of revolt" if the GEL refused to publish his work. Axelrod was startled, nevertheless, when, in the spring of 1898, he received another

---

71. Axelrod to Plekhanov, n.d., *Perepiska*, ed. Nicolaevsky, Berlin, and Woytinsky, II, 5; see also *ibid.*, I, 207–208; Kopel'zon (Grishin) to Axelrod, Feb. 23, 1898, Axelrod Archive, I.I.S.H.; Plekhanov to Axelrod, Apr. 23, 1898, *Perepiska*, ed. Nicolaevsky, Berlin, and Woytinsky, II, 9.

72. Axelrod to Plekhanov, Mar. 13, 1898, *Perepiska*, ed. Nicolaevsky, Berlin, and Woytinsky, I, 206; Ginsburg (Kol'tsov) to Axelrod, Mar. 1, 1898, Axelrod Archive, I.I.S.H.

73. Axelrod to Plekhanov, Mar. or Apr. 1897, *Perepiska*, ed. Nicolaevsky, Berlin, and Woytinsky, I, 174; Plekhanov to Axelrod, Jan. 11, 1898, *ibid.*, p. 182; Axelrod to Plekhanov, n. d., *ibid.*, p. 200.

manuscript from Prokopovich, entitled "Response to Axelrod's Brochure: 'On the Question of the Contemporary Tasks and Tactics of Russian Social Democrats.' "[74]

In this work Prokopovich contended that Axelrod's position, based on the GEL's draft program of 1885, was irretrievably outdated. At the time of the formation of the GEL, its major aim had been to rally support among the intelligentsia; hence its emphasis on political agitation. But in the meantime a labor movement had emerged in Russia that was concerned primarily with the immediate and direct needs and interests of workers. It was not prepared to allow the intelligentsia to hand it a political task. Prokopovich stressed that he did not oppose political action on principle; ultimately the working class would surely turn to it. But he warned that premature concern with politics would only provide the government with a pretext for robbing the movement of its best people through repressive measures.[75]

The veterans were dismayed by Prokopovich's attack on Axelrod, but what outraged them was his statement, made in a private letter, that when he joined the union he had not known that it subscribed to the GEL's draft program of 1885 and that he did not agree with the program.[76] Plekhanov reacted with fury to Prokopovich's confession of ignorance. He urged the immediate expulsion from the union of Prokopovich and his wife, E. D. Kuskova, who shared his views. Axelrod was as angry as Plekhanov and was prepared to break with the youngsters, but he feared that precipitous action against Prokopovich without first consulting the members of the organization would make it appear as though the Economists were being sacrificed to the "arbitrary will of a dictator." If that were to happen, the GEL's position in the movement would deteriorate immensely.[77]

Then, in a frank analysis of the turmoil, Axelrod for the first time conceded that ever since the decision had been reached to publish agitational material the GEL had faced a dilemma. The veterans granted

74. Zasulich to Plekhanov, Nov. 20, 1897, *Gruppa "Osvobozhdenie truda,"* ed. L. Deich (Moscow, 1924–1928), IV, 186–197. This is the manuscript to which Axelrod referred in his letter to the editors of *Rabochee delo*.

75. Plekhanov, *Vademecum*, p. 54.

76. *Perepiska*, ed. Nicolaevsky, Berlin, and Woytinsky, II, 6.

77. Plekhanov to Axelrod, probably late in Apr. 1898, *ibid.*, pp. 12–14; Plekhanov to Axelrod, Apr. 26, 1898, *ibid.*, p. 18; Axelrod to Plekhanov, n. d., *ibid.*, I, 200; Axelrod to Plekhanov, Apr. 26, 1898, *ibid.*, II, 15.

the need for such literature, but because of their preoccupation with theory they were temperamentally incapable of producing it in large quantities. Yet they had too little confidence in the youngsters to entrust them with the task. Although he himself had devoted much time to popular literature, he had done so "without inner fire, but, on the contrary, often with repugnance." If Plekhanov really wanted to put down the "mutiny" he should devote a few months to raising the prestige of the union by writing on Russian affairs and giving lectures. Axelrod believed, in other words, that Plekhanov should take to heart certain criticisms made by the youngsters.[78] As for Prokopovich, Axelrod proposed that his case be resolved by a congress of the union.

Zasulich was even more forceful and outspoken in urging moderation on Plekhanov. She pointed out that the balance of power within the union had shifted in favor of the youngsters who also could count on substantial support in Russia.[79] Even though Plekhanov could not persuade his colleagues to agree to his statement of expulsion, he sent a copy of it to Kuskova.[80] No formal action was taken against the couple, however, and they soon left for Russia and quit the union.

There were several reasons for the cautious conduct of Axelrod and Zasulich. For one thing, Grishin had persuaded Prokopovich to request that his controversial manuscript be withdrawn, thus depriving the GEL of a major source of irritation. Also, as Axelrod pointed out in a letter to Plekhanov, there was a real danger of martyrizing Prokopovich. None of the youngsters agreed with everything he had written, but many were prepared to defend his right to express his views without being penalized. "There was a growing feeling," Jonathan Frankel has written, "that the restriction of free discussion and the literary censorship which the group imposed on the union made a mockery of the democratic principles which they all professed."[81] The failure to enforce Plekhanov's hard line forestalled an open division in the spring of 1898, but by now feelings ran so high that the split was only delayed, not avoided.

78. Axelrod to Plekhanov, Apr. 27, 1898, *ibid.*, pp. 18–20; Axelrod to Plekhanov, Apr. 26, 1898, *ibid.*, pp. 16–17.
79. Zasulich to Plekhanov, May 25, 1898, *Gruppa*, ed. Deich, VI, 207–208.
80. This emerges from Axelrod to Plekhanov, Apr. 27, 1898, *Perepiska*, ed. Nicolaevsky, Berlin, and Woytinsky, II, 20.
81. Frankel, "Economism," p. 278. See this excellent article for more details on the conflicts between the youngsters and veterans.

Tensions heightened again in November 1898, when the first congress of the union was convoked, and the opposition triumphed on every issue. The GEL announced that except for Number 5/6 of *Rabotnik* and two brochures by Lenin, it would no longer edit the union's publications. Several candidates were enrolled in the organization, all of them belonging to the opposition, and Krichevsky, P. F. Teplov, and Ivanshin were elected editors of the union's publications. They soon proceeded to substitute *Rabochee delo* for *Rabotnik* as their working-class organ.

Defeats on the various organizational issues seriously wounded the GEL. But the veterans were even more distressed by additional evidence of ideological deviation from orthodoxy on the part of the youngsters. At the first meeting Kol'tsov called on the delegates to include a statement of principle in the statutes to be drafted for the union and advanced for that purpose the doctrine promulgated in the manifesto of the recently formed (in March 1898) Russian Social Democratic Workers' party (RSDRP), that the "immediate task" is the "conquest of political freedom." The youngsters, however, sided with Grishin, who contended that "in Russia the immediate task of the party is not the conquest of political freedom; very many comrades in Russia hold this view." The resolution was defeated by a vote of seven to four.[82]

In the course of the discussions another member of the opposition, Somov, declared that "now, of course, in the light of Bernstein's views, the Social Democratic program must be interpreted in the broadest sense."[83] Although Somov did not officially represent the youngsters, it is easy to see why the veterans became ever more doubtful about the ideological purity of their antagonists. Axelrod could not restrain himself from publicly stating that "between us there are basic differences of opinion. May all of us here at the congress really refer to ourselves as Social Democrats?"[84]

The full depth of Axelrod's bitterness can be detected in a private letter he wrote to Kautsky in December 1898, in which he described in

82. "Materialy k istorii pervogo s'ezda," *Proletarskaia revoliutsiia*, no. 74 (1928), 164–167.
83. MS of the first congress of the union, Bk. I, 28, quoted in Keep, *Rise of Social Democracy*, p. 64.
84. "Materialy k istorii," p. 166. On Plekhanov's disappointment with the events at the congress, see Plekhanov to Axelrod, May 4, 1899, *Perepiska*, ed. Nicolaevsky, Berlin, and Woytinsky, II, 86.

detail the conflicts among Russian Marxists. In tone and content he was thoroughly uncompromising; he gave no hint—as he had in a previous letter to Plekhanov—that the veterans were in any way to blame for the friction. He claimed that the youngsters, whom he dubbed "unrecognized literary geniuses," were only concerned with publishing a large quantity of "mass literature": one young comrade bluntly told him that "We need many brochures, even if they are bad; better bad but a large assortment, than competent ones in limited quantity."

At the end of the letter Axelrod leveled a new charge against the youngsters: "Incidentally, it is true that our 'independents' are grasping at Ede [Bernstein] in order to construct a new tendency. He is not to be envied, but rather pitied, in having these adherents. For they misuse his ideas and offer a hodgepodge of tendencies that stands in relation to Ede's train of thought roughly as 'true socialism' stands in relation to the French [socialism] of the forties; that is, it is a lifeless and mindless caricature."[85] The charge that the youngsters were toying with Revisionism was even more firmly believed by the veterans after Bernstein claimed in the spring of 1899—on what basis is obscure—that "many, if not most of the Russian Social Democrats active in Russia, including the editors of the Russian workers' journal, have declared themselves decisively in favor of a point of view very close to mine."[86]

It is difficult to document Bernstein's assertion. Even Plekhanov, when he first learned of it, was not sure which journal Bernstein had in mind, and he perceived at this time basic differences between the positions of the Economists and the Revisionists.[87] The fact is that not one Social Democratic journal suspected by the GEL of Economism followed a consistent ideological line. Thus, the first issue of *Rabochaia mysl'*, generally acknowledged as the most outspoken organ of the Economists, carried two articles that differed with each other "if not in principle, then certainly in emphasis and outlook" in discussing the importance of economic as against political action.[88] In 1899 *Rabochaia mysl'* also

85. Axelrod to Kautsky, Dec. 6, 12, 1898, Kautsky Archive, I.I.S.H.

86. Eduard Bernstein, *Die Voraussetzungen und die Aufgaben der Sozialdemokratie* (Stuttgart, 1899), p. 170.

87. Plekhanov to Axelrod, Mar. 1899, *Perepiska*, ed. Nicolaevsky, Berlin, and Woytinsky, II, 72.

88. Allan K. Wildman, *The Making of a Workers' Revolution: Russian Social Democracy, 1891–1903* (Chicago, 1967), p. 125. See Chap. V for a careful and incisive analysis of the content of this journal.

printed a "Supplement" that included an article by Bernstein as well as another on Revisionism in general, which seemed to betoken an "ideological kinship" between the Russian journal and the new doctrine.[89] But this material had not yet appeared when Axelrod first contended that the Economists were toying with Revisionism. There were, to be sure, some hints that individual Russian Social Democrats identified as Economists—Ivanshin, for example—had expressed sympathy for Bernstein's views,[90] but it was difficult to assess the extent to which the new tendency had found support within the movement at large.

In certain essential respects Economism and Revisionism had less in common than is often assumed, although both stressed the importance of the workers' day-to-day victories. Economism was, historically, the doctrine of a nascent labor movement that allegedly had not yet (in the late 1890's) matured sufficiently to be able to devote itself primarily to political agitation. The Economists did not so much argue that Marxism was wrong as that it was still irrelevant in Russia. Revisionism, however, may be said to have been the ideology of an advanced labor movement that, according to Bernstein, had outgrown Marxist dogmas. He never called for a repudiation of politics even as a temporary tactic. If anything, Bernstein favored a more sophisticated involvement by Social Democrats in German political life. For example, he encouraged his party to make alliances with progressive groups from the middle class.

Not only did the veterans find it hard to prove that the youngsters were Revisionists, but by 1899 it was not even easy to locate avowed and unreserved Economists. The youngsters treated ideological matters with caution in their new journal, *Rabochee delo*. They refrained from criticizing the GEL's doctrines directly and pointedly declared their support for political action. But at the same time some of their phraseology was ambiguous; thus the suspicious veterans remained uneasy. For example, in the policy statement of *Rabochee delo* the editors wrote

89. *Ibid.*, p. 141.
90. Zasulich to Plekhanov, n. d., *Gruppa,* ed. Deich, VI, 226. A case could be made, however, for the claim that some of the so-called Legal Marxists were heavily influenced by Bernsteinism. The Legal Marxists were those Marxists in the late 1890's who published works in the legal press even though they might—and usually did—also engage in illegal activities. But the Legal Marxists were a small group of intellectuals with no following in the movement. See Richard Kindersley, *The First Russian Revisionists: A Study of Legal Marxism in Russia* (Oxford, 1962).

that "the political struggle of the working class is only the most developed, broadest, and most effective form of economic struggle," which could be interpreted as a restatement of *Ob agitatsii*'s thesis.[91] More troubling to the veterans was the editors' disingenuous claim, which we have already mentioned, not to know whom Axelrod meant when he spoke of Economists in the union.

The youngsters were obviously feeling their way in the ideological realm, but there can be no doubt that by the spring of 1899 they began to turn away from Economism. This change of mind was related to the changing mood noticeable among workers in Russia, who were manifesting interest in politics earlier than the Economists had expected. The process of politicization apparently began in February 1899, when a number of workers was dismayed by the harsh police repression of student activists in St. Petersburg. The high point of this development occurred during the student demonstrations early in 1901, which were inspired by political demands and which received considerable support from St. Petersburg workers. By this time, according to Allan Wildman, "there was not a trace of this dangerous heresy [Economism] in the Social Democratic movement."[92] Even *Rabochaia mysl'* now declared its solidarity with the strategy of political struggle.

Yet the campaign against Economism did not abate. On the contrary, late in 1899 it entered a second phase in which first Plekhanov and then Lenin assumed the roles of chief defenders of orthodoxy. During this second, far more virulent phase, Axelrod retreated to the background, although he privately supported Plekhanov and Lenin.[93]

The anomalous development of a renewed attack against a declining —or, more accurately, disappearing—heresy is not easy to explain. In large part, it was no doubt the result of the continuing feud between the youngsters and the veterans, which in the spring of 1899 again manifested itself in an open clash. As so often before, the immediate cause

91. *Rabochee delo*, no. 1 (Apr. 1899), 3.
92. Wildman, *Making of a Workers' Revolution*, p. 144.
93. Although Axelrod did not write any further extensive critiques of Economism, he did continue to insist that the triumph of that tendency would signify "the death of the movement." Pavel Axelrod, *Bor'ba sotsialisticheskikh i burzhuaznykh tendentsii v russkom revoliutsionnom dvizhenii* (2nd ed., St. Petersburg, 1907), p. 125. This volume is a collection of some of Axelrod's articles, most of them written at the turn of the century.

of the friction was money. Early in 1899 the Russian Social Democratic Club of New York sent Axelrod 700 francs. Dr. S. M. Ingerman, the club's spokesman, wrote Axelrod that since the Americans could not evaluate the various controversies within the union they were sending the money to their long-standing friends, the GEL. Axelrod therefore initially presumed it proper for the GEL to dispose of the contribution as it saw fit. The union leadership, however, viewed the matter differently. Grishin, its new secretary, sent Axelrod an official letter requesting the 700 francs, which, he claimed, were intended for the entire foreign movement.[94]

Axelrod turned for advice to Plekhanov, whose stand was unequivocal. "Under no circumstance," he wrote, "must the money be handed over (for the time being) to the union. Who knows, perhaps there will be a split."[95] Axelrod had come to believe, however, that the ownership of the 700 francs was open to question, and therefore on April 20 he made a dramatic proposal: the GEL should disband and leave the union. Zasulich had told him that she was too ill to remain active. "For my part," he wrote Plekhanov, "I produce too little literature. And you are occupied with other matters. It follows that there is no group and we have no raison d'être." If the group were dissolved, the money would automatically be turned over to the union.[96]

Plekhanov replied with the haughtiness and anger of a man who found it incomprehensible that anyone would dare challenge a decision he had reached. It seemed to him, he told Axelrod, that either the money belonged to the GEL or it did not. If it did not, then Axelrod had no grounds for being offended by Grishin's having requested it; indeed, "you should be grateful that he did not take you to court. He has an absolute right [to do so]. From your letter I do not see how you can escape from this dilemma." Plekhanov urged Axelrod to try to obtain further clarification from Ingerman about the club's intentions. In the meantime, he felt the group should keep the money because it was sorely needed. Then he rejected Axelrod's suggestion that they leave the union: "I shall remain in the union as long as I am not driven out or as long as *I* have not driven out my enemies. For me this is definitely decided."

94. *Perepiska,* ed. Nicolaevsky, Berlin, and Woytinsky, II, 70.
95. Plekhanov to Axelrod, Mar. 1899, *ibid.,* p. 73.
96. Axelrod to Plekhanov, early Apr. 1899, *ibid.,* p. 77; Axelrod to Plekhanov, Apr. 20, 1899, *ibid.,* pp. 78–79.

Plekhanov foresaw a major contest in the union, which had nothing to do with money, and that, apparently, accounted for his determination to stay in the organization. "The struggle against Bernsteinism in Russia is the most urgent task of the moment. *Nachalo* [the journal of the Legal Marxists] is entirely on Bernstein's side."[97] Until this time, Plekhanov had viewed Revisionism as basically a danger to the international Social Democratic movement, but now he felt it threatened the movement that he himself had founded. His fury was therefore all the greater, though he presented no evidence that Revisionism had actually made many converts among Russians. What seems to have happened is that because some Russian Social Democrats had dared oppose him—and the youngsters were clearly doing so in requesting the money—Plekhanov suspected them of the most heinous offense: adoption of the Revisionist heresy. In the words of his biographer, Plekhanov "chose to subsume Economism as a variety of Revisionism."[98] If he could make the charge stick, he would be in a position to discredit his opponents thoroughly. He ended his letter to Axelrod on an imperious note: "If you want to participate in the impending struggle—fine; if not—I alone will follow this road along which my duty as a revolutionary takes me."[99]

Axelrod was so wounded that he wrote his reply not to Plekhanov, but, as was his custom at such times, to his wife, Rosalii Markovna. He reminded her that he had asked Plekhanov several times for advice about the matter of the 700 francs and each time was told simply that he should keep the money. "In response to all my questions, proposals, requests for definite instructions I receive not even a philippic but almost an accusation of having betrayed my revolutionary duty." He found this particularly astonishing because Plekhanov was finally calling attention to the "disease of Bernsteinism" in the Russian movement and doing so in virtually the identical words that he himself had frequently used. Still, he indicated that, if Plekhanov would now write a critique of Bernsteinism that could be published by the GEL, he would agree not to dissolve the group.[100]

---

97. Plekhanov to Axelrod, Apr. 21, 1899, *ibid.*, pp. 80–81.

98. Baron, *Plekhanov*, pp. 195–196. For an interpretation different from mine of Plekhanov's assessment of the dangers of Economism and Revisionism in the Russian movement, see *ibid.*, pp. 196–207.

99. Plekhanov to Axelrod, Apr. 21, 1899, *Perepiska*, ed. Nicolaevsky, Berlin, and Woytinsky, II, 81.

100. Axelrod to R. M. Plekhanova, Apr. 25, 1899, *ibid.*, pp. 82–85.

The GEL decided to retain the American money, causing a further heightening of the dissension.[101] In May 1899 Plekhanov spoke with equanimity of the likelihood of an open split between the veterans and the youngsters and successfully urged Axelrod to write his letter criticizing *Rabochee delo:* "This impudence deserves to be punished . . . In general, we must tell them *publicly* everything we think of them."[102] In the summer of 1899, however, Plekhanov's mood changed abruptly. One of the leading youngsters, Ivanshin, had treated him with surprising courtesy, and from this Plekhanov concluded that the opposition wanted peace. It even appeared that the GEL and the union were about to reach a formal agreement settling their differences.

Plekhanov and Grishin worked out the settlement, which on the whole was favorable to the GEL, and several members of the union objected to it. The major obstacle turned out to be the group's demand that it be allowed to bring six new members into the organization, all of them sympathizers, in order to "establish an equilibrium in the numerical strength of the union." With good reason this proposal was said to violate democratic procedure, as it would have given the veterans strength beyond their actual support in the Social Democratic movement. To iron out the points at issue, the youngsters proposed the convocation of a congress. Plekhanov responded with an ultimatum: if the draft agreement were not accepted by twelve o'clock noon, September 28, the GEL would break "all comradely relations" with the union.[103]

In the midst of this turmoil there burst another bombshell that impelled Plekhanov to abandon all attempts at reaching an understanding and to launch the second phase of the campaign against the youngsters. This new state of mind was inspired by a reading of the "Protest" of seventeen Social Democrats in Siberia, written by Lenin, against the so-called Credo. The history of the Credo has often been told and need not be repeated here.[104] It is sufficient to mention that the Credo, based on a talk given by Kuskova, was hastily printed and distributed without the

101. See "Otvet administratsii S. rus. sots. dem." (Reply of the Administration of the Union of Russian Social Democrats), May 26, 1899, Axelrod Archive, I.I.S.H.
102. Plekhanov to Axelrod, May 4, 1899, *Perepiska,* ed. Nicolaevsky, Berlin, and Woytinsky, II, 86.
103. The relevant documents are reproduced in *Sotsial-demokraticheskoe dvizhenie: materialy,* ed. A. N. Potresov and B. I. Nicolaevsky (Moscow, 1928), pp. 279–280.
104. Keep, *Rise of Social Democracy,* pp. 65–66; Baron, *Plekhanov,* pp. 196–197; Leopold Haimson, *The Russian Marxists and the Origins of Bolshevism* (Cambridge, Mass., 1955), pp. 86–87.

author's knowledge. It is a choppy, badly written, and disorganized statement with a peculiar ideological thrust: it was totally hostile to the GEL and favored the Economist—and even Revisionist—approach. Although the seventeen protesters acknowledged their uncertainty as to whether the views in the Credo enjoyed a following of any consequence among Social Democrats in Russia, Plekhanov decided that the time had come for him to attack the youngsters. "The Group for the Emancipation of Labor," he declared, "must come forth again more militant and brilliant than it has ever been before."[105]

For the next few months he worked on what surely turned out to be his most explosive and questionable publication, the *Vademecum*. It appeared in February 1900 and stunned the Russian Social Democratic community, not only because *Rabochee delo* had already published Lenin's "Protest" and explicitly disavowed the views of the Credo, but also —and primarily—because of its venomous nature. He committed the indiscretion of reproducing three private letters that had been sent to Axelrod a year and a half earlier, all of which revealed Economist sympathies. He also included Prokopovich's article criticizing Axelrod, which the author had previously indicated he did not want published. No less shameful were his comments in the preface. There could no longer be any doubt, he claimed, that in 1898 Economists predominated among the youngsters. Then he proceeded to fulminate against them: in their ideological position there was discernible "neither *socialism* nor *democracy*"; the youngsters were "political castrates and narrow-minded pedants"; they had "not mastered *even the ABC of contemporary socialism*"; the editors of *Rabochee delo* "incline toward eclecticism, vainly striving to reconcile Karl Marx and V. I. [Ivanshin], one of the editors."[106]

Axelrod's role in the preparation of the *Vademecum* was not one of his more memorable contributions to civilized political discourse. He dutifully sent Plekhanov the various letters and Prokopovich's manuscript, knowing that his colleague intended to publish them. He did have some misgivings about the publication of one of the letters, but these were tactical rather than principled.[107] Plekhanov was in so fero-

---

105. Plekhanov to Axelrod, Oct. 25, 1899, *Perepiska,* ed. Nicolaevsky, Berlin, and Woytinsky, II, 98.
106. Plekhanov, *Vademecum,* pp. vi, xxx, xli.
107. Axelrod to Plekhanov, Dec. 6–7, 1899, *Perepiska,* ed. Nicolaevsky, Berlin, and

cious a mood, however, that he did not listen to any arguments in favor of moderation. "I am doing the preface [to the *Vademecum*] only in order to defend you," he wrote Axelrod. "If we do not bring out the brochure, then it means that we acknowledge that you are wrong. But as a member of the Group for the Emancipation of Labor *you are infallible and you must not and cannot err* (you know, I am beginning to incline toward Jacobinism)."[108]

Axelrod had developed so intense an antipathy toward the young opponents that he did not even object to this extraordinary display of arrogance. After the *Vademecum* appeared he admitted to Plekhanov that, with the exception of Vl. Dm. and Vera Bonch-Bruevich, the entire Russian colony in Zurich was shocked, a reaction he dismissed as the same "old story . . . Evidently, the theoretical part of the brochure has penetrated their heads as little as peas thrown at a stone wall." He himself was delighted with it and had read it three times. He no longer believed that the conflict over popular literature was a central factor in the recent controversies; the major cause of the friction, which fully justified Plekhanov's campaign, was that in a "moral-political sense" the youngsters were "untrustworthy . . . That is why I am so skeptical about the congress."[109]

Axelrod's skepticism was well grounded. At first the discussions at the congress, held in April 1900, were conducted in a peaceful and civil manner. Then Iu. Steklov, who was to achieve fame after 1917 as the editor of *Izvestiia,* spoke in behalf of the veterans and accused the youngsters of "political opportunism," a charge that his adversaries were not prepared to let pass without a reply. They countered by criticizing the GEL, whereupon Steklov declared "that I am deeply disturbed when urchins, who have not looked in the eyes of a police officer, dare to abuse old, honored revolutionaries." With this statement, pandemonium broke loose on the floor of the congress. One of the youngsters, Bukhgolts, shouted "Comrades, we are being insulted," and threw himself at Steklov. Only the intervention of I. P. Goldenberg, who seized Bukhgolts, saved Steklov from physical assault. Then everyone jumped from his seat, and "twenty Economists" furiously moved toward Steklov, who remained in

Woytinsky, II, 100; Plekhanov to Axelrod, Dec. 8, 1899, *ibid.*, pp. 102–103; Axelrod to Plekhanov, n. d., *ibid.*, p. 107.

108. Plekhanov to Axelrod, Feb. 24, 1900, *ibid.*, p. 118; see also editor's note, *ibid.*, p. 119.

109. Axelrod to Plekhanov, n. d., *ibid.*, p. 124.

the middle of the room in close reach of a chair that he was ready to wield in self-defense. Fortunately for Steklov, he did not have to prove his prowess as a fighter. Although he refused to heed Teplov's advice to apologize for the insult, the youngsters did not deliver any blows. He and his friends were allowed to leave the hall. And so ended another brotherly socialist congress designed to restore harmony to the movement.

In the street Steklov met Plekhanov, who had left the congress as soon as the commotion had erupted. "You see, Iurii Mikhailovich," said Plekhanov with great agitation, "it is impossible to have anything to do with these gentlemen. Once they reach the point where they want to hit us, I consider it impossible to participate any further in the congress." Steklov tried to dissuade him, suggesting that his would-be assailants had compromised themselves by their conduct and that he had scored a major moral victory because he had not retracted his remarks. The youngsters also urged Plekhanov and his followers to return to the congress, promising that there would be no further incidents. But Plekhanov was adamant. He formally broke with the union and founded a new movement, The Revolutionary Organization "Social Democrat," and Axelrod followed his lead.[110]

The conflict between the veterans and youngsters now reached new heights of vindictiveness and pettiness. They quarreled over the disposition of a printing press, the archives, and other properties. Failure to reach agreement prompted the GEL to keep under lock and key the sixth issue of *Rabochee delo,* which had already been printed. The union countered by refusing to pay the rent for the room in which the GEL kept the press and the copies of the journal. Since the group had almost no financial resources, it was forced to compromise: the property was divided, and *Rabochee delo* was released, pending a final resolution of the dispute by a court of arbitration, which apparently never met.[111]

The consequences of the three-year campaign by Plekhanov and Lenin against Economism and Revisionism could only be deleterious to Russian Marxism. It introduced a method of political debate that, as Axel-

110. Iu. Steklov, "V ssylke i v emigratsii (ideinye konflikty)," *Proletarskaia revoliutsiia,* no. 17 (1923), 219–220.
111. For details, see Kol'tsov to Axelrod, Apr. 22, 27, 1900, Axelrod Archive, I.I.S.H.; *Sotsial-demokraticheskoe dvizhenie,* ed. Potresov and Nicolaevsky, pp. 305–315.

rod was to realize within a few years, was bound to destroy the possibility of an orderly settlement of differences. Opponents were discredited by attributing to them views they did not hold or by grossly distorting those they did. By 1903 this tactic proved successful in crushing the youngsters, and means that were successful once could be used again. And, indeed, the history of Russian Marxism after 1903 is so replete with controversies in which polemics, misrepresentation, slander, and vilification played such a great role that it is often difficult to ascertain their real source or nature.

This abrasive form of political discourse owed its origins to the rancor engendered during the first phase of the Economist conflict, when there existed essential differences of opinion. The conduct of both veterans and youngsters during the discussion of issues contributed heavily to creating an atmosphere of distrust and hostility. A larger share of the responsibility must be assigned to Plekhanov and Axelrod, who were older, more established, and more experienced and could therefore have been expected to act with greater understanding and flexibility. Their fatal flaw was their overbearing arrogance, born not so much of a lust for power as of total identification of their personalities with the movement they had created. They were, as a result, unable to acknowledge that a challenge to them might be anything other than a willful effort to derail the movement from its proper path. Axelrod suffered from this defect to a lesser extent than Plekhanov, but even he refused to meet the youngsters halfway. After 1903, when he was no longer as closely tied to Plekhanov, Axelrod showed considerably more tolerance toward people who differed with him on ideological matters. By that time, however, the damage to the movement had been done.

The youngsters exacerbated the dispute by frequently hiding the truth. Time and again they insisted that the decisive causes of the friction were related to organizational and personal matters. As late as 1900 the editors of *Rabochee delo* claimed "that the opposition arose and established itself firmly *mainly,* if not exclusively, because of organizational [questions]."[112] That is to say, the opposition's demands for a greater voice in running the affairs of the union and little else provoked the hostility of the veterans.

Yet in the very pamphlet in which they made this assertion they also

112. *Otvet redaktsii "Rabochago dela,"* p. 20.

admitted that they were at odds with the GEL over ideological issues. They disagreed with Axelrod's contention, stated in 1898, that the creation of a political organization of the proletariat was justified in Russia only if it accepted as its immediate goal the overthrow of the autocracy. Nor did they share Axelrod's optimistic view of the reliability of certain groups of landowners and zemstvo activists as oppositional forces. The youngsters held, instead, that the working class must direct itself first to the acquisition of such political rights as freedom of association, press, speech, and the inviolability of person, all preconditions for the further development of the labor movement. "Thus, the overthrow of absolutism is for us the result of a process of direct, practical struggle for immediate political demands."[113]

The advocacy of these views did not justify labeling the youngsters Economists or Revisionists. But until 1899 they did not openly and unambiguously concede that they differed at all with the GEL on theoretical questions. This was a serious mistake, for Axelrod and Plekhanov were too close to them not to realize that they entertained reservations about orthodox doctrines. Convinced that the youngsters were prevaricating, the veterans were led to assume the worst: that their adversaries harbored misgivings about many cardinal principles of Marxism.

The youngsters, in their denials of heterodoxy, probably acted out of a desire to avoid conflict and the belief that the substantive disagreements that did exist were minor. They were also convinced that if the veterans, especially Plekhanov, were not so quarrelsome harmony would prevail.[114] But this posture, which reflected their failure to appreciate the older men's sensitivity about matters of theory, was bound to engender distrust and sharpen the conflict. Candid discussion of views might not have eliminated controversy, but it would have reduced the chances of groundless charges and countercharges.

In sum, the clashes of the late 1890's, which were so momentous in their impact on the development of Russian Marxism, were rooted in a wide range of personal, political, and ideological factors. To single out any one as the sole cause or to hold either group wholly responsible is

113. *Ibid.*, pp. 22–25. Actually these views are similar to those the editors of *Rabochee delo* expressed in 1899 in the first issue of their journal. The main difference is that in 1900 the youngsters explicitly acknowledged that they had reservations about certain aspects of Axelrod's political position and tactics.

114. See the suggestive comments in *Sotsial-demokraticheskoe dvizhenie,* ed. Potresov and Nicolaevsky, p. 278.

to do violence to a complex series of events. Ideology and personality were too deeply entangled. It seems fair to conclude that, had the initial participants in the Economist conflict suspected how damaging their conduct might ultimately be to the movement, they would have recoiled in horror. We have here almost a classic example of human actions leading to totally unintended results.

Contemporaries were as baffled by the events at the time as are modern-day readers. On April 18, 1900, a group of sixteen Russian Social Democrats met in Paris to formulate a position on the recent split between the union and the GEL. The only resolution that could command majority support states that they should maintain relations with both parties "in view of the complete impossibility of ascertaining at the present moment the causes" of the rift.[115]

115. *Ibid.*, p. 306.

VI | The Birth of Menshevism

The GEL's resignation from the union appears on the surface to have been an act of courage. The group could boast neither adequate financial resources nor regular channels of communication with revolutionary circles in Russia, and it did not command sufficient manpower to form another organization that could hope to exert wide influence. Abandonment of the youngsters seemed to doom the veterans to political impotence. In actuality, however, the behavior of Plekhanov was not that heroic: the GEL knew that fresh forces were on the way from Russia.

In March 1900 Lenin, Alexander N. Potresov, and Iulii Martov, all talented, energetic, and experienced revolutionaries, met with two representatives of the Revisionist tendency in Russian Social Democracy, Peter Struve and M. I. Tugan-Baranovsky, in Pskov to discuss the founding of a new journal.[1] They planned to edit the journal in the West in conjunction with the GEL. By the end of April Potresov had arrived in Western Europe, to be followed three months later by Lenin. Martov remained in southern Russia until sometime in March 1901 to help set up a network of local committees sympathetic to the literary undertaking.[2]

Although Lenin, Potresov, and Martov considered themselves ortho-

1. For a comprehensive discussion of the complicated negotiations between the orthodox and Struve, who was at this time moving away from Social Democracy and becoming sympathetic to what was then called the "democratic opposition," see Richard Pipes, *Struve. Liberal on the Left, 1870–1905* (Cambridge, Mass., 1970), pp. 250–270. An agreement to cooperate was finally signed, but because of Struve's arrest in St. Petersburg in March 1901 the orthodox began to publish *Iskra* on their own. When Struve returned to the West at the end of 1901 the orthodox Marxists were no longer interested in collaborating with him. See *ibid.*, pp. 271–273.

2. Israel Getzler, *Martov: A Political Biography of a Russian Social Democrat* (Cambridge, Eng., 1967), pp. 45–47.

dox and expected to enter the lists against the union, it should be noted that before they arrived in Western Europe they had expressed misgivings about some of the positions taken by the GEL, especially by Axelrod. At the time, the differences did not generate friction between them, but some certainly portended later events.

Thus, in February 1899 Lenin told Potresov that although he agreed with the essentials of Axelrod's *The Historical Situation* he did not think that Axelrod had stressed sufficiently the "class character" of the proletarian movement. Instead of speaking of "*Unterstützung und Bundesgenossenschaft* [support and confederation]" with the liberals, Social Democrats ought to think of "utilizing" them. Axelrod's words implied "equality of rights" for the liberals, whereas he believed that they "ought (in this I am in full agreement with you) to march along in the rear, sometimes even 'while grinding their teeth'; they absolutely have not grown up enough [to be granted] equality of rights, and never will grow up enough, given their cowardice and splintered condition, and so on."[3] Axelrod had evidently been mistaken in his belief that in their talks in 1895 he had succeeded in definitively changing Lenin's mind about the role of the liberals.

Martov also found fault with a number of Axelrod's ideas. He believed that Axelrod had completely rejected the notion, stated in *Ob agitatsii,* that Social Democrats should exploit the daily antagonisms between workers and employers. In addition, he was so hostile to Axelrod's position on an accommodation between the proletariat and the bourgeois opposition that he planned to write an article criticizing it. But Lenin advised him that in view of the Economist and Revisionist controversies, of which Martov had been ignorant, it would be unwise to attack one of the defenders of orthodoxy. Martov agreed, so as not to give the appearance of siding with the "young practicals" or approving what Lenin called their strange ideas.[4]

Finally, the three were dismayed by the *Vademecum.* It was not that they disagreed with Plekhanov's general stand, but they could sanction neither the publication of private letters nor the vehemence of his attack. They feared that such methods would only produce further splits in the movement, which they were eager to avoid. Their negative reaction to

3. Lenin to Potresov, Feb. 26, 1899, *Sotsial-demokraticheskoe dvizhenie: materialy,* ed. A. N. Potresov and B. I. Nicolaevsky (Moscow, 1928), pp. 36–37.
4. Iu. Martov, *Zapiski sotsial-demokrata* (Berlin, 1922), pp. 399–402.

the *Vademecum* apparently motivated their insistence that the editorial office of the new literary venture be located outside Switzerland (first in Munich and then in London), the center of émigré quarrels.[5]

Although the decision offended Plekhanov and Axelrod, from the standpoint of efficiency it was undoubtedly wise. From the beginning there were bitter conflicts, and had the editors lived in the same vicinity it is likely that little would have been accomplished. The history of these feuds need not be detailed here, for it has already been excellently done by other historians.[6] It should be noted, however, that during the period 1900–1903 the main clashes were between Plekhanov, who displayed arrogance and pettiness unusual even for him, and Lenin, who was generally supported by Martov and Potresov. Axelrod and Zasulich, though they tended to side with Plekhanov, tried to exercise a moderating influence on him and rarely engaged directly in the debates, at least not with passion. Had anyone in the years 1900–1903 been prescient enough to prophesy a split among the six, he would surely have argued that the major protagonists would be Lenin and Plekhanov. That it turned out otherwise suggests that personal antagonisms may have played less of a role in the final schism than is often asserted, but this is a question to which we shall return in due course.

After extensive discussion and negotiation the group resolved to found a newspaper, *Iskra,* and a theoretical journal, *Zaria.* Of the six editors, five had one vote, and Plekhanov, at his own insistence, received two, which, it was assumed, would give him a controlling voice, as he could count on the support of Zasulich and Axelrod.

But Plekhanov miscalculated. For the decision not to edit the new publications in Switzerland gave the younger members of the editorial board an opportunity to exert major influence in determining their content; it had the same effect on shaping the overall course of party affairs. Although Plekhanov and Axelrod made occasional trips to Munich for policy discussions, most of the business had to be conducted by mail, a procedure that was bound to leave the day-to-day work to

5. B. N. [Nicolaevsky,] "Iz epokhi 'Iskri' i 'Zari,'" *Katorga i ssylka,* VI (1927), 30.
6. Samuel H. Baron, *Plekhanov: The Father of Russian Marxism* (Stanford, 1963), Chap. XII; Dietrich Geyer, *Lenin in der russischen Sozialdemokratie. Die Arbeiterbewegung im Zarenreich als Organisationsproblem der revolutionären Intelligenz 1890–1903* (Cologne, 1962), Chap. VII; Leopold Haimson, *The Russian Marxists and the Origins of Bolshevism* (Cambridge, Mass., 1955), Chaps. VII, VIII; J. L. H. Keep, *The Rise of Social Democracy in Russia* (Oxford, 1963), Chap. III.

those regularly in the office. After April 1902, when for almost a year the headquarters were in London, visits by the veterans became even rarer. This arrangement suited Lenin perfectly, for he was by far the strongest personality in the younger group and the most gifted organizer of them all. He assumed responsibility for procuring financial support for the group's activities, conducted correspondence with followers of *Iskra,* and, most important, created a network of agents under his personal direction.

Lenin saw the role of the party newspaper as much more than a means of indoctrination and dissemination of information: it was also to serve as a "collective organizer" for the party. That is to say, the people who supplied *Iskra* with material and who distributed it in Russia were also to establish local committees loyal to the editorial board and persuade existing committees to support it fully. Under Lenin's guidance, there was instituted the so-called "state of siege," which refers to the attempts by the paper's agents to secure a dominant position for the *Iskra* group in the Social Democratic movement. Those who indicated a desire to remain independent of the Iskrovtsy were attacked as enemies of the party, and if this failed to discredit them, a whole range of other techniques was used, most of which also violated the canons of fair play. The agents were masters at deception and intrigue, and by 1903 they helped make possible Lenin's successes at the Second Congress of the party.[7]

In addition to creating a pliant party organization, Lenin figured importantly in the other activities of the émigré Marxists. Aside from his work on *Iskra*—one of the best revolutionary papers ever published—and *Zaria,* he contributed much to drafting the party program and preparing the party congress. He also did an enormous amount of writing on a variety of subjects. Lenin was always a prodigious worker, but until 1917 he never again matched his achievements of the two years from 1901 to 1903.

Axelrod made no major impact on party affairs during this crucial period. He infrequently wrote for *Iskra,* and the one article he agreed to write for *Zaria* was completed too late for inclusion. His failure to submit a "foreign chronicle" he had promised *Iskra* prompted Lenin to

---

7. For a good description and analysis of Lenin's techniques, see Allan K. Wildman, "Lenin's Battle with *Kustarnichestvo:* The *Iskra* Organization in Russia," *Slavic Review,* XXIII (Sept. 1964), 479–503.

pester him for it. In July 1901 Lenin asked him to collaborate with Plekhanov on a draft program for the party, a request he readily agreed to carry out, but after spending some time on it he could not continue, so that his contribution was minor.[8] Nor does Axelrod seem to have participated in any significant way in the organizational work of the Iskrovtsy. All in all, the years 1900–1903 were a strikingly barren period in his life, particularly when his lack of productivity is compared to the achievements of most of the other editors.

By nature Axelrod was not nearly as productive as Lenin and Martov, and even during his most active years he could not have kept pace with them. But there were special reasons for his failure to exert greater influence on party affairs during the *Iskra* period. In 1898 his wife had become ill. Wrongly diagnosed at the outset as typhus, the ailment turned out to be tuberculosis. Zasulich was right in predicting that Axelrod would be crushed: "Pavel will be lost without her. It is impossible to imagine his living without her."[9] He was not only emotionally attached to her, but he also relied on her to help manage the kefir shop, in which he now had to spend more time.

These pressures, together with the unpleasantness of the feuds with the youngsters, adversely affected his health, which was never robust. In March 1900 Axelrod complained that for more than a year "I have . . . [suffered] from a kind of physical ailment that affected my disposition precisely the way paralysis would, or the withering of a limb, an organ."[10] Then, for the next three years Axelrod suffered from frequent attacks of neurasthenia. By early 1903 his wife's condition had seriously deteriorated: in addition to tuberculosis she had contracted a heart disease, a nervous disorder, and chronic sciatica. The illnesses kept Axelrod from party work, and he found it "agonizing . . . that during such a period as we Russians have experienced since the spring of 1901, I have remained inactive."[11]

8. Lenin to Axelrod, Dec. 7, 1900, *Leninskii sbornik*, ed. L. Kamenev (Moscow, 1924–1938), III, 115; Lenin to Axelrod, July 9, 1901, *ibid.*, pp. 192–193; *Pis'ma P. B. Aksel'roda i Iu. O. Martova, 1901–1916,* ed. F. Dan, B. I. Nicolaevsky, and L. Tsederbaum-Dan (Berlin, 1924), p. 45.

9. Zasulich to Plekhanov, n. d., 1898, *Gruppa "Osvobozhdenie truda,"* ed. L. Deich (Moscow, 1924–1928), VI, 210.

10. Axelrod to Kautsky, Mar. 18, 1900, uncatalogued, I.I.S.H.

11. Axelrod to Lenin, Oct. 15, 1900, *Leninskii sbornik*, ed. Kamenev, III, 64; Axelrod to Munich section of editorial board, June 6, July 12, 1901, *Pis'ma*, ed. Dan, Nicolaevsky, and Tsederbaum-Dan, pp. 39, 42–43; Axelrod to Lenin, Aug. 1902, *ibid.*, p. 77; Axelrod to Kautsky, Jan. 28, 1903, uncatalogued, I.I.S.H.

Considering the handicaps, it is amazing that Axelrod was able to participate at all in the work of the editorial board. A careful examination of his private correspondence reveals that he did more than he seems to have realized. As the person closest to the leaders of the German party, he was asked to seek financial aid from them. To his surprise, the Executive Committee of the German Social Democratic party turned him down on the ground that there were many Russian revolutionary groups and not all could be subsidized. Axelrod appealed to Kautsky to use his influence with the committee; after all, the Iskrovtsy represented the sole orthodox current in Russian Marxism.[12] This was the first of many attempts by Axelrod to persuade the German socialists that the circle with which he was identified was the only spokesman deserving support. Apparently he did not succeed in securing funds in 1901, but Axelrod's propaganda for his group was not completely wasted. Within a few years the Germans began to show interest in the activities of the Russian Marxists and to give them some material support.

More important, Axelrod took part in the editorial chores by regularly assessing manuscripts. He made extensive comments on them, proposing substantive as well as stylistic changes. He also gave the younger editors advice on matters of policy, though his opinion of their work was very positive. On receipt of the third issue he told them: "*Summa summarum*—the issue is excellently put together, and, I hope, it will reinforce and extend the impression made by the first issues." On the basis of its performance the editorial board had "a historical right to leadership over our movement."[13]

Yet there were numerous occasions when Axelrod criticized articles in *Iskra;* it is interesting that his objections were usually directed toward pieces written by Lenin. Thus, he indicated that he was "a bit shocked" by Lenin's demand, made in the third issue, that the *otrezki* (cutoffs) be returned to the peasants. The otrezki were the slices of land that had been tilled by the serfs before 1861 and were assigned to the landlords at the time the peasants were emancipated. Axelrod granted that the demand was a splendid agitational ploy, but he found it utterly utopian, a judgment that many came to share. After all, in the preceding

12. Axelrod to Kautsky, May 14, 1901, uncatalogued, I.I.S.H.
13. Axelrod to Lenin, Nov. 10, 1900, *Leninskii sbornik,* ed. Kamenev, III, 90–91; Axelrod to Lenin, Nov. 17, 1900, *ibid.,* pp. 104, 106; Axelrod to Munich section of editorial board, May 5, 1901, *ibid.,* p. 170; Axelrod to Munich section of editorial board, June 6, July 12, 1901, *Pis'ma,* ed. Dan, Nicolaevsky, and Tsederbaum-Dan, pp. 37, 41.

four decades the otrezki had been divided and then partly rented or sold, and it would have been immensely complicated now to return them to the peasants. Axelrod thought the rest of Lenin's article was excellent.[14]

From time to time Axelrod had misgivings about the way Lenin expressed himself. For example, he believed that Lenin's article in the fourth issue, in which he outlined his organizational principles for the first time, suffered from "diplomatic weaknesses."[15] A few days later, when asked whether a particularly polemical article by Lenin against Struve and the liberals should be published in *Zaria*, Axelrod declared once again that he was not pleased with the way Lenin formulated his views. It seemed to him premature to "speak in such a tone about how we want to use the liberals." But Axelrod was troubled by more than the tone of the article, for he also indicated that there was "a whole series of very important questions" that ought to be thrashed out by the editors. He sensed that Lenin "still had not entirely detached himself from certain primitive elements of Social Democracy."[16]

To Axelrod the basic flaw in Lenin's thinking was his failure to understand that the liberals, however weak, could bring about changes beneficial to the working class. For example, the zemstvos, in which liberals were a major force, by their very existence tended to promote "political ferment." It was true that the government might make some minor concessions in an attempt to split the opposition, as Lenin predicted, and that the moderate parties would "gain first and foremost from the existence of an extreme party," as claimed by Struve. The latter was no "slip of the tongue," as Lenin thought, but rather "a fully calculated lesson for the liberals, very useful for them and for us." Axelrod reminded his young colleague that even in the West reforms had been "halfhearted concessions designed to divide the opposition. And in

14. Axelrod to Munich section of editorial board, May 5, 1901, *Leninskii sbornik*, ed. Kamenev, III, 169; for a good analysis of Lenin's proposal concerning the otrezki, see Keep, *Rise of Social Democracy*, pp. 81–84.

15. Axelrod to Munich section of editorial board, July 7, 1901, *Pis'ma*, ed. Dan, Nicolaevsky, and Tsederbaum-Dan, p. 41. Axelrod was referring to the article "S chego nachat'?" (Where to Begin?) in V. I. Lenin, *Sochineniia* (3rd ed., Moscow, 1926–1937), IV, 107–113.

16. Axelrod to Plekhanov, n. d., but late in July or early Aug. 1901, *Perepiska G. V. Plekhanova i P. B. Aksel'roda*, ed. B. I. Nicolaevsky, P. A. Berlin, and W. S. Woytinsky (Moscow, 1925), II, 157. Axelrod wrote this letter in response to one by Plekhanov, which was also critical of Lenin. *Ibid.*, p. 154.

actuality, did this prevent or does this prevent the radical democracy or revolutionary proletariat from utilizing them, in part as positions from which to attack the existing system, [and] in part as weapons and evidence to illustrate its internal contradictions and instability [?]" Despite these misgivings, Axelrod refused to vote against the publication of Lenin's article on the ground that there ought to be a *"freie Diskussion"* of issues in *Iskra.* Lenin took into account some of the criticisms and toned down a few of his formulations, but the article still bristled with hostility toward the liberals.[17]

There is other evidence of conflict between Axelrod and Lenin during this period. In the first few months of 1902 Plekhanov and Lenin were at loggerheads over the drafting of the party program, and Axelrod, though he tried to urge compromise on Plekhanov, generally sided with him.[18] But the episodes pained him, probably because the quarrels were as often caused by collisions of powerful personalities as by theoretical differences. At one meeting Axelrod appeared to be trying to avoid taking sides. Just as the editorial board was about to vote on one item of the program, on which Axelrod had declared his agreement with Lenin, he said that he had a headache and needed to go out for a walk. It seemed to Lenin that Axelrod was leaving simply for fear of offending Plekhanov, and in a state of agitation he exclaimed, "It is impossible to work like this." Then he publicly deplored the introduction of personal considerations in reaching decisions on party matters.[19]

The wrangling was too much for Axelrod. Late in May 1902 he drafted a letter of resignation from the editorial board. He intended to explain his action by pointing out that he was prevented from writing by poor health and from participating actively in the editorial work by being so far from Munich.[20] He confessed privately, however, that he was motivated by other factors. He told Lev Deich that "by nature I am

17. Axelrod to Munich section of editorial board, July 19, 1901, *Pis'ma,* ed. Dan, Nicolaevsky, and Tsederbaum-Dan, pp. 48–50. The article in question was Lenin's "Goniteli zemstva i annibaly liberalizma" (Oppressors of Zemstva and Hannibals of Liberalism), *Sochineniia,* IV, 119–157. On this article, see Pipes, *Struve,* pp. 276–277. Lenin to Axelrod, July 26, 1901, *Leninskii sbornik,* ed. Kamenev, III, 219.

18. For details on the conflict between Plekhanov and Lenin over the program, see Baron, *Plekhanov,* pp. 223–230, and Haimson, *Russian Marxists,* Chap. VIII.

19. N. Krupskaia, "Iz vospominanii (1901–1902 g.g.)," *Leninskii sbornik,* ed. Kamenev, III, 47.

20. The draft of Axelrod's letter of resignation is reproduced in *Perepiska,* ed. Nicolaevsky, Berlin, and Woytinsky, II, 178.

not suited for the present politicking." He also complained that the younger editors had made it clear to him that they did not take his opinions seriously. "And to remain (officially) on the editorial board under such conditions—means consciously to condemn myself to a humiliating role of a zero." Although his resignation would give rise to a rash of rumors and might harm the movement, the responsibility rested with those who "with their crude disregard of me as a person and my rights make it impossible for me to remain any longer on the editorial board." He suspected that some of his colleagues actually wanted him to resign. If they did not, then they must make it clear that he would be a member enjoying all the rights exercised by the other editors and that his views would not be disregarded.[21]

Axelrod did not specify how his views had been ignored, but in referring to the "crude disregard of me as a person" he probably had in mind Lenin's recent attack on him at the meeting of the editorial board. A comment Plekhanov made in reply to the letter just quoted lends weight to this interpretation: "Your opinion is not taken into consideration simply because . . . [Lenin] is very obstinate. *Your role on the editorial board is not involved here.*" Plekhanov then pleaded with Axelrod not to go through with his resignation, for that would make it all the more difficult to fight against Lenin's obstinacy, "which can do much harm."[22] Axelrod heeded his friend's advice and did not send the letter.

One of the most puzzling aspects of this period in the history of Russian Social Democracy is the failure of the older Marxists publicly to voice serious criticisms of Lenin's ideas on the organization of the party, which he had first developed in 1900 but elaborated most extensively in 1902 in *What Is To Be Done?* which was soon to be one of the most important and controversial works of the movement. One Soviet historian has made much of the fact that at the time of its appearance the pamphlet did not give rise to disagreement, and in her memoirs, Krupskaia, Lenin's wife, claimed that in 1902 the future Mensheviks, especially those who were close to Lenin, were "thrilled" with it.[23] These assertions deserve to be scrutinized because they imply that the criticisms of *What Is To Be Done?* advanced by people such as Axelrod after

21. *Ibid.,* p. 177; Axelrod to Plekhanov, July 2, 1902, *ibid.,* pp. 179–181.
22. Plekhanov to Axelrod, July 5, 1902, *ibid.,* p. 181.
23. See V. Nevskii's review of the first volume of *Letopis' revoliutsii,* in *Proletarskaia revoliutsiia,* no. 15 (1923), 317–318; Krupskaia, "Iz vospominanii," p. 46.

1903 were motivated not by principle but by opportunistic considerations.

This implication is particularly noteworthy in view of the fundamental theoretical innovations Lenin introduced into the body of Marxist
doctrine. Lenin reached his conclusions gradually, beginning in 1899,
as a result of his disillusionment with the industrial proletariat, which
had grown into an independent force and was adopting trade union
tactics. In 1899 he also learned of the Credo as well as of the adoption
of Revisionism by a few Russian Social Democrats. These events pre-
cipitated a profound crisis in Lenin, leading him to speculate on the
need for new organizational procedures and, ultimately, to compose
What Is To Be Done?[24]

Although designed basically as a critique of Economism, the pamphlet
turned out to be a blueprint for the organizational structure of the Russian Social Democratic party. Lenin's major theoretical point was that
the working class could not spontaneously develop socialist consciousness. Without help from the intelligentsia, proletarians would become
trade unionists and fall prey to bourgeois ideology. "The theory of socialism," he wrote, "was developed by the intelligentsia and could be
brought to the workers only by them . . . only from outside the labor
movement." This blunt formulation is a striking modification of Marx's
view that class consciousness of the workers would spontaneously emerge
as a result of the economic conditions under which they lived. But in
itself, the statement, while it may have seemed overly dogmatic and un-
sophisticated, probably did not trouble Axelrod too much. After all, he
had, in response to the Economists, argued that the intelligentsia must
imbue the workers with Social Democratic principles.

The novel point in *What Is To Be Done?* was Lenin's attempt to
create an organizational framework based on his views, which implied a
commitment to permanent tutelage of the proletariat by the intelligentsia. Thus, in effect, the pamphlet declared a lack of faith in the capacity
of the proletariat as a class ever to attain that degree of consciousness
necessary for it to take a decisive part in the coming revolutionary
events without outside leadership.

Specifically, Lenin repeated his thesis that an all-Russian newspaper

---

24. On Lenin's crisis, see the analysis by Richard Pipes, "The Origins of Bolshevism: The Intellectual Evolution of Young Lenin," in *Revolutionary Russia*, ed. Richard Pipes (Cambridge, Mass., 1968), pp. 45–50.

such as *Iskra* should serve as the center of the party network. This center must be composed chiefly of "professional revolutionaries" who were thoroughly schooled in Marxism and engaged in no work other than preparing for the revolution. They were not, moreover, to be elected representatives of a specific constituency. They were self-appointed leaders who took upon themselves the selection of other people capable of serving in leading positions in the party. The center was to guide the movement, as Leopold Haimson has put it, "on the narrow and precipitous path that alone would lead to the socialist era." Mass labor organizations such as trade unions could be of service to the revolutionary party, but they were not to enjoy membership in it nor to participate in the determination of its policies.[25]

Axelrod's failure to repudiate these elitist views publicly in 1902 is not easy to explain. He and Plekhanov discussed their reservations about the brochure, and although their exact nature is not known, they seem to have been serious. "In general," Axelrod wrote early in 1902, "in certain respects . . . [Lenin's] work seems to me [to suffer from] important defects and a kind of maximalism." Plekhanov proposed that they exert pressure on Lenin to make changes, but Axelrod declined, a decision he regretted by March 1902.[26] At a personal meeting with Lenin, Axelrod apparently did raise some objections to the pamphlet, but, as he complained to Martov in May 1902, they were ignored: "Indeed, I was struck by how little our general remarks were taken into account." He acknowledged that he had presented his comments in condensed form, which may have made it difficult for Lenin to perceive the changes he was recommending. It is possible that Axelrod did not spell out his objections because he himself did not yet understand all the implications of Lenin's views, which were, after all, rather alien to anyone steeped in Social Democratic thought. Yet, Axelrod could not help being impressed by how little Lenin "tries to grasp the critical comments of his *close* comrades."[27]

25. I have deliberately confined myself to a brief discussion of Lenin's *What Is To Be Done?* because there are several excellent analyses of it. See Haimson, *Russian Marxists*, pp. 133–138; Adam Ulam, *The Bolsheviks. The Intellectual and Political History of the Triumph of Communism in Russia* (New York, 1965), pp. 176–182; Bertram D. Wolfe, *Three Who Made a Revolution. A Biographical History* (New York, 1948), pp. 156–166.

26. Axelrod to Plekhanov, end of Feb. or early Mar. 1902, *Perepiska*, ed. Nicolaevsky, Berlin, and Woytinsky, II, 165; Plekhanov to Zasulich, n. d., *ibid.*, p. 167.

27. Axelrod to Martov, May 30, 1902, *Sotsial-demokraticheskoe dvizhenie*, ed. Potresov and Nicolaevsky, p. 90.

When all the bits of evidence indicating that Axelrod objected to *What Is To Be Done?* are pieced together, they still amount to a meek protest. The truth is that throughout the *Iskra* period, whenever he differed with Lenin—and occasionally the disagreements touched on subjects he felt strongly about—Axelrod went out of his way not to offend. Why was he so timid? In part, he was no doubt motivated by a reluctance to quarrel with a friend; generally Lenin responded in kind. In his letters he was always solicitous about Axelrod's health and often warmly invited him to visit Munich.[28] However much they differed in political styles or over ideological matters, neither wanted a showdown.

But probably the most important reason for Axelrod's failure to speak more forcefully was his fear of destroying the unity of a group that was entitled to the leadership of Russian Marxism. Whatever Lenin's personal or ideological shortcomings, he still professed to be defending orthodoxy. Much of the pamphlet was in fact an attack on the Economists, whom Axelrod had for several years regarded as the chief threat to the movement. When Lenin asked Axelrod to read the first section of it in manuscript form, he referred to it as "my pamphlet (book?) against the Economists," which Axelrod evidently believed. In it Lenin made several favorable references to Axelrod's writings, as he had on earlier occasions, and to his polemics with the Economists in the late 1890's.[29] Even as modest a man as Axelrod might be softened by well-designed flattery.

In considering unity so important Axelrod was not unique among the Iskrovtsy. There is no doubt that the other editors were able to iron out their numerous differences only because they wished to prevent the disintegration of the group.[30] In view of all that we know about the friction among them, their ability to collaborate for as long as they did must be taken as a sign of remarkable self-restraint.

Whatever the reasons for Axelrod's failure to speak out in 1902 and 1903 against Lenin's organizational views, there is no merit to the sug-

28. Lenin to Axelrod, Dec. 14, 1900, *Leninskii sbornik*, ed. Kamenev, III, 122; Lenin to Axelrod, June 1, 1901, *ibid.*, p. 181; Lenin to Axelrod, July 9, 1901, *ibid.*, p. 192.

29. Lenin to Axelrod, Dec. 23, 1901, *ibid.*, p. 284. In 1901 Lenin referred to Axelrod's *The Historical Situation and the Reciprocal Relations between Liberals and Social Democrats in Russia* as an "extremely thorough elucidation" of the political significance of the zemstvos in the struggle for political freedom. See Lenin, *Sochineniia*, IV, 152.

30. For a discussion of one interesting conflict over a matter of party ethics, see Getzler, *Martov*, pp. 66–67. On the other clashes, see the sources cited in note 6, above.

gestion that he was ever sympathetic to them. Evidence in support of this conclusion can be found in a response he wrote early in 1903 to a request by Victor Adler for information about recent developments in Russia and the role of Russian Social Democracy. Although it was never completed, probably because his wife's condition suddenly deteriorated and they spent several months in Italy, the draft he produced contains an extensive account of his views on the major issues of the day.[31]

By far the most noteworthy statement in it deals with his conception of what the revolutionary party in Russia could "do and achieve." Its main purpose, Axelrod declared, was "politically to enlighten and organize the laboring masses so that they will be able as much as possible to participate in the struggle against absolutism as a conscious and independent force." Then, more significantly, he contended that the "revolutionaries from the intelligentsia" should "strive socially and politically completely to dissolve [verschmelzen] into the proletariat, to merge themselves in its struggle for emancipation. And in this way they should transform the revolutionary party, the party of action par excellence into a workers' party, so that the revolutionary and labor movements will coincide, will more truly become one and the same thing." This conception of Social Democracy is drastically at variance with the organizational views developed by Lenin in What Is To Be Done? Axelrod clearly regarded the prevailing situation, under which the party was composed and run by a small group of intellectuals, as a temporary interlude that must give way to the creation of a genuine labor movement controlled by the workers themselves.

Having said this, Axelrod added a statement that reveals that, despite his reservations, he really had not yet fully grasped the contents of Lenin's brochure nor the significance of Lenin's achievement in setting up his network of agents and local committees in Russia: "The efforts and activities of the Social Democrats have been and are directed toward this goal [creation of a workers' party]. As a matter of fact, they have gone quite far toward the realization of this goal." Within a year he was to retract this assertion in its entirety.

For the rest, Axelrod's assessment of the Russian political situation was very much in accord with his views of 1897 and 1898, though he ac-

31. Perepiska, ed. Nicolaevsky, Berlin, and Woytinsky, II, 189; Axelrod to Adler, Feb. 17, 25, 1903, Kautsky Archive, I.I.S.H. Axelrod sent these letters to Kautsky because he planned to use them as the basis for an article for Die Neue Zeit.

knowledged that developments had not proceeded in quite the way he had anticipated then. Since 1901 discontent with the autocracy had been manifesting itself with increasing intensity, but the Social Democratic party had not been strong enough to figure prominently in the disorders. (Elsewhere he placed much of the blame for the party's weakness on the Economist controversy, which he believed had confused the movement.[32]) Even the zemstvos and the landlords, on whom Axelrod had counted heavily, had not demonstrated much initiative in these events. To his surprise, students had given the protests their impetus, but he did not believe that their social base and program were broad enough for a sustained national effort. The disorders, however, could trigger oppositional activity in other social strata.[33]

Despite the ferment, Axelrod did not expect a major disturbance comparable in scale to the great French Revolution "either this year or next." If the Social Democratic movement was inadequately prepared and organized, the liberals were even less so. They had entered the "illegal arena of struggle" as a "mere literary group," and then they had developed a very modest program. "And even for this appearance [on the historical scene] liberalism had to select as its spokesman someone from the ranks of the Marxists [meaning Struve]." Still, it seemed to him that the widespread disaffection signified that "Russia is already on the eve of its period of bourgeois revolution" or in the very early stages of that period. Axelrod foresaw a long and complicated process during which the tsarist Empire would gradually change.

He agreed basically with the analysis of the liberal journal *Osvobozhdenie,* which predicted that the initial concessions to popular pressure would probably be the establishment of a *Rechtsstaat* (state based on the rule of law) and the convocation of a constituent assembly of representatives from the zemstvos and city officials, a kind of assembly of notables. For the labor movement such concessions would be far from sufficient, but in characteristically realistic fashion Axelrod refused to

32. Axelrod to Martov, Mar. 31, 1901, *Pis'ma,* ed. Dan, Nicolaevsky, and Tsederbaum-Dan, p. 20.
33. Axelrod also developed this theme in "Zarozhdenie u nas burzhuaznoi demokratii kak samostoiatel'noi revoliutsionnoi sily" (The Origins of Our Bourgeois Democracy as an Independent Revolutionary Force), written in 1902 for *Zaria* but published four years later in Pavel Axelrod, *Bor'ba sotsialisticheskikh i burzhuaznykh tendentsii v russkom revoliutsionnom dvizhenii* (2nd ed., St. Petersburg, 1907), pp. 1–32.

dismiss them as worthless: "Now I do not want to deny that the introduction even of such a representative institution could be of great significance for the further development of Russia, and the existence and deliberations of even such an assembly would already signify an essential rupture with tsarist absolutism . . . [or] at the very least a deep and wide breach in that structure."

Axelrod reiterated that in order to extend these reforms "all elements of the opposition should form a coalition and temporarily put aside those considerations that divide them." It was almost with a note of regret that he argued against a "general covenant of love [*allgemeinen Liebesbund*]" between oppositional groups on the basis of a common program, but in view of past class conflicts, which could not be forgotten, such a strategy was "nothing less than utopian."[34]

In 1903, then, Axelrod continued to advocate essentially the same ideas he had held throughout the 1890's. Ever since 1900, however, Lenin had moved further and further away from the principles of European Social Democracy by setting forth his new organizational views. This divergence underlies and informs the clashes between them during the next decade and a half.

It is difficult to think of any other event that in its own time appeared as insignificant as the Second Congress of the Russian Social Democratic Workers' party (RSDRP), and yet turned out to be one of the major turning points in history. Late in July and during August of 1903, close to sixty revolutionaries representing at best a few thousand supporters met, first in Brussels, and then in London, for the purpose of uniting at least twenty-six groups into a firmly consolidated political party. The congress was to adopt a program, elect party committees, and decide a series of tactical and organizational questions. Very few of those in attendance were aware that the organizers did not represent a unanimous bloc and were shocked beyond belief when the six editors split into two warring factions, which soon came to be known as Bolsheviks (majoritarians) and Mensheviks (minoritarians). The shock was made greater by the complicated nature of the debates, which were almost incomprehensible to some delegates. As soon as the congress adjourned, participants and others in the movement began to search for an explanation

34. Axelrod to Adler, Feb. 17, 1903, Kautsky Archive, I.I.S.H.

of the split. The consequences of the confusion that resulted were staggering and are still with us. Even now disagreement abounds on what would appear to be relatively simple questions.

Did the rift take place primarily because of personal differences among the six editors of *Iskra*? Were they involved in nothing more than a power struggle? Or were they motivated in their maneuvers and debates at the congress by concern with vital ideological matters? And if the latter was the case, what was the nature of the doctrinal conflict?

A cursory examination of the detailed protocols of the Second Congress tends to substantiate the conclusion that the delegates were involved in nothing more than a feud over influence in the party. For on the first issues under discussion, some of which were of major theoretical importance, the editors were solidly united. They all opposed the proposal of the General Union of Jewish Workers in Russia and Poland (known as the Bund) that the party be organized as a federation of national parties, a scheme that was designed to grant the Bund autonomy in matters of specific interest to the Jewish community. Not one of the editors supported the youngster, A. S. Martynov (Pikker), who during the discussion of the party program delivered a long and perceptive speech criticizing *What Is To Be Done?* "If earlier our movement suffered from disorder and primitive techniques of work [*kustarnichestvo*]," Martynov averred, "then during this period [1900–1903], as a counterpoise, there was promoted . . . a conspiratorial, Jacobin plan of organization, which in essence is suitable not for a class party of the proletariat but for a radical party leaning on ill-assorted revolutionary elements."[35] Another youngster, Akimov (Vladimir Makhnovets), offered numerous amendments to the program, all designed to introduce democratic procedures, but none was accepted.

The mood of the early sessions is best illustrated by Plekhanov's well-known remark that "Every democratic principle must be considered not by itself, in the abstract, but in its relation to that principle which may be called the fundamental principle of democracy, namely, *salus populi suprema lex*. Translated into the language of the revolutionary, this means that the success of the revolution is the highest law." Plekhanov went on to declare that for the sake of the revolution he would violate every democratic principle, including that of the "inviolability of the

---

35. *Vtoroi s'ezd RSDRP: Protokoly* (Moscow, 1959), p. 119. For a vivid account of the congress, see Wolfe, *Three Who Made a Revolution*, pp. 230–248.

individual." The speech was greeted by applause, though some delegates hissed.[36] Beyond this, there was virtually no negative reaction to
Plekhanov's remarkable statement, which must have pleased Lenin
enormously. Axelrod, who could hardly have been overjoyed, said nothing: this was one occasion on which he did not heed Plekhanov's earlier
request to warn him against succumbing to his Jacobin inclinations.
Whether his silence stemmed from a sense of loyalty to an old friend or
from reluctance to break the unity of the Iskrovtsy is difficult to say.

Given the degree of harmony among the six editors on these vital issues, it is strange that they should have fallen out over what appeared
to be the minor question of defining a party member. In part the acri-
monious exchange on the floor of the congress was a consequence of a
clash that had taken place between Martov and Lenin at a caucus of the
Iskrovtsy, when they quarreled over the selection of individuals to the
future Central Committee (C.C.). Martov tried to prevent Lenin from
packing the committee with a majority of his followers, which was not
the sort of challenge that could be accepted with equanimity by Lenin,
who was determined to achieve a preeminent position in the unified
party.[37] By the time the Iskrovtsy returned to the congress feelings ran
high, and in the tense atmosphere the protagonists were bound to be
particularly sensitive to the slightest suggestion of deviation from doctrine.

During the debate over party membership Axelrod, who was a delegate with a consultative voice—that is, without a vote—for the first
time spoke at some length. Even though a few of the arguments he advanced resembled those of the Economists Martynov and Akimov, he
found it necessary to repeat them, presumably because he believed that
one could not attach much weight to criticisms from that quarter. Even
if they were right, they only wanted to replace one heresy with another.
But in the debate over party membership the danger to the movement
came from within the orthodox camp itself. Precisely because the new
threat was not an open attack, but a distortion of orthodoxy in the
name of orthodoxy, it was that much more difficult to detect and combat. It is probably for this reason that he decided to speak up. In addition, public opposition to Lenin did not burden him with the same

36. *Vtoroi s'ezd RSDRP*, pp. 181–182.
37. Getzler, *Martov*, pp. 77–78.

personal problems as public criticism of Plekhanov, a friend of more than twenty years.

The momentous debate began on August 15, at the twenty-second session of the congress, when Lenin and Martov introduced rival drafts of the first paragraph of the Organizational Statutes, which was to define a party member. Lenin's formulation stated that membership entailed recognition of the party program and support "by material means and personal participation in one of the party organizations." Martov's draft was identical to Lenin's except that his replaced the phrase quoted with the words: "by material means and regular personal assistance under the direction of one of its organizations." To the uninitiated the difference may seem trivial, but the first speaker on the question, Egorov (E. Ia. Levin), immediately went to the heart of the matter by asserting that the two formulations represented divergent concepts of the party. Lenin's narrows it, and Martov's broadens it "to the point where it opens the door to 'democratism.' We must not forget that we, being a conspiratorial organization, are at the same time bound to the masses. I fear that 'b' does not necessarily follow 'a.' "[38]

Axelrod, the second to speak, elaborated the argument briefly stated by Egorov. He emphasized the importance of distinguishing between the concepts of party and organization. "But here the two concepts are lumped together. This blending is dangerous." He recalled that Zemlia i volia and Narodnaia volia, both centralized and conspiratorial organizations, had tried to surround themselves with as many sympathizers as possible, all of whom could join the party though not necessarily the organization. This principle seemed to him even more applicable to a Social Democratic movement. In elucidating this point he gave an example that later provoked some sarcastic comments. Suppose, he said, that there is a professor in Russia who considers himself a Social Democrat, but does not wish to participate regularly in the activities of one of the party's organizations. Although Axelrod did not elaborate, he obviously thought the academician might consider formal membership too risky. If Lenin's definition were adopted, such a person would be excluded. Thus, "we will throw overboard some of those people who, even though they cannot be taken directly into the organization, never-

38. *Vtoroi s'ezd RSDRP,* pp. 262, 425. It is surprising that Egorov subsequently voted for Lenin's draft, but after the congress became a Menshevik.

theless are members of the party." The example might seem farfetched, but we know of one well-established professor who rendered the Marxists valuable services, and there may well have been others of a similar inclination.[39]

Axelrod clearly stated that the main task confronting Russian Marxists was the creation of an organization of the "most active elements of the party, an organization of revolutionaries." He granted that not all persons belonging to the party would be suitable for "a fighting organization, strictly organized, consisting of professional revolutionaries." But he pointedly reminded the congress that the Social Democratic party was a class party: "We must not consider leaving outside the party people who consciously though perhaps not entirely actively are affiliated with this party."[40]

Lenin intervened only three times in the discussion, and he tried to appear reasonable and conciliatory. He defended his wording by stressing that he merely intended to stimulate the drive to organize a party and assured the delegates that he did not mean to suggest that *only* professional revolutionaries could belong to it. "We need very diverse organizations of all types, ranks, and shades, beginning with extremely narrow and conspiratorial and ending with very broad, free *lose Organisationen*." This did not represent a departure from the position he had taken in *What Is To Be Done?* in which he had argued that the organization should consist *chiefly* of professional revolutionaries. But he ended his first speech on this question with the following revealing sentence: "The necessary sign of a party organization is confirmation of it by the Central Committee."[41] The C. C. was surely to be composed of professional revolutionaries, and, as we have noted, Lenin made every effort to control its membership. There could therefore be little doubt that he intended to exercise a decisive voice in determining the composition of the party as a whole.

In his response to Lenin's seemingly conciliatory statement, Axelrod revealed that he, too, could be ambiguous and give the appearance of sweet reasonableness. He declared that Lenin's formulation of the first

---

39. Axelrod may have had in mind Professor M. M. Tikhvinsky of the Polytechnical Institute in Kiev. Tikhvinsky collected "considerable sums of money" for the party and performed other services for the movement. See Nikolay Valentinov, *Encounters with Lenin*, tr. Paul Rosta and Brian Pearce (London, 1968), p. 3.

40. *Vtoroi s'ezd RSDRP*, pp. 262, 267.

41. *Ibid.*, p. 265.

paragraph was "in principle a direct contradiction of the very essence of the tasks of a proletarian Social Democratic party" (he could hardly have leveled a more serious indictment), but he immediately added that in view of Lenin's explanation that there could be a "periphery of circles" belonging to the party, he might have been "knocking at an open door." Thus, although there remained some unresolved questions, "it may still be possible to bargain a little."[42]

The discussion continued for several hours. Martov, of course, made a spirited defense of his draft, and several speakers supported him.[43] But Plekhanov once again gave free rein to his Jacobinist proclivities: he declared that the debate had convinced him that Lenin had the better case. He publicly criticized and ridiculed Axelrod and in the process distorted his friend's position. He could not understand, he said, why any professor sympathetic to Social Democracy should find it humiliating to join one of the party's local organizations, which was not at all what Axelrod had said. Then Plekhanov quoted a comment Engels had once made to him: "When you deal with a professor, you must first prepare yourself for the very worst," which was greeted with laughter. Continuing to poke fun at Axelrod's "extremely unfortunate" example, Plekhanov quipped that "we do not need" the kind of "professor of Egyptology" who, because he "has memorized the names of all the Pharaohs," considered it beneath his dignity to join the party.

In a more serious but no less nasty vein he also declared that "Axelrod was wrong" about the organizational structure of the revolutionary movement in the 1870's. At the time there was "chaos, anarchy" among those groups that did not belong to the organization, a situation that Social Democracy must avoid. Toward the end of the speech he disclosed his main reason for supporting Lenin's formulation: it would not prevent workers from joining the organization because they did not fear strict discipline. It might keep out many intellectuals afflicted with "bourgeois individualism. But this is good. These bourgeois individualists are usually also the representatives of every kind of opportunism."[44]

In his longest speech on the subject, Lenin showed far more flexibility than Plekhanov, and he did not make any offensive personal remarks. On the contrary, he went out of his way to respond to Axelrod's "ami-

42. *Ibid.*, p. 267.
43. For Martov's argument, see Getzler, *Martov*, pp. 78–79.
44. *Vtoroi s'ezd RSDRP*, pp. 271–272.

able (I say this without irony) proposal . . . 'to bargain a little.' I would readily respond to this appeal, for I do not at all consider our difference so vital that the life or death of the party depends on it. We will certainly not perish because of one bad point in the statutes." His wording was, nevertheless, preferable to Martov's, which would open the door "to all elements of disorder, vacillation, and opportunism." As the party grew in size, it would be increasingly threatened with an influx of unreliable people, who ought to be kept out. It would be better to exclude ten workers (though he did not think that "genuine workers" would be driven away) than to allow one "babbler" into the party. "Our task," Lenin concluded, "is to protect the steadfastness, firmness, purity of our party. We must strive to raise the title and importance of a party member higher, higher, and higher—and therefore I am against Martov's formulation."[45]

These were scarcely the comments of a man who believed the issue was of minor significance, as he had suggested at the beginning of the speech. And when, to his surprise, he lost to Martov's wording by a vote of twenty-three to twenty-eight, he was furious, all the more so because Zasulich and Potresov sided with the majority, which put Lenin in a minority among the editors of *Iskra*. He now resolved to create his own "hard" faction, split with the "soft" Iskrovtsy, and gain control over all the important organs and committees to be selected by the congress. Lenin's subsequent moves, which bore the earmarks of a naked power play, dominated the remaining sessions. Because these moves were filled with drama and stirred the passions of a great many delegates, people tended to forget that the initial conflict among the Iskrovtsy on the floor of the congress involved substantive ideological questions.

Luck and shrewd tactics made it possible for Lenin to turn his minority into the narrowest of majorities. The Bund withdrew from the congress because it had not been granted autonomy: this removed five of the majority's twenty-eight votes. Then Lenin introduced a resolution to dissolve *Rabochee delo* and recognize *Iskra* and its organization as the only legitimate spokesman for Russian Social Democracy abroad. Martov and his supporters, who considered themselves loyal Iskrovtsy and opponents of the Economists, could not vote against this motion. When it carried, the two delegates from *Rabochee delo,* who had also voted for

45. *Ibid.,* pp. 275–278.

Martov's formulation of the first article, walked out. Henceforth Lenin could count on majorities in support of his proposals, but his margin of victory was always small. He never received more than twenty-five of the remaining forty-four votes. Even though he could not claim the support of a majority of the delegates who had originally come to the congress, and even though he had lost on the one issue that had divided the editors, Lenin proceeded to name his followers the Bolsheviks and his opponents the Mensheviks. As Bertram Wolfe has aptly pointed out, it was a stroke of brilliance for him to have used these terms, for they gave the impression that he represented the predominant sentiment of the congress. At the same time, his opponents were remarkably inept to have acquiesced in being called Minoritarians, especially because strictly speaking the designation was inaccurate.[46]

At the congress Lenin set off the greatest excitement and resentment by calling for the election of a new editorial board for *Iskra*, composed of three people, Plekhanov, Martov, and Lenin himself. Martov and the three who were to be purged—Zasulich, Axelrod, and Potresov—announced that they would temporarily absent themselves from the sessions to give the delegates freedom to discuss the sensitive issue. Plekhanov and Lenin could do no less, and on their departure "there arose an incredible noise in the hall, nothing could be heard."[47] The delicacy of the matter cast the delegates into acute discomfort: they had been asked to discard people who had already become legendary figures in the revolutionary movement.

Lenin's supporters argued that removing three of the editors should not be regarded as an adverse judgment on them. Occasional changes in personnel were necessary in any party, and the delegates should only be concerned to select the men most capable of serving the cause. Given the previous dispute and the rumors that were circulating, however, this line of reasoning persuaded few people. As V. E. Mandel'berg put it: "By electing from the old editorial board three individuals . . . we thereby enter into and *cannot but enter* into an analysis and judgment about the role of one or another editor in the creation of *Iskra* . . . By electing three from the six people of the old editorial board, you thereby acknowledge that the other three are unnecessary, superfluous. And you have neither the right nor the basis for doing this." N. A. Krasikov, one of Lenin's

46. Wolfe, *Three Who Made a Revolution*, p. 244.
47. *Vtoroi s'ezd RSDRP*, p. 359.

loyal supporters, unintentionally lent weight to this assessment when he told the assembly that "a board of six might turn out, as a board, to be incapable [of functioning]." This statement, like many others during the discussion, was received with "noise" by the audience.[48]

Krasikov doubtlessly based his comment on information Lenin had given out at the secret caucus of his followers. Exactly what transpired at that meeting is not known, but it is likely that Lenin made the charges there that he incorporated in a memorandum shortly after the congress adjourned. In it he pointed out that not one of the forty-five issues of *Iskra* had been edited by anyone other than Martov or himself. Outside of Plekhanov, no one had discussed any theoretical questions in the paper. "Axelrod did not work at all": he had published nothing in *Zaria* (which was a half-truth, as he had completed an article too late for inclusion in what turned out to be the last issue) and only three or four pieces in *Iskra*. Similarly, Lenin concluded, Zasulich and Potresov had contributed next to nothing.[49]

It is hard to conceive of Axelrod as not having been profoundly distressed by the affair. His lack of productivity had bothered him for some time. Lenin's insensitivity to his plight was therefore sure to offend him, but Plekhanov's having backed Lenin must have been devastating. It was only a year earlier that Axelrod had intended to resign. At that time Plekhanov had done his best to dissuade him because he needed an ally against Lenin, and he felt "that you sometimes can prevent our comrades from taking a false step."[50] Now Plekhanov not only ignored all that, but by supporting Lenin's move to oust the three editors he actually bolstered the case against Axelrod. It is perhaps a measure of the depth of Axelrod's pain that he never mentioned the episode in any of his published works or—and this is even more telling—private letters.

Lenin, sensing that he had overreached himself, finally delivered a speech defending his proposal. His initial statement that the elections to the editorial board were not designed to tarnish anyone's reputation evoked one of the stormiest outbursts at the congress: "Shouts: 'Untrue! Untrue!' Plekhanov and Lenin protest against the interruptions. Lenin requests the secretary to note down in the protocols that comrades

---

48. *Ibid.*, pp. 363, 364, 367.
49. Lenin, *Sochineniia*, VI, 57–58.
50. Plekhanov to Axelrod, July 1, 1902, *Perepiska*, ed. Nicolaevsky, Berlin, and Woytinsky, II, 178.

Zasulich, Martov, and Trotsky interrupted him, and requests that [the secretary] jot down how many times he was interrupted." Lenin publicly affirmed a disclosure made a day earlier by one of his lieutenants, N. E. Baumann, that Martov approved the changes in the editorial board. This added to the confusion, as Martov promptly issued a categorical denial. The only person, Lenin said, who had ever raised any objection to his suggestions was Axelrod, and he had not done so formally but privately. "It goes without saying that a protest to the editorial board does not call for private remarks."[51] When it suited his purposes, Lenin could adhere strictly to formal procedures.

The proposal to elect only three editors was ultimately adopted by a vote of twenty-five to two, with seventeen abstentions, which was not a resounding victory for Lenin. When the congress proceeded to elect Plekhanov, Lenin, and Martov as editors, another crisis erupted. Martov, in an exhibit of admirable courage and candor, refused to serve. Although before the congress was convoked he had urged Lenin to stage a coup d'état and create central organs under the control of the Iskrovtsy, he had justified these measures as necessary during the "state of seige" and because of the threats to orthodoxy that he believed to exist. Once a strong party with the proper ideological orientation was created he apparently felt these methods could be discarded. He certainly never assumed that Lenin would direct his coup at old, trusted members of the organization. "To all intents and purposes," he told the delegates in explaining his refusal to serve as editor, "the entire authority of the party is transferred to the hands of two people [Lenin and Plekhanov], and I value the title of editor too little to agree to be with them in the capacity of a third."[52] When Kol'tsov, who had received three votes, also refused to serve, the congress voted to allow the two editors-elect to co-opt a third.

In effect, the party had been split. There were still long deliberations and extensive haggling over the composition of the Central Committee and the procedure for electing it. But Egorov spoke for many delegates when he expressed surprise that people were still paying lip service to matters of principle when discussing voting procedures. Was it not obvious by now that the congress was simply trying to find ways of securing the major positions on the central organs for a certain group

51. *Vtoroi s'ezd RSDRP*, pp. 372, 373.
52. Getzler, *Martov*, p. 82; *Vtoroi s'ezd RSDRP*, p. 375.

of people? "Let us acknowledge," he bluntly declared, "that principles were long ago lost at this congress, and let us call things by their real names." Amid general laughter, Egorov added that everyone knew that there existed at the congress a "compact majority" of twenty-four votes that casts its ballots "as one man, at the signal of its leader."[53] Then the compact majority proceeded to elect a Central Committee of three people—twenty delegates refused to vote—and after hastily adopting a series of resolutions, the congress adjourned.

Although Lenin had outmaneuvered his opponents and gained control of the major party organs, his victory was less momentous than he seems to have believed. A substantial group of party members supported the Mensheviks,[54] who, proclaiming that "we are not serfs," refused to cooperate either with the newspaper or the party committees and began to form their own organizations. Among the Menshevik opponents of Lenin could be counted most of the gifted writers and many seasoned party activists.

Then, in quick succession, Lenin suffered two major defeats. First, from October 25 to 31, 1903, there took place a meeting of the Foreign League of Russian Revolutionary Social Democracy, which had been formed in 1901 as a counterpoise to the union and had been recognized by the Second Congress as the only foreign organization of Russian Social Democrats. The deliberations touched on all the issues that had arisen at the recent meeting, but with one important difference: instead of a minority, the Mensheviks held a small majority of the votes. By now the bitterness had become almost unbearable to the protagonists and occasionally reached the level of the absurd. Thus, Bonch-Bruevich, one of Lenin's followers, complained: "I call attention to the fact that when Comrade Martov addresses us he calls us 'Gentlemen!' . . . But we in our statements call him 'comrade.'" It is significant that the league adopted a resolution drafted by Axelrod, Potresov, Martov, and Zasulich critical of Lenin's "bureaucratic centralism," and this time the Bolsheviks refused to participate in the vote.[55]

53. *Vtoroi s'ezd RSDRP*, pp. 378–379.

54. Actually, the terms Menshevik and Bolshevik were not generally used—at least not without quotation marks—until sometime in 1904, but for convenience I shall employ them to describe the factions from the time of the adjournment of the Second Congress.

55. *Protokoly II ocherednogo s'ezda zagranichnoi ligi russkoi revoliutsionnoi sotsial-demokratii* (Geneva, 1904), pp. 76, 84–89.

The second blow inflicted on Lenin was delivered by none other than Plekhanov, who early in November decided to co-opt the four former editors of *Iskra* onto the new editorial board. He had apparently concluded that the party could not be run on the basis of Lenin's dictatorial methods and had also learned that Lenin—whom he now called Robespierre—had begun to intrigue against him.[56] Plekhanov's decision prompted Lenin to resign from *Iskra,* giving the Mensheviks control of the newspaper. Martov was elated, claiming that "Lenin was crushed,"[57] surely one of the most premature pronouncements ever of a politician's demise.

The Mensheviks had, nevertheless, staged an impressive recovery which inspired them with confidence about their faction's future. In November 1903 Fedor Dan, a leading Menshevik, proclaimed: "In Russia itself our position also has many supporters, and their number will continue to grow, all the more so when the Russian organizations begin to feel directly the impact of modern 'centralism' [Lenin's organizational scheme]. And unfortunately it will not take long before this happens."[58] But the recovery of the Mensheviks had taken a heavy toll. The charges and countercharges, boycotts of party committees, and endless intrigue had made a shambles of the party. The substance of the dispute had become almost totally submerged in a torrent of name-calling and mutual recrimination. In addition, the reputation of many party leaders had been blemished, most notably that of Plekhanov, who had suddenly undergone so dramatic a change of heart. As Dan wrote to Axelrod, the "most respectable" of Plekhanov's followers no longer held him in esteem. "Plekhanov's 'historic' change did not particularly enhance his reputation."[59]

The fierce infighting during the weeks immediately following the Second Congress detracted from the Menshevik cause in particular. By constantly attacking Lenin as a would-be dictator as well as crude, tactless, ruthless, and intolerant, the Mensheviks augmented his importance. No Russian Social Democrat could doubt any longer that he was a figure

56. On the various intrigues and developments immediately following the Second Congress, see Keep, *Rise of Social Democracy,* pp. 133–148.
57. Martov to Axelrod, Nov. 4, 1903, *Pis'ma,* ed. Dan, Nicolaevsky, and Tsederbaum-Dan, p. 97.
58. Dan to Kautsky, Nov. 12, 1903, Kautsky Archive, I.I.S.H.
59. Dan to Axelrod, Nov. 15, 1903, Axelrod Archive, I.I.S.H.

to be reckoned with. The concentration on personal vilification further played into Lenin's hands by seeming to confirm his insistence that the Mensheviks were motivated not by principle but wounded feelings, hurt pride, and private resentments. As early as September 13, 1903, Lenin wrote Potresov that none of the issues that had emerged at the congress was serious enough to warrant a split. In public he constantly referred to his opponents as opportunists given to distortion and unworthy conduct. In her memoirs Krupskaia reveals the opinion of those around Lenin that Axelrod's distress resulted only from his removal from the center of the movement.[60]

It should also be noted that the protocols of the Second Congress were not published until early in 1904, so that during the first few months after the split even those party members who might have taken the trouble to read the voluminous document could not do so. Social Democrats who had not attended the congress relied on eyewitness accounts, which tended to make short shrift of the dispute over the first paragraph of the Organizational Statutes and emphasize instead the conflict over the composition of the Central Committee and the relationship between various committees.[61]

None of the leading participants seems to have been able to converse coherently about the events leading up to the rift. O. A. Ermanskii, who became fairly important in the Menshevik movement, described his confusion when he tried to find out the causes of the schism. Soon after learning of the controversy he went to the West to question the protagonists. He visited Lenin, Plekhanov, and Martov, among others. "To all the questions about the causes of the schism," Ermanskii related, "I received answers that made a depressing impression on me: [talk about] such [matters] as 'fives,' 'threes,' co-optations, etc. Such were the conversations with *dii majores*. The meetings with *dii minores* made an even more painful impression on me."[62] It seemed to Ermanskii that the question uppermost in the minds of the protagonists was the composition of the various committees (to which the numbers referred) that

60. Lenin to Potresov, Sept. 13, 1903, *Sochineniia*, VI, 41–43; Krupskaia, "Iz vospominanii," p. 41.

61. See, for example, the two letters by delegates reprinted in B. N—skii [Nicolaevsky], "K istorii II s'ezda RSDRP," *Katorga i ssylka*, no. 27 (1926), 125–130; see also N. Trotsky, *Vtoroi s'ezd ros. sots.-dem. rabochei partii. Otchet sibirskoi delegatsii* (Geneva, 1903), p. 13.

62. O. A. Ermanskii, *Iz perezhitogo (1887–1921 g.g.)* (Moscow, 1927), p. 68.

would run the party. A sordid power struggle appeared to have divided the leaders of Russian Marxism.

Insofar as there was any discussion of issues, it touched on peripheral subjects. For several months Martov allowed himself to be diverted by the Leninists into a "debate on the merits of 'hard' and 'soft' centralism." Other Menshevik writers, while admitting that the party's organizational work between 1901 and 1903 had been flawed by the use of ruthless tactics, believed that formal changes in the party structure alone could correct the defects.[63]

As long as the issue between the factions was defined in these terms, the possibility of speedy reconciliation could not be ruled out. Consequently, during the endless meetings on tactics in the fall and winter of 1903, the Menshevik leaders paid much attention to the terms that might be acceptable. Axelrod was an active participant in these discussions, frequently traveling to Geneva to attend sessions of the secret bureau of the Menshevik faction.[64] He was not in principle opposed to reconciliation, but late in September 1903 he warned his colleagues not to ignore the "interests, strivings, and mood of the opposition that had declared its solidarity with us." On no account should they enter into an understanding that appeared merely to satisfy their personal grievances. Although they might not be able to secure concessions that would realize all their "rational demands," it was essential that they wrest concessions from the Bolsheviks that would "open up for us a legal path for the full satisfaction of our demands." In other words, he was willing to yield on some points (which he did not specify) as long as a party structure was created that would permit the Mensheviks to introduce changes they considered necessary. At the very minimum and as a start, he proposed that the old editorial board be restored and that new members—obviously Mensheviks—be co-opted into the Central Committee. To underline his resolve to democratize the decision-making process, he insisted that any understanding be ratified by a meeting attended "at the least" by all those in the oppositional camp who lived in Geneva. The central point

---

63. Getzler, *Martov*, p. 86; Martov's preface in M. Cherevanin [F. A. Lipkin], *Organizatsionnyi vopros* (Geneva, 1904), pp. 4–14; see also the resolutions adopted by a group of Menshevik leaders in September 1903 in *Pis'ma*, ed. Dan, Nicolaevsky, and Tscderbaum-Dan, pp. 94–96, which stress the need to change the composition of the major party committees, but do not touch on any ideological questions.

64. Axelrod, Martov, Dan, Potresov, and Trotsky were the members of the bureau. See *Pis'ma*, ed. Dan, Nicolaevsky, and Tsederbaum-Dan, p. 104.

of Axelrod's line of reasoning was to stress that for the Mensheviks the jockeying for influence in the movement was far more than a hankering after power and prestige.[65]

But instead of reaching agreement, the factions stepped up their campaigns against each other. Under the circumstances, Axelrod sensed that the dialogue between the Mensheviks and Bolsheviks had taken a dangerously wrong turn. To rectify the situation, he undertook a long and detailed analysis of the conflict. His two-part article on the subject appeared in *Iskra* in December 1903 and January 1904 and immediately caused a stir in the movement.

Considering the climate of hostility in which the article was written, the reader finds striking its lack of polemics and personal innuendo. Axelrod directed his remarks at both factions and tried to place his discussion in the broadest possible context. Thus, the name of Lenin, the archvillain as far as the Mensheviks were concerned, is not even mentioned. Axelrod was not concerned to expose the moral defects or political mistakes of individuals; rather, he charged the entire orthodox leadership with responsibility for the chaos in the party.[66] In effect, he now repudiated the methods of conducting party affairs to which he himself had acquiesced for three years.

In addition he did not want the impression to remain abroad that the friction at the Second Congress was caused by the technical question of formal organization of the party. His choice of a title—"The Unification of Russian Social Democracy and Its Tasks"[67]—indicates his belief that the crisis in the party was generated by issues touching on no less than the ultimate nature and direction of the movement. Despite its nonpolemical style, the essay was clearly designed to respond to *What Is To Be Done?* and the party institutions Lenin had founded during the previous three years.

65. Axelrod to Potresov and Martov, Sept. 23, 1903, *ibid.*, p. 93.

66. At the Fourth Congress in 1906 Axelrod pointed out that at the time of publication his article was misunderstood as a critique of the Bolsheviks only. "I often declared then in private discussions and at meetings, and I now repeat, that in my article I criticized our entire party. The schism at the Second Congress and the organized tactics of the Bolsheviks . . . only served to stimulate . . . criticisms that I undertook in the article, with the aim of substantiating and outlining the main features of our tactics in the era of struggle against the autocracy." *Chetvertyi (ob'edinitel'nyi) s'ezd RSDRP: Protokoly* (Moscow, 1959), pp. 256–257.

67. Pavel Axelrod, "Ob'edinenie rossiiskoi sotsialdemokratii i eia zadachi," *Iskra*, no. 55 (Dec. 15, 1903), no. 57 (Jan. 15, 1904).

Axelrod's central theme was that there had emerged in the party a contradiction between its subjective aims and the objective reality of its composition and activities. From the beginning, Russian Marxists had aspired to the same result as international Social Democracy: "The development of the class consciousness and political initiative of the laboring masses, the unification of them into an independent revolutionary force under the banner of Social Democracy." Relevance to this subjective goal had always been the yardstick by which Russian Marxists judged their tactics and, indeed, all their activities. Objectively, however, what kind of organization had they actually created?

By concentrating on technical problems, Russian Marxists had spawned a party apparatus inconsistent with Social Democratic ideals. Party members had been encouraged to specialize in ever smaller functions, all of which were rigidly defined and hierarchically arranged. Endless party offices, departments, sections, chancelleries, and workshops had been created. In short order, most of the activists had been converted into "section and department chiefs, officials in chancelleries, sergeant majors, noncommissioned officers, privates, [and] guards." This large army, Axelrod continued, was divided into a "whole series of scattered anthills, each isolated from the other, and swarming about in one corner, without any links with the other." There could be no thought of political work in a genuinely "socialist-revolutionary sense . . . when all party members had been transformed into screws and wheels of an apparatus that is run by an omniscient center according to personal discretion."

This was the sharpest indictment of Lenin's views and activities anyone had made so far. It struck many readers as plausible because it did more than describe a deplorable situation: for the first time the background of the crisis was exposed. Axelrod interpreted the plight of the party—that is, its domination by the intelligentsia—as the result of a "spontaneous historical process, which had given rise to the Social Democratic movement in Russia and had determined for quite a long time its character and social content." Or, as he phrased it elsewhere in the article, "history did not come close to dealing with us as we had wished. The major role it assigned to our movement, behind our backs, was not ends but means: [history] furnished us not with basic principled tasks but with historically more elementary tasks . . ." And without first attending to the means, the formation of a party, "it was not *objectively* possible consistently and thoroughly" to concentrate on the primary goal, the creation of a politically mature working class. Thus, there "was introduced into the development of Russian Social Democracy the contradiction that runs through all its phases like a red thread."

The "organizational fetishism" had emerged at a time when the party was threatened by the divisive, anti-Marxist tendencies of Economism, Revisionism, and opportunism. The deficiencies of these tendencies had become evident at the turn of the century, when large numbers of people had begun to agitate against the autocracy. Because they were inadequately organized and had little understanding of the importance of a broad campaign against the regime, the masses might easily have been absorbed by a bourgeois organization and the Marxists relegated to insignificance for some time to come. The attempts of the Iskrovtsy to put an end to "organizational anarchy" and unite all Social Democrats into a centralized party were therefore an understandable and even necessary phase. The success of the campaign against the heretics, however, led many of its advocates to believe that centralism was the answer to all the movement's problems. Centralism became for them a fetish that could eliminate all the party's "flaws and defects"; in "centralism they see a kind of talisman that works . . . panacean wonders." In Axelrod's view, the psychological predisposition toward centralism underlay the behavior of many delegates at the Second Congress: it explained why they were so passionately aroused when the debates dealt with details of the statutes, the composition of committees, and the relations between various party organs.

What the majority of the delegates had not realized was "that the viability of the new organization will be directly proportional" to the kind of ideals with which it is imbued. In elaborating this point, Axelrod again compared the Russian and Western labor movements. The European movements were largely composed of workers, who had been able to develop class consciousness on their own. In Russia, by contrast, Social Democratic ideas had to be brought to the masses *"from without"* by an alien social element, the radical intelligentsia, which constituted a bourgeois stratum. But if the intelligentsia were to exercise permanent tutelage over the proletariat, "we would be facing a revolutionary political organization of the democratic bourgeoisie which would use the Russian workers as cannon fodder." In saying this, Axelrod turned upside down the Leninist thesis that the proletariat, left to its own devices, would not advance beyond bourgeois trade unionism. For he argued that the maintenance of Lenin's organizational structure would also subordinate the workers to the bourgeoisie.

The Russian workers could avoid this undesirable outcome, Axelrod declared, only through maximum involvement in the activities of public institutions and their own party. "The active intervention in social and political life is . . . the best, not to say only, school for the development of the class consciousness of the proletariat." Every effort should be made to draw as many workers as possible into "active participation in those spheres of social life, in which until recently even in the West only the representatives of the upper classes were the bosses." In other words, the proletariat's capacity to act independently and responsibly would grow to the extent that it was provided with the experience of coping with specific issues and making and acting upon political decisions.

Axelrod conceded that in urging radical intellectuals to create a party in which they themselves would cease to dominate he was making an unprecedented demand, but he believed it to be realistic all the same. This could not have happened in the West, he explained, because Social Democracy had developed after the intelligentsia had abandoned its "revolutionary-democratic idealism" and become tied to the politically influential bourgeoisie. On the other hand, the Russian middle classes persisted in a state of "political passivity," and the revolutionary intelligentsia was therefore estranged from them. Alienated and isolated, these radicals could be counted on to devote themselves to the cause of the only class committed to fundamental change: the proletariat.[68]

Axelrod's and Lenin's concepts of the party could not have been more at variance with each other: Lenin favored a small, restrictive membership, Axelrod the largest one possible; Lenin advocated a hierarchical structure with control exercised at the top, Axelrod decision making by the rank and file; Lenin stressed the importance of discipline in the organization, Axelrod the development of the political initiative of the masses. Both distrusted spontaneity, and both looked to the intelligentsia to blunt it, but in Lenin's view it was the party professionals who were to be prepared for the revolution, whereas in Axelrod's it was the masses. In short, their conceptions were bound to come into conflict because one was an elitist and the other a democratic approach to politics.

With his article in *Iskra* Axelrod laid bare the ideological dimension

68. *Ibid.*

of the controversy between Menshevism and Bolshevism. As he saw it, the dispute revolved around much more than the most effective way to build a potent political machine. In fact, had this been the only issue the disagreements between the factions would not have been critical. After all, the Mensheviks agreed with the Bolsheviks—and continued to do so even after the Second Congress[69]—that under the conditions prevailing in Russia a centralized party was unavoidable.

According to Axelrod, the argument did not involve the organization of the party so much as the organization of the proletariat. Thus formulated, the haggling over the first paragraph of the Organizational Statutes assumes fundamental ideological importance, for it touched on the question of the class character, and therefore political orientation, of the movement. Axelrod made specific his belief that Menshevism deserved to be maintained as a separate political tendency only insofar as it strove to transform Russian Marxism. His faction, he wrote in May 1904, could justify "its right to existence only by infusing a new spirit into the positive work in Russia itself," by beginning to "revolutionize our party practices."[70]

There is one problem which, though always implicit in nearly all the writings of Russian Marxists, became more pivotal than ever before as a result of Axelrod's emphasis on the proper organization of the proletariat: if the socialist revolution could not be staged in the near future, why should the workers risk joining the Social Democratic movement? Why not let the middle class bear the brunt of the struggle? In the *Iskra* article Axelrod anticipated these questions, and the brief answer he gave was similar to a point he had often made—that the extent of the workers' social and political gains when the old regime was liquidated would depend on the influence they had exerted on the course of the bourgeois revolution.

A few months before he wrote the article, in a speech at the Second Congress, Axelrod dealt more elaborately with this theme, and in the process he developed a new and potentially appealing thesis. Although

69. See the resolution Axelrod, Martov, Potresov, and Zasulich introduced at the Second Congress of the Foreign League of Russian Revolutionary Social Democracy. The Mensheviks emphasized that under prevailing conditions in Russia a "strictly centralized organization" was needed. *Protokoly II ocherednogo s'ezda zagranichnoi ligi*, p. 84.

70. Axelrod to Potresov, May 21, 1904, *Sotsial-demokraticheskoe dvizhenie*, ed. Potresov and Nicolaevsky, p. 121.

the "objective course of economic development" did not make it possible for Russia to skip over the capitalist phase into socialism, nevertheless, he suggested, conditions were such that the Russian proletariat could "at least skip over the phase of ideological and political subordination to the bourgeois political parties." In the West the working class had been doomed "blindly to follow the left factions of the bourgeoisie" for a long time after the elimination of the "feudal-monarchical system" because it had been disorganized and politically unaware during the bourgeois revolution. Afterward, the revolutionary ideologists were forced to expend considerable energy and time freeing themselves and the masses from this tutelage. Since the Russian working class would be trained to act as an organized force during the bourgeois revolution, it would skip this historical stage and thus "speed the triumph of socialism over capitalism."[71]

Some twenty years earlier Plekhanov had made a similar point, but he had not spoken of the possibility of skipping a stage.[72] Axelrod seems to have been the first to use this terminology, anticipating Trotsky by about a year. Had he suspected that in so doing he would prompt other Marxists to recommend bypassing any number of stages, it is likely that he would have refrained from using that expression, but it is easy to see why he was tempted to make a point of the possibility of shortening the "road to socialism."

The Mensheviks responded to the publication of Axelrod's article in *Iskra* with elation. Nikolay Valentinov, who was then at the center of Social Democratic intrigue and had a phenomenal memory for details, recalled that the piece "made a tremendous impact on the Menshevik camp and . . . [was] spoken of as 'famous.'" Martov, he wrote, referred to it as a "magnificent Marxist analysis of the development of our party."[73] Trotsky hailed it as marking "the beginning of a new era in our movement" because it imparted the need for changing "the center of gravity of [our] work."[74] Peter Garvi, in later years one of the more

71. *Vtoroi s'ezd RSDRP*, p. 405.
72. G. V. Plekhanov, *Sochineniia*, ed. D. Riazanov (2nd ed., Moscow, 1923–1927), II, 337–338; see also the analysis in Jonathan Frankel, "The Polarization of Russian Marxism (1883–1903): Plekhanov, Lenin and Akimov," in *Vladimir Akimov on the Dilemmas of Russian Marxism*, ed. Jonathan Frankel (Cambridge, Eng., 1969), pp. 10–11.
73. Valentinov, *Encounters with Lenin*, pp. 117–118.
74. N. Trotsky, *Nashi politicheskie zadachi* (Geneva, 1904), p. 25.

important Menshevik *praktiki,* explained that Axelrod's analysis made such a strong impression because it was only after reading it that Russian Social Democrats appreciated the depth of the conflict between Menshevism and Bolshevism. "It was," Garvi exulted, "as though lightning had cut through the thick darkness and had lit up with a dazzling light an entire neighborhood—to the furthest distance. It was then that Menshevism became conscious of itself, understood the schism, found its ideology, hoisted its banner."[75] *Iskra* immediately adopted Axelrod's theme and hammered it home in issue after issue.

Since Garvi was an admirer and eventually a close friend of Axelrod, it might be argued that his judgment should be discounted. But the article's effect on some of the leading Bolsheviks was intense, apparently because they feared it might influence party activists and win them over to Menshevism. Although Lenin by 1904 had developed a strong dislike for Axelrod and referred to him as a "scarecrow," he nevertheless grudgingly granted him "some prestige in the party." It is therefore not surprising that when Lenin received the second half of Axelrod's article he became "so furious that he was like a tiger" and called it the "nastiest muck I've ever had to read in all our party literature . . . Axelrod has spat on three years' work of *Iskra,* on everything it has achieved . . . Only a dolt or a madman could dare write such nonsense."[76]

Even before he read the second section Lenin wrote the Central Committee that the first portion was "very much viler" than an article Martov had recently published on the Second Congress. "Apropos of this article [by Axelrod] I again and again appeal to all members of the [Central Committee]: is it really possible to let this go without a protest and struggle? Do you really not feel that, enduring this silently, you are transformed into neither more nor less than transmitters of scandals . . . and into spreaders of calumny (concerning bureaucrats, i.e. you yourselves and the entire majority)? And under such 'ideological leadership' you consider it possible to do 'positive work'?" Krupskaia, too, disdained "Axelrod's absurd article . . . The baiting of Lenin's ideas proceeds along all lines."[77]

75. P. Garvi, "P. B. Aksel'rod i men'shevizm," *Sotsialisticheskii vestnik,* no. 15/16, Aug. 18, 1925, 11. For another laudatory statement, see Parvus to Axelrod, Jan. 1904, *Sotsial-demokraticheskoe dvizhenie,* ed. Potresov and Nicolaevsky, pp. 108–109.
76. Valentinov, *Encounters with Lenin,* pp. 115, 120, 137.
77. Lenin, *Sochineniia,* XXVIII, 320. Lenin was referring to Iu. Martov's "Nash

In response to the *Iskra* article Lenin issued his sharpest attack to date on the Mensheviks. *One Step Forward, Two Steps Back: The Crisis in Our Party* was so polemical that his colleagues on the Central Committee were shocked and made him agree in writing never again to publish anything in the name of the Central Committee without its approval.[78] Despite the abundance of vilification in the pamphlet, it is significant for openly admitting to differences of substance between the Bolsheviks and Mensheviks. During the first few months after the congress Lenin wavered considerably in his assessment of the split, as he had in his comments at the meetings themselves. On the one hand, as we have already noted, he denied that the dispute concerned basic principles. But, late in October 1903, he conceded that the controversy over the first paragraph was "not at all insignificant." Early in December he reiterated this point when he said that the "only real controversy of principles that definitely divided both 'sides' (i.e. majority and minority Iskrovtsy) was the controversy over paragraph 1 of the party statutes." The differences between him and Martov over the composition of the committees "touched on comparatively very private details" and did not produce "any definite groupings among the Iskrovtsy."[79]

Although in *One Step Forward* Lenin denounced Axelrod and his colleagues for opportunism on the organizational question and accused them of moving the party toward "anarchist individualism," he could not confine himself to verbal assaults. Somehow he had to answer Axelrod's charge that his conception robbed the party of its proletarian content. He did this by turning the tables on the Mensheviks and charging them with having abandoned Marxist orthodoxy. He identified them as the reformist wing of the Russian party and asserted that in all countries this wing represented a social group not only alien to the proletariat but hostile to its interests as well. He indicated, moreover, that he did not object to being called a Jacobin. "A Jacobin," he declared, "who is inseparably linked to the *organization* of the proletariat which is conscious of its class interests—this is a revolutionary Social Democrat." Then, in an obvious attack on Axelrod, he proclaimed that "a Girondist

s'ezd" (Our Congress), *Iskra*, no. 53 (Nov. 25, 1903); Krupskaia to L. M. Knipovich, Jan. 1, 1904, *Leninskii sbornik*, ed. Kamenev, X, 149.

78. Keep, *Rise of Social Democracy*, p. 141.

79. *Protokoly II ocherednogo s'ezda zagranichnoi ligi*, p. 48; Lenin, *Sochineniia*, VI, 130–131.

who yearns for professors and high school students, who is afraid of the dictatorship of the proletariat and who sighs over the absolute value of democratic demands—this is an *opportunist.*"[80] If Lenin's pamphlet did not raise the debate to lofty theoretical heights, it did attempt a higher level of rebuttal than mere invective.

The pamphlet is also of interest for its implicit recognition of Axelrod as a presence worthy of contention. In fact, only with the publication of his article in *Iskra* did he emerge as an independent leader of Russian Social Democracy with a distinct ideological position and a secure personal following. Until 1903 Axelrod lived under the shadow of the more brilliant and renowned Plekhanov. But the break between them at the Second Congress gave Axelrod a measure of personal freedom he had never before enjoyed. He no longer felt the need to obtain Plekhanov's approval before airing his views; this sense of independence must have been reinforced by Plekhanov's critical remarks immediately after the congress. Privately he called Axelrod a "cripple, a man who had become completely valueless to the party."[81] Given the incredible intrigue of those months, when gossip and slander seemed to be the order of the day, it would have been miraculous if someone had not informed Axelrod of Plekhanov's slur against him.

In any case, in his letters to his colleague Axelrod now expressed himself less discreetly than in the past. Thus, in the spring of 1904, when Plekhanov leveled some rather farfetched charges against Trotsky and the other editors of *Iskra*, Axelrod did not hesitate to reply with rebukes of his own. "Does the expression of opinions different from yours really signify [an attempt systematically] to 'outvote' you? I confess that I do not understand this." He denied Plekhanov's "fantastic assumption" that he and the other Mensheviks were trying to embarrass him and refused to violate his own conscience by supporting him on issues about which they disagreed. Finally, Axelrod warned Plekhanov that his conduct would have the "consequence of intensifying even more the anarchy and discord within the party."[82] The letter attracts attention not because Axelrod disagreed with Plekhanov, but because of the self-con-

---

80. Lenin, *Sochineniia,* VI, 219, 303, 305.
81. Valentinov, *Encounters with Lenin,* p. 193.
82. Axelrod to Plekhanov, Mar. 31, 1904, *Perepiska,* ed. Nicolaevsky, Berlin, and Woytinsky, II, 199; for the background to this letter, see Isaac Deutscher, *The Prophet Armed: Trotsky: 1879–1921* (New York, 1954), pp. 86–87.

fident and even imperious tone in which he registered his disagreement.

From early 1904 on, Axelrod was his own master in political affairs. Although he esteemed other Menshevik leaders, especially Martov, Potresov, and Dan, and regularly consulted them, they did not have sufficient standing as theorists to be able to inhibit him from voicing his own opinions. In a sense, Axelrod may be said to have begun a new career as an independent revolutionary leader in 1904, at the age of fifty-four.

Axelrod's manner of conducting political discourse proved to be a source of strength for him. He seems to have been one of the few leaders of Russian Social Democracy who during this early period could regularly discuss politics without displaying excessive passion or abuse. An episode described by Valentinov deftly illustrates this characteristic.

During the first months of 1904 Valentinov frequently addressed émigré meetings, always defending Lenin and criticizing the Mensheviks. He generally reserved his strongest attacks for Axelrod. On one of his trips to Geneva, Axelrod, quite by chance, rented a room in the hotel where Valentinov was staying. Again, by chance, the two were seated next to each other at lunch, where they met. Axelrod not only was very polite, but invited Valentinov to visit him. "Do come to my room for coffee," Axelrod said. "I have plenty of various things to eat for breakfast. Do a great favor to an old man. I left Russia long ago, so I probably don't know enough of what's happening there, great and small." Valentinov could not refuse. They talked at length, but Axelrod, aware that his guest was a confirmed Bolshevik, deliberately avoided all reference to the split in the movement.

Valentinov was embarrassed by Axelrod's behavior. "He punished me for the rude things I had said about him at meetings by being kindness itself. The lesson was pretty painful." He tried to apologize, but Axelrod cut him off: "Don't let us bring that up! All kinds of things are said in anger. There's nothing wrong with that. In my youth I was very argumentative, too." Lenin, on hearing about the encounter, reproached Valentinov for apologizing. "Akselrod," Lenin said, "is very good at buttering people up on the sly. You should not have apologized to him. It was a blunder, a great blunder! They [the Mensheviks] are always calling us all the names under the sun, so they should not complain if we hit back. We must not stand on ceremony with them. It was a blunder, I'm telling you." Lenin looked upon his political adversaries as persons with whom cordial, or even correct, relations were inconceivable. Axelrod, however, believed in a far more flexible and conciliatory approach, which was especially appreciated by younger members of the movement.

A year after the initial encounter, Valentinov, who had by then broken with Lenin, met Axelrod again. They spent a whole day discussing party affairs; Valentinov finally asked Axelrod why he had avoided the subject of Lenin and the schism at their first meeting. "It says in the Bible," Axelrod answered, "that there is a time for everything. When I talked to you in Geneva I immediately understood that the time had not yet come for you to see the side of Lenin which makes him a dangerous man in the Social Democratic Party, which is a democratic party."[83] Axelrod's point was well taken. A number of party activists in this early period of the factional dispute did abandon the Bolsheviks and join the Mensheviks, but the shift was far from enough to destroy the Bolsheviks as a faction.

The competition between the factions for popular support continued into 1904 when it became abundantly clear that reconciliation was not within easy reach. Late in January there took place a meeting of the council of the RSDRP, set up by the Second Congress for the purpose of settling disputes between the Central Committee and the Central Organ (C. O.—*Iskra*). Two members from the C. C., two from the C. O., and an impartial president constituted the membership of the council. Plekhanov had been elected president by the congress. Lenin and his loyal supporter, F. V. Lengnik, were sent by the C. C. and Axelrod and Martov by the C. O., which was now controlled by the Mensheviks. They talked for hours, not about substantive issues but about procedural matters. In fact, at none of the meetings were ideological questions raised. The assumption of each participant was, understandably, that unless confidence in party organs and mutual respect were restored the factions would not be able to collaborate.

But it was precisely confidence and mutual respect that could not be restored. At the end of two days of incredible bickering, involved parliamentary maneuvers, and numerous calls for harmony, Martov accused Lenin of planning a coup d'etat in the party. Lenin countered by

83. Valentinov, *Encounters with Lenin,* pp. 36–38.

charging the Mensheviks with financial irregularities and inefficient distribution of *Iskra*. The leaders of Russian Marxism parted company more divided than ever before.[84]

Soon after the Second Congress adjourned, both factions tried to enlist the support of the chief spokesmen of international socialism. Lenin acted first by sending one of his trusted lieutenants, M. M. Liadov, to France and Germany to present the Bolshevik side of the case. Liadov reported that the French Marxists "attached no significance to our affairs." In Germany Liadov saw August Bebel, Isaac Singer, Ignaz Auer, Georg von Vollmar, and Kurt Eisner, among others, all of whom looked upon the Russians as "children who were only learning to walk. They did not want to take us seriously."[85]

The Russians prized most of all the approval of Karl Kautsky, who, after Engels' death in 1895, had become the most authoritative exponent of Marxism and the major theorist of the Second International. Kautsky followed developments in Russia with interest, not only because he recognized the potential importance of the Marxist movement there, but also because of his personal closeness to several Russians, who were especially eager to obtain his advice. "Whenever a controversial question arose," wrote the Menshevik Rafael Abramovich, "whenever a problem emerged, the first thought [among Russian Social Democrats] was always: What would Kautsky say about this? How would Kautsky resolve this question?"[86]

On his trip to Germany in the fall of 1903, Liadov made a point of visiting Kautsky, but he did not succeed in winning the German over to the Bolshevik side. Kautsky told Liadov that he had been close to Axelrod and Plekhanov for many years, whereas he knew nothing about Lenin. "Of course," Kautsky declared, "we cannot believe your assertion that Plekhanov and Axelrod have suddenly become opportunists. This is absurd."[87]

The Mensheviks also tried to gain Kautsky's endorsement on the as-

84. "Protokoly zasedanii soveta RSDRP 28–30 ianvaria 1904 g.," *Leninskii sbornik*, ed. Kamenev, X, 181–282.

85. M. Liadov, *Iz zhizni partii v 1903–1907 godakh* (Moscow, 1956), pp. 10, 15.

86. Rafael Abramovich, "Karl Kautsky und der Richtungsstreit in der russischen Sozialdemokratie," *Ein Leben für den Sozialismus: Erinnerungen an Karl Kautsky* (Hannover, 1954), p. 83.

87. Liadov, *Iz zhizni partii*, p. 16.

sumption that his prestige would assure victory to the group he supported. Kautsky was grateful for the information provided him by
Russians from both camps, but he was reluctant to pass judgment on
the conflict. For one thing, he wanted to hear more about it from Axelrod, his old and trusted friend, who had long been his principal in-
formant on Russian affairs. Kautsky was as perplexed as many Russians
by the dispute over the organizational question: it seemed too trivial to
have caused so much turmoil. The German Social Democratic party had,
after all, survived a conflict about fundamental theoretical questions
with much less vindictiveness and without the emergence of two organized factions moving toward a formal split.

Axelrod attempted to enlighten his friend, but, unfortunately for the
Menshevik cause, he did not immediately apprise Kautsky of the thesis
he had developed so masterfully in his *Iskra* article. Had he done so, he
might have succeeded in persuading Kautsky of the seriousness of the
cleavage between the factions, and perhaps of the advisability of intervention on behalf of the Mensheviks, for the German theorist's outlook
was certainly much closer to that of the Mensheviks. In his letters to
Kautsky, however, Axelrod tended to describe the conflict in personal
terms. Preoccupied with intraparty intrigues during the year and a half
after the Second Congress, he did not write his friend often, but when
he did, he concentrated on polemics against Lenin rather than on dispassionate analyses. He accused Lenin of employing "Bonapartist methods together with a healthy dose of Nechaevan ruthlessness" in order to
establish an "administrative dictatorship" under his aegis, even at the
price of confusing and disrupting the party.[88]

As late as May 1904 Axelrod wrote that there were "still no clear, defined differences concerning either principles or tactics," that the organizational question itself "is or at least was" not one of principle, such
as "centralism, or democracy, autonomy, etc.," but rather one of differing opinions as to the "application or execution of organizational principles . . . we have all accepted." Lenin had used the debate on this
question "in a demagogic manner" to "fasten" Plekhanov to his side
and thus win a majority "against us." Axelrod added that he had been
suspicious of Lenin's moves from the beginning of the congress; now
he was convinced that Lenin had come to the meetings already armed

88. Axelrod to Kautsky, May 22, 1904, Kautsky Archive, I.I.S.H.

with "Bonapartist plans," although they were fully revealed only at the last session. And Lenin's tactics since the congress, such as calling the Mensheviks "heralds of opportunism, Economism, [and] anarchism," were bound to lead to "a system of lies, accusations, and demagogic intrigue" within the party.

Almost parenthetically Axelrod posed the crucial question: how could one man cause so much chaos in the party? He explained that without knowledge of the "important objective background," one could not grasp the present state of affairs and Lenin's imposing influence, but rather than tire his friend, Axelrod offered to take up this question in another letter, if Kautsky was really interested.[89]

Axelrod's failure at this time to pass on to Kautsky the analysis he had developed in *Iskra* is puzzling. By temperament he was not inclined to polemics, and in his public utterances he had managed, more than any other Menshevik leader, to refrain from them. But his comments to Kautsky would suggest that Lenin's success at the congress in having him ousted from the editorial board of *Iskra* and the subsequent attacks on the Mensheviks had shocked and unsettled him far more profoundly than he cared to admit in his published works. His animus against Lenin must have become so intense that, at least when corresponding with close friends, he was incapable of the objectivity and coolness for which he was noted. It is not that his comments to Kautsky about Lenin were far off the mark; they were simply far from being the full story.

Kautsky continued to be baffled by the intensity of the dispute. Still, when Liadov asked him to comment on the controversy, he attempted to assess recent developments in the Russian party. Kautsky declared that, had he been a delegate to the Second Congress, he would have voted against Lenin on the organizational question, and that Lenin had initiated a "pernicious discord" by insisting that the three veteran editors be dropped from *Iskra*. As an act of friendship, Kautsky sent a copy of his statement to the Menshevik leaders, who were elated and begged for permission to publish it in *Iskra*. Kautsky consented, though he was sure that he had not done much more than issue a call for unity. His supposition was basically correct, for in his letter to Liadov he had also emphasized that he could see no reason for the split. Obviously

89. *Ibid.*

acting on the information he had received from Axelrod, Kautsky maintained that the controversy derived from differing conceptions of what was politically expedient rather than from a "clash of principles" between dictatorship and democracy. He went so far as to warn that adoption of Lenin's organizational proposal would cause less harm to the movement than would continuing dissension among its members.[90]

The Mensheviks, in their eagerness to claim Kautsky as their champion, did not seem to have realized that this last point tended to diminish the significance of the dispute. Blinded by wishful thinking, they expected the letter to help their cause immeasurably. Potresov told Kautsky that it would be of "extraordinarily great importance" in "pulling the rug from under Lenin's feet." It would calm the membership of the party and perhaps "direct the discussion into other channels." Potresov was not exaggerating in order to curry favor with Kautsky. Privately he also lauded the letter: "Thus, the first bomb has been exploded and—with God's help—Lenin will fly into the sky." Dan thought that it would encourage many comrades to abandon Lenin and "go over to Axelrod" without the "tragicomic fear of having been guilty of 'opportunism.'"[91] Axelrod at first agreed with Dan and Potresov,[92] but seems soon to have become doubtful whether Kautsky's letter would have the galvanizing effect his colleagues expected from it. It is quite possible that when he received a further private communication on the split from his friend he pondered Kautsky's letter in *Iskra* with greater care than he had previously.

In this new letter, written early in June 1904, Kautsky confessed that he was still puzzled by the controversy. He admitted to having a vague feeling that there were substantive differences—by which he meant theoretical differences of a fundamental nature—underlying the dispute between the factions, for the "organizational question alone cannot explain such bitter conflicts," but the information supplied him so far by Axelrod did not enable him to determine the "deeper cause" of the

90. "Kautskii o nashikh partiinykh raznoglasiiakh" (Kautsky on Our Party Differences), *Iskra*, no. 66 (May 15, 1904).

91. Potresov to Kautsky, May 22, 1904, Kautsky Archive, I.I.S.H.; Dan to Kautsky, June 2, 1904, *ibid.*; Potresov to Axelrod, May 27, 1904, *Sotsial-demokraticheskoe dvizhenie*, ed. Potresov and Nicolaevsky, p. 124.

92. Axelrod to Potresov, May 21, 1904, *Sotsial-demokraticheskoe dvizhenie*, ed. Potresov and Nicolaevsky, p. 121.

rift. When he understood it, he would be in a position to pass judgment on the possibility of a reconciliation.[93]

Only now did Axelrod realize that Kautsky had not yet grasped the nature of the controversy between Bolshevism and Menshevism. For the first time he undertook seriously to explain to his friend the issues that separated him from Lenin. It is significant that he refrained almost completely from personal attacks on his adversary and also published his remarks in *Iskra*. Although he began by praising Kautsky's letter to Liadov, he obviously intended, if not to reply to it, then certainly to add to it and to qualify what Kautsky had written. Axelrod's basic argument was similar to his statement in *Iskra* six months earlier, but Kautsky, who did not know Russian, was unfamiliar with the ideas current at that time. Axelrod's most telling new point was that Lenin's emphasis on "centralism" and "discipline" amounted not only to "Jacobinism" or "Carbonarism" but to a "very simple copy or caricature of the bureaucratic-autocratic system of our Minister of the Interior." The implication was plain: a party organized in accordance with Lenin's views, if it ever gained power, would substitute one form of despotism for another. Axelrod took the further step of sending Kautsky translations of his earlier articles as well as other documents. He regretted burdening him with so much work, "but you are, since Engels, the most qualified arbiter in the camp of international Social Democracy, and especially with respect to Russia."[94]

Kautsky refused, however, to involve himself further in the affair. He had written his letter, he asserted, on the basis of his German experiences; whether or not his views were applicable to Russia was for the Russians to decide. It would be "a bit too bold" for him to attempt to enlighten them about their own party.[95] Axelrod considered it understandable that Kautsky was reluctant to enter directly into the Russian controversy, but he feared that the "blockheads and Praetorians" would force him to do so. In any case, he felt that "It is high time that at least the intellectual and literary representatives of international Social De-

93. Kautsky to Axelrod, June 14, 1904, Axelrod Archive, I.I.S.H.

94. Axelrod to Kautsky, June 6, 1904, Kautsky Archive, I.I.S.H. For the published version, see *Iskra*, no. 68 (June 25, 1904); Axelrod to Kautsky, June 23, 1904, Kautsky Archive, I.I.S.H.

95. Kautsky to Axelrod, July 4, 1904, Axelrod Archive, I.I.S.H.

mocracy in the West stop being quite so indifferent toward the situation in our party."[96]

Despite Axelrod's entreaties, Kautsky remained adamant. During the next few years he often made the point that in principle it was wrong for him to intervene in the conflict, a rather parochial attitude considering the German's professions of internationalism. Actually, by allowing his letter to be published in *Iskra*, he had intervened. Moreover, in that very letter he had declared, "If there is anything I can do to settle this dispute, then I would be glad to offer my services." What Kautsky no doubt meant by invoking the principle of nonintervention was that it would be improper for him to take sides. After 1917, however, when he came to believe that there were vast ideological and moral differences between Menshevism and Bolshevism, he did not hesitate to take sides, and in a most emphatic manner. The truth was that during the first, pivotal few months after the Second Congress Axelrod and his colleagues laid so much stress on personal factors in their discussions of the split that they failed to convince Kautsky and most of the other German Social Democratic leaders that substantive issues of any importance were at stake.[97] Hence there seemed to be no grounds for taking a public stand in favor of either side.

Whether a quick, unequivocal intervention by Kautsky in support of the Mensheviks would have had significant results is, of course, a moot question. All that can be said is that Kautsky's standing in the international socialist movement was so high, the balance of power between the Mensheviks and Bolsheviks so precarious, and the party activists so perplexed by the rift, that it might well have. It can reasonably be assumed that a pronouncement by Kautsky in favor of the Mensheviks would have influenced other leaders of the German party, by far the most important in the Second International. In the face of such a formidable array of disapproval even a man as resourceful as Lenin might not have succeeded, at that early phase in the history of the RSDRP, in mobilizing a following large enough to enable him to maintain the Bolshevik faction as a viable force. But by the summer of 1904 the opportunity for

96. Axelrod to Kautsky, July 10, 1904, Kautsky Archive, I.I.S.H.
97. Dietrich Geyer, "Die russische Parteispaltung im Urteil der deutschen Sozialdemokratie 1903–1905," *International Review of Social History*, III (nos. 2, 3, 1958), 195–219, 418–444.

intervention in support of the Mensheviks had been lost, in large measure by the Mensheviks themselves.

Though Axelrod failed to persuade the German Marxists that the schism was rooted in ideology, by mid-1904 he had succeeded in convincing many Russian Marxists that Menshevism was definitely distinguishable from Bolshevism. "The last year," Potresov wrote in May 1904, "has clarified the situation for us and has taught us much . . . We now realize (we—those grouped around Axelrod) that in starting to centralize our party [in 1901] we did not understand the need to join with a whole series of workers' organizations." Potresov conceded that neither he nor his colleagues had previously appreciated "what was probably the most important organizational question: how should the centralized organization become closer to the masses, how can it best expedite the process of forming worker agitators from the working class itself?" There was now no doubt in his mind that the party faced two alternatives: "We will either understand that we must reorganize ourselves and then we will be able to achieve much in the impending struggle for emancipation, or we will shrink into a conspiratorial association with great pretension but damned little political influence—and then we will become a genuine Social Democracy only . . . after the collapse of absolutism. It is a burning question, a tragic situation."[98]

Considering that the Bolsheviks did not explicitly repudiate any of the central tenets of orthodoxy, it would not have been easy for Axelrod and his comrades to declare themselves a distinct ideological current. In addition, Menshevism was never—either in 1904 or subsequently—a firmly united movement. There were so many changes in policy and the faction was so frequently divided over important issues that there would seem to be merit to a remark Plekhanov once made half in jest: the only thing the Mensheviks had in common was the conviction that they were somehow better than the Bolsheviks.

Yet, a close examination of Russian Marxism from 1904 to 1920 reveals that to a greater or lesser degree all the adherents of Menshevism took as their point of departure Axelrod's views on the organization of the proletariat. Furthermore, as the division between the factions deep-

98. Potresov to Kautsky, May 22, 1904, Kautsky Archive, I.I.S.H.

ened after 1904, virtually every major issue on which Axelrod and Lenin disagreed was in some important way related to their differing conceptions of the party.

In sum, Axelrod's chief contribution during the first few months following the split was to define the doctrinal content of Menshevism. Although he had made known the intent and general meaning of his position on the organizational question, his views suffered from a lack of concreteness. Precisely how could the Social Democratic party mobilize the masses in autocratic Russia and promote their political initiative? What steps could be taken to transform an elitist organization into a mass movement run from below? The political ferment in Russia late in 1904 compelled Axelrod to consider these questions. His answers, touching on vital aspects of the party's tactics, widened the cleavage between him and Lenin, and between Menshevism and Bolshevism.

VII | The Deepening of the Split

From 1904 to 1907 the Russian Social Democratic party was beset by two contradictory tendencies. On the one hand, the increasing political ferment after the outbreak of the disastrous Russo-Japanese War in February 1904 produced a widespread demand that the factions reunite in order to exploit more effectively the demonstrable weakness of the autocracy. The factional feuds were everywhere condemned as an unpardonable waste of energy at a time when conditions favored a concerted campaign against the old order. But, ironically, on the other hand, the turbulent events only deepened the disagreements between the Bolsheviks and Mensheviks. Each stage in the revolution forced the Marxists to formulate new tactical positions, and, except for a brief period in the fall and winter of 1905, these positions were so divergent as to pull them further apart. In the end, tactical differences proved to be of far more lasting significance than the pressures for unity.

Axelrod eventually assumed the role of leading tactician for the Mensheviks, as Lenin had done for the Bolsheviks. The alternatives proposed by the two during the years 1904–1907 reveal both the extent of the disagreement between the factions and that the movement considered several possible courses of action during the Revolution of 1905.[1] Moreover, the lessons each faction drew from the revolution largely shaped the battle for supremacy between them that dominated the internal history of the movement from 1907 to 1917.

One of the most salient developments of 1904 was the intensification

---

1. For an excellent analysis of the Revolution of 1905 and the tactics of both factions, see Oskar Anweiler, "Die russische Revolution von 1905," *Jahrbücher für Geschichte Osteuropas*, III (no. 2, 1955), 161–193.

of oppositional activity on the part of Russian liberals. Initially, they generally supported the government in its war effort, but as news of the unexpected defeats reached Moscow and St. Petersburg and they recognized the incompetence of the military establishment, "society" became restive. In August 1904 one perceptive observer reported that "practically all strata of the educated population in Russia regard the government's struggle against the revolutionary opposition with total apathy, if not with *Schadenfreude*."[2] The assassination that month of the reactionary Minister of the Interior, V. K. Plehve, and the appointment to his post of the more moderate Prince P. D. Sviatopolk-Mirsky not only failed to pacify "society," but on the contrary tended further to embolden the liberal opposition.

In response to an appeal of the liberal Union of Liberation numerous local zemstvos organized banquets in November to commemorate the fortieth anniversary of the introduction of legal reforms. At the banquets resolutions were to be adopted calling for a constitution and civil as well as personal rights for every person in the Empire. That same month a zemstvo congress was also to meet in the capital; it turned out to be a "revolutionary assembly which publicly stated the need to abolish the autocracy in Russia. The country's population instinctively sensed its historic significance."[3] Never before had Russian liberalism, or any oppositional movement, been so successful in arousing public expressions of hostility to the prevailing order. To a good many Marxists it seemed as though the bourgeoisie had finally come of age politically.

The situation was bound to engage Axelrod's attention, for he had long been interested in the relationship between Social Democrats and liberals. At the time he was busy increasing his personal following among the growing number of young practical workers in Switzerland, over whom he exerted much greater influence than any other Menshevik leader. The young people found Plekhanov aloof and arrogant and therefore tended to gravitate to the more genial, tolerant, and gracious Axelrod, who was reputed to be an effective propagandist with small circles of revolutionaries. Axelrod seems to have learned an important

2. "The Coming Storm: The Austro-Hungarian Embassy on Russia's Internal Crisis, 1902–1906," ed. and tr. Abraham Ascher, *Survey: A Journal of Soviet and East European Studies*, no. 53 (Oct. 1964), 155.

3. Richard Pipes, *Struve. Liberal on the Left, 1870–1905*. (Cambridge, Mass., 1970), p. 369.

lesson from his earlier disputes with young comrades, for he now took care not to act in a superior manner and always treated them as colleagues.

One Menshevik who visited him during this period recalled that Axelrod's approach was to "teach and to learn," which could not but raise the self-esteem of his guests. He would "greedily" inquire about the condition of the party in Russia and then elaborate his views on the basis of the information he received. Although Axelrod's "passion for proselytizing" was always manifest, he did not lecture his guests or dogmatically insist that they accept his ideas. Rather he strove to direct the thinking of his listeners along lines he considered fruitful. In the process he appeared receptive to new ideas and did not hesitate to modify his position. The small groups of visitors usually left his house in full agreement with him, but at the same time feeling they had contributed significantly to the clarification of his point of view. "Thus, P. B. Axelrod acquired among Russian practicals at one and the same time ideological followers and friends."[4]

After 1904 Axelrod always enjoyed the good fortune of being surrounded by a group of loyal and devoted friends. There was little that they would not do for him: they helped care for him when he was ill, and several acted as secretaries, noting down his ideas and preparing his manuscripts. Among the people who developed this sort of filial relationship with him were E. A. Anan'in, P. A. Garvi, W. Woytinsky, M. S. Makadziub (Anton Panin), and I. Tsereteli. Without their encouragement and help, Axelrod would have exerted much less influence on Menshevism than he ultimately did.

His first opportunity as a Menshevik to exercise his talents as a propagandist occurred in the fall of 1904, when dozens of young Russian radicals descended on Geneva, which became a "kind of mobilization center of the revolution." Some came after escaping from prison or exile; others because they wanted to take a rest from their agitational work; and still others in order to find out more about the schism. Because of the appearance of so many people, personal contact with them proved time-consuming and cumbersome. At the suggestion of Axelrod, Makadziub, who then served as his "adjutant," organized a "circle of those who were

---

4. P. A. Garvi, *Vospominaniia: Peterburg-Odessa-Vena-1912* (New York, 1961), p. 17, and *Vospominaniia sotsialdemokrata: stat'i o zhizni i deiatel'nosti P. A. Garvi* (New York, 1946), pp. 402–403.

about to leave," that is, of people who intended to stay in Switzerland briefly before returning to Russia to take up or resume political work. The circle met regularly as a "seminar on tactics," at which Menshevik leaders, mainly Axelrod and Martov, led discussions on contemporary issues. Axelrod's idea, modeled after the practices of European Social Democracy, was to direct the party's attention to immediate political objectives, but he was equally determined to involve the largest possible number of class-conscious workers in any political campaign on which the Mensheviks might embark in Russia. To emphasize mass participation in party work, the circle adopted the slogan "Down with deputizing for the proletariat."[5]

Axelrod advised "those who were about to leave" to implement an organizational and agitational scheme obviously derived from Lavrov. Once they were back in Russia, they were to concentrate first of all on small groups of ten to fifteen workers. When they had been thoroughly imbued with Social Democratic ideas, each one could then take on another ten workers, and so on down the line. In this way, Axelrod believed, the movement would be able to develop "cadres of Menshevism, which will be capable of playing the role not only of transmitters and executors of political directives from a foreign center, but also of *independently* applying in Russia the method of waging a centralized political campaign, drawing on Russian conditions themselves for their material."[6] In short, the circle of those about to leave might build the nucleus of a Menshevik movement in Russia, organized and regulated within the country itself.

While working on this organizational program, the Mensheviks abroad were obliged to tackle two urgent issues: the war and the campaign for political reform. They quickly announced their refusal to support the war effort, but nevertheless rejected the defeatist argument that military collapse would be the most salutary outcome because it would discredit the regime. Instead, they called for an immediate end to the war and for the convocation of an all-Russian constituent assembly, whose first function would be to conclude the peace.[7]

But how could the Russian proletariat effectively apply pressure on

5. Garvi, *Vospominaniia sotsialdemokrata,* p. 404.
6. *Ibid.,* pp. 405, 411.
7. According to Garvi, the Japanese government offered to subsidize the Mensheviks' agitational efforts. The offer was rejected. *Ibid.,* pp. 409–410.

the government in support of these policies? In pondering this question Axelrod conceived of an elaborate proposal for a so-called "zemstvo campaign," which aroused strong opposition among the Bolsheviks and became the first purely tactical issue to divide the factions. After broaching the idea to some associates, he subjected it to the circle for "the most detailed and thorough discussion," which lasted ten evenings.

At the Fourth Party Congress in 1906 Axelrod claimed that "almost a majority" of the Mensheviks initially opposed this plan, but Garvi, writing after 1923, disputed him and asserted that virtually the entire faction supported it.[8] Axelrod's assertion seems more reliable, not only because his statement was made shortly after the event but also because it conforms to the shifts in official Menshevik thinking in 1904 and 1905. In any case, eventually the Mensheviks in Geneva approved Axelrod's proposal, and in November 1904 the editors of *Iskra* distributed a *Letter to Party Organizations* (drafted by Dan), intended for party members only, outlining the tactics to be followed by Social Democrats during the impending agitation by local zemstvos.

Basically, the *Letter* attempted to apply Axelrod's theory of the leading role of the proletariat in the bourgeois revolution to a concrete political situation. It declared that the moment for working-class action had arrived because Russia was closer to attaining a constitution than ever before. Social Democracy should, therefore, join in the political struggle so as to strengthen its organizations and its links with the masses, heighten the latter's political consciousness, and prevent the moderates in the bourgeois opposition from wresting concessions for themselves while ignoring the masses.

As the author of the *Letter* acknowledged, the features of the plan were potentially at odds with each other. On the one hand, because the "liberal zemstvos and dumas are the enemy of our enemies" they were "our allies (of course, in a very relative sense)," and the party must attempt "to give them a little more courage and to induce them to include those demands which are put forth by Social Democracy." On the other hand, a militant approach "would compromise Social Democracy because it would transform our entire political campaign into a lever for reaction. A direct, immediate struggle, as is waged against an

---

8. *Ibid.*, pp. 415–416; *Chetvertyi (ob'edinitel'nyi) s'ezd RSDRP: Protokoly* (Moscow, 1959), pp. 258–259.

unqualified enemy, is permissible only against those organs of 'public opinion' which appear in the role of allies of reaction."

The campaign therefore needed to be sensitively executed so that the middle classes would not be alarmed. Social Democrats must limit their demands to the election of a constituent assembly on the basis of universal, direct, equal, and secret suffrage. They must first of all agitate among the masses in order to mobilize their support. After doing so, they should stage simultaneous demonstrations outside all buildings where the zemstvos were meeting. The high point of the actions was to be the dispatch of a workers' delegation inside to present resolutions. If the official bodies refused to listen, then a designated leader of the workers was loudly to protest the unwillingness of the group to heed the voice of the people. In the view of *Iskra*'s editors, a sufficiently large force of demonstrators would make a powerful impression on the liberal officials.

Every precaution had to be taken to keep the workers from panicking, regardless of provocation. They must be taught to understand that they were demonstrating not against the government or police, but in order to influence the bourgeoisie. If disorders were to occur, the zemstvo officials might be frightened into calling the police, and then "a peaceful manifestation would be transformed into a hideous scuffle and barbaric slaughter, distorting its entire intent." To avoid such an outcome, Social Democratic leaders might warn the liberals in advance about the demonstration and its peaceful aims. It might even be advisable to reach an agreement beforehand with representatives of the left wing of the bourgeoisie, securing their sympathy if not active support.[9]

For the Mensheviks, the obvious virtue of the plan was that it provided the proletariat with an activist role without violating the orthodox Marxist tenet that the working class should not by itself stage the bourgeois revolution. But its weaknesses were also obvious, and it did not take Lenin long to point them out.

Within a few weeks of the *Letter*'s appearance, he published a pamphlet attacking the Menshevik proposal at its most vulnerable point. The Mensheviks, he declared, had admitted that the liberals did not

9. *Iskra*'s letter on the zemstvo campaign is reproduced in V. I. Lenin, *Sochineniia* (3rd ed., Moscow, 1926–1937), VII, 410–416. Axelrod had devised similar tactics as early as 1892, but at that time few people considered them realistic. See his "Unpublished Memoir."

favor genuine democracy, which meant that they opposed the interests of the proletariat. It was therefore "a downright banality" and "mish-mash" to assume that the bourgeois opposition could be gently prodded to press for democratic reforms. *Iskra's* plan might have served a useful purpose a few years earlier, but now that the liberals maintained an organization and publications, their only concern was to advance their own cause. The tactic of the Social Democrats should be mercilessly to criticize them, expose their weaknesses, inconsistencies, and halfhearted policies.

The truth is that unlike Axelrod Lenin did not expect the bourgeoisie to play a progressive role in Russia under any circumstances. "Bourgeois democracy," he stated, "is by its nature not in a condition to satisfy these demands" (for full democracy) because it was unwilling completely to undermine the authority of the monarchy, standing army, and bureaucracy. It was "by nature condemned" to a course of "hesitation and halfway measures." Lenin was, in effect, restating a position he had been formulating, with growing inflexibility, since 1900: that the liberals had been transformed from a potential ally to an enemy.

The implications of Lenin's position were far-reaching. If the bourgeoisie could not be relied upon to establish a democratic system, was it realistic to proclaim the necessity for Russia to pass through a bourgeois phase before socialism could be introduced? If not, which social class would democratize Russia and modernize the economy, transforming it into a fully capitalist system? In his critique of Axelrod's plan for a zemstvo campaign Lenin did not discuss these questions, but they could not long be avoided. Once they were brought into the open, the conflict between him and the Mensheviks was bound to intensify.

Indirectly, of course, Lenin dealt with these questions even in late 1904 because he felt obliged to introduce a substitute tactic for that proposed by Axelrod. The course of action he advocated more than hinted at his readiness to deviate from the traditional Marxist view of Russia's political development. Interpreting the doctrine of the hegemony of the proletariat in the most literal sense, he called on the working class neither to support the liberals nor to demonstrate against them, but rather to direct its fire against the authorities and thus lead the attempt to overthrow the old order. If the masses were powerful enough "seriously to influence the bourgeoisie," then "such forces would be entirely sufficient for us independently to present our demands to the government." The party should therefore focus on preparing for the "decisive battle" against the autocracy by means of an "all-national armed uprising."

Lenin found it absurd to insist on avoiding a clash with the police. As soon as Social Democrats disturbed zemstvo meetings, however peacefully, the police would be called. At any rate, the use of force in the establishment of a democratic republic was axiomatic to him. Yet he warned against the premature use of arms: "If there are not [sufficient] forces, then it is better not to talk profusely about great plans, but if the forces do exist then we must oppose precisely the forces of the Cossacks and police, strive to gather such a multitude in such a place that it will be able to repel, or at least hold back, the charge of the Cossacks and the police." If the Mensheviks could not accept Lenin's tactics of 1904, they could easily agree with his conclusion: "Between the old and the new *Iskra* there is a real abyss."[10]

Lenin's criticism notwithstanding, workers in several cities followed the line prescribed by the *Iskra Letter*. In the fall of 1904 *Iskra* published accounts of local confrontations and expressed confidence that every step to the left by the bourgeoisie "made under the obvious pressure of the popular masses" would lead to an intensification of the developing conflict between the "old and the new Russia."[11] The results varied from city to city, but it is sound to conclude that the demonstrations contributed to a slight shift leftward in the resolutions passed by liberal gatherings and helped mobilize and educate workers for political work.

Toward the end of December Lenin himself seemed to acknowledge the campaign's effectiveness when he declared—without openly retracting his previous position—that demonstrations should be held at "zemstvo meetings and in connection with zemstvo meetings." After all, the government had been sufficiently alarmed by the "noisy meetings" to issue an announcement condemning zemstvos that yielded to pressure by discussing "general questions concerning the state, which

10. V. I. Lenin, "Zemskaia kampaniia i plan *Iskry*" (The Zemstvo Campaign and *Iskra's* Plan), *Sochineniia*, VII, 5–20; the Menshevik reply to Lenin has not been published, and I was unable to locate it. For a discussion of it, see Solomon Schwarz, *The Russian Revolution of 1905: The Workers' Movement and the Formation of Bolshevism and Menshevism* (Chicago, 1967), pp. 43–45.

11. "Itogi zemskogo parlamenta" (The Record of the Zemstvo Parliament), *Iskra*, no. 78 (Nov. 20, 1904).

are not within their competence."[12] Although the campaign was soon overtaken by the dramatic events of Bloody Sunday, it had occasioned a controversy over tactics in which the factions advanced arguments that, with some modifications, became central in Social Democratic deliberations throughout 1905 and 1906.

The expanding opportunities for revolutionary activity in Russia heightened the interest of international Social Democratic leaders, particularly those of the German party, in the Russian movement. Kautsky, Bebel, and Victor Adler, among others, were delighted that the hated autocracy might finally collapse, an eventuality they had long wished for. As soon as Kautsky received word of political turmoil in Russia, he expressed eagerness for detailed information. "The movement in Russia," he told Axelrod, "is at present the most important factor in international socialism." He fully agreed with the tactics advocated in the *Iskra Letter,* of which he had been apprised in a confidential note sent him by Axelrod. "It is necessary," Kautsky asserted, "to embolden the liberals with the cry: If you do not win a constitution, there will be revolution. One must not intimidate them with the cry: The constitution must be the beginning of the revolution that will wash you away."[13]

In general, during the second half of 1904, Kautsky, though he still did not openly side with the Mensheviks, was less than neutral toward the factions. In July he published in *Die Neue Zeit* two articles opposing Lenin's organizational views. Three months later he refused to print an article setting forth the Bolsheviks' case on the ground that there was no need for it because the Bolsheviks had not been attacked in the journal. In taking these actions Kautsky was more than likely prompted by his enduring friendship with the Mensheviks, especially Axelrod, and his distaste for Lenin's methods of fighting his opponents. Early the next year Kautsky was angered by Lenin's refusal to agree to an attempt by Bebel and Adler to arbitrate the factional dispute in the name of the Second International. The Mensheviks had given their approval, leading Kautsky to declare privately that Lenin's obstinacy constituted the main block to a settlement.[14] At this very moment, however,

---

12. On the various attempts to implement the zemstvo campaign, see Schwarz, *Russian Revolution of 1905,* pp. 47–49. Schwarz mentions Lenin's change of mind. See also Garvi, *Vospominaniia sotsialdemokrata,* pp. 437–438.
13. Kautsky to Axelrod, Dec. 19, 1904, Jan. 10, 1905, Axelrod Archive, I.I.S.H.
14. For details, see Dietrich Geyer, "Die russische Parteispaltung im Urteil der

a series of events occurred that not only reinforced Kautsky's unwillingness publicly to espouse the Menshevik cause but also convinced him that Axelrod and his colleagues were far less honorable than he had assumed.

In many cities in Germany sympathy meetings had been organized and money collected for the Russian revolutionary movement. The leaders of the German party urged that the funds—about 10,000 marks, which they handed over to the Mensheviks—be distributed by a joint committee, consisting of Mensheviks, Bolsheviks, Bundists, and Polish and Lettish Social Democrats, in the hope that the committee would become the "nucleus for unification of all the Social Democratic factions."

Axelrod, speaking for the Mensheviks, categorically refused to agree to the formation of the committee. In a letter filled with sardonic comments he denounced all the other Marxist groups except the Poles. He opposed giving any money to the Bolsheviks because Lenin was bent on dividing the party and promoted "chaos and disorganization" in the movement. Collaboration with the Bund and the Letts was unthinkable, as these factions "in their theoretical and political tendencies belong to the most backward and shortsighted elements of Russian Social Democracy." Furthermore, both groups were engaged in intrigue with the Bolsheviks against the Mensheviks. Only with the Poles could the Mensheviks conceive of collaborating: they were led by people "with thorough technical training and broad political vision." Also, they had earned the confidence of the proletariat in the Empire and therefore commanded greater respect than the other factions. Finally, Axelrod told Kautsky that the 10,000 marks had already been divided, and although he did not specify how it had been distributed, he indicated that nothing had been given to the Bolsheviks, Bundists, or Letts.[15]

This letter, which in tone was so uncharacteristic of Axelrod, testifies to both the bitterness and self-righteousness of the Menshevik leaders. Although they had every reason to be disgusted with Lenin, this does not seem to have been the time for factional wrangling. Axelrod, however, may have believed that, precisely because the Marxist movement could now make substantial progress in Russia, it was necessary to prevent the available funds from being misspent. This belief was doubtless

---

deutschen Sozialdemokratie 1903–1905," *International Review of Social History*, III (no. 3, 1958), 421–432.
15. Axelrod to Kautsky, Feb. 2, 1905, uncatalogued, I.I.S.H.

reinforced by the conviction that "in Russia itself . . . [the Bolsheviks] are in their last agony—if they do not receive outside help." If the German comrades would only display "some measure of confidence in us," the Mensheviks would be able to overcome the party crisis.[16]

Kautsky was taken aback by Axelrod's obstinacy. Some additional money had been collected, and he pleaded with his friend to persuade the Mensheviks not to take matters into their own hands again. If they did, he warned, the other groups would be offended, and "what could be an impulse for strengthening and unifying the movement would develop into one for further dissension and weakness." In a haughty and chilly reply Axelrod expressed disappointment that Kautsky "also" favored supporting the Leninists. Nevertheless, he and his colleagues had to remain adamant: so long as completely separate organizations did not exist, the Mensheviks could not agree to "Lenin's clique and Co." having rights equal to their own. "We therefore give up all claims to our portion [of the new contribution] and request that it be divided among the national organizations. We would be most pleased if it were entirely given to our Polish comrades."[17]

Thoroughly exasperated, Kautsky retorted that he had now concluded, on the basis of personal experience, that the Mensheviks were the main cause of the present dissension. He accused them of having disbursed the aforementioned 10,000 marks in an "autocratic manner" and of treating other Social Democratic groups with disdain. "I would not have believed this," Kautsky said, "for I am very skeptical with respect to complaints of factions that are in conflict, but your behavior with regard to the 10,000 marks showed that there is good cause for the complaints."

Kautsky did not agree that the Bolsheviks ought not receive any of the money. As fighters against absolutism they, too, were entitled to a share, regardless of whether they were members of the party or of a separate organization. Kautsky was so angry that he bluntly told his friend that as far as he could see the Mensheviks were much like the Bolsheviks. Both professed a desire for unity, yet the Bolsheviks claimed they could not work with "people such as Axelrod, Plekhanov, etc.," and the Mensheviks refused to have anything to do with Lenin if he received a

16. Axelrod to Kautsky, Feb. 15, 1905, *ibid.*
17. Kautsky to Axelrod, Feb. 6, 1905, Axelrod Archive, I.I.S.H.; Axelrod to Kautsky, Feb. 10, 1905, Kautsky Archive, I.I.S.H.

portion of the funds. "You do not understand by unification the unification of two groups each possessing equal rights, but the unconditional subjugation of one to the other." He found this attitude
incomprehensible, for "there do not exist any *substantive* differences of
importance." Unless the Mensheviks became less autocratic and more
reasonable, he warned, harmony could not be reestablished within the
party. He urged Axelrod to show these remarks to his colleagues and also
let it be known that it would be best if the unpleasant matter of the
money did not become public. Kautsky's statement was meant to convey,
unofficially, the sentiment of a sizable segment of the German party
leadership, for appended to it was this postscript from Bebel: "Am in
agreement with the above."[18]

What reply, if any, Kautsky received is not known, but Axelrod's
reaction to the rebukes can be gleaned from a draft letter in his archive.
He denied any unfairness on the part of the Mensheviks in distributing
the money from Germany and again contended that "the legalization of
Lenin's group and Co. [by giving them a portion of the funds] we consider simply impossible and irreconcilable with the basic interests and
honor of our party." Axelrod explained that if the German comrades
carefully studied the situation they would realize that the Bolsheviks
did not even belong "to the category of honest people, that they ought
to be thrown out of the ranks of Social Democracy."

Then Axelrod made a statement that reveals how shaken he had been
by Kautsky's charges. Despite all Axelrod had written about the ideological meaning of the controversy over the organizational question, his
emotions again beclouded his reason, and he reverted to the position he
had taken in his first letters to Kautsky about the split: that there were
no substantive differences between the factions and that Lenin, impelled
by "purely personal motives," was prepared to disrupt the party and
stage a coup d'etat. Desperately anxious to discredit Lenin, Axelrod
resorted to the age-old device of describing his adversary as being totally
without principle. In a final, almost pathetic plea, he asked: how could
Kautsky show so little trust in "old comrades" who had demonstrated
their honesty for the past thirty years?[19]

Even if Kautsky had seen this letter—and he may have received a
version of it—it is unlikely that he would have changed his mind. To

18. Kautsky to Axelrod, Feb. 14, 1905, Axelrod Archive, I.I.S.H.
19. Axelrod to Kautsky, incomplete draft, *ibid.*

be sure, by now he had had access to writings in which the differences
between the factions were analyzed in theoretical terms, but in view of
Axelrod's and the Mensheviks' continuing insistence that personal considerations were paramount, it is not surprising that he did not attach
much weight to the theoretical explanations. Since there were "no
Revisionists" among the Russians—a judgment, he stressed to Axelrod,
based on "information [emanating] from friends of *Iskra* and . . . from
you yourself"—the Mensheviks should have the grace to make compromises and grant concessions when such trivialities were at issue.[20]

Axelrod sensed that he had pressed Kautsky too hard: the Mensheviks'
intransigence was drawing them into a conflict with the leading theorist
of European Marxism. He therefore begged Kautsky "for pardon one
hundred times," but even while apologizing profusely he could not forgo
another sting, so obsessed was he with the Bolsheviks: "If my mind were
not dominated by the thought of the injustice you do us in accusing us
of the same crime committed by Lenin, then I would probably not have
lost sight of the fact that you had already decided [that Lenin should get
some of the money] and that our resistance only causes you unpleasantness without in any way being able to change your mind."[21] Still, Axelrod did not agree to make concessions, as suggested by Kautsky.

Nor was he ready to accept as final Kautsky's refusal to draw any
distinction between the Mensheviks and Bolsheviks. Three months after
the exchange over the money he took his friend to task for not publicly
and unequivocally criticizing Lenin. Kautsky replied that if he did so
he would no longer be in a position to use his influence to achieve
unification. He then made some remarks that not only seem to disclose
the deeper reasons for his professions of neutrality but also indicate that
his earlier censorious comments about Menshevik behavior were more
than an expression of temporary annoyance. The conflict, he said, had
become an "unheard of scandal," both sides were "equally stiff-necked,"
and Russian Marxism was in danger of compromising itself before the
world. Indeed, "everyone is laughing at you," because the inner discord
had paralyzed the movement at a time that "could perhaps be decisive
for centuries." Whenever people asked him why there was so much

---

20. Karl Kautsky, "Die Differenzen unter den russischen Sozialisten," *Die Neue
Zeit*, XXIII, pt. 2 (1905), 69; Kautsky to Axelrod, May 13, Feb. 14, 1905, Axelrod
Archive, I.I.S.H.
21. Axelrod to Kautsky, Feb. 28, 1905, uncatalogued, I.I.S.H.

dissension in the Russian party, he was forced to give an answer that evoked disbelief: "Because Axelrod and Plekhanov consider Lenin an intriguer, which, on the basis of what I know about him, is probably true." If this sort of contentiousness were not quickly ended, Kautsky warned, it was probable that the Russians "would be completely disavowed" by international Marxism. Certainly, his fondness for the Menshevik leaders, a sentiment he did not extend to Lenin, was no longer sufficient to "defend you."[22]

As was true a few months earlier, Kautsky's strictures against the Mensheviks did not convey only his own feeling. Bebel was furious with the Mensheviks for withholding 750 marks (from the 10,000) to which the Bund was entitled, and he warned Axelrod that the German party was thinking of deducting that amount from its contributions to *Iskra*. Bebel also expressed amazement at the inability of Russian revolutionaries to end their feuds and concentrate on political work in Russia. "In short," he declared, "it must be openly said that the influence of the émigrés on the Russian movement, no matter how effective at one time, is at present clearly pernicious and harmful." As soon as more people in the West found out about the discord, he predicted, "the inclination to give support will completely disappear."[23]

These words were harsh enough. Fortunately for Axelrod, he was not aware of the even more drastic conclusion Kautsky had reached. Kautsky privately told Victor Adler that the leading Russian Marxists were hopelessly ill-equipped to meet the revolutionary crisis in their country. The center of Marxism had been abroad too long, far removed from practical work. Consequently, the leaders had been excessively preoccupied with theory, and this, in turn, had bred a "peculiar brand of Marxism . . . And now we need action and organization, not criticism and theory"—a striking pronouncement by the archtheorist of European socialism. He hoped that new people would emerge in Russia and "remove and replace" the entire leadership, including Axelrod, Plekhanov, and Lenin.[24]

The discussions about the money from Germany continued for several months, and neither of the major Marxist factions distinguished itself

22. Kautsky to Axelrod, May 13, 1905, Axelrod Archive, I.I.S.H.
23. Bebel to Axelrod, May 29, 1905, *ibid.*
24. Kautsky to Adler, July 20, 1905, in Victor Adler, *Briefwechsel mit August Bebel und Karl Kautsky*, ed. Friedrich Adler (Vienna, 1954), pp. 464–465.

for fairness. On August 2, 1905, the Bolshevik C.C. and the Menshevik Organization Committee (O. C.) finally settled their differences on this issue. They were brought together by the realization that there was one solution on which they could agree: to exclude the other Marxist groups and divide all foreign contributions equally between themselves.

The Executive Committee of the German party refused to go along with this arrangement and in September summoned all the Russian revolutionary organizations to send representatives to Berlin to work out a new formula. As the Menshevik delegate, Axelrod had to assent to a distribution that he did not find altogether satisfactory: the Mensheviks and Bolsheviks were each to receive 22.5 percent; the Poles, 20 percent; the Bund, 20 percent; and the Letts, 15 percent. The Bund and the Letts protested loudly at receiving smaller shares than the major factions, but as far as is known the Germans adhered to the plan. Although none of the five Marxist groups was happy with the outcome, they could all spitefully take comfort from having succeeded in denying any funds whatsoever to Socialist Revolutionaries.[25]

The stubbornness of Axelrod and his associates, as well as their dubious handling of the German money and lack of consistency about the causes of the schism, had transformed the leaders of German Social Democracy from sympathetic neutrals into hostile neutrals in a year's time. In subsequent years, when the Mensheviks protested to the Second International about other, shadier, financial dealings of Lenin, they were frequently met by deaf ears. Kautsky and Bebel had come to the conclusion that in financial matters neither faction could claim a monopoly on integrity.

Although the controversy over money during the first half of 1905 exacerbated the situation, it was by no means the only—or even the major—source of friction between the Mensheviks and Bolsheviks. When Lenin decided to convoke a party congress, the Menshevik leaders protested vehemently. He had allowed ten days for the election of delegates, an impossibly short period. Moreover, it seemed to Axelrod a "real crime at such a moment to remove a substantial number of people from the arena of battle and probably squander 25 to 30,000 francs" on the

---

25. German Social Democratic party to editors of *Iskra*, Sept. 18, 1905, Axelrod Archive, I.I.S.H.; *Pis'ma P. B. Aksel'roda i Iu. O. Martova, 1901–1916*, ed. F. Dan, B. I. Nicolaevsky, and L. Tsederbaum-Dan (Berlin, 1924), pp. 116–118.

meetings. He thought it likely that the new crisis would end in a "formal split of the party. And this would actually be the best thing—under the given circumstances."[26] The Mensheviks refused to attend and, instead, held a conference of their faction to discuss tactics.

At their congress the Bolsheviks approved the need for a centralized party, adopted Lenin's definition of a party member, and emphasized the importance of preparing the proletariat for an armed uprising. The only surprise was the acknowledgment that it might be permissible for Social Democrats to participate in a provisional government, whose membership would presumably be mainly bourgeois.[27]

The resolutions of the Menshevik conference, which met in April and May 1905, were phrased in such a way as to allow for most contingencies and satisfy a wide range of opinion. They proclaimed the need to democratize the party and specified guidelines for its reorganization, but when it came to tactics they were vague and confused. The delegates indicated that they did not oppose an armed uprising, but insisted that before military actions could be contemplated Social Democrats must engage in extensive agitational and organizational work. As the "party of the most extreme revolutionary opposition," Social Democracy must avoid participation in a provisional government. The Mensheviks asserted, nevertheless, that their approach "of course, does not at all exclude the advisability of partial, episodic seizures of power and the formation of revolutionary communes in one or another city, in the exclusive interest of influencing the spread of the uprising and disorganizing the government." Finally, the Mensheviks explicitly refrained from ruling out the possibility of a proletarian seizure of power in the near future: for this to happen, it was only necessary for the revolution to spread to the advanced countries of Europe, where conditions were already ripe for socialism.[28]

It is unfortunate that no protocol of the proceedings at the Menshevik conference remains; thus, the positions taken by individual dele-

---

26. Axelrod to Victor Adler, Apr. 14, 1905, Friedrich and Victor Adler Archive, Verein für Geschichte der Arbeiterbewegung, Vienna; Axelrod to Kautsky, Apr. 4, 1905, uncatalogued, I.I.S.H.

27. *Tretii s'ezd RSDRP: Protokoly* (Moscow, 1959), pp. 449–466; for a fine analysis of the Third Congress, see Leonard Schapiro, *The Communist Party of the Soviet Union* (London, 1960), pp. 60–62.

28. *Pervaia obshcherusskaia konferentsiia partiinykh rabotnikov. Otdel'noe prilozhenie k No. 100 "Iskry"* (Geneva, 1905); see also Israel Getzler, *Martov: A Political Biography of a Russian Social Democrat* (Cambridge, Eng., 1967), pp. 107–109.

gates are not known. Within a few months, however, it became evident that there really was no one Menshevik line on the revolution. In late 1905 and early 1906 the situation erupted into chaos, as several Menshevik leaders proposed programs drastically at variance with each other. Some were closer to the Leninist position than to that of other Mensheviks.

The proliferation of tactical proposals by Menshevik leaders must be seen, in large measure, as a response to the unexpectedly rapid changes in Russia. By mid-1905 the zemstvo movement was dominated by those who called for a parliamentary government and a constituent assembly to be elected on the basis of universal, secret, direct, and equal suffrage. In August these liberals on the left began to discuss with the radical professional unions the formation of a Constitutional Democratic party (Cadets), which came into existence in October. At the same time that the liberals intensified their oppositional activities, the revolutionary mood spread to the countryside, where peasant unrest was ignited, and various nationality groups began to voice demands for autonomy or independence. In October 1905 the workers, supported by many segments of the middle class, staged a general strike that virtually paralyzed the country. Thus, in two respects the course of events in Russia differed basically from any of the upheavals that had occurred in Western Europe since the French Revolution of 1789. In the first place, the Russian authorities were forced simultaneously to cope with four critical issues: the demand for a constitution; agitation by peasants; agitation by workers; and the pressures of the nationality groups. In the second place, because of the relative weakness of the bourgeoisie the proletariat turned out to be the most dynamic force in the revolution. This combination of four protest movements was too much for the stubborn Tsar Nicholas II, who, after some hesitation, in October granted civil liberties and pledged to convoke an elected Duma.

It seems, on the surface, as though the Russian Marxists had been right in predicting that in their country the working class would be the paramount force during the bourgeois revolution. But the proletariat's role in the events of 1905 did not take the form envisioned by the theorists. For the assumption had been that the politically conscious proletariat participating in the revolution would be under Social Democratic direction, but in fact neither Marxist faction planned the general strike or was responsible for initiating it. Still, during the work stoppage Social Democrats became active and in several ways helped maintain it. Their influence over the labor movement also increased substantially as a result of their (mainly Menshevik) role in the St. Petersburg Soviet of Workers' Deputies, an organization that emerged spontaneously for the purpose of directing the general strike. The first elective body representing the disfranchised workers, the St. Petersburg soviet acquired extraordinary authority as one of the major focuses of the revolution. Within a few days some forty to fifty workers' soviets were formed in other cities of the Empire, and several of them became important centers of the proletarian opposition. All these developments held out the promise of far more drastic changes than anyone had anticipated a few months earlier.

It was therefore understandable that leading Mensheviks, as well as Lenin, were moved to reexamine their estimates about the potentialities of the upheaval and to formulate new tactics. The situation in the Menshevik camp was further complicated by the fact that its leaders were dispersed, some having stayed in the West and some having gone to Russia in the fall of 1905.

In order to examine and explain the various tactical proposals it is necessary to move back slightly in time and review the early period of the revolution, the spring and summer of 1905. It is interesting that of the most famous Social Democrats the two who did not deviate from their theoretical beliefs, Plekhanov and Axelrod, remained in the West during the height of revolutionary activity. Physical distance doubtless enabled them to view the events with less passion and fewer illusions than their colleagues in Russia. Plekhanov was detained in Switzerland by illness, and by the time he had recovered sufficiently to undertake the journey, comrades warned against it lest he be immediately arrested. Nonetheless, he was severely criticized for failing to rush to the center of the action,[29] a fate that Axelrod feared would also befall him.

Because Axelrod's wife was mortally ill, he could not leave her. Early in November 1905, when Zasulich and Potresov invited him to accompany them on the voyage to Russia, Nadezhda was on her deathbed, having contracted cancer in addition to her other ailments. Axelrod feared that

---

29. Samuel H. Baron, *Plekhanov: The Father of Russian Marxism* (Stanford, 1963), p. 276. For a discussion of Plekhanov's views on the Revolution of 1905, see *ibid.*, pp. 261–278.

his departure would "brutally poison" the last moments of her life. However eager he was to be in Russia, he could not bear to add to her suffering. "I do not have the capacity," he wrote, "to become *'ueber-menschlich'* (or *'untermenschlich'*). And I flatter myself with the hope that the group of close comrades, with whom I have made common cause and with whom I have worked to the limit of my powers, will be able to defend me against the calumny of various party hooligans, if they take it into their heads to slander me for not now abandoning a friend who has given me the best years of her life, has done everything she could to make it possible for me to participate to the best of my powers in our historical work."[30] Nadezhda died in April 1906, and within two months Axelrod crossed the border into the Russian Empire.

Even while he remained in Switzerland Axelrod was far from inactive politically. He followed developments in Russia assiduously and frequently discussed issues with his colleagues. He seems also to have figured prominently in the preparation of pamphlets and leaflets sent into Russia. According to a report of the Swiss police, a *Buchdruckerei Paul Axelrod* was formed in Geneva for the purpose of printing revolutionary material and smuggling it into the Empire. The police report referred to Axelrod, a Swiss citizen, as the "straw man" of the printing firm and asserted that "he had worked himself up through his 'kefir' business and is now the protector of all Russian refugees and [financially] supports their revolutionary agitation."[31] In this instance the efficient Swiss police were misled. It is true that Axelrod disposed of large sums of money, but they were not derived from his modest business. Exhilarated by the news from Russia, socialists from all over sent him contributions—sometimes as much as 1,000 Swiss francs and 1,600 Dutch gulden—with instructions to use them as he saw fit.[32]

By far his most significant political contribution of 1905 was the proposal that Russian Social Democrats agitate for a workers' congress, an idea that was to receive widespread attention in Russian Marxist circles during the following two years. Apparently, he first suggested the idea

---

30. Axelrod to Zasulich and Potresov, Nov. 3, 1905, *Sotsial-demokraticheskoe dvizhenie: materialy*, ed. A. N. Potresov and B. I. Nicolaevsky (Moscow, 1928), p. 165.
31. Police report of June 27, 1906, on deposit at the Schweizerische Landesbibliothek, Bern.
32. Henrietta Roland Horst to Axelrod, Dec. 10, 1905, Axelrod Archive, I.I.S.H.; Stanislavskii to Axelrod, Nov. 17, Dec. 4, 6, 8, 1905, *ibid.*; Theodor Steiner (from Connecticut) to Axelrod, Aug. 10, 1905, *ibid.*

in letters to the O. C. elected at the Menshevik conference of April and May 1905. The committee seemed favorably impressed, though it made no formal commitment of support. Axelrod was heartened by the response and proceeded to develop his views in greater detail, which he would continue to do with modifications and refinements for the next two years. In the fall of 1905 he published a pamphlet on the subject, *Narodnaia duma i rabochii s'ezd* (The People's Duma and the Workers' Congress). He tried to anticipate all possible objections and therefore took his time in preparing the pamphlet for publication. He struggled painfully to find the right wording, so much so that his son, Alexander, urged him to be less fastidious. "Try," he said, "to write without much rewriting," advice that Axelrod was temperamentally incapable of following.[33]

Being a slow writer turned out to be an advantage, for while he was refining his proposal the Russian government made a modest concession that directly affected it. In February 1905 Tsar Nicholas had indicated willingness to create a representative assembly, and he directed his Minister of the Interior, A. I. Bulygin, to work out the electoral procedures and define the powers of the body. On August 6 the government published an edict announcing the elections of the so-called "Bulygin Duma." It was to be a purely consultative assembly with no control over the executive branch. Only a small number of people were granted the vote, and even then the electoral procedures were highly complex. No industrial workers were enfranchised.

The oppositional movement reacted with shock to this paltry concession. After much soul-searching the liberals decided to participate in the election, but nearly all the leaders of both Social Democratic factions favored a policy of boycott, though there was an important difference in the approaches advocated by the Bolsheviks and Mensheviks. Whereas the latter proposed nonparticipation, the former called for "active boycott," by which they meant the staging of violent disturbances so as to prevent people from voting.[34] Alexander Helphand (Parvus) was the most notable among the few who favored participation.

In his brochure on the workers' congress Axelrod rejected all these approaches. He denounced the Bulygin Duma because it was neither

33. Alexander Axelrod to Axelrod, July 17, 1905, *ibid*.
34. Lenin, *Sochineniia*, VIII, 145–146.

embodied with real powers nor elected by universal suffrage. But he considered the policy of boycott a purely negative response that would contribute nothing to rallying the proletariat in support of a meaningful course of action. He repudiated the notion of "active boycott" because its ultimate effect would be to weaken the working class: it would probably lead to violent clashes between workers and "sizable numbers among the masses (petty bourgeois)" willing to take part in the election, which in turn would facilitate the emergence of "a coalition of diverse elements, in which the Black Hundred [extreme right-wing elements] heroes [would] merge with those strata that place their hopes in this Duma into one unified mass led [and] inspired by the government [and directed] against the entire democracy." The first aim of the proletariat should be to prevent the formation of a reactionary coalition, and second it should transform the electoral campaign waged for the Bulygin Duma into "a weapon and lever for [the promotion of] the revolution."[35]

Social Democrats could pursue both goals by organizing a general workers' congress, to be composed of deputies elected by the largest possible number of "advanced workers." As with Axelrod's earlier proposal for a zemstvo campaign, the underlying rationale was to involve workers in political activity and to strengthen the bond between the party and the masses.

As he had no hope of gaining Bolshevik support, Axelrod called on the Mensheviks' highest organ, the O. C., to hold a meeting of a small number of reliable activists to determine how best to implement his plan. He merely offered some general guidelines. The agitational campaign for the election of workers' deputies should be based on immediate demands uppermost in the minds of the proletariat. It would not be wise to appear before the workers with ready-made slogans, but "in the capacity of spokesmen and executors of the conscious will of the masses of comrades—workers and intelligentsia." Workers' clubs throughout the country should be encouraged to discuss the movement's policies and submit specific demands that the party could incorporate into its platform. In short, Axelrod did not want the content of Social

35. Pavel Axelrod, *Narodnaia duma i rabochii s'ezd* (2nd ed., St. Petersburg, 1907), pp. 34–35. The second edition contains virtually the entire pamphlet Axelrod had published in 1905 plus certain further thoughts he had had on the subject in 1906 and early 1907.

Democratic propaganda to be dictated by the party's leadership acting on its own, but rather arrived at in consultation with the working class.[36]

This did not mean that party activists should refrain from providing direction to the discussions. On the contrary, Axelrod urged the activists or practical workers to make opposition to the Bulygin Duma the "central focus" of their speeches to working-class circles. This would surely strike a responsive chord among many people, for "hundreds of thousands of workers and peasants are now keenly interested in the State Duma designed by the government. It is not difficult to evoke passionate interest [in political issues] in these masses through agitation that explains all the deception in the government's plan and all the dangers with which the people would be threatened by its implementation and calls on the people to wage an organized struggle against the reactionary gang of enemies of the people—in the name of a powerful national assembly that has no sovereign except the *autocratic* people."[37]

Axelrod realized, of course, that the government might not allow the workers' congress to meet, but this did not seem to him a persuasive argument against his proposal. The central purposes could be achieved by the electoral campaign itself: "the political enlightenment of the laboring masses," the "raising of their fighting spirit," and the "development in them of the capacity and readiness forcefully to cope with [police] violence in the struggle for their rights and demands." It was conceivable that the agitation could "at a certain stage, in one or another center of Russia, even provide the impulse for a genuine popular uprising."[38]

If by some chance the workers' congress were permitted to meet, the benefits accruing to the labor movement would be greater still. For the first time, delegates elected by workers would decide the party's policies on vital issues, such as the nature of the economic and political concessions that should be demanded and labor's attitude toward the bourgeois opposition. In private discussions Axelrod laid special stress on the latter point. His line of argument was directly related to his conception of the revolution in Russia. As he saw it, the autocracy could not be overthrown unless a coalition was formed between the proletar-

36. *Ibid.*, p. 55.
37. *Ibid.*, p. 25.
38. *Ibid.*, p. 31.

iat and progressive liberals. As long as Social Democracy was dominated by the intelligentsia, however, any agreement with the middle class was bound to rouse the workers' suspicions because they would fear being betrayed by their leaders. But if the party was controlled from below, the workers could ensure that their interests not be ignored.[39]

Initially, in 1905, Axelrod suggested that at the time the workers' congress met the Social Democrats should also hold a party congress. He did not give a reason for this suggestion, but it is probable that he expected the Social Democratic gathering to serve as a pressure group on the workers' congress, which would probably include delegates who were not Social Democrats. By 1907, however, he had abandoned the idea of a separate congress, confident in the assumption that the workers' congress would adopt generally orthodox principles and tactics. In Axelrod's view, nothing could be more desirable:

In this case our party organization will have to merge with the new workers' Social Democratic organization into one Social Democratic party. Thus it will fulfill its last duty to the proletariat, for it will itself help its advanced elements make a revolution, the aim of which is to eliminate the regime of the intelligentsia's organized tutelage over the laboring masses awakened to conscious political life and substitute for it the regime of their organized self-government. In this ideally favorable case the workers' congress will play the role of a proletarian constituent assembly, which will liquidate our old party system and initiate a new party regime in the ranks of Social Democracy and the advanced strata of the proletariat. Such a congress would be the greatest triumph for our party.[40]

Axelrod had finally formulated a concrete proposal for solving a problem that had vexed the Mensheviks ever since 1903. As Dan confided to Kautsky in the summer of 1905, the Mensheviks were still incapable of coping with the "great crisis in the party," that is, how to make the transition from "narrow, conspiratorial organizations to broad, public, mass organizations." Activists brought up in "conspiratorial hiding places" were baffled by the new situation, which demanded unfamiliar skills. Dan was forced to admit that the bourgeois parties were much more adept than the Marxists at extending their influence beyond small groups of intellectuals. "But this problem must be solved by us," he concluded.[41] Axelrod concurred in the urgency of this task and con-

39. N. Cherevanin [F. A. Lipkin], *Londonskii s'ezd RSDRP 1907 g.* (St. Petersburg, 1907), p. 72.
40. Axelrod, *Narodnaia duma*, pp. 20–22, 48.
41. Dan to Kautsky, July 12, 1905, Kautsky Archive, I.I.S.H.

sequently derived particular satisfaction from having conceived of a way to accomplish it.

Although during the Revolution of 1905 Axelrod centered his attention on the transformation of Social Democracy into a class movement, he did not by any means slight the question of social and political reform. It was his conviction that in formulating tactics Social Democrats must never forget that the winning of political freedom was of primary interest to the proletariat. He maintained, in fact, that in the unlikely eventuality of a conflict between the "special class tasks of Social Democracy" and the general democratic demands of bourgeois progressives, the "party would have to renounce . . . [its] tasks."[42]

Axelrod demonstrated his concern for general reform when he first advanced the idea of a workers' congress. He proposed that if the government went ahead with its plan for the convocation of the Bulygin Duma, Social Democrats together with liberal-democratic groups should take the initiative in creating an illegal National Assembly (Narodnaia Duma), which was to challenge the authority of the official representative organization. The liberals and Social Democrats were to conduct agitation separately and name their own candidates for the National Assembly. The basis for their collaboration was to be common acceptance of the principles of direct, equal, and secret suffrage and resistance to any attempt by the government to interfere with the elections or the activities of the National Assembly.

After creating an effective labor organization as a result of the agitation for a workers' congress, Social Democrats should form a "central club" which would meet at the same time and place as the State Duma and the National Assembly. The central club should attempt to "rally the local proletariat and form a strong revolutionary atmosphere," which would enable the club to influence both organizations. Axelrod did not, as he later admitted, work out his plan in detail, but he had in mind the influence exerted by the Jacobin Club during the French Revolution of 1789.[43] The central club was, in a similar way, to serve

42. "P. B. Aksel'rod o zadachakh sotsialdemokratii," *Tovarishch*, no. 153 (Dec. 31, 1906–Jan. 13, 1907).

43. On this, see the first edition of Axelrod's *Narodnaia duma i rabochii s'ezd* (Geneva, 1905), p. 8. In April 1906 Axelrod suggested that he did not pay more attention to the idea of convoking a National Assembly because he assumed that the liberal intelligentsia would by and large participate in the election to the Bulygin Duma. See *Chetvertyi (ob'edinitel'nyi) s'ezd RSDRP*, p. 269.

as a pressure group for the introduction of democratic reforms, a tactic that conformed to Axelrod's view of the proletariat as the vanguard of the bourgeois revolution.

Drawing analogies between events in their country and previous revolutions was a favorite pastime of Russian Marxists, and on occasion this mode of analysis yielded insights. But it could also lead to misconceptions for the obvious reason that no two revolutions are alike. The French model of the 1790's was not at all applicable to Russia in 1905. The Jacobins were able to exercise influence because the revolutionaries had already succeeded in overthrowing the monarchy. In Russia the autocratic system was shaken but it had by no means lost control.

In any case, the October Manifesto, which promised more generous concessions than the plan for a Bulygin Duma (which was not convened), made superfluous Axelrod's proposal for a National Assembly. He never abandoned his call for a workers' congress, however, since he was convinced that no matter how much a revolution might change class relationships and the political structure of the country, the benefits won by the proletariat would be minimal unless Social Democracy ceased to be dominated by the intelligentsia.

The uniqueness of Axelrod's tactics of 1905 can be fully appreciated only if they are compared to the contemporaneous plans and ideas of other Russian Marxist leaders. As a matter of fact, among those who continued to insist on the bourgeois nature of the revolution, not one advanced a new tactical proposal for the party.[44]

Lenin devised a strategy based on his conviction that the middle classes could not be relied upon to press for far-reaching changes. In the spring of 1905 he began to argue in favor of a provisional government which he called the "revolutionary-democratic-dictatorship of the proletariat and peasantry." Viewing the peasantry as a potentially revolutionary force, he now contended that it, together with the proletariat, could form a government whose mission would be to introduce democratic reforms and arrange for the election of a constituent assembly. Although he generally held that in view of Russia's primitive state of economic development the provisional government could not

44. Martov's advocacy of a "network of institutions of revolutionary self-government" was not really innovative. In effect, he was calling for an extension of the "municipal revolutions" that had already taken place in Georgia and Latvia early in 1905 and of the action of the sailors aboard the battleship *Potemkin*, where a "military republic" had been formed in June 1905.

do more than establish democratic institutions, on occasion Lenin casually mentioned an immediate conversion to socialism. But he was thoroughly unambiguous about the immediate duty of the party: with increasing urgency he called on Social Democrats to devote all their energies to preparing for an armed uprising.[45]

Throughout most of 1905 Menshevik theorists tended to agree that if the revolution was confined to Russia, the country could not be pushed beyond the bourgeois stage. There were differences among them, however, over the question of the workers' congress. In 1907 Axelrod asserted that in 1905 a significant number of Mensheviks had been "almost as conservative" on this issue as the Bolsheviks, who were completely opposed. Of the Menshevik leaders in the West only Alexander Potresov immediately adopted the idea. The others apparently accepted Axelrod's proposal in principle, but doubted that it could be implemented and therefore disregarded it.[46] In addition, they failed to consult him for several weeks while discussing tactics, probably because they wanted to avoid exposing him to open criticism. Given the sensitivity of the man, it comes as no surprise that as soon as he realized that he was being ignored he resigned from the editorial board of *Iskra*.

For some time Axelrod had been disappointed with the editorial policy of the paper. In October 1905 he told Martov that it was a mistake to concentrate on the question of participation versus boycott of the election for the Bulygin Duma; instead, the editors should place primary emphasis on the campaign for an all-Russian workers' congress. He thought that the government would soon make some significant concessions, probably by granting greater freedom of the press, and this, he believed, would create an atmosphere favorable to legal agitation for his idea.[47] Axelrod's analysis proved to be sound, and by late October 1905 the situation in Russia seems to have been suitable for an attempt to implement his plan. This is not to suggest that it would

45. See esp. V. I. Lenin, *Dve taktiki sotsial-demokratii v demokraticheskoi revoliutsii*, in *Sochineniia*, VIII, 3–126. For an analysis of Lenin in 1905, see Alfred G. Meyer, *Leninism* (Cambridge, Mass., 1957), pp. 120–144.

46. Axelrod, *Narodnaia duma i rabochii s'ezd* (2nd ed., St. Petersburg, 1907), p. 41; *Chetvertyi (ob'edinitel'nyi) s'ezd RSDRP*, p. 270; *A. N. Potresov. Posmertnyi sbornik proizvedenii*, ed. B. Nicolaevsky (Paris, 1937), p. 52; Dan to Axelrod, Aug. 2, 1905, Axelrod Archive, I.I.S.H.; Martov to Axelrod, Oct. 1, 1905, *Pis'ma*, ed. Dan, Nicolaevsky, and Tsederbaum-Dan, p. 119.

47. Axelrod to Martov and Fedor and Lydia Dan, end of Oct. 1905, *Pis'ma*, ed. Dan, Nicolaevsky, and Tsederbaum-Dan, pp. 138–139.

have been easy; it would, of course, have required a prodigious effort by a large number of dedicated activists. Still, in pre-1917 Russia there never existed a better opportunity to forge close links between the party and the working class, and certainly no one had offered a more plausible plan than Axelrod to achieve this.

Martov went out of his way to conciliate Axelrod. He tried to minimize the differences between the other editors and Axelrod and pleaded with him not to go through with his resignation, a request Axelrod heeded. Then, on November 2, shortly before leaving for Russia, Martov assured him that he intended to do his best to implement the proposal for a workers' congress. A few days after his arrival in St. Petersburg, he reported that the newly formed soviets in the two capitals were already laying plans for such a congress.[48]

But by November several other prominent Mensheviks had returned to Russia, and quite a few were soon carried away by the revolutionary mood that infected the country. The general strike had scored a tremendous success; the government had been forced to make extensive concessions, and, most gratifying to the Marxists, workers were flocking to the Social Democratic movement, which for the first time appeared to be developing into something of a mass party.

This was not an atmosphere conducive to restraint and certainly not to proposals as moderate and superficially unexciting as Axelrod's. "We live here as though in a state of intoxication," Dan wrote to Kautsky on November 9, 1905; "the revolutionary air affects people like wine." Two weeks later he told Adler that "As far as the general strike is concerned, it engendered the most revolutionary and activist mood among the St. Petersburg workers, [and] it strongly affected the leaders."[49] The time had come, so it seemed, for proletarian action, and for a few weeks Menshevik theorists in Russia advocated ideas that were neither orthodox nor prudent.

In St. Petersburg they founded a newspaper, *Nachalo*, which succeeded *Iskra*, and throughout November and December 1905 it carried

---

48. Martov to Axelrod, Oct. 1, 1905, *ibid.*, pp. 118–121; Axelrod to Martov, Oct. 10, 1905, *ibid.*, pp. 130–131; Martov to Axelrod, Oct. 15, 1905, *ibid.*, pp. 131–132; Martov to Axelrod, Nov. 2, 1905, *ibid.*, p. 139; Martov to Axelrod, end of Oct. 1905, *ibid.*, p. 146.

49. Dan to Kautsky, Nov. 9, 1905, Kautsky Archive, I.I.S.H.; Dan to Victor Adler, Nov. 25, 1905, Friedrich and Victor Adler Archive, Verein für Geschichte der Arbeiterbewegung, Vienna.

the most radical pronouncements, hardly distinguishable from those in the Bolshevik paper, *Novaia zhizn'*. In some respects *Nachalo* was even more radical than Lenin. The leading figure on the paper's editorial board, Trotsky, set forth the theory of permanent revolution, which posed the likelihood of Russia's imminent entry into the socialist phase. "It is entirely possible," so read one lead article in *Nachalo*, "that in the event of a protracted civil war our revolution, which began as a democratic revolution, will end as a socialist revolution." The author did not think that such an outcome would violate Marxist doctrine because Russian Social Democrats had never said how long the bourgeois stage would last. Even Martynov, the former Economist, voiced such extremist views.[50] Among the important Mensheviks in Russia, Martov was one of the few who held on to the previous assessment of the revolution as essentially a bourgeois affair, but even he became a bit shaky in his convictions.[51]

As the differences between several leaders of Menshevism and Bolshevism tended to fade late in 1905, moves were undertaken to bring about collaboration between the factions. Newspapers of both groups devoted a considerable amount of space to diverse schemes to end the rift. In a number of towns Federal Councils (or Committees) were set up, which generally consisted of an equal number of Bolsheviks and Mensheviks.[52] These developments presaged the convocation of the Fourth Congress of the party, one of whose primary purposes was to be the formal reunification of the factions. Carefully regulated elections for delegates were held, and for the first time a party gathering can be said to have been genuinely representative of the broader membership of the movement.[53] The results gave the advantage to the Mensheviks, who elected sixty-two delegates against the Bolsheviks' forty-six.

By the time the congress assembled in Stockholm late in April 1906 it was clear that the factions had much less in common than the optimists had assumed. The revolutionary tide had begun to recede late in 1905, prompting many Mensheviks to reconsider their positions. The

50. *Nachalo*, no. 7 (Nov. 20, 1905); see the discussion in J. L. H. Keep, *The Rise of Social Democracy in Russia* (Oxford, 1963), pp. 274–275.
51. For details, see Martov to Axelrod, end of Oct. 1905, *Pis'ma*, ed. Dan, Nicolaevsky, and Tsederbaum-Dan, p. 146; see also Keep, *Rise of Social Democracy*, p. 276.
52. On the unification movement, see Keep, *Rise of Social Democracy*, pp. 283–284; Schwarz, *Russian Revolution of 1905*, pp. 235–242.
53. M. Liadov, *Iz zhizni partii v 1903–1907 godakh* (Moscow, 1956), p. 155.

end of the Russo-Japanese War early in the summer of 1905 had made it possible for the autocracy to bring reliable troops into European Russia and use them to crush the uprisings in various cities, including the one staged by the Bolshevik-dominated soviet in Moscow in December. Loans from France had bolstered the finanical stability of the country. The opposition had been split by the October Manifesto, which won the support of a section of the middle class. Moreover, as early as November the workers of St. Petersburg had failed to respond to several calls to strike by the soviet, indicating that the proletariat's enthusiasm for revolution was waning rapidly. When, late in November 1905, the St. Petersburg soviet was disbanded by the government, the workers took no resolute steps to defend it. Not only had party leaders been wrong in believing that the socialist revolution might be at hand; it became evident that there would probably be no bourgeois revolution. In consequence, the Mensheviks in Russia hastily retreated from their extreme views of November and December 1905, only to clash anew with the Bolsheviks.

No sooner had the year 1906 begun than the factions tangled over the question of participation in the impending Duma election. The government had given a vote to many more citizens (including certain categories of urban workers) than had been contemplated six months earlier, when the edict on the Bulygin Duma had been issued. Nevertheless, the Bolsheviks decided to boycott the election, a policy that struck Dan as "nonsense without parallel."[54] Martov was as distressed as Dan by the Bolshevik tactic. According to him, Lenin had initially appeared to favor participation, but suddenly changed his mind, endangering the chances for permanent unification of the movement. A compromise had been worked out by means of which it was agreed that selection of their course of action during the electoral campaign would be left to the various local organizations.

It was bound to be an uneasy compromise. For one thing, both the Menshevik leaders and Lenin felt too strongly about the issue not to insist on a uniform policy. In addition, it was reasonable to predict that when the boycott was discussed in the local party committees all the old bitterness and rivalries would inevitably rise to the surface. This, as Martov relates, is exactly what happened in St. Petersburg,

---

54. Dan to Kautsky, Feb. 1, 1906, Kautsky Archive, I.I.S.H.

where at first the Menshevik advocates of participation were supported by a majority. But by resorting to underhanded methods the Bolsheviks managed to push through a resolution in favor of boycott. Among other things, they had illegally packed the conference with 250 of their followers.[55]

The stand taken by the Menshevik leaders early in 1906 corresponded in almost every respect to the tactics Axelrod had advocated throughout 1905, as Martov went out of his way to acknowledge. "I wanted, above all," he wrote Axelrod in February 1906, "to give you a few more *facts* from the entire four-month period, so as to help you to take stock of your hypotheses and conclusions. For after each new cycle of revolutionary events, one invariably reached the conclusion that although our history—according to the immortal expression—moves along 'incredible paths,' still ultimately—in those questions affecting the party and the working class—it nevertheless moves 'according to Axelrod,' as we sometimes say in jest, and each time we are confronted in a new form with the old problems that you have formulated."[56]

In view of this turn to Axelrod's tactical position by the Menshevik leadership, it was natural that he should be asked to speak for the faction on the resolution concerning participation in the election, even though he was a delegate without a vote. The commission designated to formulate the resolution had failed to agree and therefore presented two versions to the floor of the congress. The debate that followed, which touched on virtually every facet of the movement's revolutionary tactics, stretched over six of the twenty-seven sessions. Axelrod's speech, the longest and most theoretical at the congress, was also the most comprehensive critique to date of the Bolshevik policies of the preceding year. He deliberately discussed many problems, contemporary as well as historical, for his aim was not merely to persuade the delegates to accept his tactical views but also to steer the movement back to traditional principles of Social Democracy, which he felt had been widely ignored. Time and again he reiterated two points that would have seemed trite and superfluous but a few months earlier: that social relations in Russia had only matured sufficiently to make possible a bourgeois revolution,

55. Martov to Axelrod, Feb. 17, 1906, *Pis'ma*, ed. Dan, Nicolaevsky, and Tsederbaum-Dan, pp. 148–149.

56. *Ibid.*, pp. 147–148. Dan agreed with Martov's assessment. See Dan to Kautsky, sometime in Apr. 1906, Kautsky Archive, I.I.S.H.

and that Social Democracy must be prepared, "under certain conditions," to enter into a coalition with the middle class in the fight against the autocracy.

One of the most notable qualities of Axelrod's speech is its imperious tone. It must have appeared to him that at the most critical phase in its history the movement had ignored him and let him down in almost a personal way. Now that events had proven him right, he felt entitled to criticize both the Mensheviks and Bolsheviks and to preach to them about their future obligations. It was, in short, the speech of an elder statesman, pleased that many of his colleagues had returned to the fold, but nevertheless anxious to dwell on their mistakes so they would not repeat them. If the congress marked Menshevism's pinnacle of strength in Russian Marxism, it also signified the peak of Axelrod's personal strength within Menshevism.

In his speech Axelrod chided those Mensheviks who had opposed his proposals for a zemstvo campaign and a workers' congress and deplored the fact that only a small minority of the faction had consistently disclaimed the Bolshevik call for preparation for an armed uprising. He was chagrined that even those Mensheviks who had in principle supported his tactical line late in 1904 "abandoned it . . . as soon as there began a new political upsurge." He felt it necessary to speak bluntly "in the interest of self-criticism of the party and elimination of all illusions concerning the real state of affairs within it." In his view, Bolshevik tactics could only be characterized as a "putschist-conspiratorial approach, as a mixture of anarchist and Blanquist tendencies, concealed under Marxist or Social Democratic phraseology." Therefore, should the Mensheviks revert to their positions of the previous few months, they "would bear the responsibility lest we, present-day Social Democrats, end our historical career by being transformed—yes, I may be permitted this expression—into something like historical impostors, who conferred an inappropriate title upon themselves."[57]

When one delegate rose to accuse Axelrod of unfairness for having reproved the workers for their actions during the zemstvo campaign, he replied that he had only intended to criticize the Social Democratic leaders. But if he considered it necessary, he added, he would not shrink from censuring the entire proletariat. Obviously referring to those who

57. *Chetvertyi (ob'edinitel'nyi) s'ezd RSDRP*, pp. 249, 267.

catered to the momentary whims of the masses and readily altered the party line to accommodate them, he announced that "I do not belong to those who regard it as their duty in season and out of season to proclaim the proletariat as sinless and infallible, to lavish upon them all kinds of praise and are not even squeamish about openly flattering them. On the contrary, I think it is our duty to point out to the workers with complete frankness that they, in the mass, are still very backward and that even their advanced elements are still only in the first stages of their political development."[58]

Axelrod's remarks were not politic, but they were courageous and reflected his steadfast commitment both to the inviolability of Marxist dogma and the educative function of Social Democracy. Neither in 1905 nor at any time thereafter did he consider it permissible to modify Marxist teachings in order to adjust them to the seeming realities of the moment. As he had sensed to some extent during the pogroms in 1881, and to a greater extent during the Dreyfus Affair in the 1890's, as a collectivity the masses could go astray, and if they did he was not ready to follow them.

Axelrod assigned high priority to the question of the Duma election. In his view the differences between the factions over this issue reflected irreconcilable attitudes as to the aims and purposes of the party and could be traced directly to disagreements that had existed for three years. For, if Marxists were to heed Lenin and devote themselves to military matters, not much attention would be paid to developing the political consciousness of the working class.

Such an eventuality might radically alter the composition of the movement since even a man like Plekhanov, who had once studied in a military academy, would become superfluous to a militarily oriented movement. "In the sphere of military-revolutionary techniques and the organization of a purely fighting, armed struggle, a brave officer or noncommissioned officer who is in the slightest degree intelligent is more valuable than a dozen Marxes put together." Thus, the people who remained active would have to acquire military skills instead of the theoretical and political training that had traditionally been valued by Social Democrats. Also, the party would have to reorganize its structure and like every military establishment create "a leading center in-

58. *Ibid.*, pp. 320–321.

vested with dictatorial power," a perversion of the Marxist idea of a labor movement.[59]

At the time of the bourgeois revolution, the proletariat, incapable of formulating clearly defined political goals, would then spill its blood in the streets only to advance the interests of the middle class, as had its Western counterpart over a hundred years earlier. But if this was to be the contribution of the proletariat, why did the intelligentsia go to the trouble of founding a Social Democratic party?[60]

Axelrod stressed that he did not mean to suggest that in principle he was opposed to an armed uprising. As a matter of fact, he had never believed that the old order might be liquidated peacefully and had conceived of the zemstvo campaign as a preliminary stage to an uprising. The party, however, "the party as such, in its *entirety*, as a *political collectivity*" could not prepare the masses in a "military-technical" sense. Its function was to revolutionize them "in the name of their class interests, on the basis and by means of the development of their social-political initiative," and to encourage liberals to take more militant action. No one political party should take it upon itself to organize an armed uprising. If the oppositional movement as a whole was agreed that taking up arms was the "main and completely feasible" policy, then a "nonparty or superparty party [should be formed] with a common, directing center as its leadership," and the Social Democratic party should be temporarily disbanded as an "organized political force."[61]

Conditions in Russia led Axelrod to believe that there was much more to be gained for the revolutionary cause from participation in the Duma elections than from an uprising. Not that he thought the government had granted the Duma in good faith. On the contrary, he was sure that it intended to deceive the people, isolate the opposition by appearing reasonable, and turn the representative institution into a counter-revolutionary tool. Nevertheless, by reacting to the Duma with hostility and by boycotting it, Social Democrats would only play into the hands of reactionaries, who would gain control of the legislature. If the Marxists acted wisely, however, they could transform the Duma into a "lever" for progress.

59. *Ibid.*, pp. 254–255, 256, 266.
60. *Ibid.*, p. 259.
61. *Ibid.*, pp. 264–265.

Not only should Social Democrats take part in the elections; they should also pursue a realistic program in the Duma that would not frighten off the liberals. Thus, Axelrod saw no reason for the party to insist that liberals elected to the Duma call for the immediate creation of a democratic republic, since such a demand at that time would be met with little support. It might even hamper progress by causing the government to become more intransigent than ever and by giving rise to dangerous illusions among the proletariat. Once the workers were to realize that they had been led to pursue unrealistic policies, they could easily succumb to despair or apathy.

As Axelrod saw it, no matter how moderate the reforms advocated by the Duma, it would inevitably antagonize the government which would stubbornly defend its privileges. Rebuffed by the autocracy, the assembly would eventually find it necessary to seek the "active support of the people." Such a development, in turn, would force the Duma to broaden its political program and, ultimately, to campaign for a genuine constitutional order. Judicious exploitation of the Duma by the proletariat could therefore contribute much to the radicalization of the progressive bourgeoisie.[62]

Axelrod did not, essentially, conceive of the Duma, which was limited in power and elected by a restricted suffrage, as a vehicle for introducing important reforms. Nor did he accept the position of most of the other Mensheviks that it should be regarded merely as a forum from which to attack the autocracy and publicize radical ideas. By its very nature as a representative institution, he thought, the Duma could be used to direct the country toward the establishment of a constitutional order. It was a seductive notion that might have succeeded had the sixty-five Marxist deputies in the Second Duma, elected a year after his speech, heeded his advice to seek realistic goals. Instead, they ceaselessly attacked the Duma as a counterrevolutionary institution and undermined the efforts of the Cadets and left Octobrists to turn the assembly into a parliamentary body that could enact at least some legislative measures.[63]

The result was that early in June 1907, three and a half months after it was convened, the Duma was dissolved by the government. The brevity of its life had provided the opposition with little opportunity to

62. *Ibid.*, pp. 275–276, 324–325.
63. See Alfred Levin, *The Second Duma* (New Haven, 1940), pp. 355–356.

utilize it even as a platform for mobilizing popular opinion against the government. Instead of serving as a lever for progress, the Duma had actually played into the hands of the reactionaries.

It is noteworthy that the reasoning behind Axelrod's thesis on participation became the theoretical underpinning for the major tendencies in Menshevism from 1907 to 1914. He urged Social Democrats to take advantage of every legal organization and all open manifestations of bourgeois oppositional activity to advance the interests of the proletariat. The legally constituted public institutions should be used as "weapons, pegs . . . in the interest of the social-political education of the workers in a proletarian class sense and of their unification under the banner of Social Democracy into an independent political organization." From this point of view, he contended with characteristic realism, the most "pitiful" form of parliamentarism represented a "great plus" compared to previous conditions in Russia. Here Axelrod sounded suspiciously like an Economist, but it must be remembered that broad political objectives were always uppermost in his mind when he advocated participation in legalized institutions.[64]

Axelrod's incisive and forthright speech was a sound analysis of party developments and was remarkably prophetic about the consequences for the movement if Bolshevik tactics were followed. It is not surprising that the delegates' reactions to it corresponded to their factional allegiance. The Mensheviks generally expressed approval, with Dan, who only a few months earlier had supported the theory of permanent revolution, leading the way. He called Axelrod's address a "splendid, almost ornamental, work" and asserted that regardless of what measures the Duma adopted it would aid the proletarian cause. "Let the Duma be moderate," he declared, "let it be reactionary, let it *decide* every question in a very reactionary spirit: the important thing is that these questions *are raised*, that the masses concentrate their attention on them." Plekhanov was equally enthusiastic, arguing that the Duma stands "on the high road toward the revolution. We must not avoid it."[65]

But Lenin pronounced it a trap. Participation in the election would force Social Democrats to lend their support to the Cadets (in many districts the most progressive candidates with any chance of winning),

64. *Chetvertyi (ob'edinitel'nyi) s'ezd RSDRP*, p. 258.
65. *Ibid.*, pp. 293, 299.

first in the elections and then in the Duma. The liberals would consequently be the only ones to benefit, and they would devote their energies to suppressing the revolutionary movement. Support for the Duma would also mislead the people into thinking that democracy would be established by peaceful means.[66]

Within a few days Lenin acknowledged in effect the shallowness of these criticisms. He made a dramatic switch when an amendment was introduced advising the comrades in the Caucasus to submit their own candidates for election to the First Duma. Returns had been received from the rest of the country indicating that despite their party's official stand against participation many workers had gone to the polls, and since there were no Social Democratic candidates they had cast their ballots for Socialist Revolutionaries and Cadets. The election had not yet been held in the Caucasus, and many delegates disliked the idea of socialist workers voting for non-Marxist candidates. To everyone's surprise, Lenin and sixteen Bolsheviks voted for the amendment, offering the lame excuse that the impending vote in the Caucasus had "no practical significance."[67] This shift presaged Lenin's complete reversal on the question of the Duma.

The rest of the Menshevik resolution in favor of participation had already been adopted by a vote of sixty-two to forty-six, with three abstentions. The congress also approved the Menshevik proposal for "municipalization" of the land rather than "nationalization," as advocated by the Bolsheviks. Further, it singled out agitation among the masses as the "basic task" of the party, not preparation of an armed uprising, and it repudiated the Bolsheviks' "partisan actions" (or "expropriations"), which were armed robberies of banks or government institutions for the purpose of procuring funds for the revolution.[68]

Although the Mensheviks had defeated them on every issue, the Bolsheviks allowed the deliberations to end on a note of harmony. They made known their objections to the resolutions of the congress, but

---

66. *Ibid.*, pp. 282–285; on the question of Social Democratic participation in the Duma, see the excellent article by J. L. H. Keep, "Russian Social Democracy and the First State Duma," *Slavonic and East European Review*, XXXIV (Dec. 1955), 180–199.

67. *Chetvertyi (ob'edinitel'nyi) s'ezd RSDRP*, pp. 356–358.

68. *Ibid.*, pp. 522–528; on the agrarian question, see Geroid Tanquary Robinson, *Rural Russia under the Old Regime* (2nd printing, New York, 1949), pp. 178–179; on the Fourth Congress, see also Schapiro, *Communist Party of the Soviet Union*, pp. 71–85.

they did not challenge their legitimacy. At the time Lenin believed that "The Social Democratic proletariat and its party ought to be united,"[69] and formally at least the congress achieved that goal by merging into a single organization not only the two major factions but also the Polish, Lithuanian, and Latvian groups, as well as the Bund. The delegates elected a Central Committee of seven Mensheviks and three Bolsheviks; later two Poles, two Bundists, and one Lett were added.

Lenin derived special satisfaction from the fact that at the party meeting "organizational differences were almost completely overcome."[70] He was moved to make this statement largely because the Fourth Congress unanimously adopted a definition of a party member virtually identical to the one which he had introduced at the Second Congress, and which had caused so much dissension. Why did the Mensheviks change their minds? Two explanations may be suggested. First, ever since the "days of freedom," instituted in October 1905, the party had shed its clandestine status, and there was no longer any compelling reason for sympathizers to hesitate to join and to fulfill the obligations Lenin's formulation required. Second, in the opinion of Axelrod and his followers, the question of the organization of the proletariat, which had always been their central concern, was no longer intimately tied to the issue of party membership but to that of the workers' congress. After all, if the masses of workers were represented at the workers' congress, which was designed fundamentally to reform the party, how significant were the rules concerning party membership adopted at the congress in Stockholm? Shortly after adjournment of the Fourth Congress it was in fact the disagreement between Axelrod and the Bolsheviks over the workers' congress that became one of the key sources of new conflict.

Immediately after the congress Axelrod moved to Terioki, Finland, some twenty-five miles from St. Petersburg. Although frequently ill, he continued to try to implement his policies. One of his more interesting endeavors involved the establishment of a coalition between Social Democrats and liberals. In October 1906, after the First Duma had been dissolved and the parties were preparing for the next electoral campaign, he had a long discussion with Vladimir Gessen about the

69. Lenin, *Sochineniia*, IX, 222.
70. *Ibid*,

possibility of collaboration. It soon emerged that Gessen, an eminent professor of law and a leading Cadet, had to contend with obstacles in his party analogous to those faced by Axelrod. "Among the Cadets," Axelrod reported, "there dominates an antirevolutionary doctrinairism to the same extent as [there prevails] in our camp a doctrinairism that emphasizes revolutionary violence." If the Social Democrats had their Lenin, Pavel Miliukov "personified Cadet Bolshevism," so firm was he in his opposition to an alliance with the Marxists. Gessen thought it might be feasible, nevertheless, to reach an agreement on a common platform for the forthcoming election. He proposed that the Marxists accept the principle that the purpose of the new Duma would be to legislate for the country. Thus, the Social Democrats would have to abandon both the notion that the Duma could serve only as a "tribune for agitation" and the demand for the convocation of a constituent assembly. Axelrod saw no "irreconcilable contradiction" between the quest for a Duma that would have the power to initiate legislation and one that would act as a sovereign legislative body, which was what he had in mind as a minimum Social Democratic demand. It seemed to him that the liberals and Marxists could subscribe to different campaign slogans and still collaborate.

Axelrod's point was well taken. The truth was that Tsar Nicholas was not inclined to grant the Duma more than a consultative role, which made both the Social Democrats and the Cadets oppositional parties. As such, they had enough in common to be able to mount a joint electoral campaign. The real problem, as Axelrod saw it, was to overcome the resistance to an agreement by the extremists in the two parties. He told Plekhanov that he was planning to negotiate further with Gessen, but he despaired of making progress. "What would be the practical sense of a new meeting if at such a time I can, in effect, only speak for myself and for the party with many reservations?" He complained that "the idea of an agreement has only little by little penetrated into . . . [the Mensheviks'] heads."[71] Even though the Mensheviks had supported Axelrod's tactics at the congress in Stockholm, many of them apparently did not understand, or favor, all their implications. And if the Mensheviks hesitated to collaborate with the liberals, what could Axelrod

---

71. Axelrod to Plekhanov, Jan. 31, 1907, *Perepiska G. V. Plekhanova i P. B. Aksel'roda*, ed. B. I. Nicolaevsky, P. A. Berlin, and W. S. Woytinsky (Moscow, 1925), II, pp. 232–233.

expect from the Bolsheviks? It is not known whether or not he conferred further with Gessen, but the evidence indicates that in some districts Mensheviks and liberals entered into informal coalitions for the elections to the Second Duma.

During his stay in Terioki Axelrod spent most of his time disseminating his ideas among the Mensheviks, and slowly, over a period of many months, he scored some impressive successes in making converts. According to Garvi, Axelrod became the "life and soul" of the so-called "Chamber of Stars," a group that informally served both as a collegial directorate of the faction and as a forum for the discussion of theoretical and political questions. Much as the ranking Mensheviks desired party unity, they knew better than to count on its durability and therefore took no chances on dispersing their forces.

Practical workers as well as prominent members of the faction attended the chamber's frequent meetings, and everyone was encouraged to speak his mind. No votes were taken, but the deliberations proved useful in clarifying issues and positions and in bringing to the attention of the theorists some of the actual difficulties the movement met in trying to mobilize the Russian workers. The meetings also made possible intensive indoctrination of practical workers in the principles of Marxism.[72]

One of the liveliest debates in the chamber took place in July 1906, soon after the dissolution of the First Duma, an event that provoked a major reassessment of tactics by the Mensheviks. The RSDRP called for a general strike to protest the government's peremptory action, but the response was pitiful. Most Mensheviks saw the workers' failure to strike as a stunning defeat for the party. All along they had believed that in the course of the revolution the movement was broadening its base and, as N. Cherevanin (F. A. Lipkin) put it, was "naturally" being transformed into a mass organization, but now it turned out that it could not even persuade the workers to demonstrate their resentment at one of the government's most retrograde moves.

There were many plausible explanations for the workers' apathy: they were weary; they feared new repression by the government and retaliation by employers in the form of lockouts and dismissals; they were disappointed in the strike as a political weapon; they were still indifferent to general political issues; they were unwilling to act on

72. P. A. Garvi, *Vospominaniia: Peterburg 1906* (New York, 1961), pp. 99–101.

their own without support from the peasants; and they wished to regroup their forces for the final attack against the regime. But however persuasive these explanations, the Mensheviks could not escape the conclusion that they were totally out of touch with the temper of the masses.[73] Many argued that Russian Social Democracy represented only a few intellectuals, as it had in 1903.

Under these "depressing circumstances" the Mensheviks in Terioki, and soon in other parts of the Empire, revived an "almost forgotten" proposal designed to eliminate the party's isolation from the masses—the convocation of a workers' congress. "From this moment [July 1906]," Garvi recalled, "until the state coup of June 1907 and the introduction of the Stolypin reaction, the question of the workers' congress remained at the center of . . . [the chamber's] discussions and did not cease to be one of the main points of our sharp polemical [conflicts] with the Bolsheviks, who immediately greeted the idea with hostility—especially because it was at that time particularly closely linked to the problem of party reform."[74]

Axelrod was, naturally, eager to take advantage of the opportunity to develop his ideas in the chamber, all the more so because he could again come into direct contact with Russian workers, a long-cherished dream. In addition to addressing public meetings, Axelrod discussed his proposal with small groups of party activists almost every day. By the middle of August 1906 he reported an encouraging response by a circle of "influential comrades," but in "the sphere of the party bureaucracy" he had encountered a lack of enthusiasm that apparently was not motivated by strong feelings either for or against the plan. Half in jest, he compared their attitude to the lukewarm way the tsarist bureaucracy had reacted to the idea of convoking a Duma and creating a liberal cabinet. He publicly made this analogy at a meeting of the Chamber of Stars, hoping thus to shame his listeners into accepting his point of view.[75]

Garvi, who spent a considerable amount of time in Terioki in 1906, remembered vividly how Axelrod was gradually able to win support for the workers' congress. He made a strong impression on his listeners not

73. *Ibid.*, pp. 104–105; see also Cherevanin, *Londonskii*, pp. 66–67.
74. Garvi, *Vospominaniia: Peterburg 1906*, p. 106.
75. Axelrod to Plekhanov, Aug. 15, Sept. 1, 1906, *Perepiska*, ed. Nicolaevsky, Berlin, and Woytinsky, II, 219–220, 222–223.

only by the force of his arguments, but especially by his zeal, which people found irresistible.

How can one convey the lively agitation, the deep conviction, the apostolic passion that distinguished the speeches of the founder of Russian Social Democracy at these interviews with advanced St. Petersburg workers? P. B. Axelrod was no orator: he spoke quietly, he presented his ideas in a very complicated and frequently in a ponderous form—but there was something infectious in the integrity and sincerity of the tone, in the unquestionable validity of the idea, in the almost maniacal enthusiasm for the idea of working-class independence. We did not notice either the absence of good organization in his expositions . . . or the frequent repetitions, or the extensive digressions with examples from the history of revolutions and the Western labor movement for the purpose of emphasizing his positions. We were captivated and, as it were, uplifted.[76]

Not everyone who listened to Axelrod, however, became a convert. Lenin turned up at one meeting and attacked the proposal for a workers' congress as unnecessary, useless, impractical, and artificial.[77] Occasionally workers also voiced objections in the style of Lenin. After a speech by Garvi in favor of the congress, a Bolshevik worker exclaimed: "Here Comrade Iurii [Garvi] tells us that the workers' congress is the best means of assuring the independence of the proletariat in the bourgeois revolution; otherwise, we workers will play the role of cannon fodder in it. So I ask: what is this insurance for? Will we really make the bourgeois revolution? Is it possible that we will spill blood twice—once for the victory of the bourgeois revolution, and the other time for the victory of our proletarian revolution? No, comrades, it is not found in the party program [that this must be so]; but if we workers alone will spill our blood, then only once, for freedom and for socialism."[78] Such expressions of impatience with Menshevik tactics were not rare among workers and ultimately proved to be a major reason for the decline of Menshevism.

Nevertheless, in 1906, the advocates of a workers' congress attracted a heartening number of supporters from the working class. During the summer numerous meetings were held in St. Petersburg, and at times

76. Garvi, *Vospominaniia: Peterburg 1906*, p. 110.
77. S. Markov, "Moi vospominaniia o V. I. Ulianove (Lenine)," *Proletarskaia revoliutsiia*, no. 36 (1925), 51.
78. Garvi, *Vospominaniia: Peterburg 1906*, p. 111.

lively discussions of the issue took place, which was precisely one of the objects of the proposal.[79] Here was a concrete, relatively uncomplicated question that could engage the attention of workers who had not even been schooled in the intricacies of Marxism.

Now that interest in his idea was manifest and the party had been formally unified at the congress in Stockholm, Axelrod devised a different manner of realizing it than the one he had proposed in 1905. He no longer thought it necessary for the initiative to come from above, that is, from the central groups of the party, but rather envisioned a three-stage campaign, in which determinative pressure would come from the general membership. The first stage was to be comprised of widespread discussion of the idea in workers' circles, clubs, and workshops with the purpose of developing concrete plans for the organization and agenda of the congress; the second, of literary and "organized oral propaganda" in Social Democratic circles and among the "more or less conscious workers"; the third, of pressure on the C.C. from below by means of resolutions and letters urging it to convoke the congress.[80]

In the summer of 1906 Axelrod judged conditions suitable only for the first stage, but in several localities the issue aroused so much interest that votes were taken on it. Some committees had actually passed motions in favor of the congress as early as the end of 1905. A group of Social Democrats in the Moscow district went so far as to call on all factories to elect representatives to a workers' congress "that should define actions with regard to our enemies and our temporary allies."[81] In December 1905 the Fourth Congress of the Donets Union of the RSDRP passed, on its own initiative, a resolution in favor of a workers' congress. In the same month a sort of local workers' congress was convoked in Ekaterinburg; it represented some 50,000 laborers in the Perm *guberniia* and passed resolutions consistent with Social Democratic principles.[82]

In the fall of 1906 similar expressions of support were issued by a conference of the RSDRP of the Irkutsk district and by local Social Democratic branches in Moscow. That September a comrade, probably Makadziub, wrote to Axelrod: "I arrived in Odessa and at once became

79. *Ibid.*, p. 110.
80. Axelrod to Plekhanov, Sept. 2, 1906, *Perepiska,* ed. Nicolaevsky, Berlin, and Woytinsky, II, 224–226.
81. *Iskra,* no. 112 (Oct. 8, 1905).
82. See Martov's speech in *Piatyi (Londonskii) s'ezd RSDRP: Protokoly* (Moscow, 1963), pp. 528–532.

convinced that the question of a workers' congress has already attracted general attention."[83]

To be sure, at some gatherings in St. Petersburg the proposal was rejected and denounced as "harmful demagoguery."[84] But the significant point is that it had become the subject of widespread and intense debate, so much so that the Second Conference of the RSDRP (also known as the First All-Russian), meeting at Tammerfors November 16–20, 1906, found it necessary to take a stand on it. "The conference believes," ran the official announcement, "that active steps toward the organization of a workers' congress are entirely intolerable and are a breach of party discipline so long as a party congress has not taken a decision on the matter." The resolution further declared that, while the question might be taken up in the party press and at meetings, consideration of it "must not go beyond the bounds of a purely principled discussion."[85]

It is not clear how the Mensheviks at this conference voted on the resolution. It has been asserted that they held a majority and therefore must have voted against any moves designed to convene a workers' congress. Actually they controlled thirteen out of thirty-two votes and were able to push through some resolutions only because they were supported by the five Bundist delegates. Since most Bundists opposed the workers' congress, it is probable that on this issue the Mensheviks were simply outvoted.[86]

The point is of some interest because the evidence tends to suggest that by late 1906 the Mensheviks generally supported the workers' congress, though there were differences of emphasis among them. Indeed, by this time the subject was charged with controversy, the two factions having lined up on opposite sides. During the last few months of 1906 and the first three of 1907, the proposal was analyzed in some fifteen brochures,[87] several of which contained numerous articles that scrutinized the problem from every angle imaginable. The debate demonstrated even more undeniably than the polemics of 1903 and 1904 the

83. P.[Panin?] to Axelrod, n. d., but probably Sept. 1906, Axelrod Archive, I.I.S.H.

84. See *Sotsialdemokrat*, no. 4 (Oct. 20, 1906), 7; *O vserossiiskom rabochem s'ezde. Sbornik statei* (Moscow, 1907), pp. 119–122.

85. *Kommunisticheskaia partiia sovetskogo soiuza v rezoliutsiiakh i resheniiakh s'ezdov, konferentsii i plenumov Ts. K.* (7th ed., Moscow, 1954), I, 143.

86. Schapiro, *Communist Party of the Soviet Union*, p. 76; on the Bund's position, see *Di Geshikhte fun Bund*, ed. Y. Sh. Herts *et al.* (New York, 1960–1966), II, 410.

87. Lenin, *Sochineniia*, XI, 142.

radically divergent attitudes toward the working class that were competing for supremacy in the Russian Marxist movement.

Two major tendencies emerged among the proponents of a workers' congress. The first, developed mainly by Iu. Larin and V. Shcheglo in St. Petersburg, generally followed Axelrod's line of argument that the initiative in convoking the congress should be taken by the Social Democratic movement and that the delegates should be limited to representatives of the labor vanguard, that is, class-conscious workers.

Another group, centered in Moscow and represented by "El.," Akhmet Tsalikov, and L. Solomin, among others, argued for the convocation of a nonparty all-Russian congress, to be composed of workers representing the entire working class, not simply its advanced stratum. El. contended that the revolution had activated huge numbers of workers, as was illustrated by the rapid growth of trade unions, and that they were craving for a political organization in which they could play a decisive role. He commended Axelrod for proposing to rebuild the Social Democratic movement "from below," but rebuked him for not going far enough. This criticism had some substance since Axelrod spoke primarily of mobilizing the advanced workers, yet at the same time he always emphasized that the agitation for a workers' congress would serve an educative function and imbue a growing number of workers with class consciousness. Thus, regardless of their differences, all the advocates of a congress agreed on the need to broaden the base of the party and to Europeanize it by including a large number of laborers in its ranks and reducing the influence of the intelligentsia.[88]

One of the more interesting positions of qualified support for the idea was taken by Trotsky, who, despite his theory of permanent revolution, still considered himself a follower of Axelrod. In a long, private letter Trotsky explained his attitude and in the process bared sentiments that account for his behavior at a crucial period in his career. He held that a congress would serve a useful purpose only if it were organized by a firmly united party. Many Mensheviks, he feared, looked upon the workers' congress as a "panacea that would save the party," but he did

---

88. Iurii Larin, *Shirokaia rabochaia partiia i rabochii s'ezd* (Moscow, 1907); V. A. Shcheglo, *O rabochem s'ezde* (St. Petersburg, 1906); El., "Dva techeniia v vopros o rabochem s'ezde," in *Vserossiiskii rabochii s'ezd. Sbornik statei* (Moscow, 1907), pp. 5–20. The last volume contains articles by A. Tsalikov, L. Solomin, A. Argunin, N. D'iakonov, I. Bezzemel'nyi, and A. Arkhangel'skii, all favoring a workers' congress.

not believe the party needed to be saved. The proof of the health of Russian Social Democracy lay in the fact that both factions were "struggling for influence over the proletariat," that is, both were leaning on the same social class. Having defined party health so formalistically, Trotsky saw Axelrod's advocacy of party reform as bound to weaken the existing organization by unnecessarily antagonizing the Bolsheviks, who resented criticism of the party structure. Before any step was taken to organize a workers' congress, Trotsky cautioned, "the party must move toward an agreement binding on both sections."

Trotsky was haunted by the specter of a formal split in the party, which was what he most wanted to avoid. "To turn one's back on the party—this slogan seems to me more dangerous than dozens of Jacobins or opportunistic phrases. *The unity of the party on the basis of the unity of the class struggle, unity at all costs!* I stand on this position, I cannot do otherwise . . . 'Long live the party!' And I am firmly convinced that the hand of our teacher P. B. A. [Axelrod] will be the first stretched out to this banner." He also did not doubt that Axelrod would take charge of the organization of the workers' congress, for this "requires the ability to disregard small and petty considerations of a formal revolutionary or formal party character in the name of a broad formulation of the genuine revolutionary and party tasks."[89] This same unswerving loyalty to the party inspired Trotsky in the 1920's and crippled him in the struggle against Stalin.

In stating that the party was basically a proletarian movement and that unity should precede the convocation of a congress, Trotsky, of course, differed sharply from Axelrod, in whose mind the situation was precisely the reverse. But Trotsky did contend that a workers' congress could be a weapon for increasing party strength during a revolutionary period, and on this point the two men were in accord.

The ruminations and disputes of 1906 about a workers' congress may today appear quixotic. After all, the participants were aware that the plan could not be implemented while the autocracy was solidly in control. Yet, before many years had passed, in 1917, the all-Russian soviets performed tasks that resembled those Axelrod had assigned to the workers' congress. The central bodies of the soviets represented laborers of all persuasions, their debates and resolutions helped clarify political

89. Trotsky to Axelrod, Sept. 2, 1906, Nicolaevsky Collection, Hoover Institution.

issues for the people at large, and they influenced the Provisional Government.

The similarity between the soviets and the proposed workers' congress was not fortuitous. In 1915 and 1916 Axelrod's plan had been revived by the Labor Groups attached to the War Industry Committees. The latter were formed on the initiative of A. I. Guchkov, a leader of the Octobrists, for the purpose of promoting efficiency in factories producing military supplies. The Bolsheviks and the Mensheviks in exile rejected participation in the committees, but several Menshevik "practicals" (most notably Garvi and K. A. Gvozdev) seized the opportunity to engage in organizational activities among workers. It did not take the practicals long to go beyond Guchkov's initial intentions and propagate political demands in the new organizations and, in particular, to call for a workers' congress. Thus, the idea of electing workers' deputies to some sort of representative body was very much in the air in the months immediately preceding the collapse of the autocracy.[90]

In 1917 the Bolsheviks supported the soviets as institutions expressing the will of the masses, at least so long as they believed them useful for promoting the socialist revolution. In 1906, however, all Leninists rejected the idea of a workers' congress. With striking candor, one Bolshevik confessed that however desirable it might be, under capitalism the majority of workers could never be imbued with class consciousness and therefore could not be granted a voice in party affairs. He claimed that even in advanced Western countries only a minority of the work force belonged to the Social Democratic organization. But this was no reason for pessimism: "It is not improbable," he wrote, "that even on the eve of the social revolution the Social Democratic party will unite within its ranks only a minority of the entire population, but it will nevertheless be the vanguard, the leader of the entire working class because it is the only conscious spokesman of its class forces and will."[91] In 1906 even Lenin shied away from stating so baldly that the socialist revolution might be the work of a relatively small group of workers.

90. "K istorii 'Rabochei gruppy' pri tsentral'nom voenno-promyshlennom komitete," *Krasnyi arkhiv*, no. 57 (1933), 43–84, but esp. 65–66; "K istorii gvozdevshchiny," *ibid.*, no. 67 (1934), 28–92, but esp. 40, 48–49, 57; A. Shliapnikov, *Kanun semnadtsatogo goda* (3rd ed., Moscow, 1923), pt. II, 147.

91. G. L. [G. D. Leiteizen], *Rabochii s'ezd ili s'ezd rabochii partii* (St. Petersburg, 1906), p. 14.

For about a year Lenin did not comment on Axelrod's proposal in public, but there is no question about the fierceness of his hostility toward it. In October 1905 he drafted an outline for an attack on Axelrod's brochure *Narodnaia duma i rabochii s'ezd,* in which he referred to the scheme as the "prototype of *all Iskra* absurdities," as "comedy, phantom . . . chaotic ideas . . . scholastic pedagogy."[92] A year later he even belittled the notion of discussing the proposal: "The labor party is not a club for intelligentsia 'discussions,' but a fighting proletarian organization. Discussion, discussion, but it is necessary to live and act." Though decked out in new trappings, the scheme amounted to nothing more than an old form of opportunism, Economism, which would eventually lead to the subordination of the working class to the bourgeoisie.[93]

That the Bolsheviks were deeply disquieted by the discussions of the workers' congress emerged distinctly at the Fifth Party Congress (May 13–June 1, 1907) in London, where they tried once and for all to put an official stamp of disapproval on the idea and squelch all further consideration of it. Soon after the Fourth Congress, Lenin, who had maintained his faction intact, began to call for another party congress in the hope of recapturing control of the organization. One point of disagreement between the factions had been removed in 1906 when Lenin completely changed his mind on the question of participation in the Duma election. He now argued that the Duma could be used not as a legislative body but as a platform for Social Democratic agitation.

But other sources of conflict remained. Lenin still refused to go along with the Menshevik tactic of collaborating with Cadets in certain districts in order to defeat reactionary candidates to the Duma. After the elections to the Second Duma in February 1907, moreover, he accused the Mensheviks of deliberately having formed coalitions with the liberals in St. Petersburg, thereby splitting the local Social Democratic vote in exchange for concessions for their candidates. The Mensheviks, in turn, were made increasingly uneasy by the Bolshevik expropriations, which continued despite their having been condemned by the Fourth

---

92. *Leninskii sbornik,* ed. L. Kamenev (Moscow, 1924–1938), V, 386–389.
93. Lenin, *Sochineniia,* XXX, 179.

Congress. These tensions notwithstanding, the Mensheviks finally agreed to another congress. They anticipated a new wave of revolutionary activity and therefore believed it important to preserve unity.[94]

In large part because of their greater financial resources, the Bolsheviks were able to elect more delegates than their rivals. The Bolsheviks controlled about ninety votes and the Mensheviks about eighty-five, but as the former could count on the support of forty-five Polish and twenty-six Lettish delegates, they generally carried a majority. The fifty-four Bundists tended to side with the Mensheviks, so the votes on some crucial issues were quite close. Lenin pressed his advantage to the limit. The relative civility that had marked the previous congress was nowhere apparent.

At the thirtieth session the congress was to have discussed a resolution on the State Duma. Instead, the assembly suddenly and unexpectedly took up the question of the workers' congress. The maneuver had plainly been planned, for G. D. Leiteizen, the principal Bolshevik speaker on the subject, arrived at the session with a copy of Axelrod's brochure from which he proceeded to quote. Plekhanov asked that the debate be delayed on the ground that he had not even seen the resolution the Bolsheviks were proposing. The Bolsheviks refused; Leiteizen explained that since the Mensheviks were familiar with the Bolshevik position, no delay was necessary. A. I. Gusev called attention to the urgency of the matter: "This question not only interests us; it torments us. We must resolve it right now."[95]

But before the discussion could begin, the Bolsheviks had to unveil their resolution. Although the Mensheviks had expected a repudiation of Axelrod's proposal, they were stunned by the harsh and repressive form of the resolution. It firmly declared that the "idea of a nonparty workers' congress, seized by the anarcho-syndicalists for a struggle against Social Democratic influence among the laboring masses, is absolutely harmful for the class development of the proletariat." While affirming the right of party members to discuss the issue in the party press, paragraph four stated that "it is at the same time not permissible either for individual members or organizations of the Social Democratic Labor party [to engage] in agitational and organizational work among the

94. On the Fifth Congress, see Schapiro, *Communist Party of the Soviet Union,* pp. 86–99.
95. *Piatyi (Londonskii) s'ezd RSDRP,* pp. 495–497.

laboring masses for the purpose of preparing a workers' congress." This paragraph, clearly a limitation of the personal rights of individual party members, outraged the Mensheviks and provoked Trotsky into delivering a sharp attack on the Bolsheviks.

What, exactly, he asked, did the authors of the resolution mean by agitation? Would it be permissible to write pamphlets? At that point Plekhanov interjected: "That depends on their price!" Would it be in order to organize conferences for the discussion of the question of the workers' congress? "You see, the party statutes do not prohibit freedom of movement. (Laughter) And could circles be organized for the discussion of the question of the workers' congress? And what is the difference between oral and written agitation? . . . You have no confidence in the validity of your resolution, this is a cry of weakness. (Applause) You see, the Mensheviks will then be able to shout at you, as [Wilhelm] Bracke shouted at Bismarck after the Reichstag's adoption of the Exceptional Laws against the Socialists: 'Wir pfeifen auf ihr Gesetz.' (Applause)."[96] The Bolsheviks yielded and agreed to strike this point from the resolution, which prompted the Mensheviks to shout: "You are afraid."

Actually, the Mensheviks, after hearing the resolution, did not want to discuss it at all. They bitterly resented having been denied time to prepare themselves, and, as one delegate fatalistically put it, "It makes no difference, the Bolshevik resolution will be adopted. Why discuss? We will only lose time." Amid applause and shouts, Gusev tried to rouse further debate from the Mensheviks. It would not do for the resolution to appear to have been steamrollered through the congress. The assembly therefore voted to proceed and gave Leiteizen the floor.[97] It was an inauspicious beginning, and one might have supposed that the tone and level of the deliberations could only improve. As it happened, they did not.

After surveying briefly the history of the proposal for a workers' congress, Leiteizen asserted that it "undermines the idea of scientific socialism . . . [and aims] at the creation of a nonparty organization as a counterpoise" to Social Democracy. He also claimed that it was not true that the party had failed to broaden its base, as Axelrod had charged. Trade unions, which drew upon the masses for their membership, had expanded the influence of the party enormously. Nor could it be said

96. "We do not give a damn about your law." *Ibid.*, pp. 555–556.
97. *Ibid.*, p. 499

that the Bolsheviks looked askance at all nonparty proletarian organizations: witness their enthusiasm for the soviets. (This example was misleading, for initially many Bolsheviks had been extremely cool toward the soviets because they viewed them as potential rivals to the party.) As for the proponents of a workers' congress, they had committed the offenses of pitting "workers without consciousness" against the party, spreading "corruption" among them by dwelling on the schism and the party's alleged lack of contact with the masses, and wanting to turn back the wheels of history. "Your entire agitation is agitation against the party. And you want to create another, broad labor party . . . We must fight against a tendency that fights against Social Democracy." Plekhanov could contain himself no longer and shouted: "The trouble is that you're a bad Marxist." To which Leiteizen replied: "Your student, Comrade Plekhanov." "A bad student!" snapped Plekhanov.[98]

Axelrod spoke in favor of the Menshevik resolution, which recommended preparatory agitation for a workers' congress. He began by expressing indignation that the subject had been raised because a discussion of it "at our congress will have the character of a trial by the party of the 'idea' of a workers' congress, a trial in which the representatives of the coalition of Bolsheviks and the national organizations appear as the prosecutors and judges." Axelrod was, nonetheless, well prepared for his extemporaneous remarks. For two years he had talked and written about almost nothing else, so that he readily formulated a rebuttal to Leiteizen's claims and charges and did it with the same self-assurance and forthrightness that had impressed the Fourth Congress a year earlier.

He branded as "self-delusion" Leiteizen's assertion that even though many workers did not belong to the party it was indeed a genuine working-class organization. "I contend," Axelrod said, "that our party has been since its origin and remains until this time the revolutionary organization not of the working class, but of the petty bourgeois intelligentsia (noise, protests from the Bolsheviks, shouts: Listen!) for the revolutionary influence over this class." In recent months, to be sure, a number of workers had been enrolled in the movement, but often this had been done out of "factional calculations," that is, because a certain group wanted to gain control over a local committee. In addition, those

98. *Ibid.*, pp. 499–503, 548. Plekhanov had previously made a public statement favoring the workers' congress. See his "O chrezvychainom partiinom s'ezde" (On the Extraordinary Party Congress), *Sotsialdemokrat,* no. 1 (Sept. 17, 1906).

workers who had been admitted constituted "a sort of class of plebeians, whereas the intelligentsia plays the role of an aristocracy, a class of party members controlling internal and external affairs of our party state, guarding the plebeian lower orders against all pernicious influence from without." The workers did not feel that they possessed rights in equal measure to those of other party members. "Our party must undergo radical changes so that it can begin to be a genuine homeland for the workers themselves. It is very regrettable that all this has still to be proven."[99]

Once again, as at the congress in Stockholm a year earlier, the Mensheviks rallied behind Axelrod. But as the philosophical Menshevik had predicted, the Bolsheviks could not be moved by arguments. Rather, they were angered by Axelrod's charges and responded with personal attacks. M. Tomsky, for example, said: "Yes, the matter is clear. Comrade Axelrod, cut off from Russian life by his long stay abroad and [his custom of] viewing Russia through German spectacles, has not noticed the growth of our party and until this moment has a conception of it characteristic of a high school boy." For good measure, he accused Axelrod of subscribing to the heresy of syndicalism, and the Mensheviks in general of bankruptcy: "You have fallen into the gutter, Comrade Mensheviks . . . When the worker Mensheviks here talk about the bourgeois intelligentsia, it is clear to me that they are speaking about their own leaders."[100]

Shortly thereafter the congress adopted the Bolshevik resolution condemning the idea of a workers' congress, agitation for which would "inevitably lead to the disorganization of the party and promote the subordination of the laboring masses to the influence of bourgeois democracy." The vote was 165 to 94, with 21 abstentions. Nearly all the Mensheviks, as well as a few Bundists, opposed the resolution.[101]

On the other major tactical issues the congress also divided along factional lines, and the Bolsheviks secured majorities for practically all their resolutions. The most important of these concerned the Social Democratic attitude toward the bourgeois parties. It unleashed especial wrath on the Cadets, who were depicted as deserters from the revolutionary cause. The only exception to the string of Bolshevik triumphs

99. *Piatyi (Londonskii) s'ezd RSDRP*, pp. 503–520, 543–549.
100. *Ibid.*, pp. 527–528.
101. *Ibid.*, pp. 556–557, 561, 612–613.

was the adoption, by the surprisingly decisive vote of 170 to 35, with 52 abstentions, of the Menshevik resolution condemning "partisan actions and expropriations." Most of the Bolsheviks could not bring themselves to sanction these forays, but Lenin did not heed the decision of the congress and the squeamishness of his followers.[102]

The reader of the protocols of the London congress of the RSDRP is likely to be struck by the air of unreality in which the meetings were conducted. The underlying assumption of virtually every tactical resolution endorsed by the delegates was that the revolutionary movement in Russia still embodied a palpable threat to the regime. No one raised the question of the party's tactics should the government quash the opposition, but two weeks after the congress adjourned (June 16, 1907) Stolypin engineered a coup d'etat. He dissolved the Duma, disfranchised many citizens, exiled the Social Democratic deputies to the Duma, imposed severe restrictions on the press and trade unions, ordered the arrest of hundreds of revolutionaries, and placed most of the country under a state of emergency.

At first, some Menshevik leaders, who had again settled in the West, thought that the draconian measures of the government would stimulate a new wave of revolutionary ferment. "Eternal irony of fate!" Martov wrote from Paris to Axelrod in Zurich, "It seems to me that in the end the coup that has been staged will be beneficial to the revolution since it will remove much of the ambiguity and bring the nation back to that starting point of the revolution when a small group of privileged people stood in opposition to the aggregate of all the objectively progressive classes." Such a development would be a "brilliant justification of those revolutionary perspectives which we depicted in our platform before the [London] congress . . . [as well as] our predictions that the . . . [Cadets] will again 'become more radical,' and, finally, our tactics in the Duma."

In the same letter Martov passed along some information he had received from Dan, which provided the basis for a more realistic assessment of Russia's political future. Dan, who had returned to Russia, reported that the entire St. Petersburg organization of the Mensheviks had been crushed and that he therefore was incapable even of attempt-

102. *Ibid.*, pp. 582, 610–616; see also Alfred Levin, "The Fifth Social-Democratic Congress and the Duma," *Journal of Modern History*, XI (Dec. 1939), 484–508.

ing to elicit working-class response to the coup. The Bolsheviks had raised the question of a strike, but it had been met with no reaction from the proletariat.[103] The Marxists who had assembled in London seem to have been unaware of the extent of working-class apathy. They apparently had no idea how much proletarian morale had been damaged by the economic recession of 1904 and the revolution itself, which left extensive unemployment in its wake. Under the circumstances, workers were reluctant to rally to the call for political strikes.

Within a few months even the most optimistic Mensheviks recognized that the movement in Russia was in disarray. All the reports told the same story. In November Dan wrote Axelrod that of the members of the St. Petersburg center who had not been arrested, many had left the movement, others had abandoned political work altogether, and a few had been absorbed by Bolshevik committees. Dan could not collect enough money to start a newspaper and asked Axelrod to send him 2,000 or 3,000 francs for the purpose.[104] Over a decade later Martov accurately summed up the effect of Stolypin's repression: "Now the forces of the party collapsed like a house of cards."[105]

Although disappointed by the course of the revolution, Axelrod in 1907 could look back on the intraparty developments of the previous three years with some satisfaction. The Mensheviks, after having equivocated during 1905, had followed his lead on one issue after another and thus remained faithful to his conception of orthodoxy. In 1907 he admitted that this agreeable outcome had surprised him and that he had previously contemplated leaving the party because it had followed tactics he considered both "anti-Social Democratic and unsound."[106] Now, however, he could once again play a determinative part in the

103. Martov to Axelrod, June 26, 1907, *Pis'ma*, ed. Dan, Nicolaevsky, and Tsederbaum-Dan, pp. 163–164.

104. Dan to Axelrod, Nov. 12, 1907, Axelrod Archive, I.I.S.H.; Dan to Axelrod, n. d., but late in 1907, both from Terioki, *ibid.;* for a similar assessment, see Potresov to Axelrod, Oct. 16, 1907, *Sotsial-demokraticheskoe dvizhenie: materialy*, ed. A. N. Potresov and B. I. Nicolaevsky (Moscow, 1928), pp. 171–173.

105. L. Martov, *Geschichte der russischen Sozialdemokratie: Mit einem Nachtrag von Th. Dan: Die Sozialdemokratie Russlands nach dem Jahre 1918* (Berlin, 1926), p. 231.

106. Pavel Axelrod, *Dve taktiki: Doklad, prochitannyi na s'ezde v Stokgol'me* (St. Petersburg, 1907), pp. x–xii.

formulation of Menshevik policy. For the next twelve years at least, official Menshevism never again strayed from the major tactical or theoretical positions adopted in 1906 and 1907.

In this period, also, the distinctions between Bolshevism and Menshevism were refined to a far greater extent than they had been in the first year and a half after the schism. This was partly due to the curious dynamic at work in the clashes between the factions. Whenever a spokesman of one group proposed a policy, the leaders of the other felt obliged not only to criticize it but to advance a new policy of their own with an extensive theoretical rationale. In consequence, the disagreements began to encompass an ever wider range of issues, none of which had seemed to be in contention in the early stages of the feud. Although Bolshevism and Menshevism were, ideologically, both variants of revolutionary Marxism, by 1907 each represented a self-contained set of attitudes toward Russia's future development.

The experiences of the revolution had taught the Mensheviks the futility of concentrating on preparation for an armed uprising. Not only was such a course likely to provoke massive repression, as had occurred; it would also distort the nature of Social Democracy by transforming it from a movement dedicated to the political activation of the working class into a conspiratorial party organized along hierarchical, military lines. Another, related lesson that the Mensheviks drew from the events of 1905 and 1906 was that the advocacy of maximalist demands was bound to split and therefore weaken the opposition to the autocracy.

Menshevik hostility toward the liberals was, in general, substantially less intense than that of the Leninists, as had been the case prior to the revolution. It is true that frequently Axelrod's colleagues stridently criticized middle-class progressives and during the revolution rejected the notion of working-class participation in a bourgeois government after the fall of the Tsar. But they usually tempered their criticism, making it plain that they had not written the liberals off as an oppositional force. The divergent attitudes of the factions toward the middle class proved in time to be of decisive importance. After the collapse of tsarism early in 1917 the Mensheviks supported the essentially middle-class Provisional Government, and several of them even served in it, which was a major reversal of policy.

Finally, the Revolution of 1905 again made it evident to the Mensheviks that their ties to the working class were extremely tenuous and that, in fact, their assessments of the mood and aspirations of the proletariat were thoroughly flawed. They acknowledged that new efforts were necessary in order to move closer to the masses. The intrafactional debate over the workers' congress may, therefore, be said to have marked a turning point of sorts in the history of Russian Marxism. It once again brought the organizational question to the surface, and, more important, it finally laid to rest the claim that in 1903 the differences over this matter had not turned on the fundamentals of the party's ideology. Bolshevik critiques of Axelrod's proposal were so explicit and candid in articulating the elitist, conspiratorial conception of the party that there could no longer be any doubt that Lenin and his followers intended to create an organization that had little in common with the initial aspirations of Russian Marxists. At the same time the widespread Menshevik support for a workers' congress underlined the determination of Axelrod's faction to refashion the movement into a mass party. During the period of reaction from 1907 to 1914, when tactics were perforce not of paramount concern, the issue of the organization of the proletariat again proved to be the principal source of ideological discord within Russian Social Democracy.

VIII | The Failure of Conciliation

Shortly after the Fifth Party Congress Axelrod returned to Zurich in a grim mood. It was only then that he had to make the painful adjustment to living without his wife. During the first year after her death he had been somewhat distracted from his sorrow by the feverish party work in Terioki, where he was constantly surrounded by close friends who looked upon him as their ideological mentor and took pains to publicize his views. It had also been a year of high optimism: a new wave of revolutionary activity was expected at any moment. Stolypin's coup d'etat, however, had dashed those hopes, and Russian Marxism now seemed scarcely more influential than it had been in 1904. Instead of planning a new offensive against the regime, the Mensheviks found themselves starting anew to build an effective working-class movement.

Axelrod now suddenly faced serious financial difficulties, which was particularly distressing because he had finally enjoyed a few years of modest comfort. In his absence a new milk company, with access to "huge" amounts of capital, had been established in Zurich and proved to be a powerful competitor. Because he lost many customers, his income plummeted. By 1908 his debts ran in excess of 15,000 francs, a substantial sum, and he was threatened with bankruptcy. It was fortunate that the owner of the new company, impressed by the "popularity of our firm and our kefir," offered to buy the business in exchange for information on the proper preparation of the product and the right to use Axelrod's name. It was also fortunate that the competitor was unaware of Axelrod's financial straits; this enabled the latter to prolong the negotiations and ultimately to strike a good bargain. When late in 1908 he sold the business, the buyer agreed to give him a sum large enough to pay off his debts and support himself and his son for a year, as well as an annuity of 2,000 to 3,000 francs for ten years thereafter, which was sufficient for his personal expenses. For the first time in his adult life he did not have to worry about earning a livelihood, and at last he was free of the "damned kefir."[1]

Before the negotiations were completed he succumbed to a severe attack of neurasthenia. For extended periods he could not work at all. On days when he felt a little stronger he could write for two or three hours at best. "It is terribly difficult," he told Ingerman in 1909, "to write about . . . the [political] struggle when I feel as though I were physically and intellectually paralyzed."[2] He was so agonized by his inability to work that he asked his friends to arrange for an autopsy of his brain after his death. Only in this way, he believed, would people be convinced that his failure to contribute more to the movement was the result of illness rather than "laziness." The autopsy was performed, but the diagnosis is not known.[3]

In 1909 he moved to France, apparently in the hope that a change of scenery would afford him relief from his wretchedness. At first he lived with Dan and Martov, who after leaving Russia had rented a summer cottage near Bordeaux. The two men endeavored to make Axelrod's stay comfortable and after much prodding persuaded him to consult a neuropathologist. The doctor charged him an exorbitant fee for the "useless information" that he ought to take a complete rest, advice that Axelrod felt he could have prescribed himself. Nevertheless, the sojourn with Dan and Martov, which was followed by permanent residence in Paris with old friends, the Pomerantses, had a salutary effect on him. After a few months in France he felt stronger than he had in several years and found it possible to work for a while almost every day.[4]

The fortunes of his party in 1907 and 1908 deepened Axelrod's mood of despondency. The abusive debates at the congress in the spring of 1907 revived the factional feuding. Neither side seems actually to have accepted as genuine and permanent the unity that had been achieved in Stockholm in 1906. Both had maintained their factions intact and

1. Axelrod to Ingerman, Dec. 28, 1909, Axelrod Archive, I.I.S.H.
2. Axelrod to Ingerman, n. d., but sometime in 1909, *ibid.*
3. P. A. Garvi, *Vospominaniia: Peterburg-Odessa-Vena—1912* (New York, 1961), pp. 19–20.
4. Axelrod to Ingerman, Mar. 3, 1910, Axelrod Archive, I.I.S.H.

during 1907 flouted party resolutions. Some Mensheviks paid no more attention to the prohibition on agitation for a workers' congress than did the Bolsheviks to the official condemnation of expropriations. Late in 1907 the Leninists embarked on an even more outrageous activity: the production of counterfeit rubles. The Mensheviks found out only because several Bolsheviks were caught red-handed by the Berlin police. Axelrod was stunned: "If all this is true, then I ask: How can we remain with them in one party?" Plekhanov reacted similarly: their conduct was so "vile" that he thought it time to "break with the Bolsheviks."[5]

Most of the Mensheviks were not prepared to go this far, but they did agree on the need to revitalize their faction as a separate organization. The first order of business, Martov decided late in October 1907, was to create a literary center abroad. He asked Axelrod to become an editor of the projected newspaper and journal, even though he might not be well enough to do much writing. Martov believed that a promise by Axelrod to serve would be of "great significance in order to gather all the Mensheviks around such organs (as you know, Dan's authority is insufficient for that)." (Dan was still in Russia trying to organize Menshevik party cells.) Despite his reluctance to act as a silent partner, Axelrod felt that he could not refuse to lend his name to the venture. Late in January 1908 he attended a meeting of Mensheviks in exile to map the policies of the new publications.[6]

At this conference the Mensheviks disagreed, as usual, on how to proceed. Three positions were advanced, by Dan, Martov, and Axelrod, respectively. Dan, who had just returned from Russia, emphasized that politically the Bolsheviks were drawing close to the Mensheviks. He therefore favored a "tactic of preservation of 'unity' at all costs, protection of the 'prestige of the party' (i.e. abstention from 'excessive' criticism, adjustment to the status quo, to the hooligan actions of the official organs and their agents, etc.), 'conquest' of party institutions—

5. P. A. Garvi, *Vospominaniia: Peterburg—1906* (New York, 1961), p. 115; Axelrod to Martov, Dec. 7, 1907, *Pis'ma P. B. Aksel'roda i Iu. O. Martova, 1901–1906*, ed. F. Dan, B. I. Nicolaevsky, and L. Tsederbaum-Dan (Berlin, 1924), p. 115; Plekhanov to Martov, Dec. 9, 1907, *Sotsial-demokraticheskoe dvizhenie: materialy*, ed. A. N. Potresov and B. I. Nicolaevsky (Moscow, 1928), p. 175.

6. Martov to Axelrod, Oct. 26, 1907, *Pis'ma*, ed. Dan, Nicolaevsky, and Tsederbaum-Dan, p. 167; Axelrod to Martov, Oct. 29, 1907, *ibid.*, p. 170; see also editor's note, *ibid.*, pp. 182–183.

with the aid of a policy of 'accommodation to baseness.' " The new publications should concentrate specifically on general agitational and political questions rather than on a factional and primarily polemical contest against the Bolsheviks. Dan hoped that by appealing to reason Menshevism would attract the masses to its side.[7] Dan's position makes sense only in the light of his assessment of the situation in Russia, which he had given Axelrod in December 1907: "There are no money, no people, no [interest in party] work . . . . Menshevism as an organization simply does not now exist in Russia, and to assemble it once again by mechanical means is impossible." The Bolsheviks, however, had succeeded in retaining at least the nucleus of an organization, and Dan feared that if the Mensheviks split with them the Leninists could easily dominate the labor movement. The only sensible course for the Mensheviks was "not to recoil from the remnants of Bolshevism" but within the party to "fight all these nasty people and slime" which "threaten to stifle us, to deprive us forever of the hope" of creating a genuine Social Democratic party. In other words, the Mensheviks should try to avoid provoking a split, while pursuing the attempt to win control of the party.[8]

Martov, standing at the opposite end of the pole from Dan, advocated a strong anti-Bolshevik line. He was guided "not so much by theoretical implacability, as by an unreservedly negative attitude toward attempts to resurrect illegal forms of activity." Martov's position also derived from his sense of outrage at the continuing criminal activities of the Bolsheviks. Apparently, it was only in early 1908 that the Mensheviks learned about the Tiflis expropriations, the most ambitious and scandalous to date. At this time Martov actually proposed a complete break with the Leninists, though it is not known whether he urged this policy at the conference.[9]

Axelrod interpreted the movement as going through a phase similar to two previous phases: the period of the founding of Russian Marxism,

7. Axelrod to Plekhanov, Feb. 2, 1908, *Perepiska G. V. Plekhanova i P. B. Aksel'roda*, ed. B. I. Nicolaevsky, P. A. Berlin, and W. S. Woytinsky (Moscow, 1925), II, 252–255; my discussion of the three positions is based mainly on this letter and on Axelrod to Martov, Jan. 13, 1908, *Pis'ma*, ed. Dan, Nicolaevsky, and Tsederbaum-Dan, pp. 179–180.

8. Dan to Axelrod, Dec. 6, 1907, Axelrod Archive, I.I.S.H.

9. On the Tiflis affair, see Bertram D. Wolfe, *Three Who Made a Revolution. A Biographical History* (New York, 1948), pp. 393–398; Israel Getzler, *Martov: A Political Biography of a Russian Social Democrat* (Cambridge, Eng., 1967), p. 120.

and that of the Economist heresy. He believed, consequently, that the principal aim must be to form a group of the "most advanced elements of the party," which would devote itself to the "ideological, organizational, and political regeneration of Russian Social Democracy as an authentic proletarian party—on the theoretical basis of Marxism." Such a course would involve neither renunciation of the existing party nor excessive concern about its unity or prestige. Ideological and tactical differences should be aired and the Bolsheviks criticized, but not so intensely as to cause a split in the near future. If the organization became thoroughly discredited, it would be necessary to found a new one, for which Axelrod proposed the name "communist." But as long as the Mensheviks retained active adherents and the slightest chance to revitalize the party, every attempt should be made to reform existing institutions.

Axelrod's wait-and-see strategy would not have been easy to execute, but it had much to commend it. It would have allowed the Mensheviks to disassociate themselves from Leninist excesses without assuming the responsibility for initiating a formal split. At the same time, it was designed to give them a breathing spell during which they could ascertain whether or not they could muster enough support from "healthy elements" to gain the upper hand in the party.

The conference adopted Axelrod's line, which was also supported by Plekhanov, who had not attended because of illness. Dan considered it a "middle course." Axelrod, however, conceived of it not as a compromise between two extremes but as a distinctive approach, "the only possible, logically necessary [one] at the present moment." Once a broad strategy had been chosen, the conferees decided to publish a newspaper, *Golos sotsialdemokrata*, which was to serve as the literary center for the revitalization of the party.

Agreement on policy was one thing, implementation another. For the first issue of the paper Martov wrote two articles that sharply attacked the Bolsheviks and exposed their terroristic and criminal activities.[10] Axelrod, with the backing of Dan and, apparently, the other editors (Martynov, Plekhanov, and P. Maslov), induced Martov to tone down his critique. In addition to undermining Axelrod's general strategy, Martov's exposé might be "used for police and demagogic purposes."

10. For an analysis of Martov's articles, see Getzler, *Martov*, pp. 121–122.

Much as he deplored the expropriations, Axelrod did not want the Mensheviks to bear the onus for police action against Lenin and his followers.

Instead, he proposed that the Mensheviks dispatch an appeal to "broad party circles" to seek an end to the criminal actions. He also considered making the Bolshevik excesses known to leaders of Western parties, but confessed that "a kind of feeling of party pride" gave him qualms about advocating this step. In the end, he and his associates decided to submit a report on the expropriations to the Executive Committee of the German party, and to Kautsky, Adler, and the International Socialist Bureau (I.S.B.).[11] No such report seems to have survived, and, given Axelrod's disinclination to attack the Bolsheviks, it is quite possible that it was never written.

Why was he so cautious? It would seem, on the surface, that the Leninists' criminal conduct presented him with the ideal means to humiliate and crush the opponent for whom he had such profound contempt. He was probably restrained by the apprehension that the revelations not only might fail to achieve their purpose, but might even boomerang. Of all the Mensheviks he had enjoyed the closest relations with the leaders of international Social Democracy, and he could not have forgotten that only three years earlier Kautsky and Bebel had condemned his faction for high-handedness in financial matters. Would they now believe the Menshevik charges against the Bolsheviks?

If Axelrod's misgivings were as we have speculated, time would show that they were well-founded. In the fall of 1908 the Bolsheviks appealed to the Executive Committee of the German party to arbitrate some outstanding issues between the factions. When Dan learned of the move, he privately told Kautsky that it was "ill-advised": instead of bothering foreign socialists, Russian Social Democrats ought to grapple with the "important political questions" that required immediate attention. If the Germans wished to intervene in Russian affairs, Dan suggested, they ought to review the overall situation in the movement, for the conflict was not confined to differences over tactical questions, but also stemmed from the Bolsheviks' "acts of banditry," a "cancerous sore" that was infecting the entire party.[12] There is no evidence that Kautsky showed

---

11. Axelrod to R. M. Plekhanova, Feb. 26, 1908, *Perepiska,* ed. Nicolaevsky, Berlin, and Woytinsky, II, 257.

12. Dan to Kautsky, Oct. 8, 9, 1908, Kautsky Archive, I.I.S.H.

interest either in investigating Dan's charges or in denouncing the Bolsheviks' actions.

In 1911, when Martov exposed details of the expropriations in a pamphlet entitled *Saviors or Destroyers,* Western socialist leaders were also not moved to expressions of indignation. It is true that the charges referred to events that had taken place a few years earlier, but they were so serious that some voicing of disapproval might have been expected. Instead, Kautsky decried Martov's "detestable brochure" and branded it a "senseless" attack, whose only purpose could be to provoke a split by "unearthing mistakes of the past." He explained that he did not approve of Lenin's actions, but despite the revelations he could not consider himself "an opponent of Lenin." It was Martov who deserved to be censured for attempting to divide the party. Kautsky then repeated his usual profession of neutrality vis-à-vis the factions. Although these opinions appeared in a private letter, they so delighted the Bolsheviks that they gleefully circulated a hectographed translation in émigré circles.[13]

Golos sotsialdemokrata was launched early in 1908, and once again the Mensheviks possessed an organizational center and an official— though modest—mouthpiece. In February of that year Dan complained that "our resources are so meager that at first we will not be able to appear more often than once a month." During its three-year existence *Golos sotsialdemokrata* appeared even less frequently, only twenty-six numbers actually being published. Still, of the 5,000 copies of the first issue, the Mensheviks managed, within two weeks, to smuggle 2,500 into Russia. Of the rest there remained only eighty in the office.[14] A reservoir of interest in what the Mensheviks in the West had to say had obviously survived.

Soon the existence of three centers of Menshevik strength inside the Empire became known. The only Menshevik organization with an underground committee had been established in Georgia. Under the leadership of N. Zhordania and N. Ramishvili, the Georgians elected two of their number, E. P. Gegechkori and N. S. Chkheidze, to the Duma. In St. Petersburg a group of intellectuals sympathetic to the

13. Kautsky to Lunacharsky, Aug. 9, 1911, Nicolaevsky Collection, Hoover Institution.

14. Dan to Kautsky, Feb. 6, Mar. 19, 1908, Kautsky Archive, I.I.S.H.; Dan to Axelrod, Mar. 14, 1908, Axelrod Archive, I.I.S.H.

Mensheviks gathered around A. N. Potresov; from 1910 to 1914 they legally published the sophisticated *Nasha zaria*, a superb guide to the thinking of Mensheviks in Russia during the period. Finally, there were a fair number of practicals, men who operated principally in the trade unions, cooperatives, and other mass organizations, insofar as this was permitted by the government.[15]

Even though these developments suggest a gradual revival of Menshevism in Russia, Axelrod's strategy of detaching the majority of the party from the Bolsheviks never had a chance to succeed. Before long Lenin raised an issue that polarized anew opinion in the movement. The savage campaign against liquidationism, unleashed in 1908, again put the factions at loggerheads over an ideological question. It looked initially like a new issue, but it soon turned out that it was merely a new version of the long-standing dispute over the organization of the proletariat. In the years 1908–1914, when the Mensheviks disagreed among themselves about numerous matters, it was their broad common position on liquidationism, as much as anything else touching on ideology, that bound them together.

Liquidationism is one of those hopelessly elusive words so often encountered in the history of Russian Social Democracy and, indeed, in the history of Russia. Lenin, who coined the term, quickly used it in a pejorative sense and called anyone he disagreed with or wanted to discredit a liquidator. He had apparently learned this technique from Plekhanov. "Plekhanov," Lenin told Valentinov in 1904, "once said to me about a critic of Marxism (I've forgotten his name): 'First, let's stick the convict's badge on him, and then after that we'll examine his case.' And I think that we must 'stick the convict's badge' on anyone and everyone who tries to undermine Marxism, even if we don't go on to examine his case. That's how every sound revolutionary should react. When you see a stinking heap on the road you don't have to poke around in it to see what it is. Your nose tells you it's shit, and you give it a wide berth."[16] Though effective as a means of character assassination, this method had the drawback of muddying the distinction between groundless charges and reality, as events would show.

Apparently the term liquidationism was officially used for the first

---

15. This classification is based on Leonard Schapiro, *The Communist Party of the Soviet Union* (London, 1960), pp. 102–103.

16. Nikolay Valentinov, *Encounters with Lenin*, tr. Paul Rosta and Brian Pearce (London, 1968), p. 182.

time at the Fifth All-Russian Conference of the RSDRP, which met in Paris January 3–9, 1909. At Lenin's instigation, and in spite of the resistance of the Mensheviks and some Bundists, the conference passed a resolution condemning the attempts of several groups of party intelligentsia "to liquidate the existing organization of the RSDRP and to replace it with a shapeless association" that would be permitted by law.[17] A few months later Lenin characterized the liquidators as being "intrepid opportunists" who argued against the "necessity of an illegal Social Democratic party and against the necessity of the RSDRP," and who opposed "the revolutionary class struggle of the socialist proletariat in general and, in particular, . . . the hegemony of the proletariat in our bourgeois-democratic revolution."

During the next four years Lenin repeatedly broadened the attack on liquidationism. He branded Axelrod as one of the leaders of the current, which he now virtually equated with Economism, reformism, and "non-Social Democratic, bourgeois tendencies," in addition to several other heresies. He also repeatedly denounced the Mensheviks as a group for subscribing to liquidationism.[18] Lenin used the term liquidationism to cover such a broad spectrum of ideas that his works do not offer a reliable guide to the ideological dispute between him and the Mensheviks after 1907. He distorted the views of the Mensheviks beyond all recognition.

First of all, it is patently untrue that the Menshevik leaders had become reformists. They had not relinquished the notions of class struggle, historical materialism, belief in the inevitability of revolution, or any of Marx's economic doctrines. They disassociated themselves publicly and privately from the ideas advanced by Bernstein. Yet, it is undeniable that after 1907 the previous differences over the organization of the proletariat between Axelrod and his comrades on the one side and the Leninists on the other assumed a new ideological dimension. This new dimension cannot be grasped, however, by reading Lenin's diatribes against liquidationism, but rather by examining the works that he thought exemplified the tendency. Aside from Axelrod's proposal for a workers' congress, Lenin singled out two articles for special

17. *Kommunisticheskaia partiia sovetskogo soiuza v rezoliutsiiakh i resheniiakh s'ezdov, konferentsii i plenumov Ts.K.* (7th ed., Moscow, 1954), I, 195.
18. On Lenin's characterizations of the liquidators, see his *Sochineniia* (3rd ed., Moscow, 1926–1937), XIV, 93, 104–110, 130–135, 165, 341; XV, 205; XVI, 35–44, 70, 126, 436, 612; XVII, 483.

vilification, one by Dan and one by Potresov, and ascribed ideas to both that they did not hold.

In a short piece entitled "The Struggle for Legality," published in 1910, Dan argued that the way for the party to counter the repressive measures of Stolypin was to increase its efforts "tenfold" to preserve and strengthen its "legal positions" through the use of all existing institutions: the courts, press, organs of self-government, and the Duma. At the same time an extensive program of agitation should be initiated among the masses, the democratic strata of the population, the international proletariat, and peoples in Western countries. It is important to note that Dan did not divorce the struggle for the "legal, open existence" of the labor movement from the general political efforts of the proletariat in Russia.

By writing on its banner "struggle for legality," Social Democratic activists of the legal labor movement thereby go beyond the bounds of "purely trade union" or "purely cooperative" or "purely educational" tasks. At the same time they inevitably go beyond the bounds of "legality." The *political* struggle is a necessary precondition even for the open existence of *nonpolitical* labor organizations; the *illegal* rallying [of the working class] is the necessary weapon in the struggle for *legality*. Perhaps this sounds paradoxical. But in actuality this is a historical fact, which the Russian laborer has already faced throughout the course of his [political] development.[19]

Lenin mercilessly attacked Dan's article, but when he explained his disagreement, it emerged that he simply reversed the Menshevik's order of priorities. "For Social Democrats," Lenin proclaimed, "the *legal* rallying [of the workers] is at the present moment one of the necessary weapons of the *illegal party*."[20] The movement should concern itself primarily with the strengthening of the underground party structure, but the legal institutions should also be utilized when feasible. Thus, the new conflict between Lenin and the leading Mensheviks had nothing to do either with liquidating the underground movement or reinterpreting Marxist doctrines. It derived, rather, from a question of emphasis: should primary stress be placed on the illegal or legal activities of the RSDRP? But the difference in emphasis was far from insignificant,

19. F. Dan, "Bor'ba za legal'nost'," *Golos sotsialdemokrata,* III, no. 19/20 (Jan.–Feb. 1910).
20. Lenin, *Sochineniia*, XIV, 259.

for it once again underscored the fact that the two factions harbored conflicting conceptions of the nature of a proletarian party.

The dispute over liquidationism actually had another aspect, as Potresov pointed out in an article that Lenin also found utterly heretical.[21] Potresov contended that liquidationism as a political current did not exist: it was the "phantom of a morbid imagination." In 1909 there was, in fact, no such thing as a Social Democratic "party" in Russia, if that word is properly defined, that is, "as an integral and organized hierarchy of institutions." No one had willed the extinction of the party, as the term liquidator implied: it had disintegrated in the wake of the counterrevolution. Although there remained an "ideological legacy," that is, the Social Democratic Duma representatives and some "uncoordinated remnants of the past," they did not add up to a meaningful political organization.[22]

Axelrod eventually involved himself in the liquidationist controversy because it touched on questions that he had long considered paramount. He also felt obliged to defend his Menshevik colleagues who were being subjected to vicious polemics. In 1910, despite poor health, he undertook a series of lectures to émigré circles. He had "taken heart," wrote Martov: "in Geneva he delivered three lectures on 'antiliquidationism' and on the evolution of Social Democracy in general with great success."[23]

Axelrod stressed two major points in his lectures. First, Lenin had turned his campaign against the so-called liquidators into a weapon for discrediting all his opponents. "For the Bolsheviks this word [liquidationism] has acquired as loose a meaning as the words 'enemy of the people' [or] 'enemy of the state' when used by the Black Hundreds." Just as the latter branded not only the anarchists, Socialist Revolutionaries, and Social Democrats, but also the Cadets and left Octobrists, as bent on destroying the Russian state, so the Leninists "liberally and without analysis" apply the sobriquet liquidator to any Marxist they wish, for one reason or another, to defame.[24]

Axelrod's second point was that close scrutiny of Lenin's "new cam-

21. *Ibid.*, p. 326.
22. A. Potresov, "Kriticheskie nabroski" (Critical Sketches), *Nasha zaria*, no. 2 (1910), 61–62.
23. Martov to Potresov, Nov. 3, 1910, Nicolaevsky Collection, Hoover Institution.
24. Pavel Axelrod, "Istochniki raznoglasii mezhdu tak-naz. partiitsami i tak-naz. likvidatorami," *Golos sotsialdemokrata*, III, no. 23 (Nov. 1910).

paign under the banner of 'anti-liquidationism' " exposed it as "a new phase of . . . the old struggle," begun in 1903, "to save the old party regime."[25] Like Potresov, he dismissed the charge that the Mensheviks favored the destruction of the party organization: as a result of the apathy of the Russian working class there was no party to dismantle.[26] He conceded that there was, nevertheless, a "grain of truth" to the contention that the Mensheviks were liquidators, but not in the sense intended by Lenin. "The active Mensheviks," Axelrod declared, "by and large are really trying to liquidate the negative elements of our past; . . . they strive to liquidate only the internal contradictions that prevent the party from escaping from the blind alley."[27] According to Axelrod, his faction, by emphasizing legal work, was merely trying to Europeanize Russian Social Democracy, a policy he had long advocated.

It should be noted that a few Social Democrats did call for an end to all underground, illegal activities. Thus, a certain N. D'iakonov, writing late in 1907 in support of the workers' congress, repudiated the idea of a secret, conspiratorial organization, which he considered appropriate only when the revolutionary bourgeoisie fought the autocracy unaided. "But when the political struggle becomes a mass struggle, the underground organization inevitably decays and disappears because it is not in a condition either to elucidate or defend the class interests of the proletariat." Only a party whose activities were public could grasp the needs and concerns of the masses.[28] In addition, at one of the Menshevik caucuses during the congress of 1907, an unnamed delegate is said to have proposed the liquidation of the "party organization and the conduct of open work in trade and other mass organizations." No one at the caucus seems to have supported this position.[29] Nor did any eminent Menshevik ever align himself with it.

Axelrod warned Garvi, in fact, that a few of the practical workers

25. E. Charskii [E. A. Anan'in], "P. B. Aksel'rod ob 'antilikvidatorstve' i ego istoricheskikh korniakh," Nasha zaria, no. 1 (1911), 67. This three-part article (two sections appeared in nos. 3 and 5) is based on interviews with Axelrod.

26. Axelrod to Martov, Sept. 3, 1910, Pis'ma, ed. Dan, Nicolaevsky, and Tsederbaum-Dan, p. 206.

27. Axelrod, "Istochniki."

28. N. D'iakonov, "Rabochii s'ezd i otkrytaia partiia" (A Workers' Congress and an Open Party), in Vserossiiskii rabochii s'ezd. Sbornik statei (Moscow, 1907), pp. 65–77.

29. N. Cherevanin [F. A. Lipkin], Londonskii s'ezd RSDRP 1907 g. (St. Petersburg, 1907), p. 79.

were going too far in opposing illegal work, thus providing the Bolsheviks with "proof of the accuracy of their slanders." Axelrod explained that though anxious to do away with the excessive conspiratorial aspects of the "stifling underground," he did not favor total abandonment of the illegal apparatus. He cautioned that the Europeanization of the party could only result from a "long and complicated process" and not a "stunning plan" or single decree, as some seemed to think.[30] Like Dan, Axelrod laid major stress on enlarging the legal scope of Social Democracy's political work in Russia without, however, denying the need for an illegal organization.

Although the emphasis had shifted slightly, the essentials of Axelrod's concept of the nature of the party had not been modified since 1903. The extent to which it had changed can be attributed to the changed situation in Russia. There was now considerably more scope for legal work, though government repression still created obstacles. Many practical workers found employment in trade unions and various cooperative associations and promptly began to train workers for an active and responsible role in their organizations. Here was a concrete possibility to promote the samodeiatel'nost' of the working class. It is not surprising that these praktiki considered Axelrod the father of liquidationism as they—not the Bolsheviks—understood the term. "We, the practicals, only concretized and applied in practice the methods . . . [Axelrod] advocated for Europeanizing the Russian labor movement under the conditions created by the semivictorious first revolution."[31] That they, as a group, were determined to do away with the party or its underground organization has never been demonstrated, but they were unquestionably resolved to found a genuine mass movement, which was enough to arouse Bolshevik suspicion and condemnation.

As much as Axelrod was appalled by the Leninist calumnies against him and the Mensheviks, he was probably even more distressed by the behavior of Plekhanov, who indulged in pettiness and meanness far surpassing his previous violations of civil conduct. In 1908 Plekhanov took umbrage at an article Potresov had written on the development of Marxism for a five-volume opus, *The Social Movement in Russia at*

---

30. Garvi, *Vospominaniia: Peterburg-Odessa-Vena—1912*, pp. 17–18; E. A. Anan'in, *Iz vospominanii revoliutsionera 1905–1923 g. g.* (New York, 1961), p. 37.
31. Garvi, *Vospominaniia: Peterburg-Odessa-Vena—1912*, p. 16.

the Beginning of the Twentieth Century, which was being edited by several Mensheviks. Plekhanov found Potresov's article deficient in several respects, but he was most disturbed that Potresov did not accord him the prominence he felt he deserved.[32] He made several efforts to have Potresov revise the article, but none of the changes satisfied him. Then he demanded that the editors of *Golos sotsialdemokrata* refuse to publish the piece, a request they could not honor because they were not, as a group, responsible for the contents of the study. Plekhanov responded to the refusal, first, by publicly resigning from the editorial board of *Golos sotsialdemokrata* and, second, by privately calling his former colleagues opportunists, the most withering insult in the Marxist lexicon.[33] Finally, in February 1910, he published a long article in which he portrayed Potresov as a Legal Marxist and liquidator and quoted extensively from private letters sent to him and his wife by Martov and Axelrod.

The revelations were damaging, as both had criticized Potresov's article. In one letter Axelrod had expressed displeasure with it and asserted that its author had "not been equal to his task." But he had failed to detect in it a "turn to Struvism" or any other evidence of heresy. Nor had he understood why Plekhanov should take as a personal affront the appearance of his piece in the same book as Potresov's. There were articles inferior to Potresov's in the collection, but their appearance did not reflect on Plekhanov's reputation. From his remarks, it is evident that Axelrod had hoped to smooth things over. He agreed that the essay was weak, yet pleaded with Plekhanov not to make an issue of it. As a solution, he had proposed that Martov and Plekhanov resign from the editorial board of the collection; thus, no prominent Menshevik would have appeared to sanction Potresov's piece.[34]

There is no need to go into the details of the ensuing negotiations between Plekhanov and Axelrod. The point is that Plekhanov felt betrayed by Axelrod's refusal to take a strong stand against Potresov's article. He claimed that Axelrod had promised to "insist" on a "delay" of its publication, which was impossible because at the time they dis-

---

32. G. V. Plekhanov, "O moem 'sekrete' " (About My "Secret") in *Sochineniia,* ed. D. Riazanov (2nd ed., Moscow, 1923–1927), XIX, 73–95.

33. Axelrod to Ingerman, probably early in 1909, Axelrod Archive, I.I.S.H.

34. Axelrod to R. M. Plekhanova, Dec. 1, 1908, *Perepiska,* ed. Nicolaevsky, Berlin, and Woytinsky, II, 268.

cussed the matter the volume containing Potresov's contribution was already in print. Plekhanov had plainly lost perspective in the matter. According to his wife, it was his "deep conviction that in coming to Potresov's defense, the editorial board of G[olos] s[otsialdemokrata] compromises itself before the entire world." Even Martov's offer to resign from the editorial board of *Golos sotsialdemokrata* did not soothe Plekhanov's ruffled feelings or prompt him to tone down his attacks on his comrades.

Plekhanov was most hurt by being let down by his old friend, Axelrod. "We very much love you," wrote Rosa Plekhanov, "George and I deeply respect you, and it is very distressing to us that in all the misunderstandings with comrades you stand completely on their side, committing great injustice to George. And one would think that the long-standing spiritual tie should have led to a complete mutual understanding. Why has it not? This is a deep tragedy."[35]

This same love and respect had not prevented Plekhanov from making public Axelrod's letters. Nor did they keep him from casting aspersions on Axelrod's integrity. After asserting that in splitting with the Mensheviks he was acting in accordance with his vow, made twenty-five years earlier, to remain faithful to his creed regardless of consequences, he discharged a barb at Axelrod: "I would wish from the bottom of my heart that each one of my former comrades in the Group for the Emancipation of Labor had the moral right to say the same about himself."[36]

Up to this point Axelrod had confined himself to private strictures against his friend.[37] Now for the first time he published an attack on him. The burden of his statement, which appeared in a special supplement to *Golos sotsialdemokrata* devoted to the contretemps, was its reproof of Plekhanov for resorting to methods of "an entirely Black Hundred and hooligan character." By calling all Mensheviks liquidators, Plekhanov was acting like a "real liquidator" himself because he was contributing to the destruction of the Russian labor movement. Axelrod saved his harshest words for Plekhanov's failure to respect the privacy of their correspondence:

35. See the exchange of letters, *ibid.*, pp. 270–287.
36. Plekhanov, " 'Sekrete,' " p. 95.
37. Axelrod to Ingerman, n. d., but sometime in 1909, Axelrod Archive, I.I.S.H.; Axelrod to Ingerman, Dec. 28, 1909, *ibid.*

I would have blushed with shame if even for an instant it had come to my mind that there existed the danger that so old and intimate a comrade as Plekhanov could put . . . [my letters] into circulation among readers who could misunderstand them because they have no notion of the content of the *entire* correspondence and were not familiar with the circumstances that had evoked them. What an example of a scandalous break of comradely trust . . . Let Plekhanov only try to imagine the kind of morals, the kind of spirit that would prevail in our party if his example were followed by all comrades.[38]

Axelrod's protest did not stem merely from hurt feelings at being the victim of Plekhanov's indiscretion; he had become increasingly sensitive to ethical issues since 1900, when he had sanctioned the publication of private letters for the purpose of undermining political antagonists. By 1910 he realized that resort to such "barbaric tactics" poisoned the atmosphere in the movement and made impossible an orderly resolution of differences.

This exchange marked the end of one of Axelrod's most intimate personal and political relationships. For a time he had overlooked the wounds Plekhanov had inflicted on him at the Second Congress, and the contacts between them had remained cordial, but this was no longer feasible. "It is difficult for me to express to you," Axelrod wrote Ingerman, "the feeling of shame and injury that I experience in looking through these products of [Plekhanov's] personal irritation and vindictiveness."[39] He was so anguished that he frequently spoke of retiring from politics. He retained his respect for Plekhanov's contributions to Marxism, nevertheless, and in 1923 dedicated his memoirs "To the memory of Georgii Valentinovich Plekhanov."

Even if the two had forgotten the bitter exchanges of 1909 and 1910, a rapprochement would not have been effected, for Plekhanov soon intensified his attacks on the Mensheviks. In order to embarrass them before the international movement, he sent letters to Kautsky claiming that there were really no differences of principle between the factions. He now contended that in the conflict then raging within the party the primary blame had to be placed on "Dan and company" rather than on Lenin.[40]

38. Pavel Axelrod, "Vynuzhdennoe ob'iasnenie," *Neobkhodimoe dopol'nenie k "dnevnikam" G. V. Plekhanova* (Paris, 1910).
39. Axelrod to Ingerman, Mar. 8, 1910, Axelrod Archive, I.I.S.H.; Axelrod to Ingerman, n. d., but sometime in 1909, *ibid.*
40. Plekhanov, *Sochineniia*, XIX, 378–388; Plekhanov to Kautsky, Dec. 27, 1910, Kautsky Archive, I.I.S.H.

Plekhanov's assessment had changed drastically since 1905 and 1906, when he believed there was an important ideological dimension to the split. Nor did it accord with the stance he took in 1907, when he urged a formal rupture with the Bolsheviks on the ground that they had hopelessly compromised themselves by perpetrating the expropriations. It is hard to avoid the conclusion that personal pique had seriously colored his political judgment.

Plekhanov's defection and attacks came at an inopportune moment for the Mensheviks, as they were again embroiled in a financial dispute with their rivals. Early in 1910 it had been agreed at a plenum of the C. C. of the RSDRP to give a large sum of money procured by the Bolsheviks[41] to three German trustees (Kautsky, Franz Mehring, and Zetkin), who were to disburse it to the C. C. if the factions managed to cooperate on their work inside Russia. Otherwise, the Bolsheviks would have the right to request its return. Someone had told Axelrod that Lenin had withheld at least 10,000 rubles, which he intended to use to further his plans to take over the party. Axelrod pleaded with Kautsky to see that Lenin carried out the plenum's decision faithfully. Luise Kautsky, answering for her husband, wrote that had Kautsky known he was expected to arbitrate the financial affairs of the party he would never have accepted the position of trustee. "He considers all of you equally honest and believes that you are terribly steamed up and excited and that you are therefore no longer in a condition to put your affairs in order with a cool head . . . Even the closest friend of the Russians, which he considers himself, must now say: 'I will not have anything more to do with this complicated Russian business.' "[42]

Even now, after all the discussions, Axelrod could not reconcile himself to Kautsky's professions of neutrality and nonintervention. He resolved to make yet another effort at enlightening his friend. He drafted a long missive, which is of interest because it reveals his motive for bombarding Kautsky with so many letters on the same topic. It was not that he wanted the satisfaction of his support, nor that he was simply concerned to defeat Lenin. He wanted the self-assurance that he

41. The reference is to the money the Bolsheviks had acquired from the "Schmitt inheritance" and the expropriations. See Wolfe, *Three Who Made a Revolution*, pp. 371–398.
42. Axelrod to Kautsky, June 5, 1911, Nicolaevsky Collection, Hoover Institution; Luise Kautsky to Axelrod, June 12, Axelrod Archive, I.I.S.H.

had done all in his power properly to inform the leaders of Marxism, for a time would come when they would realize that their prejudice in favor of the "representatives of a clique" had irreparably damaged Russian Social Democracy. A genuine internationalist, Axelrod contended that members of foreign parties ought not to refuse to intervene in Russian affairs because the degeneration of one party would inevitably cast a shadow on the Marxist movement the world over. In any case, the Germans had intervened as early as 1904 but in an "extremely one-sided manner, on the basis of blind trust in our [Joseph] Peukert [a disreputable member of the German party whom Axelrod here is likening to Lenin]."[43]

This letter to Kautsky and one in a similar vein to Clara Zetkin[44] suggest that Axelrod was not in a frame of mind conducive to the rather delicate mission he undertook about a week after he wrote them. From September 10 to 16, 1911, he attended the Jena congress of the German socialists, largely for the purpose of prevailing upon the trustees to transfer some of the money to the Mensheviks. Trotsky, who needed funds for his newspaper, *Pravda,* also went to Jena, and together they appealed to the Germans. There resulted a series of minor intrigues and a few public meetings with party leaders, but no success in obtaining funds.

Trotsky and Axelrod secretly met Kautsky and Hugo Haase at a remote restaurant, where they would not be likely to come across supporters of Zetkin and Rosa Luxemburg, who strongly favored the Bolsheviks. Later Kautsky arranged for a larger meeting that included Zetkin, but not much is known about the various discussions. Axelrod feared that his "manifestations of obstinacy" toward the Bolsheviks had upset Kautsky: "It seems to me that because of this I especially provoked his anger against me." Zetkin, who behaved "in part even more correctly than Kautsky," could not be induced to make any commitments. The two merely promised to discuss the question of the money soon and reach a quick decision.[45]

43. Axelrod to Luise Kautsky, June 14, 1911, incomplete draft, Axelrod Archive, I.I.S.H. Peukert was an anarchist held in great contempt in German radical circles because in 1887 he allegedly informed on another anarchist, Johann Neve, who was then sentenced to a fifteen-year term in prison. See Franz Mehring, *Geschichte der deutschen Sozialdemokratie* (4 vols., 8th ed. Stuttgart: J. H. W. Dietz, 1919), IV, 297.
44. Axelrod to Zetkin, Sept. 3, 1911, incomplete draft, Axelrod Archive, I.I.S.H.
45. Axelrod to Dan and Martov, Aug. [but should read Sept.] 19, 1911, *Pis'ma,* ed. Dan, Nicolaevsky, and Tsederbaum-Dan, pp. 217–218.

Axelrod's failure at the congress was a bad omen, as the Mensheviks soon discovered. For in his decisions as trustee, Kautsky, despite his protestations of neutrality, proved to favor the Bolsheviks. On several occasions he voted to deliver considerable sums of money to Lenin's group and none at all to his opponents. Kautsky's behavior may be attributed to several factors. First, he could not be shaken in the opinion he had reached in the years 1903–1905: that there were no differences between the factions sufficiently significant to justify a schism. Plekhanov's rash of attacks could only have served to confirm these convictions. And insofar as Kautsky did detect any divergencies, by this time he seems to have been sympathetic to Lenin's overall strategy, though he still did not approve of his strong-arm methods. In 1909 Kautsky declared his lack of confidence in the revolutionary commitment of the Russian middle classes and pinned his hopes on the peasantry and proletariat as the groups likely to stage a bourgeois revolution.[46] Finally, all the trustees probably believed that since Lenin had obtained the funds they were holding, he was entitled to at least a portion.

The fact of the matter—so painful and incomprehensible to Axelrod —was that the Mensheviks had still not convinced most of the leaders of international socialism that they merited support. The extent of Western puzzlement is revealed in a long letter Axelrod received in the summer of 1911 from Adolf Braun, one of the editors of the major Austrian journal, Der Kampf. Braun asked for an article explaining the roots of the turmoil and discord in the Russian party and emphasized that he and other European Marxists deplored the conduct of the émigrés: "While the enemy proceeds against the labor movement and against socialism with a ruthlessness surpassing that of its predecessors, within the circle of émigrés differences of all dimensions appear to be the most important concern, and a large share of the efforts of the most able, the best and experienced people are expended—we mean: squandered—on struggles between comrades. For those of us who do not know Russian this is an extraordinarily painful experience."

Braun was also puzzled by the constant emergence of new ideological tendencies. To be sure, some of the "talmudic" discussions of fine theoretical points were interesting, but they did not appear remotely

46. See Paul Lösche, Der Bolschewismus im Urteil der Deutschen Sozialdemokratie 1903–1920 (Berlin, 1967), p. 57.

related to the political tasks at hand. He hoped that Axelrod would be able to enlighten Western readers on these subjects. "The editors of *Der Kampf* know that there does not exist a man more capable and skillful at answering these questions."[47]

The letter from Braun agitated Axelrod. He read it with care, underlining passages and writing marginalia in response to specific questions, and immediately forwarded his acceptance of the assignment to Braun, adding that he would write the article as a series of letters because this would permit him "to express [himself] somewhat more freely."[48]

Axelrod spent the next few months in mental agony. He set aside everything else and devoted himself to the letters. He wrote endlessly, filling up some nineteen notebooks, but he never managed more than a first draft of a single letter, and none of the material ever saw the light of day. A full year after he had committed himself to writing for *Der Kampf*, he was still at work on the manuscript, but as he confessed to his friend Garvi, he was psychologically incapable of completing it. "You say that I should not force myself to work. Oh, how happy I would be if I could [force myself]. But the trouble is that 90 percent of the time this is as impossible for me as it is for a person whose legs are partly paralyzed to walk and move forward. In this case no efforts help."[49]

Axelrod had suffered from this kind of "paralysis"—or neurasthenia —before, but it caused him special distress in 1911 and 1912 because he was disconsolate over the fact that eminent Western socialists still harbored misconceptions about the controversy within the Russian movement. "Out of pure indignation at the chaos . . . [in our party the European leaders] declare themselves absolutely helpless and powerless, and consider themselves justified in assuming a stance of complete indifference and passivity vis-à-vis the struggling factions and groups."[50]

By now Axelrod had even reached the grim conclusion that the German trustees were merely tools of the Bolshevik policy of disorganizing the party.[51] He hoped that his letters to Braun would, once and for all, alert Western socialists to the actualities of the Russian

47. Braun to Axelrod, July 30, 1911, Axelrod Archive, I.I.S.H.
48. Axelrod to Braun, Aug. 3, 1911, *ibid*.
49. Axelrod to Garvi, Aug. 17, 1912, Nicolaevsky Collection, Hoover Institution.
50. Axelrod to Braun, n. d., incomplete draft, Axelrod Archive, I.I.S.H.
51. Axelrod to Alexander Stein, Sept. 24, 1911, Nicolaevsky Collection, Hoover Institution.

movement and thus contribute to "surmounting [the party strife] and to the rapid creation of conditions that would make possible the liquidation of our present factional internecine war."[52] He had set an ambitious task for himself, and it may well be that his recognition of its enormity and consequent fear of failure produced so much anxiety in him that he could never complete it.

The drafts have survived; they disclose Axelrod's views about the general situation in the party, which had undergone some striking changes. Although he repeated the explanation of the split he had maintained ever since his *Iskra* article of 1903 and 1904, he now manifested a deep concern with the moral aspect of the factional controversy. According to Valentinov, as early as 1904 Axelrod had contended that "Between us and Lenin and his band there is an entire abyss. It is not only a question of theoretical divergencies, but moral and psychological [ones]."[53] In 1911 and 1912 he underlined this point by stating that even though his historical account of the origins of the schism might explain the roots of the party's failure to develop into a democratic mass movement and its factionalism, it was by no means to be construed as a justification of Bolshevik methods. "I feel completely free," he wrote, "from the inclination to follow the example of that 'historical school' which, on the authority of Marx, seeks to legitimize and justify 'the baseness of today in terms of yesterday's baseness.' Baseness remains baseness, regardless of whether it was committed yesterday or today, regardless of whether it has deep roots or no roots in the past, no matter whether it has an 'historical basis' or none at all."[54]

This statement delineates Axelrod's conception of the relationship between ends and means. Much as he yearned for the overthrow of the autocracy and the establishment of socialism, he refused to sanction all means to achieve these goals. Though as a Marxist he believed in the inevitability of socialism, he repudiated the argument that inevitability made the means irrelevant. Nor could he agree that the immorality of the oppressor justified immorality by the oppressed. These attitudes reveal how much he had been influenced by the ethic of nineteenth-century liberalism, which upheld the notion of a universal code of behavior and insisted on the responsibility of each individual for his

52. Axelrod to Garvi, n. d., but probably early in 1912, *ibid.*
53. N. Vol'skii [Valentinov] to Kautsky, Apr. 4, 1932, Kautsky Archive, I.I.S.H.
54. Axelrod to Braun, n. d., incomplete draft, Axelrod Archive, I.I.S.H.

actions. It is altogether likely that his early religious training formed the basis for his acceptance of these liberal views. Axelrod did not explicitly acknowledge these influences or develop the philosophical position in detail. But that position undoubtedly affected his judgments and conduct: it led him to detest the robberies and defamation of character for which the Bolsheviks had become notorious. Within a few years it also engendered within him a powerful revulsion against the Bolshevik system of rule.

However contemptuous Axelrod was of Bolshevik tactics and conduct, he nevertheless supported various attempts to reunify the factions. Like many radicals, he found it difficult to believe that he faced implacable enemies on the left. He continued to look upon the Leninists as Marxists with whom collaboration should be possible. He had also convinced himself that many Bolshevik activists were disgusted with their leader's "Nechaevian-Bonapartist tactics" and would not join Lenin in his drive to carry out a "coup d'etat in the party." Early in 1910 Axelrod actually described the Bolshevik faction as being in a "critical situation . . . The ruling Bolshevik circles find themselves in a position analogous to that in which the government of Nicholas II found itself after the Japanese war"—that is, they were rapidly losing the confidence of the masses. Regardless of his personal inclinations, Lenin, as Axelrod saw it, now had no choice but to seek reconciliation with his opponents. Axelrod urged the Mensheviks to take advantage of the situation "in order to achieve [party] reform which will *facilitate* the work of comrades in Russia striving to revive the party."[55] In short, he still clung to the belief that by remaining in the party the Mensheviks might become its dominant voice.

Axelrod thoroughly approved therefore of the steps taken to end the schism by the plenum of the C. C., which met early in 1910 in Paris. The delegates condemned the expropriations, endorsed the need for a mass party, resolved to establish a single party press, and, as we have already noted, provided for the trusteeship over some of the money held by the Bolsheviks.[56] Axelrod considered the settlement so promising that he rebuked the Menshevik practicals for refusing to nominate two representatives to the *Semerka*, a group of seven who were to serve

55. Axelrod to Ingerman, Mar. 8, 1910, Jan. 1, 1911, *ibid.*
56. Schapiro, *Communist Party of the Soviet Union*, pp. 116–117.

inside Russia as the arm of the C. C. of the unified party.[57] The practicals, less trusting than Axelrod or the other Mensheviks abroad, had predicted that the Semerka would become another battleground for interfactional discord.

The agreement reached at Paris did not significantly alter the situation. The refusal of the practicals to cooperate provided Lenin with an excuse to heighten his campaign against the liquidators, while the dispute over money continued and neither side moved to create a single party press. But in the meantime, in 1910 and 1911, there emerged signs that Axelrod's broad strategy of 1908 was yielding results. The industrial depression had ended, and the revival of the economy brought with it a revival of working-class activism. Axelrod and his colleagues were most gratified by the news that the Mensheviks in Russia seemed steadily to be winning popular support.

The Mensheviks in exile were fully informed of these developments at a meeting called by the editors of *Golos sotsialdemokrata*. Several practicals as well as Potresov and Trotsky attended the gathering, which was held in Weggis, a village near Lucerne, in August and September 1911. The most important decision reached at the informal conference was to begin preparatory work for the convocation of a "unification conference of the entire party." As a conciliatory gesture, Trotsky, who had severely upbraided the liquidators, agreed to collaborate with Potresov on *Nasha zaria*.

The only document extant from that meeting is a list of working-class organizations active in Russia. Prepared by Martov on the basis of information supplied by the practicals, it discloses that the ties between the Mensheviks and legal workers' groups, though not extensive, were far from negligible. In St. Petersburg, for example, there were eleven active clubs with more than 3,000 dues-paying members, five trade unions with a total membership exceeding 7,000, seven trade union newspapers, and two general publications (*Nasha zaria* and *Delo zhizni*). One of the union papers registered a circulation in excess of 6,000. In other cities, of course, there were fewer organizations, and frequently all were subjected to government harassment. Nevertheless, in many larger cities (Riga, Kharkov, Odessa, Kiev, Baku, Tiflis,

57. Garvi, *Vospominaniia: Peterburg-Odessa-Vena—1912*, pp. 17–18.

Voronezh, and Vilno, among others) working-class willingness to organize and to subscribe to Menshevik doctrines was obviously growing.[58]

Axelrod, who attended the Weggis meeting, probably had this report in mind when, late in December 1911, he told friends in New York that however inadequate the links between his group and revolutionaries inside Russia, he was not ready to despair. The circle around *Golos sotsialdemokrata* could claim a stronger foundation than the GEL of the 1880's and 1890's. He was confident that the Mensheviks would be able to root out the "moral-political depravity . . . and ideological chaos that the Bolsheviks introduced into our movement."[59]

But in planning new attempts at unification and purification Axelrod and his colleagues had failed to reckon with Lenin's determination not to collaborate with men who might challenge his authority and policies. Throughout 1911 he moved relentlessly toward a formal split of the party. Martov's attacks on the Bolshevik expropriations and the refusal of the leaders of international socialism to approve of the Menshevik's offensive provided both a pretext and setting for the final rupture. In January 1912 Lenin presided over a conference in Prague attended almost solely by his most trusted followers; there he persuaded the assembly to expel the Menshevik liquidators from the party. Even though the gathering, according to Trotsky, did not represent more than one-fifth of the membership of Russian Social Democracy, it declared itself the "Sixth Conference of the Russian Social Democratic Labor Party" and proceeded to elect a new Central Committee of seven people, six of whom were committed Leninists.[60] Lenin could at last look upon himself as the undisputed leader of a political party.

Lenin's bold move pointed to the desirability of some kind of unified action on the part of the other factions. This was true for reasons other than the advisability of keeping him from dominating the movement. New elections to the Duma were scheduled for 1912, and if the party remained splintered the working-class vote would be hopelessly dispersed. Moreover, in order to wage an effective campaign the Russians

58. Martov's summary is on deposit in the Nicolaevsky Collection, Hoover Institution.

59. Axelrod to New York Group of Social Democrats, Dec. 1911, *ibid*.

60. Wolfe, *Three Who Made a Revolution*, pp. 529–532; Trotsky to New York Group of Assistance, Mar. 2, 1912, Nicolaevsky Collection, Hoover Institution.

needed a subsidy, which the Germans were willing to provide only if the various groups united.[61]

Trotsky took the initiative in summoning a unification conference, and Axelrod was one of the first to whom he appealed for support. Though fond of each other, the two had drifted apart since 1905, when Trotsky had ceased to consider himself a Menshevik. Despite this, Axelrod found it difficult to ignore appeals from his former "student." Indeed, it was characteristic of him that when he learned that Trotsky was in financial stress, personally and professionally, he went to considerable pains to procure funds for him. Axelrod even dipped into his own pocket when he heard that Trotsky had incurred large expenses as a result of illness. Trotsky was deeply moved by his friend's generosity: "Dear Pavel Borisovich, if only I could be firmly convinced that you did not take this money from your own more than modest budget."[62]

Though warmly disposed toward the man, Axelrod could not muster any enthusiasm for Trotsky's unification plan. He doubted whether the so-called liquidators in Russia would find it possible to collaborate with people (especially Trotsky) who had so violently attacked them, and he bluntly told Trotsky that he had little faith in a conference that was being prepared simply in the name of unity and loyalty to the party. Serious differences persisted over the question of Europeanizing the movement, and unless agreement could be reached on this issue he did not see how the factions could collaborate for any prolonged period.[63]

Still, Axelrod did not want to stand in the way of possible reconciliation so that when the Caucasian district committee selected him as a delegate to the conference he decided, after some hesitation, to accept. Most of the groups finally agreed to send representatives, more out of a sense of duty, one suspects, than from any conviction that much could be accomplished. The Leninists refused to attend, as did Plekhanov, the latter on the ground that nonparty and antiparty groups were participating. He would not, he told Trotsky, contribute to such a

61. Philipp Scheidemann to Russian Social Democrats, Sept. 5, 1912, Nicolaevsky Collection, Hoover Institution.

62. Trotsky to Axelrod, Feb. 12, 26, 1912, *ibid.*

63. Axelrod to Zasulich, May 6, 1912, *Sotsial-demokraticheskoe dvizhenie,* ed. Potresov and Nicolaevsky, pp. 220–221; Axelrod to Trotsky, July 15, 1912, Nicolaevsky Collection, Hoover Institution.

"scandalous violation of our . . . statutes."[64] Probably Plekhanov's real reason was that he despised Trotsky.[65]

Shortly after the conference, which met in Vienna, Axelrod seemed optimistic about its achievements. With satisfaction he reported to Kautsky that an Organization Committee had been elected to conduct the forthcoming electoral campaign. It had also been decided to establish a legal publication in St. Petersburg, to create a mass party, and to prepare another, broader conference for the purpose of bringing additional party sectors into the August Bloc, as the new group came to be called. "In short," Axelrod concluded, "the conference can with complete justification be considered the common representative of the party, that is to say, of the party *in Russia.*" Axelrod further pointed out that in Moscow the Mensheviks and Bolsheviks had reached agreement to support one candidate, a Bolshevik. Whether or not Axelrod was really pleased with the outcome, as these comments suggest, is difficult to say. The purpose of his letter to Kautsky was to convince the German party to help subsidize the campaign, and he knew that his appeal would be successful only if he could assure his friend that the August Bloc represented the entire movement.[66]

As it turned out, the Germans refused to subsidize the bloc because it did not embrace all the factions, but its existence no doubt prevented a free-for-all among the Marxist groups during the campaign. They all —including, ultimately, the Bolsheviks—collaborated reasonably well. The Mensheviks elected seven deputies to the Duma and the Bolsheviks, six. But the bloc did not enjoy a long life. As D. B. Riazanov perceived, "Only personal hatred for the scoundrel Lenin keep together most of the Mensheviks, Bundists, and Trotsky."[67] That was hardly enough to sustain a political coalition of such diverse groups. By February 1913 Trotsky was denouncing *Luch,* the paper that the August Bloc had agreed to publish in St. Petersburg. Instead of representing all the constituents of the bloc, he claimed, *Luch* was promoting an unadulterated liquidationist line. He further charged that the paper had refused to

64. Trotsky to Axelrod, May 27, 1912, Nicolaevsky Collection, Hoover Institution.
65. On Plekhanov's animosity toward Trotsky, see Isaac Deutscher, *The Prophet Armed: Trotsky, 1879–1921* (New York, 1954), pp. 62, 86–87.
66. Axelrod to Kautsky, Sept. 6, 1912, Nicolaevsky Collection, Hoover Institution.
67. Riazanov to Kautsky, Dec. 14 [1912], Kautsky Archive, I.I.S.H.

publish his articles and had not even bothered to answer his letters of protest. He pleaded with Axelrod to use his influence with the liquidators in St. Petersburg to mend their ways. Otherwise, he would be forced to split with those who "usurped the August conference." It would pain him not to be in the same camp as Axelrod, "But I cannot reproach myself in any way with disloyalty toward my allies."[68]

Axelrod, however, considered Trotsky partly to blame for the crisis. He agreed that *Luch* had expressed views that were unacceptable, but it seemed to him that Trotsky had unnecessarily exacerbated the situation by loosely applying the term liquidator and by aggressively challenging the editors of the paper. Axelrod certainly could not agree with Trotsky that *Luch* should be curbed: the August conference had specifically granted every group the right to state its position publicly.

The main reason for Axelrod's cool response to Trotsky's entreaties was probably that by now (spring, 1913) he had concluded that the conference had not managed to eliminate the old prejudices and mutual distrust. Much more drastic measures were needed to create a "healthy" Social Democracy, specifically, the restructuring of the party by drawing into it large numbers of politically conscious and mature workers.[69] The bloc had made almost no headway in this endeavor.

By mid-1913 the August Bloc had in effect disintegrated, and Russian Social Democracy was again hopelessly splintered. Ill feelings between the Leninists and the Mensheviks reached new levels of intensity as the former began to overtake the latter in popular support. For a variety of reasons, the workers in the two capitals were growing increasingly militant and turning to the Bolsheviks, who advocated "extremist objectives and tactics." In the period 1912–1914 they defeated their major rivals in several important elections in legal working-class organizations.[70] These victories undermined the Menshevik strategy, first laid down by Axelrod in 1908, of capturing the allegiance of the masses and thus gaining control of the party. In addition, Trotsky and Plekhanov, each with a small following, remained aloof from both major parties. It should also be noted that two small groups, the Bolshevik Conciliators

68. Trotsky to Axelrod, Feb. 21, 1913, Nicolaevsky Collection, Hoover Institution; Trotsky to Axelrod, n. d., but sometime in Apr. 1913, *ibid*.
69. Axelrod to S. Iu. Semkovsky, Mar. 24, 1913, *ibid*.; Axelrod to Trotsky, Apr. 17, 1913, *ibid*.
70. See Leopold Haimson, "The Problem of Social Stability in Urban Russia, 1905–1917 (Part One)," *Slavic Review*, XXIII (Dec. 1964), 630–639.

and the Bolshevik *Vperyodists,* had broken with Lenin.[71] Finally, there were the national parties: the Poles, Bundists, Letts, and Latvians, and even among them there existed diverse factions.

The last attempt to unify the numerous sects (a total of eleven) was made by the International Socialist Bureau late in 1913. Responding to a request from several Russian groups, the I.S.B. agreed to initiate and conduct negotiations with delegates appointed by each faction. The O. C. of the August Bloc, which still maintained a nominal existence, chose Axelrod as its representative. He was reluctant to undertake the mission because he resented the failure of S. Iu. Semkovsky, secretary of the O. C., and A. N. Chkhenkeli, a Menshevik deputy in the Duma, to discuss with him the assignment or party affairs in general.[72]

In the end he could not withstand the entreaties of Semkovsky, who early in 1914 wrote him that "all the factions within the August Bloc look upon you as their teacher and representative." Semkovsky also assured Axelrod that he would be fully supported by a majority of the O. C. As a final argument, Semkovsky claimed that Menshevik fortunes were improving, and this was therefore a propitious moment for unity. The circulation of the Bolshevik *Pravda,* according to Semkovsky, had dropped from 90,000 to 28,000, while the circulation of the Menshevik *Novaia rabochaia gazeta* had risen from 14,000 to 24,000. "One can observe a change in the mood of the masses [who had been] enticed by the revolutionary phraseology of Leninism."[73] The source of Semkovsky's figures is not known, but his general conclusion does not correspond with the available information on the period. Nevertheless, his remarks seem to have made a strong impression on Axelrod.

Axelrod's reluctance to accept the assignment did not stem merely from his having been slighted by his colleagues, but also from a suspicion that he held a different point of view from the O. C. He imagined it would concur with Trotsky in the belief that the Bolsheviks were genuinely interested in overcoming the schism, a belief he no longer

71. The Bolshevik Vperyodists, who split with Lenin in 1909, "made a fetish of illegality" and condemned any kind of legal work in trade unions or the Duma. The Conciliators or Party Bolsheviks opposed Lenin's policy of splitting with anyone who differed with him. Early in 1910 they joined with several other factions in an attempt to promote the unity of the party. See Wolfe, *Three Who Made a Revolution,* pp. 520–524.

72. Axelrod to Potresov, Feb. 2, 1914, *Sotsial-demokraticheskoe dvizhenie,* ed. Potresov and Nicolaevsky, pp. 264–265.

73. Semkovsky to Axelrod, Feb. 6, 1914, Nicolaevsky Collection, Hoover Institution.

shared. As a result, he insisted that this skepticism be emphasized in the talks with European socialist leaders.

Axelrod continued to favor unity, but he was afraid that if the O. C. rejected his approach of openly questioning Lenin's sincerity, the I.S.B. would believe that both factions were equally interested in a settlement. Then, if the discussions ended in failure, as he expected, the Mensheviks would be as burdened with blame as the Leninists. He soon learned, however, that a majority of the O. C. supported his approach, which induced him to accept the assignment.[74]

Fortunately, his health had taken a turn for the better, and he was able to plunge into the wide range of activities required by his new position. As a first step, he wrote to Camille Huysmans, secretary of the International Bureau, "We yearn with heart and soul for as speedy and complete a unification as possible." He promised to cooperate with the I.S.B., but warned that Lenin and his followers would do their utmost to nullify the endeavors of the committee. Axelrod pleaded with Huysmans to see that the Western representatives thoroughly familiarized themselves with the controversies plaguing the Russian party and suggested that each faction submit documents in French to the I.S.B. well in advance of the meetings. He pointed out that in the past Western socialists had presumed to speak on Russian affairs without having examined the issue carefully. "And the consequence of this was that precisely those elements of Russian Social Democracy who bear the major guilt for our discord received direct and often even indirect support from some circles of our Western brother parties . . . This danger can only be avoided by means of substantial preparation [on the part of the I.S.B.]." Axelrod concluded optimistically: at the least, the International's efforts would provide a "stimulus" for unification.[75]

The tone of this message may appear to have been tactless, but within a few weeks Axelrod received information that must have reinforced his conviction that his instincts were sound. V. Pozin, a Menshevik then staying in Brussels, where Huysmans also lived, told him that the secretary of the I.S.B. often corresponded with Lenin and tended to

74. Axelrod to Kautsky, Apr. 8, 1914, *ibid.;* Axelrod to Semkovsky, Feb. 19, 1914, *ibid.;* see also editors' note, *Sotsial-demokraticheskoe dvizhenie,* ed. Potresov and Nicolaevsky, p. 396.
75. Axelrod to Huysmans, Mar. 1914, Axelrod Archive, I.I.S.H.

assess developments from the Bolshevik standpoint. Pozin urged Axelrod to keep Huysmans informed about political trends in Russia, particularly about the Menshevik position on specific issues, since, "aside from the German comrades," no one in the West really knew much about the Russian party.[76]

Axelrod did not share this confidence in the Germans. He therefore traveled to Berlin, where he spent several weeks lecturing and speaking to prominent members of the German party. At one gathering Kautsky, Rudolf Hilferding, Victor Adler, Otto Bauer, and Hugo Haase shocked him by discussing the Russian situation in "the most nonsensical fashion" and inadvertently revealing that they "do not even have any notion of how much they are lacking the most necessary premises for an assessment of our affairs."

Later, he talked at greater length with Haase, Hilferding, and Kautsky and pronounced these discussions as "not in vain." Axelrod's approach was to concentrate not on theoretical issues but on the immediate prospects for the Russian party, hopeful that on this basis it would be possible to reach an understanding with Lenin. He indicated that at the discussions on unification he would be willing to forget past differences, but he also predicted that Lenin would rake them up.[77]

The effectiveness of Axelrod's endeavors cannot be measured directly, but the I.S.B. definitely made a determined effort to obtain as much information as possible about the state of affairs in the Russian party. The Bureau sent emissaries to several countries to interview members of the various factions. A leading Belgian socialist, Emile Vandervelde, was even dispatched to St. Petersburg, where he talked to many Social Democrats. He told Martov that he himself sympathized with the Mensheviks and asked whether they would agree to let the Bureau serve as arbiter with power to impose a settlement. Martov replied in the

---

76. Pozin to Axelrod, n. d., but probably May 1914, Nicolaevsky Collection, Hoover Institution. For the correspondence between Lenin and Huysmans during this period, see *Correspondance entre Lénine et Camille Huysmans 1905–1914*, ed. Georges Haupt (The Hague, 1963), pp. 133–143. The letters in this volume do not reveal the agreement between the two men that Pozin claimed to exist, but apparently Pozin based his assessment on personal conversations with Huysmans. Actually, Lenin considered the secretary of the I.S.B. hostile to the Bolsheviks. See *ibid.*, p. 126. The fact is that leaders of both factions regarded anyone who did not fully support them as their opponent.

77. Axelrod to Semkovsky, May 19, 1914, Nicolaevsky Collection, Hoover Institution.

affirmative for his faction, though he doubted that Vandervelde ever raised the possibility with the Bolsheviks.[78] It seems clear, nevertheless, that the I.S.B. had decided to force a settlement on the Russians. To this end, it called for a conference in Brussels of the delegates of the various factions for July 16 and 17, 1914. The agreement reached by the conference would then be ratified by the Congress of the International, which was scheduled to meet two weeks later in Vienna.

All eleven factions sent representatives to the conference at Brussels. The three Bolsheviks (Lenin did not attend) immediately demonstrated the soundness of Axelrod's warnings that Lenin did not desire unity. Their belligerence completely ruled out the possibility of an amicable settlement freely arrived at by the Russians themselves. Kautsky's resolution calling for a merger of the factions was supported by representatives of nine groups (among them Axelrod); neither the Bolsheviks nor the Letts voted for it. Proceeding from the premise that "at the present time there are no tactical differences that are sufficiently great to justify a schism," the resolution stipulated the following general conditions for unity: acceptance of the program of the Russian Social Democratic party; acceptance of majority rule in the movement; renunciation of blocs with bourgeois parties; and agreement to participate in a congress that was to resolve outstanding issues in the dispute. It is significant that the resolution also stated that "the organization of the party must at present be secret"; and the Mensheviks' endorsement of this plank once again proved that they did not repudiate the underground section of the movement.[79]

All in all, the I.S.B. had arrived at an equitable approach for solving the factional discord. Lenin's obstinacy therefore stunned the leaders of the International. Huysmans voiced the sentiment of many when he declared that "whoever does not vote for the resolution is responsible before the International for wrecking the attempt to achieve unity." He resolved to inform the congress in Vienna that the Bolsheviks and Letts had thwarted the efforts of the I.S.B.[80]

The Bolsheviks' report to the conference, which was drafted by Lenin and read by Inessa Armand, contained, ironically, a theme that

---

78. Martov to Axelrod, June 2, 1914, *Pis'ma*, ed. Dan, Nicolaevsky, and Tsederbaum-Dan, pp. 290–291.
79. Kautsky's resolution is reproduced in Lenin, *Sochineniia*, XVII, 682–683.
80. *Ibid.*, p. 745.

Axelrod had also occasionally developed during the previous decade and most recently in 1912: that the division between the two major factions was wider than any that existed in Western Social Democracies.[81] According to Lenin, the liquidators—by which he meant the Mensheviks, as well as others—intended to destroy the party and create an entirely new movement. Consequently, his disagreement with them had nothing to do with the best way to organize the party, but with "the question of the *existence* of the party. Here there cannot be any question either of any kind of conciliation, or agreement, or compromise . . . In contemporary Russia, where even the party of the most moderate liberals is illegal, our party can only exist as an illegal party."[82]

Under the circumstances, unification imposed by the Congress of the International would probably not have lasted for any length of time. But, as Leonard Schapiro has argued, a vote by the congress in favor of Kautsky's resolution would have put Lenin in a precarious position.[83] His bullheaded behavior had so distressed a number of his followers that they were ready to quit the faction. And the Mensheviks would at last have realized their long-cherished dream: the unequivocal backing of the International.

Events on the international scene, however, intervened. The outbreak of war precluded the convocation of the congress and further steps toward unity. The Mensheviks and the factions supporting them had drafted a letter to all Russian workers informing them of the Bolsheviks' refusal to cooperate and urging them to rally around a single banner. But the message appeared only once—in a relatively obscure publication of the Bundist émigrés.[84] Within a few months the military conflict gave rise to new disagreements of such magnitude that they soon spread to all Social Democratic parties, and schism became a world phenomenon.

81. Axelrod to Braun, 1912, incomplete draft, Axelrod Archive, I.I.S.H.

82. Lenin, *Sochineniia*, XVII, 545. That Lenin planned to subvert the I.S.B.'s efforts emerges clearly from a letter written to Lenin on July 16, 1914, by I. F. Popov, the Bolshevik representative in Brussels. See "Bol'sheviki na Briussel'skom soveshchanii 1914 g.," *Istoricheskii arkhiv*, no. 4 (1959), 25; see also pp. 31–35 of this article.

83. Schapiro, *Communist Party of the Soviet Union*, pp. 138–140.

84. *Sotsial-demokraticheskoe dvizhenie*, ed. Potresov and Nicolaevsky, pp. 399–400.

IX | The Crises of Violence: War and Revolution

The outbreak of the First World War early in August 1914 shattered the illusions of European Marxists by exposing the impotence of their movement. Despite the appeals of socialist leaders for a peaceful settlement of the crisis caused by the assassination of Archduke Francis Ferdinand, and their threats of militant action by an aroused proletariat, European statesmen continued to act in what they conceived as the national interest of their respective countries. After war erupted, Marxists discovered, to their dismay, that the doctrine of international proletarian solidarity was of little practical significance. It did not take long for several major socialist parties to pledge support to their governments in the impending struggle. When put to the test, national bonds proved stronger than class loyalties.

Many Marxists—and their number grew as the duration of the conflict surpassed expectations—looked upon the failure of international socialism to take effective steps against the war as an admission of weakness, cowardice, and, above all, depravity. The highest principles of socialism had been sacrificed. Furthermore, the German party, which, by virtue of its power, theoretical preeminence, and political experience, was expected to set an example, had been the first to repudiate internationalism. The shock was so profound and feelings ran so high that in the end the most militant opponents of the war found it impossible to remain in the same movement with those who supported the war, the so-called defensists. The International, which had existed since 1889, in effect collapsed.

The failure of the International and of individual socialist parties to act decisively against the war in 1914 seems, retrospectively, less perplexing than the surprise and despair of Marxists on discovering the

302

impotence of their movement. The history of Marxism after 1900 yields little reason for confidence in a militant response to war by the European working class. It is true that Social Democrats frequently denounced capitalism and imperialism as the root causes of war and condemned resort to force. But the consensus among socialists broke down over the specific measures the proletariat might take once war had been declared. The question of a general strike was discussed at several congresses of the International, but the only resolution ever passed by the highest body of the proletariat urged all national parties to do their utmost to prevent an outbreak of hostilities in case of an international crisis. When the crisis materialized in 1914, the national parties found themselves without precise guidelines.

If the vagueness of the International made a unified response from the European proletariat unlikely, the circumstances surrounding the war's beginning and the nature of the opposing coalitions virtually assured a diversity of reaction. Although Germany fired the first shot, it could not be proven that the imperial government had deliberately followed an aggressive policy with war as its object. Without too much difficulty, the governments of all the belligerent countries could make out plausible cases for the moral and political legitimacy of their cause. The situation was further complicated for socialists because each country could claim to stand for progress. In this connection it was not difficult to invoke the authority of Marx and Engels, who had often supported wars that they felt were promoting the forward march of history.

Thus, the German leaders contended that their country, surrounded by hostile nations, was defending Europe against "Asiatic barbarism." In the eyes of some Russian socialists the tsarist autocracy merited support because it had cast its lot with Western democracies against reactionary Prussianism. Aside from these considerations, there was a practical factor that Marxists in Western countries could not ignore: the masses—including large numbers of workers—turned out to be patriotic. In August 1914 the leaders of the French and German socialist parties could not but feel that if they advocated open opposition to the war they would quickly lose their following.

Because of these complexities and the painful decision forced upon socialists, the war produced not only the most enduring of the many divisions that plagued Marxism but also ideological chaos within all Social Democratic movements.[1]

Axelrod's first reactions to the declarations of war and the events surrounding them were emotional rather than reflective. He was particularly stunned to learn that the German party had voted for war credits (that is, to grant the government the right to borrow money for military expenditures). It seemed to him that a "mighty earthquake had swept over the international proletariat . . . the enormous authority of German Social Democracy had disappeared [in a flash] . . . What can one still believe?" He was apprehensive about the impact the action of the German party would have in Russia. Only six days earlier, on July 29, he had predicted that war might inspire a revolution in his country. Now he feared that the Russian working class, influenced by the German example, might yield to patriotism. He was also vexed by the possibility of an early defeat of democratic France and Belgium by authoritarian Germany. "Therefore," he later confessed, "I *momentarily* wished for some military victories 'by Russia' for the Entente."[2] Axelrod did not express these judgments and speculations in writing at the time, probably because he realized that they were impulsive.

Not until October 1914, by which time he had regained his composure, did he formulate a comprehensive position on the war and make a public statement on the subject. In the course of ten weeks his views had changed substantially. He no longer favored victories by either side, though he revealed unmistakable pro-French and pro-Belgian sympathies.

Axelrod's statement was largely provoked by Lenin's contention that since the conflict was "historically inevitable," Marxists had no business distinguishing between aggressors and defenders, or between socialist

1. The following are some of the more useful studies dealing with the question of socialism and war: Merle Fainsod, *International Socialism and the World War* (2nd printing, New York, 1966), pp. 1–17; Max Victor, "Die Stellung der deutschen Sozialdemokratie zu den Fragen der auswärtigen Politik, 1869–1914," *Archiv für Sozialwissenschaft und Sozialpolitik,* LX (1928), 147–179; Carl E. Schorske, *German Social Democracy, 1905–1917* (Cambridge, Mass., 1955), pp. 66–69, 79–87, *et passim;* G. D. H. Cole, *The Second International, 1889–1914,* which is vol. III, pt. 1 of *A History of Socialist Thought* (London, 1960), Chap. II; Julius Braunthal, *Geschichte der Internationale* (Hannover, 1961–1963), I, 327–363.

2. *Die Zimmerwalder Bewegung: Protokolle und Korrespondenz,* ed. Horst Lademacher (The Hague, 1967), I, 84; Georges Haupt, *Le congrès manqué: l'Internationale à la veille de la première guerre mondiale* (Paris, 1965), p. 262.

parties who supported expansionist governments and those who rallied behind governments of countries under attack. Axelrod agreed with Lenin's analysis up to a point: that the war had been caused by "contemporary capitalism, by the imperialist policies of the ruling classes of many European states, each of which is striving for economic monopoly and political domination of the world." But this explanation did not demonstrate that the conflict was inevitable or that it had to begin at the time and in the manner that it did. It seemed to Axelrod a distortion of Marxism to accept so fatalistic a view of the historical process. Had the proletariat managed to organize itself into a powerful political movement prior to 1914, it could have influenced the course of events even to the point of preventing the war.

To buttress his contention, Axelrod cited Marx's discussion of the law of impoverishment. Although Marx had indeed spoken of a "law" of economics in describing the increasing impoverishment of the masses, he had not argued that this was an irreversible process that man could not modify. Rather, the law described a tendency of capitalist development that could be affected or negated by contradictory tendencies that were likely to emerge in a capitalist economy. The state could, for example, introduce measures to blunt the impact of the law of impoverishment, a course that Marx neither ruled out nor opposed. "Thus," Axelrod concluded, "historical necessity, which people now like to cite so irrelevantly, did not signify for Marx a passive attitude toward a concrete evil—pending the socialist revolution. On the contrary, it calls forth a more active struggle of the proletariat against the real manifestations of this evil."

It is not necessary to go into the question of whether or not Axelrod correctly interpreted Marx's concept of historical necessity. There is certainly ample evidence to show that Marx often judged specific issues in the manner claimed by Axelrod. The interesting point is that the Menshevik was selective in his adherence to a rigid conception of historical determinism. On some issues, as we shall see, he continued to be rigidly deterministic, but not on the war. People in positions of power faced alternatives and had the freedom to choose among them. "We must," he argued, "analyze the concrete conditions in which each country found itself before the declaration of war."

Axelrod applied this commonsensical approach to the situation in Europe in July 1914 and concluded that Germany had provoked the conflict and thereby had forced several countries to defend their sovereignty "to the death." Again, as in 1912, he could not evade moral judgments; nor would he ask the Belgian and French socialists to do so in reaching a decision on the war. Should the Belgian comrades have refused to take up arms in defense of "their elementary existence" on the ground that the war was "in the final analysis a historical necessity"? He quoted approvingly a point made by Jules Guesde, the French socialist: if the house occupied jointly by a worker and a capitalist catches fire, the worker must try to extinguish the flames for it is also his home. Moreover, French workers had every reason to prefer a French republican regime to rule by semiabsolutistic Germany: "The French socialists could not but actively participate in the defense of their country."

Toward the German socialists Axelrod was not so charitable. He granted that the German party and proletariat were moved to support their government by honorable sentiments of patriotism, but this could not justify their stand because the conflict had been caused by the adventurist policy of the German ruling class.

Even though Russia was an ally of France and Belgium, Axelrod did not approve his country's war effort which he felt was being used to promote reactionary interests. The nobility and the bourgeoisie greeted the war with enthusiasm in the belief "that Russia's victory will enhance not only the state's but *their own power*." Both groups hankered after conquered territory and were counting on military triumphs to divert the proletariat from its quarrels with the Tsar. The agrarian interests also hoped to gain advantageous trade agreements with Germany after its defeat.

Accordingly, Axelrod lavished praise on the RSDRP for repudiating the war. The working-class organizations had, unfortunately, been crippled by a series of strikes in the spring and summer of 1914 and the subsequent wave of government repression. "Thus it came to pass that Russian Social Democracy, *weakened* and *disorganized* at the time of the outbreak of the war, was not able to discharge its international duty: to offer resistance to the war with all means." But the Duma delegations of both Marxist parties had been "politically and morally strong enough" publicly to renounce the war and to inform the people that the autocracy was waging war at their expense. He applauded their decision to quit the Duma before the vote on war credits, an action, he claimed, that in Russia was an even stronger protest than a negative vote.

Axelrod's position on the war was too complicated to be described as defensist or defeatist, yet it comprised a bit of both tendencies. He sympathized with the decisions of the French and Belgian socialists to defend their countries, but refused to sanction support of the Tsar by Russian socialists. By the same token, he opposed the idea of total victory or defeat of either side. He conceded that there had been a time when national wars were a vehicle for effecting desirable social and political change. But in the twentieth century a crushing defeat of a major power could only amount to a "great misfortune for all human-ity" because the economic devastation it would produce would impede the economic development of Europe as a whole. At the same time, however, he suggested that a minor defeat for tsarist Russia, one that would not affect the "organic development of the country, would be of assistance in the liquidation of the old regime." For the rest, Axelrod hoped for a speedy negotiated peace providing for a return to the status quo ante bellum.[3]

Axelrod's refusal to advance a straightforward, uncomplicated line on the war irritated many Russian Marxists. In 1916 he complained that "Since the outbreak of the war until the present I have been quite isolated, even within the narrow circle of my colleagues."[4] It seemed to him that nearly everyone misunderstood his position. Yet the real source of his isolation was the widespread belief that his guarded and judicious statements concealed indecision, vagueness, and, most serious, insufficient dedication in opposing the war.[5]

Early in 1915 a certain A. Popov from Petrograd arrived in Geneva to

3. The discussion of Axelrod's earliest reactions to the war is based on the following: Raf. Grigor'ev, "P. B. Aksel'rod ob internatsionale i voine," *Golos*, nos. 86, 87, Dec. 22, 23, 1914; this article is a summary of comments Axelrod made in an interview, an account of which first appeared in the *Bremer Bürger-Zeitung* late in October and early in November 1914. (I could not locate this version of the inter-view.) Grigor'ev's article also appeared in *Novyi mir*, nos. 249, 250, Jan. 4, 5, 1915; see also Pavel Axelrod, "Russland und der Krieg," *Berner Tagwacht*, Oct. 26, 27, 1914.

4. Axelrod to Kautsky, n. d., but probably in 1916, Nicolaevsky Collection, Hoover Institution.

5. For some of the attacks on Axelrod, see Lenin to A. G. Shliapnikov, Jan. 31, 1915, *Leninskii sbornik*, ed. L. B. Kamenev (Moscow, 1924–1938), II, 224; Lenin to Shliapnikov, Feb. 11, 1915, *ibid.*, p. 227; V. I. Lenin, "Russkie Ziudekumy" (Russian Südekums), *Sotsialdemokrat*, no. 37, Feb. 1915.

make contact with antiwar socialists and was dismayed by a long conversation he had with Axelrod. Popov had not expected "a simple scheme and elementary straightforwardness," but he was not prepared for the "endless series of conditional sentences in which he formulated the reasons for his point of view," or the "net of reservations with which he covered it." Popov considered Axelrod's attitude toward the defensists weak and compromising: on the one hand, he urged an ideological struggle against them, but on the other, warned against any steps that might lead to a new Menshevik schism. As Popov's account clearly indicates, Axelrod's primary concern was to prevent a further disintegration of Social Democracy; consequently, he went out of his way to avoid actions or statements that would either lead to new splits or make more difficult the restoration of the International.[6]

A strong case can be made for Axelrod's desire to maintain unity "at all costs," as Popov put it. In withholding dogmatic opinions on the war that might offend some socialists, Axelrod had his eye on the future. He knew that the international socialist movement could not hope to be effective in promoting peace unless it remained united. Moreover, sooner or later the war would end, and the proletariat would only be able to influence the peace settlement if it commanded an organization—the International—that could speak for the entire working class of Europe. These considerations, however, were not calculated to appeal to people whose passions had been inflamed by the agonies of military conflict. Such persons could not respond to subtle distinctions or qualified positions on complex issues. Most Russian socialists opted for firm, bluntly defined positions, however crude, unrealistic, or inconsistent with Marxist teachings. But by this time Axelrod had become accustomed to standing alone politically, and although he did not relish the role of dissenter he would not pare down his views to please others.

Among Russian radicals, Lenin's attitude toward the war was the most militant. In early September 1914 he charged that the war was nothing but an imperialist conflict in which workers were senselessly killing each other in behalf of the bourgeoisie of their respective countries. He denounced Social Democrats who supported their governments as opportunists and traitors to the working class. He also argued that the

6. A. Popov (N. Vorob'ev), "Stranichka vospominanii o rabote v 'mezhduraionke.' S predisloviem A. Shliapnikova," *Proletarskaia revoliutsiia*, no. 22 (1923), 103–104.

failure of the Second International to call for decisive measures against the war was indisputable evidence that its leaders had succumbed to "petty bourgeois opportunism" and that therefore the organization did not merit resurrection. Finally, he maintained that for the Russian proletariat "the least evil" would be a defeat of tsarism and called for defeatist propaganda in all countries and among all armies in order to prepare the masses for social revolution. In short, rather than concentrate on a "struggle for peace," Marxists ought to attempt to transform the international conflict into a civil war against the bourgeoisie.[7]

In the rest of the Russian Social Democratic community a wide range of opinion emerged. Trotsky occupied the extreme left; although he did not subscribe to Lenin's "revolutionary defeatism," he was otherwise very close to him ideologically. As Trotsky saw it, mankind faced only one set of alternatives: "permanent war or proletarian revolution." Martov, shattered by both the moral and political implications of the war, was appalled by the conduct of the German socialists and indicated a readiness to attack them even if this led to a deterioration of the relations between Russian Marxists and their Western colleagues. He refused to sanction the notion of civil peace in any country and considered entering a "working arrangement with Lenin," who during the early part of the war extravagantly praised the Menshevik's pronouncements. But Martov could not go quite that far. He distrusted Lenin too much and, like Axelrod, was unwilling to split the International.[8]

The most startling position on the war was held by Plekhanov, who favored the Entente and urged socialists in countries opposing the Central Powers to vote for war credits, establish civil peace, and enter coalition governments. Not only were the Allies fighting a war of national defense, which legitimated their cause from a Marxist standpoint; they were also striving to prevent the economic enslavement of Europe and Russia by German reactionaries, who intended drastically to curtail the socialist movement. His utterances were colored by a strong trace of "love for Russia," which was altogether baffling in view of his longstanding adherence to internationalism.[9]

7. V. I. Lenin, *Sochineniia* (3rd ed., Moscow, 1926–1937), XVIII, 44–46.
8. Isaac Deutscher, *The Prophet Armed: Trotsky, 1879–1921* (New York, 1954), pp. 213–218; Israel Getzler, *Martov: A Political Biography of a Russian Social Democrat* (Cambridge, Eng., 1967), pp. 138–141.
9. Samuel H. Baron, *Plekhanov: The Father of Russian Marxism* (Stanford, 1963), pp. 371–378.

Plekhanov's "patriotic" point of view, as it has been called, found little support among the Mensheviks in Russia.[10] Although Potresov advocated a sort of defensism that received the approval of several well-known publicists and leaders of the workers' intelligentsia, his stand differed from Plekhanov's in several important respects. He argued that as far as the interests of world socialism were concerned the defeat of the Central Powers was preferable to a collapse of the Allies, for the anti-German coalition was the bearer of historically progressive principles, that is, democratic ideals. Potresov therefore approved of "civil truce" for France and England, but not for Russia because his country was still bound by an autocratic form of government. As the mounting military defeats revealed the incompetence of the government in Russia, Potresov and his colleagues began to clamor with increasing vehemence for a reorganization of the state structure. This line of argument clearly implied that once Russia was democratized socialists should adopt a positive attitude toward their country's war effort.[11]

The dominant Menshevik group, both inside Russia and abroad, was the so-called Internationalists, who favored prompt conclusion of a democratic peace without annexations or indemnities.[12] By early 1915 Axelrod had moved considerably to the left on the war, so that even though he continued to maintain an independent position on several issues he was sufficiently in accord with the Internationalists to join their ranks and to become one of their chief spokesmen—Martov was the

10. B. Dvinov, *Pervaia mirovaia voina i rossiskaia sotsialdemokratiia* (New York, 1962), p. 75.
11. B. I. Nicolaevsky, introduction to *A. N. Potresov: Posmertnyi sbornik proizvedenii* (Paris, 1937), pp. 67–70.
12. It should be noted that there existed important differences within the Internationalist group. For example, the Siberian Zimmerwaldists (Irakli Tsereteli, Dan, W. S. Woytinsky, among others) "were prepared to admit that under certain conditions the defense of one's country was justifiable." This theme became a basic feature of the doctrine of Revolutionary Defensism, which was the official policy of the leaders in the soviets after February 1917. See Rex A. Wade, *The Russian Search for Peace: February–October 1917* (Stanford, 1969), p. 19; see also his "Irakli Tsereteli and Siberian Zimmerwaldism," *Journal of Modern History*, XXXIX (Dec. 1967), 425–431. There was also disagreement, as already noted, over the question of working-class participation in the War Industry Committees. The Menshevik Internationalists in exile were opposed, whereas some in Russia favored participation in order to be in a stronger position to agitate for political change. See Leonard Schapiro, *The Communist Party of the Soviet Union* (London, 1960), pp. 152–154; see also George Katkov, *Russia 1917: The February Revolution* (Oxford, 1967), pp. 16–22, 231–237; M. Balabanov, *Ot 1905 k 1917: massovoe rabochee dvizhenie* (Moscow, 1927), pp. 379–395.

other—in the West. Axelrod never explicitly repudiated the views he had expressed in the late fall of 1914 (except for his hope for Russian victories), but as the enormity of the slaughter and the inability of the powers to stop the war became manifest the emphasis in his activities and writings shifted markedly. Instead of merely exploring the causes of the conflict or assigning responsibility for its outbreak, he paid increasing attention to injecting life into the peace movement.

He had returned to Zurich shortly after the declaration of war, probably because of the freedom of action Switzerland's neutral status would allow him. Early in 1915 he collaborated with Martov, Semkovsky, Martynov, and I. S. Astrov on a newspaper that publicized the point of view of the Internationalists and the Foreign Secretariat of the Menshevik O. C. (*Izvestiia zagranichnago sekretariata organizatsionnago komiteta RSDRP*). By and large, the editors worked harmoniously, but there were occasional differences between Axelrod and Martov. In the summer of 1915, for example, Axelrod threatened to resign from the Foreign Secretariat if his colleague did not quit the editorial board of *Nashe slovo*, which, largely under Trotsky's influence, was following a line close to Lenin's.[13]

In the paper Axelrod characteristically addressed himself to strategy and tactics. The party had come to expect specific proposals from him whenever a crisis developed, and in December 1914 Iurii Larin wrote him from Stockholm: "All our comrades in Petrograd very much entreat you to write what you think about the situation and the position that ought to be adopted; I will pass everything along."[14] After receiving several more such requests in the spring of 1915 Axelrod outlined the steps he thought socialists should take to hasten the war's conclusion.

It was plain to him that the socialist proletariat in all countries had to initiate a "war against the war in order to put an end as soon as possible to the international slaughter." But before such a common campaign could be launched socialist parties would have to agree on conditions of peace and tactics. He therefore urged socialists from neutral countries to convoke an international conference for the purpose of devising a program and a course of action that could prove acceptable to Marxists of different views. He considered it a grave mistake

13. Alfred Erich Senn, *The Russian Revolution in Switzerland 1914–1917* (Madison, 1971), p. 77.
14. Larin to Axelrod, Dec. 12, 1914, Nicolaevsky Collection, Hoover Institution.

for Social Democrats from belligerent states to play a major part in organizing the initial meeting because most of them lacked the necessary detachment for such an undertaking.

It seemed to him, nonetheless, that socialists in each party could make a real contribution to promoting peace. They could endeavor to eliminate the "psychological obstacles" preventing restoration of international proletarian solidarity, that is, the "nationalist poison that has gripped the labor parties and their leaders." The Russian Marxists were well-suited to take the lead in the campaign against this "internal enemy" because their party, and especially its leaders, had never succumbed to nationalist passions. Axelrod urged "advanced workers" to seize every opportunity to enlighten other members of the movement about the harmful effects of nationalism, but he ruled out demonstrations and strikes as premature and risky. Only after "opposition to the struggle for peace within the International itself" was overcome would it be appropriate to move to a more militant stage.

Axelrod's plan was predicated on the assumption that it would be possible to win over the official leadership of the various parties to a peace program and discontinuation of collaboration with the regimes of the warring states. As a last resort he was willing to break with the existing parties—and by implication with the Second International— but he did not think that the situation called for such drastic action.[15]

Several European socialists were, in the meantime, attempting to work out measures to end the war. As early as September 27, 1914, a number of Italian and Swiss Marxists met in Lugano and issued a general statement reminding socialists to "uphold the old principles of the International of the proletariat." In March 1915 the International Socialist Women's Conference at Bern adopted a centrist line: it condemned the war, but refused to split with the so-called "social chauvinists."[16] Plans were laid for a much larger conference to be held in September 1915 in Zimmerwald, Switzerland. Axelrod took a dim view of these meetings, in part because he knew that although Italian and Swiss socialists were the organizers, Lenin had played an important part behind the scenes,

15. Pavel Axelrod, "S chego nachat'?" *Izvestiia zagranichnago sekretariata organizatsionnago komiteta rossiiskoi sotsialdemokraticheskoi rabochei partii*, no. 2, June 19, 1915.

16. Fainsod, *International Socialism*, pp. 45–46, 57.

and he was afraid that Lenin would try to "transfer into the International . . . [his] favorite methods of factional conflict."[17]

Above all, Axelrod did not favor formal meetings that bypassed the existing organs and decisions of the Second International. As he explained late in 1915, he had always advocated *"private international conferences"* that would prepare the way, by means of propagandistic and agitational activity, for a formal international socialist conference. For this reason he had refused to participate in the discussions at Lugano.[18] But Robert Grimm, the Swiss socialist who was one of the chief organizers of the Zimmerwald meeting, assured him that a formal gathering of oppositional socialists "does not necessarily imply a split." Axelrod remained dubious, but, unwilling to appear unreasonable, he yielded to Grimm's entreaties. Axelrod's agreement to participate was probably also motivated by the news of the sinking of the *Lusitania* with its loss of over 1,100 lives, which he heard the day he gave his assent. He supposed that in view of all the "barbaric ruthlessness" of recent months he should accept the sinking as normal in time of war. "And yet! I fear that this outrage will unleash a completely elemental, primitive racial hatred."[19] Given this mood of despondency, he found it hard to reject what seemed to be the only hope for socialists to contribute toward ending the conflict. His decision to participate in the socialist conference at Zimmerwald was well intentioned and politically sound, but he had good reason to doubt whether he would long be able to collaborate with the Bolsheviks. The more he thought about the war, the more he disagreed with the Leninists, who were among the most active participants in the international meetings.

Axelrod delivered a series of lectures on the socialist response to the war in Zurich in 1915 in which he discussed yet another difference of opinion with Lenin. Lenin described the controversy over the war among European Marxists as essentially a continuation of the long-

---

17. Axelrod's attitude emerges from letters by Angelica Balabanova to Axelrod, Nov. 13, 27, 1914, Nicolaevsky Collection, Hoover Institution, and from Axelrod's letter to Grimm, May 20, 1915, *Die Zimmerwalder Bewegung*, ed. Lademacher, II, 70–74.

18. Axelrod to Grimm, Dec. 1915, *Die Zimmerwalder Bewegung*, ed. Lademacher, II, 371–373.

19. Grimm to Axelrod, May 8, 1915, *ibid.*, pp. 64–65; Axelrod to Grimm, May 11, 1915, *ibid.*, pp. 66–67.

standing feud between the orthodox and the Revisionists, in which the latter assumed the mantle of opportunists for having misled the workers into believing they must remain loyal to the state because imperialist expansion would bring them higher wages. Axelrod took a more complex view of the situation: after all, some Revisionists had adopted an anti-war position, and some orthodox Marxists had become fervent defensists. Moreover, the patriotic feelings that impelled workers to fight for their country had existed long before the birth of Revisionism.

To Axelrod the division over the war reflected a conflict between nationalism and internationalism that European socialists had never faced squarely. Theorists had consistently neglected nationalism, generally by dismissing it as an ideology invented by bourgeois writers and politicians in order to evoke popular support for the capitalist state. But Axelrod now divined that nationalistic feelings were deeply rooted in human psychology and occasionally spoke of them as an "atavistic tendency."[20] People naturally tend to build up emotional ties to the communities in which they live, and sentiments of this kind can determine human conduct, as was amply demonstrated by the readiness of citizens to die for their country. Thus nationalism contained the potential for an independent effect on the historical process. Even a socialist revolution, Axelrod prophetically warned, would not automatically eradicate nationalism.

He did not recommend accommodating to the "disease" of nationalism. He contended, on the contrary, that a major defect of the Second International had been its failure to combat it; this was especially regrettable because the war demonstrated that there existed an "irreconcilable conflict" between chauvinism and the "development of modern productive forces." For the most part, the economy had been internationalized, while political loyalties and behavior remained local or national. Axelrod perceived only one way of overcoming the contradiction: "through a thorough and consistent internationalization of the tactics of the labor movement." The proletariat's struggle for emancipation must be *"organized in common."*

To effect such a change, he proposed restructuring the International into a supranational body vested with palpable authority over national parties. "The relations between national labor parties and organizations

20. Axelrod to Kautsky, Jan. 5, 1917, Nicolaevsky Collection, Hoover Institution.

and the International must *approximate* those that existed between the [socialist] movement in Baden, Bavaria, or Prussia and the all-national party in Germany." Only in that way would the International be in a position to influence the policies of national governments: during international crises it would be capable of "opposing [individual states] and suppressing their belligerent intentions by unleashing a revolutionary storm and . . . the socialist revolution."

But before so far-reaching a reform could be effected, Marxists, as Axelrod realized, had to grapple with a more immediate problem: the war. He urged that a sustained effort be made to secure the agreement of all parties to the formula "neither victory nor defeat" as the basis for a peace campaign. Such a campaign, he reiterated, could succeed only if *all* socialist parties acted together; Axelrod therefore called for the restoration of the old International, including the "social chauvinists."[21]

Axelrod had singled out a central weakness of the Second International—its inability to enforce decisions—and his discussion of the psychological roots of nationalism, though sketchy, was a novel mode of analysis for Marxists that a fair number of Social Democrats found appealing and persuasive. Tsereteli, who spent much of the war in exile in Siberia, recalled that long sections of Axelrod's writings on the conflict were secretly distributed among "leading circles" of the Russian, German, and Austrian parties. "People wrote to me in Siberia about . . . [Axelrod's pamphlet] as though . . . [its appearance] were an event, and sent me . . . extracts from it."[22] But if some socialists were impressed by Axelrod's analysis and recommendations, many others were scandalized. They had no patience with proposals that counseled more debate and compromise and could tolerate no one who had a kind word for socialists favoring civil peace. Because of the intensity of these feelings, Axelrod's suggestion that the old International be restored was unrealistic, as he was soon to discover.

Nashe slovo, the paper edited by Trotsky in Paris, immediately attacked the proposal that all socialist tendencies be represented at forthcoming peace meetings. The militants around *Nashe slovo* were primarily concerned to unite socialist opponents of the war, and the

21. Paul Axelrod, *Die Krise und die Aufgaben der Internationalen Sozialdemokratie* (Zurich, 1915), and "Iz besedy s P. B. Aksel'rodom o nashikh raznoglasiiakh," *Nashe slovo*, nos. 87, 90, May 12, 16, 1915.
22. Tsereteli to Woytinsky, Feb. 1931, Nicolaevsky Collection, Hoover Institution.

idea of collaborating with defensists like Plekhanov even after the war was anathema.[23] Lenin ridiculed Axelrod for phrasemaking. He found the analysis of the sources of nationalism reminiscent of the landowners' endless discussions in 1861 about the profound roots of serfdom in Russian history; their scholarly disquisitions only played into the hands of reactionaries, as did Axelrod's. The Menshevik leader did not appreciate the extent of the international ties the proletariat had forged in recent years, ties that must now be utilized as the basis for "international revolutionary actions. Axelrod is against such actions. He is for reminding us about the one-thousand-year roots of the knout and against actions directed at the abolition of the knout."[24]

These additional differences with Lenin and Trotsky notwithstanding, Axelrod continued to participate in the antiwar movement. He attended the conference at Zimmerwald, which finally met in September 1915 in defiance of the Bureau of the Second International. The organizers had successfully resisted Leninist pressure to exclude the centrists, with whose position Axelrod sympathized, and this was sufficient assurance to him that the gathering would adopt acceptable policies. In fact, the centrists managed to dominate the meeting, which denounced the war as "the outcome of imperialism," but refrained from advocating defeat of any one country or an official break with the old International.[25]

In his speech at Zimmerwald Axelrod pleaded with the delegates not to oversimplify the differences over the war among socialists. He pointed out that there were important distinctions between the French and German socialists who supported their country's military effort and that those who mercilessly condemned all defensists were guilty of moralizing. After all, the refusal of the Russian party to follow the example of the "Western brother parties [in voting for war credits] was in no way the result of special moral or intellectual superiority of its leaders, nor of extraordinary theoretical training or superb political sagacity." The Russians had acted as they did because of the "objective revolutionary situation in which the tsarist Empire has found itself for a few years." The workers in his country understood that the notion of "national defense" was an "illusion"; only the destruction of the

23. "Ot redaktsii," *Nashe slovo*, no. 90, May 16, 1915.
24. Lenin, *Sochineniia*, XVIII, 308.
25. Fainsod, *International Socialism*, pp. 65–73.

reactionary regime and the establishment of democracy could, in their view, save Russia from decline.[26]

Axelrod's general statement on the war was consistent with the position he had upheld for some ten months, but his comments on Russia's internal situation suggest that his thinking had changed somewhat. With increasing frequency and vehemence he designated fundamental political change in Russia as a prerequisite for the attainment of peace. At Zimmerwald he declared that the slogan of Russian Social Democrats must be "A democratic constituent assembly for the liquidation of the war and the absolutist regime." As the Russian proletariat could not realize this policy by itself, it had to appeal for help to European workers and middle-class progressives in Russia.[27]

Axelrod's call for decisive political change in his country, though vague, placed him in a difficult position. On the one hand, he believed that such a change would and should bring the bourgeoisie into power. On the other, he was aware of the determination of the middle class to pursue the "war till victory," a policy unacceptable to him. Thus, he favored a bourgeois form of government without supporting the bourgeoisie on the outstanding issue of the day. Axelrod and his close associates tried to extricate themselves from the dilemma by proposing a strategy that can only be described as well-nigh impracticable. Referring to the "enormous significance" of a transfer of power to the bourgeoisie, they urged workers to collaborate with the middle class if it should attack the government, but simultaneously to unite with the proletariat of other countries in a struggle for peace.[28]

Axelrod was reacting to the marked rise in the oppositional mood in all belligerent countries by employing increasingly militant rhetoric, but when it came to concrete action he refused to budge from his centrist position. This became apparent at the next conference of anti-war socialists, which gathered in Kienthal in April 1916. The Zimmerwald left, led by Lenin, introduced a resolution demanding that all ties with the Second International be severed. Axelrod was the chief spokesman of the centrist opposition to the motion. He urged the delegates to vote for a resolution proposing the convocation of the Bureau of the

26. *Die Zimmerwalder Bewegung,* ed. Lademacher, II, 83–91.
27. *Ibid.,* p. 91.
28. Pavel Axelrod, Astrov (I. S. Poves), Iu. O. Martov, A. S. Martynov, S. Iu. Semkovsky, *Proletariat i voina* (Switzerland, 1915), pp. 9–10.

Second International, which had already shown some signs of activity in favor of a peace campaign. "For a long time," he told the conference, "Lenin has been asserting that the International is dead. I have also frequently stated that we are undergoing a great crisis. But I do not place myself in the same position as the doctor who says about one of his patients: 'I am going to perform surgery immediately, even if he dies from it.' I agree more with the other doctor, who says: 'We want to wait awhile and permit the man to recover a bit.' "[29]

After much wrangling and parliamentary maneuvering, the conference adopted a compromise resolution that marked a definite shift to the left by the socialist peace movement. It vigorously condemned the policies of the Bureau of the Second International and refused to take a clear-cut stand on whether or not to agitate for its convocation or to participate in its activities if it met. The resolution was passed by a vote of twenty-one to one. But Axelrod could not sanction the merest suggestion that a break with the Second International might be desirable. He abstained (along with a few other delegates) and thereafter always maintained that he was a *Zimmerwaldian,* but not a *Kienthaler.*

The outcome of the conference depressed Axelrod. More than at any previous time during the war, he felt utterly alone. His views on the "further development of the International," he complained, "are completely misunderstood," and consequently he was the object of widespread criticism. The right wing of the Russian movement attacked him for not supporting Russia's war effort; the left, for arguing that the failure of the International to act in 1914 did not result from the treacherous behavior of individuals or social groups but from its longstanding inability to counteract the appeal of nationalism. Axelrod smarted under the attacks. He could not work and felt he was undergoing a "slow and protracted process of dying."

His one consolation was that once again he found himself in the same camp as his old friends Kautsky and Bernstein. It was a source of pride to him that people regarded him as a *Kautskyaner.* "My mode of thinking," he wrote to Kautsky, "my general conceptions and practical-political tendencies appear to me to be by and large very close to yours, even if not in all details. I have developed extraordinary sympathy for Ede [Bernstein] because of his brave and, in the best sense of the word,

29. *Die Zimmerwalder Bewegung,* ed. Lademacher, II, 365–366.

idealistic position. Precisely for that reason I think that even in practical matters I would very much agree with him."[30]

Kautsky tried, as he had in earlier years, to raise Axelrod's spirits: "You have felt tired for a long time and still you have accomplished so much good."[31] But Kautsky's words of encouragement were not enough to cheer him up. In addition to the political disappointments, he was also suffering a personal tragedy. His second daughter, Sonja, who had been ailing for many years, was finally confined to a sanatorium. Although her illness appears to have been physical, it seems to have been compounded by the emotional stress of her unhappy relationship with her husband, Rudolph Laemmel, whom she had married against her father's advice.

Laemmel, by his own admission, was a contentious person. "When I was eight years old," he told Axelrod, "I was regarded as an extremely dangerous lad and all students were publicly forbidden to have any dealings with me." In addition, he had failed in his profession—that of mathematician—and he placed much of the blame on this fact for his not having made a "good marriage." His son-in-law's treatment of Sonja troubled Axelrod, and on one occasion he accused Laemmel of turning their son against her. For over a year Axelrod constantly worried about his daughter, but there was little he could do for her. She died in June 1917, at the age of thirty-five.[32]

In the meantime, in March 1917, the revolution had begun in Russia. Like other Russian socialists in exile, Axelrod yearned to be at the center of action. Iurii Larin seems initially to have taken charge of planning the return to Russia of Marxist émigrés. By March 17 he had concocted an ingenious, if somewhat farfetched, scheme for transporting Axelrod and others from Switzerland to Petrograd. Underestimating the imagination and daring of the Kaiser's advisers, Larin ruled out the possibility that the German government might allow revolutionaries to pass through their country. He had learned, however, that boats traveled regularly from Bergen, Norway, to Petrograd. In order to reach Norway

---

30. Axelrod to Kautsky, n. d., but probably summer, 1916, Nicolaevsky Collection, Hoover Institution; Axelrod to Kautsky, Jan. 5, 1917, *ibid.* In 1915 Bernstein, who initially supported Germany's war effort, became an opponent of the war.

31. Kautsky to Axelrod, Dec. 16, 1916, Axelrod Archive, I.I.S.H.

32. Laemmel to Axelrod, Aug. 17, 1916, *ibid.;* Laemmel to Axelrod, Sept. 18, 1917, *ibid.*

from Switzerland Larin suggested an overland trip through France into Spain, followed by a crossing by boat to New York, and another back to Norway. Neither Germany nor Great Britain prevented North American ships from reaching Europe. But Larin realized that during such a long journey war might break out between the United States and Germany, in which case Axelrod and his colleagues would have to travel from New York to Siberia. As a last possibility, if war between the United States and Germany were declared before the émigrés departed from Switzerland, they would have to go from Spain to Vladivostok by way of Africa. There can be no doubt that the Mensheviks explored all contingencies in their eagerness to participate in the revolution.[33]

All the involved plans ultimately proved unnecessary. When it dawned on the German government that additional revolutionaries could intensify the growing turmoil in Russia, it allowed the exiles to pass through the country in two sealed trains.[34] Unlike Lenin and his followers, Axelrod and Martov (as well as a number of other radicals) at first made their acceptance of the offer conditional on the willingness of the Provisional Government to return some German prisoners as a quid pro quo. The Mensheviks instinctively recoiled from a one-sided arrangement that could expose them to charges of being German agents. The continuing inaction of the Russian authorities so infuriated them that they took advantage of the German offer, although they expected to be criticized for it.[35] But it was too frustrating to be away from Russia at so crucial a period: Axelrod "could not bear it any longer and wanted to participate in the revolution."[36] He took the second train, which arrived in Petrograd on May 22. As a Swiss citizen, he enjoyed the privilege of sitting at an open window.

Axelrod was met at the Finland Station by Peter Garvi, who led the veteran Menshevik to a public square to face a large, waiting crowd. Garvi solemnly announced the name of the new arrival, but few heard him. "Yet this was unimportant. P. B. Axelrod uncovered his almost gray head, and the crowd let loose with a gust of emotion: shouts, applause." Axelrod began to address the people, but his voice was weak

33. Larin to Axelrod, Mar. 17, 1917, Nicolaevsky Collection, Hoover Institution.
34. For details, see *Lenins Rückkehr nach Russland 1917. Die deutschen Akten*, ed. Werner Hahlweg (Leiden, 1957). The introduction is a succinct and thorough account of the negotiations preceding Lenin's journey through Germany.
35. On Axelrod's and Martov's return to Russia, see Getzler, *Martov*, pp. 147–149.
36. "Zaiavlenie P. B. Aksel'roda," *Rabochaia gazeta*, no. 46, May 3, 1917.

and did not reach most of his audience. This, too, did not matter. For the "crowd saw—and I shall never forget it—this good, humane, and wise person, filled with emotion and joy, . . . [his] half-gray hairs, fluttering in the spring breeze—and it reacted in a stormy [fashion]." Garvi could not help being pleased at having arranged Axelrod's "first meeting with the people."[37]

Even before he arrived Axelrod had outlined a political strategy for the Menshevik party. He held it as axiomatic that "the struggle for peace is the paramount task of revolutionary democracy" and that the government could not embark on a course of "internal reconstruction" until the war was ended. He warned, nevertheless, against precipitous action on the peace issue and repudiated the idea—then being discussed—that Russia conclude a separate peace with the Central Powers. Though superficially appealing, advocacy of a separate peace might discredit the socialist movement in the eyes of the populace, including the proletariat, who, he believed, did not desire a cessation of hostilities at any price. It would also lead to conflict between the Mensheviks and the new liberal government and thus might conceivably strengthen the hand of those social groups pressing for victory as well as those who still favored the old order. Just as in 1905, Axelrod urged the Mensheviks to shun policies likely to cause a break with the progressive middle classes.

In addition to these considerations, Axelrod also took seriously the commitments Russia had made to its allies during the war. He regarded a separate peace with Germany as a betrayal of Belgium and France, much of whose territory was still under foreign occupation. Nor could he sanction "a victory of semiabsolutistic Junker Germany over revolutionary Russia . . . the moral to be drawn from this would be: 'One must not criminally violate a *Burgfrieden* [civil peace] when the country is in danger.'" The entire world proletariat would come to the conclusion that support of the bourgeoisie in time of war was the correct policy.[38]

But Axelrod by no means advocated continuing the war policies of

37. P. A. Garvi, "Iz neopublikovannykh vospominanii," on deposit at the Inter-University Project on the History of the Menshevik Movement, Columbia University.
38. "P. B. Aksel'rod o bor'be za mir," *Izvestiia*, no. 60, May 7, 1917; "P. B. Aksel'rod o taktike s.-d. v russkoi revoliutsii," *Rabochaia gazeta*, no. 48, May 5, 1917; "Pis'mo P. B. Aksel'roda o bor'be za mir," *Rabochaia gazeta*, no. 18, Mar. 28, 1917.

the tsarist regime. While still in Switzerland, in fact, he and several other Mensheviks published a letter protesting the attempts of French and English socialists to persuade the Provisional Government to fight until victorious.[39] It seemed to him that the revolution had made it possible for Russia to take the initiative in pressing for a speedy end to the war on the basis of no annexations and no indemnities. The proletariat should exert pressure in various ways to achieve this goal. In the first place, the Petrograd soviet should mobilize a popular campaign designed to force the Provisional Government to discuss a joint renunciation of conquests and common approaches to arranging an armistice with the Allies. If the Allies worked in unison, the revolutionary regime could not be accused of betraying past commitments.

In the second place, Axelrod proposed the convocation of an international congress of labor parties in order to develop a concerted program of action for peace on a world scale. The Petrograd soviet could again play a leading role "in the capacity of initiator . . . and organizer . . . It ought to circulate an appropriate appeal to the socialist proletariat of all countries and in particular to the proletariat of Austria, Germany, and France." If the official groups of the existing parties and the International refused to lend support to the meeting, the workers would be justified in electing new representatives. In other words, Axelrod would now sanction splits in European Social Democratic parties if they resisted following a peace policy.

As he realized, the German socialists held the key to success of his course of action. If they were to reject the "international struggle for peace" and the German army continued to threaten Russia with conquests and "new disasters," then "Russian Social Democracy would have to face point-blank *the question* of the defense of the country." No more should be required of the German comrades than that they participate in the international conference, an act that by itself might engender a "revolutionary outburst in Germany as well as in France."[40]

The editors of *Izvestiia*, the organ of the Petrograd soviet that reprinted Axelrod's views, underlined their endorsement of his plan. Stories had apparently been circulated about disagreements between

---

39. Pavel Axelrod, Astrov (I. S. Poves), Iu. O. Martov, A. S. Martynov, S. Iu. Semkovsky, "Ein Brief an Genosse Tscheidse," *Berner Tagwacht*, Apr. 5, 1917.
40. "P. B. Aksel'rod o bor'be za mir"; "P. B. Aksel'rod o taktike."

them, for the editors were moved to declare that "This puts an end to all sorts of contrary rumors, zealously set afloat by various liars."[41]

Like most Mensheviks, Axelrod held that "it is quite clear that the present revolution is not a purely proletarian [event], but also a bourgeois [event]." He rejected the Leninist slogan "Down with the Provisional Government" as "criminal," on the ground that the working class could not possibly govern the country under prevailing conditions. The proletariat ought to support the new government, but at the same time endeavor to participate in all "fields of social and state activities and in the daily organic work of democratizing all spheres of national life." Although the attempt to democratize Russia's institutions might compel socialists to oppose the government on some issues, such opposition must not extend beyond "the bounds of the defined character of the revolution."

When it came to tactics, Axelrod called for flexibility. Thus, while he argued against the service of socialists in the Provisional Government, he indicated that if it were necessary in order to save the revolution, he would approve of it as the "lesser evil. Everything depends on the conditions of the moment." He would even entertain the possibility of a "purely proletarian government," but only if first there were a general proletarian revolution in Europe. He did not foresee such a development in the near future, however, especially as long as the war continued. And, quoting Engels, he warned that premature seizure of power by the working class would pose "a great danger for the proletariat."[42]

Few traces of Axelrod's activities during his three-month stay in Petrograd have survived. It is known that he was elected to several high posts in the Menshevik party, including chairman of the O. C., and that he served on a number of commissions created to formulate party policy on specific issues. He was frequently so absorbed in party work that he did not return to his lodgings until two or three in the morning and on one occasion not until eight o'clock. "It was," he wrote, "as though I had been gripped by a whirlwind." Because of the "enormously tense atmosphere in Petrograd" the news of the death of his daughter did not wound him as much as it would have in Switzerland.

41. *Izvestiia*, no. 60, May 7, 1917.
42. "P. B. Aksel'rod o taktike."

But the revolutionary euphoria did not last long, and in time he suffered much anguish over his loss.[43]

Despite his presence at meetings and his high reputation in Menshevik circles, Axelrod exerted relatively little influence on the day-to-day decisions of his party in 1917. Of the revolutionaries who moved to the fore during those tumultuous days, some could quickly resolve complicated issues and act on them, others could mesmerize large gatherings with their oratory, and still others excelled at political infighting. Axelrod possessed none of these gifts. His aptitude for slowly developing broad tactical positions was irrelevant to a period when virtually every day a new crisis of major proportions had to be dealt with summarily. He therefore seems to have assumed the role of elder statesman and guardian of party unity. Thus, in July 1917, when he was elected honorary chairman of the Petrograd Menshevik organization, he limited himself to exhorting his comrades "to look for those points which unite them with their adversaries [in the Menshevik movement], not those which divide them."[44]

Another probable reason for the limited extent of Axelrod's contribution to political affairs in Petrograd was that once again he found himself at odds with his colleagues. He had no rapport with Plekhanov, who believed in fighting the war for victory and polemicized against Axelrod's proposal for an international peace campaign. He also could not agree with Martov, who objected to the Menshevik party's decision in April to join the coalition government and called for a peace offensive even at the price of a break with the Allies. Martov held that Russia should fight only if attacked and then should do so on its own. After July Martov demanded the formation of a new government based on the parties represented in the soviets.[45]

It appeared on the surface as though Axelrod was in full accord with the official Menshevik leaders—principally Dan and Tsereteli—who clung to the view that Russia was in the throes of a bourgeois revolution. Moreover, the Petrograd soviet, in which the Mensheviks exercised a dominant influence, had pressed for an international conference to take

---

43. Axelrod to Kautsky, n. d., but sometime in the summer 1917, Nicolaevsky Collection, Hoover Institution; Axelrod to Luise Kautsky, Oct. 10, 1917, *ibid.*

44. *Izvestiia,* no. 121, July 19, 1917.

45. G. V. Plekhanov, "Nemnozhno logiki" (A Little Logic), *Edinstvo,* no. 32, May 6, 1917; Getzler, *Martov,* pp. 150–152, 155.

up the peace question, and on April 22 the International Socialist Bureau announced that such a meeting would be held in Stockholm on May 15. These moves presaged the possibility of restoring the Second International and exerting proletarian pressure for an armistice, just as Axelrod had planned.

Despite these hopeful signs, he voiced serious reservations about the actions of the Menshevik leaders in Petrograd. On October 10, 1917, he confided to Kautsky that while in Zurich he had often been irritated when Mensheviks in Russia were criticized: "now I must acknowledge that after closer observation . . . I also became critical of them." In effect, some of the Mensheviks' actions "have helped the Bolsheviks achieve domination over the masses." Axelrod deplored, specifically, the failure of responsible socialists in the summer of 1917 "to concentrate the interest and attention and energy of the masses who were in a revolutionary mood on two points that I consider most important: the preparation for the election of the constituent assembly and the struggle for peace within an international framework." He complained to Kautsky that the Mensheviks were just beginning to pay serious attention to these matters. "If only this has not happened too late."

In addition, he feared that even now his party's leadership would approach the preparation of elections and peace talks in a halfhearted manner. There was a real danger, in his view, that Russia might be "on the eve of a retrograde movement," by which he meant a "new violent flaring up of the revolutionary flame," clearly a reference to some new action by the Bolsheviks. Axelrod based this apprehension on casual observation of crowds in the streets and their demands. "The dominant slogans on the flags in yesterday's demonstrations were: 'Down with the 10 capitalist ministers, all power to the Soviet of Workers and Soldiers' . . . and 'Peace between nations,' 'Long live the International.' " It seemed evident to him that the Provisional Government—which was subject to Menshevik pressure because it both included some of their number and existed only by grace of the socialist-dominated soviet—had done too little to capture the support of the war-weary people.[46]

Given the excitement of the times, Axelrod's perceptions were exceptionally unerring. Indeed, the Provisional Government had failed to resolve any of the major problems, and in the months from March until

46. Axelrod to Kautsky, Oct. 10, 1917, Nicolaevsky Collection, Hoover Institution; Axelrod to Kautsky, n. d., but sometime in summer, 1917, from Petrograd, *ibid.*

November its authority declined steadily. Although civil rights had been granted and a democratically elected constituent assembly promised, these progressive and important steps did not suffice to stem the tide of discontent. On many vital issues the government either postponed action or did not act at all.

For example, because of the turbulent situation throughout the country it delayed the election of the constituent assembly and thus failed to create a governmental authority that could claim to be legitimate on account of genuine popular support. By the summer of 1917 peasant disorders, usually accompanied by land seizures, were widespread, but the government still reached no final decision on agrarian legislation. One nationality group after another declared its autonomy or independence, and the authorities proved incapable of stopping the trend. Nor could they cope with the tendency of local soviets to assume control over their regions or of workers to seize factories. But most serious of all, the new regime did not appear committed to pursuing a consistent peace policy. It was known, in fact, that most of the cabinet ministers favored continuing the war if for no other reason than that a German victory would bring about the restoration of the Romanovs. The Russian troops, however, were in no mood or condition to fight and suffered defeat after defeat. By the fall of 1917 the rate of desertion had reached alarming proportions. In general, the worsening situation only aggravated the conflicts between the various political forces and precluded the emergence of a stable polity. It is no exaggeration to say that by the time the Bolsheviks staged their coup d'etat on November 7 the country had reached an advanced stage of disintegration.

The Menshevik party was forced to tread a narrow path throughout 1917. Its official leadership, the centrists led by Tsereteli and Dan, were hemmed in on one side by the right wing of the movement, which advocated more vigorous prosecution of the war, and on the other by the left, which valued peace more than treaty obligations to the Allies. The centrists were also constrained by their ideological convictions and their memories of 1905. In the summer of 1917 they probably could have assumed control of the government with the help of their allies, the Socialist Revolutionaries, for at the time the two parties maintained a solid grip on the soviets in Moscow and Petrograd. But they now rigidly adhered to the view of Russia's historical development that Axelrod himself had propagated for so long: that the country's backward economic and social levels ruled out a proletarian revolution. Furthermore, the centrists were unshakable in their conviction that excessive radicalism on the part of labor had caused the failure of the Revolution of 1905, and they were determined not to repeat the mistake.

Because the Menshevik party was so prominent and influential, it was natural for people to hold it responsible for the country's woes. Among the urban population its stock began to fall, and in September 1917 the Leninists for the first time won majorities in the soviets of the two capitals, which indicated that popular opinion in the cities had shifted to the left.

Axelrod was particularly distressed by the Mensheviks' failure to act more forcefully to internationalize the peace campaign. The difference between Axelrod and his Menshevik colleagues on this matter was actually not so much over aims as means. The Petrograd soviet had taken the initiative in calling for an international peace conference of socialists in Stockholm and had obtained permission from the Provisional Government to dispatch delegates. This latter concession was by no means a paltry achievement. Socialists in the United States, France, Belgium, and Great Britain were unable to secure passports.

But although the Mensheviks had sponsored the drive for a conference, they did not prevent the Provisional Government from issuing statements that could only have weakened the impact of any decisions that might have been reached in Stockholm. Early in August the government announced that "the determination of the question of war and peace belongs exclusively to it in unity with the governments of the Allied Powers." Then, in October, M. I. Tereshchenko, the Foreign Minister, declared that the decisions of the Stockholm conference "could not have decisive importance for the state power and governments."[47] Axelrod readily understood that if the revolutionary government of Russia refused to commit itself to support the decisions of the meeting, little could be expected from the statesmen of the other belligerent countries.

Nevertheless, because he had invested so much hope in the conference, he accepted the appointment of the Central Executive Committee of

---

47. *Izvestiia*, no. 133, Aug. 2, 1917; *The Russian Provisional Government 1917: Documents*, ed. Robert Paul Browder and Alexander F. Kerensky (Stanford: Stanford University Press, 1961), II, 1143.

the Petrograd soviet to help make preparations for it. He was also chosen to represent the Menshevik party at the meetings. The other members of the soviet delegation, W. Rozanov, A. N. Smirnov, I. P. Goldenberg, H. Erlich, and N. S. Rusanov, left for Stockholm early in July. Axelrod's departure was delayed by illness.

While recuperating in Petrograd, he participated in the discussions of the Central Executive Committee about the instructions that should be sent to the delegation in Stockholm; on one question he and the committee split. The committee held that the soviet delegation should avoid all discussion of responsibility for the outbreak of the war or the disintegration of the International. Consideration of these matters might embitter relations between socialists from different countries and therefore hinder the formulation of a common plan of action. Axelrod, however, believed that these questions constituted an integral part of the agenda. Before the International could be revived a candid analysis of past errors and a public condemnation of those mistakes which had led to its collapse were necessary. It seemed to him especially important that the French and Belgian socialists be criticized for their refusal to participate in the International's efforts to establish contacts between comrades from warring countries. Although the Executive Committee concurred in Axelrod's assessment of the actions of the Allied socialists, and privately told him so, it refused to alter its stand.

On the ground that a basic principle was at stake, Axelrod declined to serve as the soviet's delegate. "With all his gentleness and warmth in his relations with comrades," Tsereteli wrote, "Axelrod displayed an iron will when his convictions on the correctness of one or another political move were concerned." After resigning as representative of the soviet, he accepted a mandate to attend the conference as a delegate of the Menshevik party without specific instructions.[48]

Why was Axelrod so stubborn about this question since there was merit to the argument that a discussion of the old controversies would only impede dispassionate consideration of the paramount issue, the launching of a peace campaign? The answer is probably to be found in Axelrod's assertion that "Both wings—the right and the left—are neces-

48. I. G. Tsereteli, *Vospominaniia o fevral'skoi revoliutsii* (The Hague, 1963), I, 302–306.

sary for the success of the conference. The ultras and the doctrinaire people on both sides must be rendered harmless."[49]

The need to enlist the support of *all* socialist tendencies was driven home to Axelrod by Adler, a leading proponent of the conference and one of the best-known spokesmen of European Marxism. In a private letter written late in the spring of 1917 Adler admitted that he harbored no illusions about the potential impact of the meeting. "You yourself do not believe that we can make peace; still, from Stockholm there can be issued a call for peace from the entire proletariat of the world who are sick of the war, a call that would make it difficult for the nations to continue the war." The Russian comrades must assume the decisive role, for the revolution had heaped prestige on the working class, but they could not act effectively unless they ended their discord over the war. "If we are to wait until you, dear Axelrod and Martov, are to agree with Lenin and Trotsky, and in the end even with Riazanov on a sensible tactic, then the war might last another twenty years and hundreds of thousands of human beings will be slaughtered." Adler appealed to Axelrod to work for a common effort by all Russian socialists in favor of peace on the basis of "no annexations, no indemnities, and the right of self-determination."[50]

Although he agreed with Adler, Axelrod knew that the left wing of the socialist movement was so enraged at the rightists for collaborating with their governments that if the conference did not take some sort of position against the civil truce there would be no chance of promoting a common campaign for peace. By mentioning the failure of the socialists in France and Belgium to support the early moves for peace, Axelrod probably hoped to mollify the German Majority Socialists, who were bound to be severely censured. Thus, socialists in both camps would be subjected to criticism, a procedure that would appear fair. Also, the militants would not be able to argue that the International had disregarded the errors of national parties. This risky approach was probably the only one that stood a chance—however slight —of unifying the divergent tendencies.

Just as Axelrod was about to depart for Stockholm, an incident took

49. Axelrod to Kautsky, n. d., but sometime in summer, 1917, from Petrograd, Nicolaevsky Collection, Hoover Institution.
50. Adler to Axelrod, June 14, 1917, Archive of the Second International, I.I.S.H.

place that prompted him to delay his trip once again. The newspapers carried an announcement that Plekhanov had sent a dispatch to the French socialist party accusing anyone who participated in the Stockholm meeting of "state treason." In great agitation, Axelrod met with a group of Petrograd Mensheviks and requested an "energetic protest against this treacherous blow at the cause of the struggle for peace by the international proletariat." By a vote of eighty-four to four the group adopted a resolution describing Plekhanov as "completely isolated" in the movement.[51] Armed with this vote of confidence, Axelrod left for Stockholm on August 10. He was never to return to his native land.

After arriving in Stockholm, Axelrod immediately immersed himself in the work of preparing the conference. Although he suffered from a series of minor ailments, he seems to have weathered them remarkably well. Rusanov, one of the soviet representatives, observed the diversity of Axelrod's activities with surprise. Despite his advanced age, Axelrod regularly went swimming and took long walks, which he used as forums for examining and reaching conclusions on the political questions under review in various committees. During his first few weeks in the Swedish capital he attended even more meetings than he had in Petrograd; they often kept him occupied from early morning until late at night.[52]

The membership of the forthcoming conference remained the thorniest problem. The Leninists, backed by many Zimmerwaldists, opposed the participation of socialists who had supported the civil peace. Axelrod still adhered to the view that the International would be an effective instrument only if all tendencies were represented at its meetings. The difference between him and the Bolsheviks erupted into open warfare at the Third Zimmerwald Conference, which was held secretly on September 5–12, mainly for the purpose of determining policy in the broader conference.

It is unfortunate that the minutes of the proceedings were never printed and none of the participants published a detailed account of the discussions. Several, however, have referred to a particularly stormy session during which Axelrod wrangled with Karl Radek, a sympathizer

51. *Novaia zhizn'*, no. 96, Aug. 9, 1917.
52. N. S. Rusanov, *Kak my podgotovliali stokgol'mskuiu konferentsiiu: Vospominaniia chlena stokgol'mskoi delegatsii N. S. Rusanova* (n. d., n. p.), p. 143, on deposit in the Russian Archives, Columbia University; Axelrod to Luise Kautsky, Oct. 10, 1917, Nicolaevsky Collection, Hoover Institution.

of Lenin and representative of the National Committee of Polish Social Democracy. Radek savagely berated the coalition government of Russia for its "sins," charging it with cowardice, lack of principle, and the implementation of "objectively reactionary" policies. V. V. Vorovsky (Orlovsky), the Bolshevik delegate, broadened the assault: he specifically accused Axelrod and Martov of having participated in a capitalist war government and in the repression of soldiers and workers, and of having helped prepare military offensives.

Axelrod was unable to control his rage. He is alleged to have replied with a four-hour tirade in which he castigated the Bolsheviks so severely that Georg Ledebour of the German Independent Socialist party shouted out a demand for an apology. Instead of apologizing, Axelrod left the meeting immediately after his speech. In a way, all the contenders had wasted their breath: the continuing refusal of the Entente governments to grant visas for the conference at Stockholm made the entire question of participation irrelevant. The Third Zimmerwald Conference ended its deliberations by calling for a general strike against the war, which never materialized.[53]

The Bolshevik seizure of power on November 7, 1917, made senseless any further negotiations for a unified socialist campaign against the war. Not only had the Bolsheviks decided to break with the Second International; they immediately indicated their intention of concluding a separate peace. Now that he was no longer needed in Stockholm, Axelrod hoped to return to Russia "in order to take a direct part in the struggle of my party friends against the putschists and their wretched activities." But the Menshevik C. C. pleaded with him to stay in Stockholm in order to "defend the interests of our revolution before the International."[54] Axelrod's son, Alexander, who was then in Petrograd, also urged him to remain in the West. "Most friends do not consider

---

53. O. A. Ermanskii, *Iz perezhitogo (1887–1921 g.g.)* (Moscow, 1927), pp. 173–174; Angelica Balabanova, "Die Zimmerwalder Bewegung 1914–1919," *Archiv für die Geschichte des Sozialismus und der Arbeiterbewegung*, XII (1926), 400–401; P. E. Korolev, "V. I. Lenin i tsimmerval'dskoe ob'edinenie (fevral'-oktiabr' 1917 goda)," *Voprosy istorii KPSS*, no. 2 (1960), 153. Korolev had access to the notes of N. A. Semashko (A. V. Alexandrov), a Bolshevik who attended the Third Zimmerwald Conference. Semashko's notes are in the Central Party Archives of the Institute for Marxism-Leninism. For an analysis of the various meetings and discussions in Stockholm, see Fainsod, *International Socialism*, pp. 147–164.
54. Axelrod to Greulich, Jan. 12, 1918, uncatalogued, I.I.S.H.; Axelrod to Otto Bauer, Nov. 27, 1917, postcard that was never mailed, Axelrod Archive, I.I.S.H.

it wise for you to come here," he wrote. He appreciated his father's eagerness to return, but "political life here has already declined so much, and developments are so brutal, vulgar, and ruthless that one is seized with the 'greatest despair.'" In the expectation that the situation would deteriorate further Alexander warned his father that if he came back he might never be permitted to leave the country again. "You will not be able to find any peace of mind for work, and participation in party work is very difficult, too exciting, and worrisome for you." In his son's opinion, Axelrod could make his greatest contribution by devising a "Marxist analysis of our peculiar Russian revolution."[55]

Axelrod soon came to agree with his son, especially when he heard of the misconceptions about Russia rampant in radical circles in the West. The need to counteract these misconceptions was probably driven home to him by some letters he received from Kautsky, who was better versed in Russian affairs than most Western socialists and who after 1914 had begun to grasp the nature of Leninism. On November 10, 1917, he wrote Axelrod that in his view the Bolshevik coup did not necessarily spell disaster for democracy in Russia. He still hoped that the "sensible Bolsheviks" would realize that compromise was unavoidable. "Either an understanding between the forces of democracy or there will be chaos, the dissolution of Russia."[56] But within a few weeks Kautsky became anxious about the course of events. He now acknowledged his ignorance of developments in Russia and pleaded for news: "We are totally in the dark and cannot find our way." Moreover, he had received contradictory reports on the position of Axelrod and his colleagues toward Lenin's regime. He had a foreboding that the "situation is not pretty," an attitude he complained that no one in Berlin shared. "Lenin has brought off the trick of becoming the most popular person in *all* parties from the most extreme left to the most extreme right. This always signifies that his position, based on illusions, will be short-lived."[57]

Though it upset him, the lack of skepticism toward the Bolshevik regime among Western socialists did not really surprise Axelrod. In an obvious reproach, he reminded Kautsky that for over a decade he had

55. Alexander Axelrod to Axelrod, n. d., but shortly after the Bolshevik seizure of power, Axelrod Archive, I.I.S.H.
56. Kautsky to Axelrod, Nov. 10, 1917, Nicolaevsky Collection, Hoover Institution.
57. Kautsky to Axelrod, Dec. 22, 1917, *ibid.*

refused to accept his analysis of Bolshevism. "But never before," Axelrod admitted, "did I find this so distressing and painful as at the present moment."[58] At about the same time he told another friend that the "Bolshevik crime against our revolution and against the entire International" was being glorified in the West and especially in Central Europe as a "world historical event that will soon free humanity not only of the war but also of capitalism and all its miseries." Consequently, "international duty" demanded that the falsity of the legends proliferating about the Bolsheviks be exposed. "Herein lies the reason for my remaining here [in Stockholm]."[59]

Axelrod's assessment of the Bolshevik seizure of power was unremittingly negative. To his way of thinking, it was basically counterrevolutionary and "a historical crime without parallel in modern history." He could not entertain the possibility that history might fail to avenge itself on those who had violated its rules by taking power in a country not yet ripe for socialism. He therefore predicted that the life of the Bolshevik regime "will be short; its days or weeks are numbered. But it is very doubtful whether the revolution can still be saved and Russia can escape ruin."[60]

Axelrod's dogmatic view of the historical process had misled him dismally in trying to forecast the longevity of Bolshevism. His analyses of Lenin's triumph and policies, however, were incisive. He now dedicated himself to making them known, and the spurt of activity it inspired, which lasted about four years, would have been extraordinary even for a younger and healthier man. He lectured frequently, edited a journal on contemporary Russia, traveled throughout Europe to enlist the aid of leading socialists, addressed international conferences, and sustained a spirited correspondence with comrades and friends throughout the world. It seemed to him that only if Western Marxists understood the full dimension of the Russian catastrophe would there be any hope of rectifying the damage that had been done. The zeal with which Axelrod attempted to impart this conclusion to his European comrades can only be compared to that of a missionary.

His crusade began in Stockholm with a series of lectures on the year 1917. The main theme was that from the moment the old regime col-

---

58. Axelrod to Kautsky, n. d., but early in 1918, *ibid.*
59. Axelrod to Greulich, Jan. 12, 1918, uncatalogued, I.I.S.H.
60. *Ibid.;* Axelrod to Kautsky, n. d., but sometime early in 1918, *ibid.*

lapsed Lenin had sought a *"monopoly* of government power" for his party. The methods he had used in his drive for power were precisely the same as the ones he had applied to interparty conflicts ever since 1903. "The revolution has only created an enormous arena for these party practices, for an unbridled application of these methods of struggle vis-à-vis comrades with a different point of view." Once again he emphasized that in its essence Bolshevism violated fundamental principles of traditional Marxism.

First, the revolution had not been the work of the class-conscious proletariat. Lenin had exploited the yearnings of war-weary soldiers, most of whom were peasants in civilian life, and of urban workers who had only recently moved to the cities. "It is possible to assert with certainty that the Bolshevik agitation inflamed the most primitive instincts and passions of the masses and opened the door to all sorts of dubious and demoralized people. Creatures of the old tsarist regime, provocateurs, gendarmes, members of the so-called 'Black Hundreds,' representatives of the 'lower regions,' gangsters, all sorts of adventurers and place-hunters [*Streber*] clutch at the coattails of the Bolsheviks and also play an important role among them."

The Bolsheviks' claim that they represented proletarian interests was belied by their actions shortly before they took power. If Lenin's primary concern, Axelrod contended, had been to effect a radical solution of the social, political, and economic problems of the country, he would have joined with other socialist groups who had indicated a readiness to initiate far-reaching changes. At the Council of the Republic, a sort of preparliament which first met on October 20 and was to serve as a deliberative and consultative body until the constituent assembly was convoked, there emerged a majority of Mensheviks, Socialist Revolutionaries, and other radicals who supported "resolute measures on all questions" relating to foreign policy, agriculture, and other domestic areas. The legitimacy of the body had been acknowledged by the cabinet which had sent before it two of its members, the Foreign Minister and the Minister of War, to report on and explain their policies. Alexander Kerensky had declared his willingness to resign if the council wished. Moreover, the Cadets would surely not have accepted the council's proposals; thus, had the left formed a stable bloc the bourgeois representatives would have quit the government. But at the very start of the council's sessions the Bolsheviks publicly declared their refusal to participate and left the hall. The radical opposition to the government was therefore split and incapable of decisive action.

In other words, late in October Axelrod seems not to have been averse to the exercise of power by a combination of socialist parties. Because he never returned to this theme it is impossible to determine precisely the kind of political regime he envisioned. All he suggested was that a government composed of representatives from all socialist parties could have ended the war, instituted radical changes in the agrarian sector, and, above all, consolidated the democratic gains of the March Revolution. Whether or not such measures could have been successful in stabilizing the situation at this late stage is doubtful, for the masses had become too militant and impatient to trust the old leadership. Yet Axelrod was right in asserting that Lenin's refusal to make the effort of collaborating with other radical groups revealed his intention of taking power alone.

Axelrod made another, perhaps more telling, point in charging that throughout 1917 the Bolsheviks had not been interested in making positive contributions to the democratic revolution. They paid little attention to practical questions either in the soviets or in other administrative sectors. Rather, they devoted their energies to agitation and to denigrating other socialists, who appeared unable to cope with the most pressing problems. "By virtue of the fact that they could concentrate their activities on agitation, they secured great advantage over the Mensheviks among the masses." In short, the Bolsheviks did their utmost to intensify the frustrations of the masses and then capitalized on them. Once authority collapsed, they were ready to pick up the pieces. "Thus, the Bolshevik coup cannot be considered a spontaneous event, as the only occurrence that could result from the objective process of development of the revolution. The Bolsheviks . . . consciously strove for . . . [a seizure of power] and planned it from the beginning of the revolution."

In saying this, Axelrod did not deny that Lenin's opponents had played into his hands by neglecting to pursue more vigorously the goal of internationalizing the campaign for a democratic peace and by failing to convoke a democratically elected constituent assembly. Axelrod insisted, nonetheless, that the democratic revolution could have been saved had it not been for the "gigantic efforts" of the Bolsheviks to play a "world historical role under the Marxist banner." Now he dreaded that the Leninists, having obtained power by force, would be compelled to resort to ever more violence to retain it. And since in his opinion they would soon be overthrown, he feared that their example would be used by their reactionary successors as a justification for new "bloody orgies and policies of oppression and for depriving the people of their rights."[61]

Axelrod unquestionably discussed Bolshevism and its tactics in a one-sided and somewhat polemical fashion. His criticisms of the non-Bolshevik socialists were mild; he did not even mention the dogmatism of the Mensheviks and their hesitation to take power. Nor did he lend sufficient weight to the vacillation and weakness of Kerensky, which contributed so much to the collapse of authority. He also sadly under-estimated the staying power and resourcefulness of the Leninists. There were still other factors that he failed to take into account, but it must be remembered that his purpose was political, not scholarly. Consider-ing his intention, the perspicacity of his analysis is noteworthy. In fact, the three central themes he developed are still widely accepted by Western writers on the Revolution of 1917: first, that the Provisional Government's failure to cope with vital issues rendered it ineffective in its efforts to prevent political disintegration; second, that Lenin's seizure of power was not the natural consequence of the course of events, but rather the result of a planned action by a determined minority exploiting the chaotic conditions in the country; and third, that the Bolshevik victory could not lead to the emergence of a social order based on the principles of traditional Marxism.

During the initial period of the Bolshevik regime, Axelrod's opinions about the revolution corresponded fairly closely to those of the most influential Menshevik leaders in Russia, even though the latter favored a tactic of partial accommodation. By mid-November 1917 Martov and his Internationalist group had gained ascendancy in the party, and they succeeded in persuading the C. C. to attempt to negotiate for an all-socialist government ranging from the Popular Socialists to the Bol-sheviks.[62] The decision was based on a number of considerations: a

61. Paul Axelrod, "Herostraten," in *Die russische Revolution und die sozialistische Internationale: Aus dem literarischen Nachlass von Paul Axelrod*, ed. I. Tsereteli and W. Woytinsky (Jena, 1932), pp. 133–158.

62. Until 1906 the Popular Socialists were a small group on the right wing of the

desire to avoid both one-party rule by the Bolsheviks and a return to the *immobilisme* of the Kerensky coalition; fear of losing working-class support to the Leninists; and, finally, the fact that there existed a sizable group of Bolsheviks opposed to the seizure of power by one party.

It soon emerged, however, that Lenin was not interested in negotiating with the Mensheviks. Nevertheless, at an Extraordinary Congress of the party, early in December 1917, the Internationalists won ten of nineteen seats on the C. C. A few people on the right wing, such as Potresov and Mark Liber, refused to participate in the new C. C. Henceforth the basic political line of the party in Russia was set by Martov, Rafael Abramovich, and Dan (the last having adopted Martov's position).[63]

Although communication with the West became difficult in the fall and winter of 1917, the Mensheviks corresponded occasionally with Axelrod, who was now the chief foreign representative of the party. In a letter written on December 1, 1917, Martov urged him to explain to the German socialists still in Stockholm (Haase and Ledebour) why the Internationalists were not taking part in Lenin's revolution: "Although the masses of workers are for Lenin, his regime more and more becomes a regime of terror not of the proletariat but of the 'sansculottes'—ill-assorted masses of armed soldiers, 'Red Guards,' and sailors . . ." Martov added that the Bolshevik attempt to govern the country against the will of the huge majority of peasants and bourgeoisie could not lead to anything but failure. He asked Axelrod to let the Germans know that by suppressing all freedoms granted in March 1917 the Bolsheviks were preparing the way for a Bonapartist regime.

The tactics Martov and his colleagues proposed for dealing with the Bolsheviks indicates that they had not shed their illusions about their adversaries. They intended to concentrate on "exposing and unmasking Lenin's policies in the hope that the better elements among the laboring masses following him, understanding where . . . [the policies] lead, will form a nucleus capable of directing the course of the 'dictatorship' into

Socialist Revolutionary party. Thereafter they had an independent organization; they agreed with the aims of the SR's, but advocated more moderate methods of political action. See Oliver Radkey, *The Agrarian Foes of Bolshevism: Promise and Default of the Russian Socialist Revolutionaries February to October 1917* (New York, 1958), p. 65.

63. B. Nicolaevsky, *Men'sheviki v dni oktiabr'skogo perevorota* (New York, 1962), pp. 1–9.

another path." The immediate aim, according to Martov, was to unite all socialists (including the Bolsheviks) in the constituent assembly "on the basis of a solution of the peace issue, the institution of reforms in industry and agriculture, and the renunciation of terror and socialist-utopian experiments." Martov urged his Western colleagues to convoke an international socialist conference, presumably to take up the question of a peace campaign that would render unnecessary separate negotiations between Russia and the Central Powers.

Axelrod's views on the specifics of Menshevik tactics in Russia during this early period of Lenin's rule are not known. He might be expected to have questioned both the feasibility of a coalition with the Bolsheviks and Martov's estimate of the strength of their ties to the class-conscious proletariat. But these differences were not significant at the time. Indeed, Martov assumed basic agreement between them, as is suggested by the following comment he made in a letter to Axelrod: "And, you know, Pav[el] Bor[isovich], only now has that 'Jacobin' character of Leninism, which you revealed in *Iskra* No. 55 in 1903, been exposed in full measure."[64] Once again, as he had in 1907, Martov acknowledged that his friend had been right all along in his evaluation of Bolshevism.

Axelrod received further evidence to bolster his assessment of the Bolshevik revolution from Dan, who had also remained in Petrograd. Dan, too, claimed that all sorts of discredited individuals—hooligans, former agents of the secret police, Black Hundreds—"cling to the Leninist dictatorship like bees to honey." But he was sure that "The Bolshevik dictatorship is obviously falling to pieces." The reaction against anarchy and terror had begun to manifest itself, and he concluded that "all conditions have matured for the appearance of the 'white general.'" Dan also asked Axelrod to inform Western socialists about the true state of affairs in Russia. "If . . . [the Bolsheviks] are not ejected from the international socialist circle, then it means that the International tolerates all sorts of renegades and hangmen and . . . that the banner of the International can provide shelter for the direct preparation of a very fierce counterrevolution."[65]

These cries of outrage from his comrades in Russia reinforced Axelrod's determination to publicize the Bolshevik method of rule as widely

---

64. Martov to Axelrod, Dec. 1, 30, 1917, Nicolaevsky Collection, Hoover Institution.
65. Dan to Axelrod, Dec. 4, 1917, Jan. 8, 1918, *ibid.*

as possible. He made every effort to hasten the appearance of the new paper he was editing on the situation in Russia. Martov was delighted when he heard that the first issue would appear early in 1918 and in the name of the Menshevik C. C. sent him a thousand rubles for the undertaking.[66] Axelrod felt confident that his campaign to arouse the conscience of Western Marxists accurately reflected the wishes and predilections of his party in Russia.

Although the Bolshevik seizure of power did not unsettle Axelrod's commitment to Marxism, it further weakened his conviction that a movement claiming to be proletarian was necessarily virtuous. He could not even assume, as he once had, that a revolution staged by such a movement would represent progress. The crisis of 1917, like several previous events, compelled him to question some of his most cherished beliefs and to become aware of the possibility that there might be some issues, particularly moral issues, that should not be resolved either in the interest of a political ideology or political expediency. Whenever this had happened in the past, he had aligned himself on the side of justice, as he saw it.

Late in November 1917 the Jewish Press Bureau in Stockholm asked Axelrod to comment on "The Impending Peace and the Jewish Question." His statement reveals how much his approach to politics had changed since 1882, when he first confronted the Jewish question as a public figure. Now he unequivocally condemned anti-Semitism and did not show the slightest reluctance to having his views publicized. He assigned to the "international proletariat"—presumably he had in mind a resurrected International—the task of intervening, with the greatest possible vigor, in behalf of Jews wherever they were persecuted, regardless of the extent of popular prejudice. He singled out Poland, Galicia, and Romania as areas where such action would be appropriate. Not only must Jews be granted full rights of citizenship; they must also be accorded the right of "national self-determination" and of "national autonomy on a personal basis." Axelrod did not elaborate the latter point, but it is clear that he had abandoned the idea of "amalgamation" and his long-standing opposition to a principal contention of the Bund, that the Jews constituted a nation.

66. Martov to Axelrod, Dec. 30, 1917, *ibid.*

The most profound change in his outlook, however, can be found in his comments on Zionism. After pleading ignorance of the subject, he acknowledged that there was a conflict within his "soul" between two points of view. "When I indulge in the dream of a happy, united humanity, then it appears to me a pity that the Jews exert so much energy in colonizing Palestine. But in view of the hard fact of reality, of the pogroms, and of all the various forms of Jewish persecution, there stirs within me sympathy for Palestine and a wish to see in the realization of the Zionist goal a refuge for that unhappy people. Very often it seems to me that the fate of the poorest nation of the world is to be envied if only it has a place of its own and a certain territory that it can regard as its undisputed historical property." In any case, there was no doubt at all in his mind that the "concrete demand" of the Jewish socialist organization *Poale Zion* for unimpeded Jewish colonization of Palestine was "absolutely justified."[67]

These last remarks are arresting because they indicate both that Axelrod had changed his mind about the Jewish question and that he refused to condone or tolerate suffering in his time for the sake of an ideal to be realized in the future. During the next few years much of his work in opposition to the Bolsheviks was motivated by this consideration. To be sure, Lenin's perversion of Marxist doctrine also impelled him to repudiate the regime. But all of Axelrod's criticisms of the Bolshevik experience would emphasize the human suffering it would entail. The older he grew, the less willing he was to sacrifice the present to an unknown—and unknowable—future.

67. Axelrod's statement is on deposit in the Archive of the Second International, I.I.S.H. I have found only one published account of these remarks, in the Menshevik paper *Novyi luch* that appeared in Petrograd on January 27, 1918. The account is quite detailed and accurate except for one omission: Axelrod's favorable comment about Zionism.

X | Conscience of the Party

Axelrod's last years of political activity were the most trying of his revolutionary career. Ever since the early 1870's, when he first dedicated himself to the cause of radical change, he had been beset by adversity. He had frequently found himself pitted against the most influential revolutionaries—and sometimes even his closest associates—over ideological matters or tactics, and only by virtue of his persistence and persuasive powers had he been able to retain a commanding position in the movement. But after 1917 he faced the severest challenge of all: to counteract the glorifications of Communism that had become fashionable in Marxist and left-wing intellectual circles the world over. For a time, his was one of a handful of voices that warned against romanticizing Lenin's regime. With a tenacity, resourcefulness, and boldness that few thought he possessed, Axelrod attempted to prevail upon Western socialists to take an unequivocal stand against the Bolsheviks.

In this endeavor he had to deal with some fundamental and thorny problems that confounded other theorists and politicians on the left and, in due course, scholars writing on modern Russia. Was the Bolshevik Revolution a progressive or retrograde event? Did Leninist rule constitute a dictatorship *of* the proletariat or a dictatorship *over* the proletariat? Did the new order, even if repressive, contain within it the seeds of an egalitarian and humane society? Are socialism and democracy indissoluble? Or is it chimerical to believe that socialism can be attained by democratic means? Because he explored these questions in his campaign against Bolshevism, Axelrod may be said to have been an initiator of the great debate over the Communist Revolution of 1917 that has not yet ended.

Within two months of Lenin's seizure of power, Axelrod had assembled the first issue of a new journal, *Les Echos de Russie,* which was designed to make developments in Russia understood in the West. All told, twenty-one numbers appeared, the last in September 1918. After June 1918 the Socialist Revolutionaries N. Rusanov and V. Sukhomlin collaborated with him in editing that journal as well as the German-language *Stimmen aus Russland.* The content of the seven issues of the latter overlapped to some extent the French periodical.

The circulation of the two publications was not large, mainly because money was in short supply. In the summer of 1918 the Mensheviks in Petrograd sent Axelrod 6,000 rubles and promised him a monthly subsidy of 1,500.[1] But government restrictions soon hampered contact between him and his colleagues in Russia, and by the fall of 1918 the editors in Stockholm were penniless. Although Axelrod intended to resume publication after resettling in Switzerland, he was never able to obtain financial backing for the venture.

Both journals were plainly tendentious. Axelrod made no attempt to conceal his intention to destroy the "legend" that the Bolshevik order had heralded "the dawn of a new era in world history." But he made every effort to be accurate and tended to eschew unsubstantiated reports. The general situation in the country was so bleak that factual accounts in themselves gave the impression he wished to impart, that Russian society was in chaos. Many of the data were gleaned from the Bolshevik press, which Axelrod read omnivorously. He occasionally reprinted articles from Menshevik newspapers that appeared illegally after the middle of November 1917. From time to time he also reproduced letters he had received from comrades in Russia. For Westerners seeking detailed information about political developments, economic conditions, the activities of opposition parties, and the increasing political terror, the journals were a valuable and basically reliable source.

Axelrod addressed himself primarily to Western Marxists, on the theory that only by isolating the Bolsheviks within the international socialist movement could the climate for restoring democracy in Russia be created. Although aware of the odds against this strategy, he never suspected how intractable the obstacles he encountered would be.

The trouble was that for a long time many European socialists were positively euphoric about the Bolshevik achievement. On November 12,

1. Genrikh Erlikh to Axelrod, June 4, 21, 1918, Nicolaevsky Collection, Hoover Institution.

1917, the Austro-German party sent a telegram to the Congress of Soviets in Petrograd welcoming the assumption of power by "Russian democracy." The German Independents addressed a proclamation to the proletariat in their country hailing Lenin's feat as an "achievement of world historical significance. Never before has so great a task been assigned to the proletariat as at this time."[2] Even the Majority Socialists were enthralled. *Vorwärts*, their major daily paper, asserted that the new government's willingness to make peace demonstrated that it was composed of true socialists and class comrades. Early in December 1917 the editors of the paper expressed regret that the reported recommendation of Lenin and Trotsky for the Nobel Peace Prize had been made after the deadline for the submission of names. Not all Majority Socialists glorified the new rulers, but the dominant mood in the party was certainly favorable to them.[3]

Nevertheless, a few Marxists encouraged Axelrod to publish his journals. In January 1918 Kautsky wrote that he looked forward to them "with the greatest interest. It is urgently necessary that you have an impact on foreigners who do not read Russian." He warned, however, that the journals would not find many sympathetic readers. In Berlin a small circle still formed a counterweight to the "worshipers of the Bolsheviks. In Vienna there is none. Even Otto Bauer has allowed himself to be captured."[4] Hermann Greulich, the Swiss socialist, and Eduard Bernstein wrote similar notes of encouragement to Axelrod, but also predicted that his success was likely to be minimal. "Candidly, it is tragic," Bernstein confessed, "that you are being left in the lurch; often, when I read in your [publication] . . . about how scandalously you are being treated [in Russia], I cry out [in shame] that you do not even have the satisfaction of feeling that your voice evokes an echo among foreign comrades."[5]

Realizing that his journalistic endeavors were not moving Western comrades to action, Axelrod decided to appeal to them directly. In August 1918 he composed a letter "To the Socialist Parties of All Countries," which, after it had also been signed by D. Gavronsky, Rusanov,

---

2. *Bote der Russischen Revolution*, no. 9/10, Nov. 17, 1917.
3. Peter Lösche, *Der Bolschewismus im Urteil der Deutschen Sozialdemokratie 1903–1920* (Berlin, 1967), pp. 105, 117, 119–120.
4. Kautsky to Axelrod, Jan. 16, 1918, Nicolaevsky Collection, Hoover Institution.
5. Greulich to Axelrod, Feb. 1, 28, 1918, Axelrod Archive, I.I.S.H.; Bernstein to Axelrod, June 30, 1918, Nicolaevsky Collection, Hoover Institution.

and Sukhomlin, was widely distributed. It challenged the international socialist movement impartially to examine conditions in Russia and then to pass judgment on the Bolshevik regime. Although Axelrod offered his own analyses of the regime and its immediate prospects, he did not propose that his word be accepted at face value.

In an unsparing indictment he charged the Bolsheviks with the destruction of democratic institutions and the economy, the suppression of socialist newspapers, and responsibility for the widespread famine. He further accused them of waging fierce terror against political opponents of every persuasion and of having reduced the chances for a universal democratic peace by signing a separate peace with Germany. The Bolshevik regime, he concluded, had degenerated into a "gruesome counterrevolution."

Tensions between the disaffected masses and the intransigent rulers had reached a point at which "a violent revolution appeared to be the only, unavoidable remedy." As Axelrod saw it, the central question was whether a period of violence would propel democratic or reactionary forces into control of the country. "Now inasmuch as the Western comrades sanction the Bolshevik policies of oppression vis-à-vis the masses of workers and peasants, politically justify and morally support the regime of force of the People's Commissars, they render more difficult and weaken the position of those socialist parties who struggle against this regime; and [the Western comrades] run the risk in this way of helping the counterrevolutionary elements triumph over the democratic forces at the moment of the inevitable liquidation of Bolshevism."

Axelrod conceded that Western socialists had so far dismissed reports of political repression in Russia as "fairy tales," but he attributed this to ignorance rather than ill will. He suggested therefore that his charges be investigated "on the scene" by a commission of inquiry authorized by the International and composed of men with impeccable credentials. An objective report was needed because not only the future of the Russian Revolution but the "honor and fate of the International" were at stake. If Lenin were allowed to continue to exploit the moral support of Western socialists, the working-class cause throughout the world would be tarnished.[6]

6. The letter is reproduced in *Die russische Revolution und die sozialistische Internationale: Aus dem literarischen Nachlass von Paul Axelrod*, ed. I. Tsereteli and W. Woytinsky (Jena, 1932), pp. 159–162; it was originally published in *Stimmen aus Russland*, no. 4/5, Aug. 1918.

The response to Axelrod's appeal was pitiable. Only one newspaper, the Swedish *Social-Demokraten*,[7] printed the letter in its entirety, and few party leaders showed interest in the suggestion that a commission be formed. Nevertheless, Axelrod refused to give up. For the next four years all of his energies were absorbed in the attempt to mobilize the International into organizing what he called a "moral intervention" in Russian affairs. With each new crisis—the military intervention by the Allied Powers and Japan, the civil war, the virtual economic collapse of the country—he found the necessity for a commission of inquiry greater. He almost became obsessed by the idea, and the more he pondered it, the more he refined his supporting arguments. He scored some of his most telling points in the periodic pleas for action that he sent to Western socialists.

Thus, he assured Arthur Henderson, a leader of the British Labour party, that he was not asking that the Bolsheviks be condemned or tried a priori, but merely that a "nonpartisan, objective examination" of the facts be made. He warned Thornwald Stauning, a prominent figure in the Danish party, that the elite of the Russian working class, in despair because they had been abandoned by their colleagues, might easily "greet the counterrevolution . . . as liberation." A demonstration of concern by the International, however, would inspire them with "new courage and new hope." Axelrod further stated that a "moral and political 'intervention' by international Social Democracy in the internal affairs of Russia would place the Bolsheviks in a dilemma: either to give in to the demands of the proletarian masses and their parties or openly to come out in opposition to international socialism." Adoption by the Leninists of the first alternative would, of course, be an enormous victory for democracy. Adoption of the second would erode the moral position of the Bolsheviks and consequently embolden the democratic socialists in Russia.[8]

Axelrod did not advocate a planned uprising against the Bolsheviks, though he did contend that if conditions did not improve quickly violence would erupt spontaneously. His opposition to armed resistance was not motivated by "Christian-Tolstoyan principles of nonresistance to evil." On the contrary, he contended that in Georgia, where democratic socialists were in power, resort to force to ward off the Bolsheviks

7. See the complaint in *Les Echos de Russie*, no. 20/21, Sept. 1, 1918, 30.
8. Axelrod to Henderson, Sept. 7, 1918, *Die russische Revolution*, ed. Tsereteli and Woytinsky, pp. 163–167; Axelrod to Stauning, Sept. 14, 1918, Axelrod Archive, I.I.S.H.

was legitimate. But in areas where the Bolsheviks ruled, the risks were too great: "By entering the path of conspiracies and military uprisings, the democratic forces must inevitably embark on this path in coalition with all sorts of dubious elements—right up to the counterrevolutionaries, [thereby] risking absorption by these counterrevolutionary allies in the event of a victorious outcome of this kind of undertaking." Instead, he favored the same type of resistance to Bolshevik arbitrariness that he had to that of the Tsar: "organizational and agitational work among the masses, [for the purpose] of developing their political fighting capacity."[9]

However much Axelrod despised Leninist rule, he could not bring himself to associate with anti-Communists whose principles he found repugnant. This attitude is amusingly revealed by an incident related by Wladimir Woytinsky. In 1920 Axelrod and Woytinsky by chance ran into Gregory Alexinsky in Geneva. Alexinsky had been the leader of the Bolshevik delegation in the Second Duma. He later broke with Lenin, moved steadily to the right, and by 1915 had become one of the most vociferous war patriots. In 1917 he called Lenin a German agent and in 1918 joined the Whites fighting against the new government. Apparently, he still considered himself something of a radical, for he was trying to attend a socialist conference in Geneva. On seeing the two Mensheviks in the street, he stretched out his arm to shake their hands. Woytinsky hesitated, but anxious to avoid unpleasantness he offered his hand. "Suddenly, I see that Alexinsky's face had changed. His arm, extended to Axelrod, was poised in mid-air; Pavel Borisovich had crossed his hands behind his back, muttering: 'no, I cannot,' and walked past him. When we had moved away five steps, Pavel Borisovich said to me in an agitated tone: 'I did not in the least want to offend him. But, you know, I cannot . . . He himself ought to understand that I cannot.' " Axelrod could not reconcile himself to a person who had betrayed his ideals. Nor would he compromise his convictions by collaborating with reactionaries in order to defeat the Bolsheviks.[10]

As a final argument in favor of a commission of inquiry, Axelrod claimed that the Western parties stood to gain from a dispassionate

9. "Zapis' besedy Anan'ina s Pavlom Borisovichem v Tsiurikhe v 20 godu" (A Record of Conversations with Pavel Borisovich in Zurich in 1920), Nicolaevsky Collection, Hoover Institution.

10. W. S. Woytinsky, "Poslednie gody," Sotsialisticheskii vestnik, no. 8/9 (May 3, 1928), 5–6.

report about conditions in Russia: it could "prevent much harm" within their ranks. Because of the "Babylonian confusion and enormous delusion" about the Bolshevik experiment, socialists in the West were flocking to the newly created Communist parties. The friction and ideological disorder in the socialist parties that ensued led to tragic bloodshed between workers in Germany in January 1919. Precisely when the struggle for a democratic peace required a united effort by the proletariat, it was deeply divided, in large part over the Russian question. Only the truth about conditions under Lenin's rule could win the masses back to traditional Social Democracy. The Soviet leaders might refuse to allow the commission of inquiry into the country, but then, Axelrod reasoned, the Bolsheviks would surely stand condemned in the eyes of the Western proletariat.[11]

Axelrod's expectations and hopes may today appear quixotic. Indeed, there is no doubt that he was prone to wishful thinking. Rusanov, who saw much of him in 1918, recalled: "What ardent, indeed youthful enthusiasm he experienced at the smallest manifestation of what appeared to him the awakening of the working class from the Bolshevik anesthesia!"[12]

But it must be remembered that in the summer of 1918, when he first proposed a commission of inquiry, the Bolsheviks had not yet consolidated their power. The harsh peace treaty that the government had concluded a few months earlier had aroused considerable opposition in the country and even within Lenin's party. The White Guards had begun to organize an army, and it was obvious that the country would soon be embroiled in civil war. Troops from the Allied countries were landing in Murmansk, Archangel, and Vladivostok, which posed a further threat to the regime. Finally, the economy continued to deteriorate, and the radical measures introduced by the government only aggravated an already chaotic situation. Given these circumstances, Axelrod's speculations about influencing the Bolshevik regime seem not to have been all that unreasonable.

The Soviet leaders themselves were, in fact, far from confident that

---

11. Pavel Axelrod, "K voprosu o sotsialistichcskoi interventsii 1920 g.," Nicolaevsky Collection, Hoover Institution; Axelrod to Gregory Bienstock, Jan. 16, 1919, *ibid.*

12. N. S. Rusanov, *Kak my podgotovliali stokgol'mskuiu konferentsiiu: Vospominaniia chlena stokgol'mskoi delegatsii N. S. Rusanova* (n. d., n. p.), p. 141, on deposit at the Russian Archives, Columbia University.

they could survive for long without help from socialists in the West.[13] They set to wooing the European Social Democratic parties in the hope that they would at least apply pressure on their governments not to follow anti-Bolshevik policies. It was of the utmost psychological importance for the Russians to find support abroad, for the sense of isolation had added to the burden the Bolsheviks felt themselves to be carrying. It is therefore not surprising that Lenin's government reacted with acute displeasure to the news of the appeal that Axelrod and his friends had sent to the socialist parties. According to one report, Vladimir Bonch-Bruevich, Chief of the Chancery for the Soviet of People's Commissars, issued an order for the arrest of Axelrod and Rusanov.[14] It was not an order that the Soviet authorities could execute, but its mere existence suggests their sensitivity to criticism.

The open hostility of the Bolsheviks only confirmed Axelrod in the wisdom of his course of action. He was further encouraged by his comrades in Petrograd who wrote him that "We consider your work extremely important and valuable" and promised to find ways of sending him additional financial support.[15] But Western socialists continued to ignore his appeals. He thus decided on another tack: face-to-face contact with the leaders of the European parties.

Late in September 1918 he left Stockholm and for the next two and a half months traveled to Norway, France, and England, everywhere presenting his case against the Leninists. He tried to visit Kautsky, Bernstein, and Haase in Berlin, but was blocked by the German government, which refused to grant him a visa. He did, however, talk to many socialists in England and France. Though he exerted himself to the fullest, he considered his trip a failure. His impression of the European parties was "very gloomy . . . Unfortunately, the chances of an intervention by international Social Democracy in the 'internal affairs' of Russia . . . are extremely slim, if not nonexistent." He found the socialists' refusal to act "a further illustration of the moral and political degeneration of . . . [their] parties." They were in such disarray that he doubted that they were capable of affecting governmental policy on any vital issue.[16]

---

13. Leon Trotsky, *My Life: An Attempt at an Autobiography* (New York, 1931), p. 342; V. I. Lenin, *Sochineniia* (3rd ed., Moscow, 1926–1937), XXII, 322.
14. Reported in *Vorwärts*, Aug. 25, 1918.
15. Semkovsky to Axelrod, Aug. 9, 1918, Nicolaevsky Collection, Hoover Institution.
16. Axelrod to Kautsky, Dec. 8, 1918, *ibid.*

When Axelrod arrived in Zurich early in December 1918 he was thoroughly exhausted and was ill again. He hoped to find some tranquillity while recuperating in Switzerland, but the reports of developments in Europe made it impossible for him to savor the temporary withdrawal from political activity. He was revolted by the "cynical-brutal" and "barbaric" behavior of the Entente toward Germany and Austria-Hungary at the conclusion of hostilities. "And what is most horrible is that the spirit of revenge and hatred that dictates this behavior has also gripped the masses of France." He looked upon France as the leader of "international reaction" and its military intervention in Russia as being staged to help the reactionaries crush the Bolsheviks.[17] Contrary to Bolshevik charges, he repudiated, publicly and privately, the dispatch of troops to his country, a move that he feared would contribute "to the bloodiest suppression of the entire Russian democracy."[18]

The most serious blow to his hopes was the progress of the German revolution, which had broken out early in November 1918. At first he believed that this event "could . . . become really great and push the entire Western proletariat along the path of socialist revolution." Like his Menshevik comrades in Russia, Axelrod expected the ascendancy of democratic socialism in Germany to shift the center of the world revolutionary movement from Moscow to Berlin. He also assumed that the more humane policies of the Germans would have a salutary effect on the Bolsheviks.[19] But late in 1918 he realized that the revolution was threatened from two sides: first, by the "Entente plunderers," and, second, by an "absurd enthusiasm to imitate the Bolshevik caricature of the 'dictatorship of the proletariat.' " Two weeks later he concluded that the Independents, known earlier as the centrists, were merely "hangers-on" of the Spartacists, many of whom were ideologically akin

---

17. *Ibid.*

18. Axelrod vigorously denounced the military intervention in a letter to Pierre Renaudel, June 25, 1919, Axelrod Archive, I.I.S.H. In his speech at the International Socialist Conference in Bern in February 1919 he publicly expressed opposition to the intervention. See *Die russische Revolution,* ed. Tsereteli and Woytinsky, p. 169. But as late as 1963 Soviet scholars still asserted that he had favored "an armed intervention in Russia." See *Piatyi (Londonskii) s'ezd RSDRP: Protokoly* (Moscow, 1963), p. 830.

19. On the Mensheviks' attitude toward the German revolution, see Abraham Ascher, "Russian Marxism and the German Revolution, 1917–1920," *Archiv für Sozialgeschichte,* VI/VII (1966–1967), 415–422.

to the Leninists. At the same time, he looked upon the Social Democratic government of Friedrich Ebert and Philipp Scheidemann as inept and misguided. Without specifying, he held that it should have made many more concessions to the working class than it did.

When he learned of the assassinations of Rosa Luxemburg and Karl Liebknecht he gave up all hope that the German revolution might save the Russian one. "It is more than horrible," he declared, "it is a tragic misfortune and, I fear, a great calamity for the German revolution . . . [it will serve] as a new spur to the further development of a bloody war *within* the socialist proletariat. I can hardly recover sufficiently from the shock to continue this letter."[20] Axelrod's prediction proved to be only too accurate. Disappointed with the prospects in Central Europe, he again turned his attention to the international movement.

Shortly after the end of hostilities in November 1918 a number of leaders of the defunct Second International tried to resurrect the organization. But it emerged at the first conference, held in Bern early in February 1919, that the ideological conflicts engendered by the war and the Russian Revolution were insuperable obstacles. The Bolsheviks, Spartacists, and several other groups on the extreme left refused to attend because they considered the gathering chauvinistic and reactionary. The Belgian Labor party and the American Federation of Labor shunned the conference because they would not sit at the same table with Germans and Austrians who had supported their governments during the war. But even among the 102 delegates from 26 countries who did attend there arose sharp differences, especially over the Russian question.[21]

In an attempt to avoid controversy the organizers of the conference tried to prevent a direct confrontation over the issue. The Russian Revolution as such was not listed on the agenda, but the euphemistically titled discussion of "Democracy versus Dictatorship" deceived no one. Every delegate realized that when the conference took up this theoretical subject the central topic would be Lenin's system of rule. More-

20. Axelrod to Bienstock, Dec. 29, 1918, Axelrod Archive, I.I.S.H.; Axelrod to Bienstock, Jan. 7, 16, 17, 1919, Nicolaevsky Collection, Hoover Institution.

21. On the other issues discussed at the conference, see the recent account in Arno J. Mayer, *Politics and Diplomacy of Peacemaking: Containment and Counterrevolution at Versailles, 1918–1919* (New York, 1967), pp. 373–409; see also Merle Fainsod, *International Socialism and the World War* (2nd printing, New York, 1966), pp. 193–195.

over, they all knew that in large measure the response of the European working class to Russia's call to revolution would depend on the policies adopted by socialist leaders.[22]

Although Axelrod was a member of the International Socialist Bureau, he initially considered boycotting the conference because the organizers had failed to demand officially that the Bolshevik government grant passports to delegates chosen by all socialist parties.[23] He quickly concluded, however, that it would be unwise to lose an opportunity to plead the cause of democracy before so large a gathering of his colleagues. In addition, he discovered that his eight-month campaign for a commission of inquiry had been more successful than he had suspected; several delegates intended to place the idea before the conference.

Two resolutions on "Democracy versus Dictatorship" were submitted. The first, introduced by Hjalmar Branting of Sweden, chairman of the conference, asserted that "A reorganized society more and more permeated with Socialism, cannot be realized, much less permanently established, unless it rests upon triumphs of Democracy and is rooted in the principles of liberty." Branting did not call for condemnation of the Bolshevik experiment, but he did formally propose the dispatch of a commission of inquiry "composed of representatives of all Socialist tendencies . . . for the purpose of making an impartial report to the International on the political and economic situation [in Russia]." To the left-wing delegates at the conference—who represented the center of the socialist movement as a whole—even this mild resolution appeared to imply censure of the Leninists. Friedrich Adler and Jean Longuet therefore introduced a second resolution, the key to which was the statement: "We have not sufficient material for [such] a judgment." Adler and Longuet also contended that passage of Branting's resolution would make it impossible to reunite the "Socialist and Revolutionary parties of all countries conscious of their class interests."[24]

On the surface, the initiators of the two motions seemed to share a basic conviction, that more information was needed. But as the debate unfolded, it turned out that the formal language of the resolutions

22. Fainsod, *International Socialism*, p. 195.
23. Axelrod to Bienstock, Dec. 29, 1918, Axelrod Archive, I.I.S.H.; Axelrod to Paul Olberg, Jan. 17, 1919, *ibid.*
24. Fainsod, *International Socialism*, pp. 196–198.

concealed profound differences. On February 9, 1919, the sixth day of the conference, Branting recognized Axelrod as the second speaker on the resolutions. Representatives of the French left protested angrily, claiming that they should have been recognized before him. After prolonged procedural wrangling, it was discovered that three different lists of speakers had been drawn up, and Axelrod was second on one of them. Announcement of this blunder provoked an uproar in the hall. For a while the chairman seems to have lost control of the meeting, and delegates freely expressed their opinions.

Paul Mistral of the French left urged that there be no mention of the relationship between dictatorship and democracy in any resolution adopted by the conference. But his right-wing colleague, Pierre Renaudel, insisted that this was precisely the question that must be decided: "If you want to wait until the commission of inquiry has ended its investigation in Russia, then Bolshevism will long ago have swallowed up socialism." To this F. Loriot retorted: "Let us first fight against the bourgeois terror before we begin to talk about Bolshevik terror." Longuet could be heard yelling: "[Branting's] resolution is designed to give Clemenceau and Lloyd George a weapon for the struggle against Soviet Russia." By this time there was no longer any semblance of a civilized debate; from all corners of the room people shouted their views, usually in abusive language. After a few hours of this free-for-all, Huysmans, realizing that the issue could not be resolved at this last planned meeting, proposed another session for the following day. At that meeting Axelrod, who had been unable to utter a word, was to be given the floor.[25]

Axelrod's brief address was concise and candid. His most cogent point was that the conference should never have explored the Russian question under the rubric of "Democracy versus Dictatorship":

The conception of an unbridgeable conflict between democracy and proletarian dictatorship is altogether of recent vintage. At least in those circles that understand Marxism it used in earlier years to be considered as self-evident that the rule of the proletariat in the transitional period from capitalism to socialism presupposes a democratic system; only on the basis of democracy can the proletariat consolidate its power and by no means does proletarian rule require the violent destruction of democracy. Only the victory of the Bolsheviks over democracy and their success in disseminating the legend

25. *Arbeiter-Zeitung*, Feb. 11, 1919.

that their seizure of power has brought the proletariat to power provided the impulse to formulate anew the relationship between democracy and proletarian dictatorship.

Axelrod's assertions were historically accurate. Even though individual Marxists had harbored antidemocratic convictions, it is inconceivable that at any meeting of the International in the two and a half decades prior to the war the question of democracy would have been debated. The vast majority of Western Marxists had been agreed on the indissolubility of democracy and socialism.

Axelrod continued his speech by challenging the delegates to form a commission of inquiry. As on earlier occasions, he made it plain that he was only asking for a "disclosure of the truth." If his charge that Lenin's regime amounted to "a reversion to the most dangerous and wildest form of Bakuninism and Blanquism," proved to be accurate, then Western socialists would be morally obliged to come to the aid of the Mensheviks. Denunciation of White terror and military intervention in Russia, though laudable, would not suffice. Russian Social Democrats, Axelrod explained at another meeting of the International, were entitled to ask that their colleagues act as they had during the tsarist era, that is to say, that they protest against arbitrary rule and political repression.[26]

In an effort to prevent a schism at the conference, Friedrich Adler suggested that instead of voting on the two resolutions, the national delegations as units merely indicate the preference of their members. Following this procedure, sixteen delegations expressed support for the Branting resolution and five for that of Adler and Longuet. The margin of victory, however, was far less impressive than the figures suggest, for several delegations were narrowly divided.[27]

The conference also elected a Permanent Commission of the International, which included Axelrod, and charged it with selecting a commission of inquiry to investigate conditions in Russia. Nine of the projected twelve members were immediately chosen: Ramsay Mac-Donald and Charles Rowden Buxton of England, Longuet and Paul Faure of France, Justo Tomaso of Argentina, Kautsky and Rudolf

26. The speech is reproduced in *Die russische Revolution,* ed. Tsereteli and Woytinsky, pp. 168–176; for his comments at the subsequent conference (at Lucerne), see *Arbeiter-Zeitung,* Aug. 11, 1919.

27. *Bulletin officiel de la conférence internationale ouvrière et socialiste,* I, no. 11, Feb. 12, 1919.

Hilferding of Germany, and Friedrich Adler and Otto Bauer of Austria. The group represented a broad range of opinion, and Axelrod had every reason to be satisfied. As a matter of fact, the very decision to send a commission was a major personal achievement for him.

The Mensheviks in Russia were delighted by his success. "Your speech at Bern," Boris Skomorovsky gleefully wrote Axelrod from Moscow, "caused a sensation. The official publicists, led by Steklov [editor of *Izvestiia*], are in a rage. *Vpered* [the Menshevik paper] . . . expressed its solidarity with you."[28] The Menshevik C. C. succeeded in smuggling to Axelrod a series of resolutions that had been passed by local committees in Russia hailing the decision of the International.

The Menshevik leaders denounced the "filthy campaign of slander" to which the Bolsheviks had subjected Axelrod's proposal and called on their followers to receive the foreign delegation in a "worthy manner." Every industrial enterprise, party group, and trade union was urged to discuss the impending visit and elect representatives to receive the members of the commission. Local organizations were also asked to prepare appropriate banners welcoming the "guests of the Russian proletariat." The C. C. voiced "its firm conviction that the brotherly help of the resurrected labor International will offer the Russian working class the opportunity to overcome the internal counterrevolution as well as the imperialist intervention of international imperialism."[29]

But no one knew how the Bolsheviks would react to the plan to send an investigative committee to Russia. Lenin scorned the participants in the Bern conference: "Like the contemporary philistines, the leaders of the 'Bern' International repeat the bourgeois-democratic words about freedom and equality and democracy . . . without understanding that the proletariat needs the state not for 'freedom' but for the purpose of suppressing its enemy, the exploiter, the capitalist." *Pravda* prominently displayed a resolution from the Moscow Committee of the Russian Communist Party that similarly denounced the delegates at Bern.[30]

28. Skomorovsky to Axelrod, Feb. 19, 1919, Axelrod Archive, I.I.S.H.

29. A German translation of the resolutions is on deposit in the Axelrod Archive, I.I.S.H. Axelrod apparently sent copies of them to Western socialists. They were published in the Menshevik *Rabochii internatsional*, no. 1, Mar. 2, 1919. In June 1919 the Menshevik C. C. denied Bolshevik-inspired reports that it was displeased with Axelrod's work in the West. The C. C. explicitly affirmed its support for Axelrod's endeavors. See "Zaiavlenie Ts. K. RSDRP" (Statement of the Central Committee of the RSDRP), June 18, 1919, Nicolaevsky Collection, Hoover Institution.

30. Lenin, *Sochineniia*, XXIV, 398; *Pravda*, Feb. 28, 1919, quoted in S. A.

Despite these attacks and Lenin's previous strictures against socialist intervention in Russian affairs,[31] the government did not go so far as to deny the commission entrance into the country. Possibly it feared the repercussions of a negative response in the Western parties. Perhaps it sensed that it would be able to influence the commission. At any rate, the Council of People's Commissars announced that although it did not regard the conference at Bern as genuinely socialist and would not officially receive the delegation, it would not prevent it from fulfilling its mission.[32]

Kautsky was elated. This "concession," together with the news he had received in March 1919 that the Communists would now allow Mensheviks to serve in the soviets again, indicated to him that the "Bolshevik government is demonstrating an inclination to return to the path of democracy." With remarkable naïveté, he announced that "the idea of democracy is on the march again in Russia."[33] Even at this late date Kautsky occasionally viewed the undemocratic features of Bolshevism as a temporary deviation.

Axelrod took a more cautious view. He was gratified, of course, that the Soviet government would admit the commission into the country, but he predicted—with good reason, as events would show—that the visitors would be given guided tours and thus be deceived about conditions there. Consequently, he urged his comrades to insist on the right of free movement in Russia and on the "absolute freedom of contact with representatives from all social strata and all parties." Should these requests be refused, the commission should depart "under protest." He also suggested that the Western group include persons who knew Russian and were acquainted with the country. "An attempt will be made to show the foreign guests Potemkin villages, so that they will not be inclined to abandon their illusions."[34]

Mogilevskii, *Vosstanovlenie II Internatsionale 1919–1923 gg.* (Leningrad, 1963), pp. 69–70.

31. V. I. Lenin, *Polnoe sobranie sochinenii* (55 vols., 5th ed., Moscow, 1958–1965), XXXVII, 210.

32. Reported in *Rabochii internatsional*, no. 1, Mar. 2, 1919; see also Mogilevskii, *Vosstanovlenie*, p. 70.

33. Unabhängige sozialdemokratische Partei Deutschlands, *Protokoll über die Verhandlungen des ausserordentlichen Parteitages vom 2. bis 6. März 1919* (Berlin, n. d.), pp. 123, 220.

34. Paul Axelrod, "Brief an die Schwedischen Genossen," *Die russische Revolution*, ed. Tsereteli and Woytinsky, pp. 177–179; Axelrod to S. Backlund and Engberg, Mar. 4, 1919, Axelrod Archive, I.I.S.H.

Axelrod's sound advice turned out to be superfluous because the Entente Powers refused to grant passports to members of the commission. He assumed that the governments feared that the commission might expose the "recklessly reactionary conduct" of Western agents and troops in Russia and that the visitors might return with glowing reports about conditions there that would enhance Bolshevik influence in the European labor movements.[35] At the Lucerne conference of the International early in August 1919 it was decided that if passports could not be obtained by British and French comrades after some further attempts the Swedish party would send a commission composed entirely of Swedish citizens. Neither project ever materialized.[36]

This was surely one of the deepest disappointments of Axelrod's life, and for several months he pondered the reasons for the International's failure to implement his proposal. He had known all along that it would not be easy to carry out his project, "but with good will the obstacles could have been overcome. Unfortunately, this good will did not exist." He found several explanations for the lack of enthusiasm among Western socialists.

When he first proposed the idea, in mid-1918, many German Marxists were opposed because it ran counter to their government's policy of promoting "Bolshevik chaos" in Russia and thus keeping that country weak while war raged in the West. But why had the other socialist parties taken so few pains to support the commission? Why had they not tried to arouse public opinion in favor of the enterprise? Axelrod thought that socialist leaders who repudiated Leninism nevertheless wished to avoid alienating members of the movement who equated criticism of the Bolsheviks with aid and comfort to reactionaries. Also, in some countries workers did not care about events in distant Russia. In May 1919 Ramsay MacDonald privately told Gregory Bienstock, who was trying to prod the British into paying more attention to Russian affairs: "[The English workers] will not move a finger for anything that lies outside the interests of their stomachs." Moreover, although MacDonald had no use at all for Communism, he preferred Lenin to Admiral A. I. Kolchak (a dictator in Siberia and a leader of

---

35. "Zapis' besedy Anan'ina"; Axelrod, "Sotsialisticheskoi interventsii."
36. "Bericht des Internationalen Sekretariats," Brussels, Apr. 8, 1920, Axelrod Archive, I.I.S.H.

anti-Bolshevik forces), and these seemed to him the only alternatives open to the Russians.[37]

The main reason for socialist indifference to the commission of inquiry, however, probably lay elsewhere. The Russian Revolution had not only thrust many socialists "under the power of Bolshevik legends," as Axelrod put it;[38] it had also reinforced the profound crisis of self-confidence in Marxist circles that had set in as a result of Social Democracy's failure to stop the war. Many socialists who remained dubious about the Leninist experiment nevertheless began to lose faith in convictions they had held for decades. After all, Lenin's undemocratic methods had made possible the revolution for which Marxists had yearned. Western socialists inevitably wondered whether these methods might not also be necessary in Europe.

We have noted that at the Bern conference Social Democrats initiated a reexamination of the relationship between democracy and socialism. At subsequent meetings of the International this reexamination continued apace. In a privately distributed "Circular Letter" Huysmans reported on the second conference of the International held in Lucerne: "In broad circles of the international socialist movement there prevails the view that the experience of the war and especially of the revolution that followed the war make it necessary for the International not only to subject to reexamination the general political principles that up to now have guided the labor movement, but also to formulate a position on the question of which political system corresponds to the principles and aims of Social Democracy." Although the delegates at Lucerne, according to Huysmans, were not ready to "throw overboard" the principles of democracy and replace them with the doctrines of the dictatorship as practiced in Russia, there was still a widespread feeling that the "orthodox forms of democracy did not constitute the last word in political development." Many delegates thought it might be possible to formulate a "compromise between both extremes" and had therefore voted to create a commission to study the question.[39] It was probably the tenuousness of their commitment to liberal democracy at this time,

37. Bienstock to Axelrod, May 3, 1919, Nicolaevsky Collection, Hoover Institution; see also "Zapis' besedy Anan'ina"; Axelrod, "Sotsialisticheskoi interventsii."
38. Axelrod to Ingerman, Aug. 14, 1920, Nicolaevsky Collection, Hoover Institution.
39. "Rundschreiben no. 6," Oct. 23, 1919, Axelrod Archive, I.I.S.H.

as much as anything else, that accounts for the tepid response of Western Marxists to Axelrod's call for "moral intervention" in Russian affairs.

Even after it became evident that the International would not be able to send a commission, Axelrod attended as many conferences as possible to plead his cause. He also continued to hammer away at the theme in the Western press.[40] In the summer of 1922 he was granted the reward of seeing his idea partially realized. At that time the Communists, in response to pressure from Western socialists, allowed Emile Vandervelde to enter the country in order to defend several Socialist Revolutionaries who were being tried for an attempt on Lenin's life and other alleged terrorist acts. Vandervelde's intervention did not result in an acquittal, but his firsthand account of the workings of Soviet justice did disconcert a number of European radicals and seems to have been decisive in preventing a rapprochement between the Two and a Half International and the Third International. According to Tsereteli, "this example [of socialist intervention] not only demonstrated the practicability of P. B.'s idea, but it wrote one of the finest pages in the history of the International."[41] It was, however, a pale version of the kind of intervention Axelrod had hoped for.

In the meantime, Axelrod had been subjected to another cruel disappointment. The Mensheviks in Russia had undergone an ideological about-face. For close to two years he had been almost completely cut off from his comrades. Suddenly, in April 1920, their letters began to reach

40. "Discours de Paul Axelrod à la conférence de Lucerne," *La République Russe*, Nov. 6, 1919; "L'enquête socialiste en Russie (Interview avec le camarade P. Axelrod)," *ibid.*, Mar. 1, 1920; "L'opinion de P. Axelrod sur la décision du 'Labour Party,'" *ibid.*, Mar. 15, 1920; "Lettre de Paul Axelrod" and "Interview de P. Axelrod," *ibid.*, June 1, 1920; "Le camarade Axelrod nous en expose les tragiques conséquences," *Le Populaire*, Nov. 7, 1921; "Le secours international à la Russie affamée et les socialistes de l'Occident. Une conférence de Paul Axelrod," *Pour la Russie*, Nov. 24, 1921.

41. I. Tsereteli, "P. B. Aksel'rod (cherty dlia kharakteristiki)," *Sotsialisticheskii vestnik*, no. 15/16 (Aug. 18, 1925), 17. Vandervelde described his experiences at the trial in Emile Vandervelde and Arthur Wauters, *Le procès des social-revolutionnaires à Moscou* (Brussels: Libraire du Peuple, 1922). For a brief account of the trial, see Leonard Schapiro, *The Origin of the Communist Autocracy* (London, 1955), pp. 166, 169. The impact of the trial on socialists who tended to be sympathetic toward the Soviet Union is discussed in André Donneur, *Histoire de l'Union des Partis Socialistes pour l'action internationale* (Sudbury, 1967), pp. 267–278. For a discussion of the ideological position of the Two and a Half International, see note 57, below.

him, and "they unfortunately contained a variety of unpleasant news." He was most disturbed by the decision of the Menshevik C. C., made under the influence of the German Independents, to leave the Second International. He immediately resigned as foreign representative of the Menshevik party and from the standing committee of the Second International. He regretted both resignations, but felt that he could not represent the party so long as he disagreed with it about a fundamental question of policy.[42]

Huysmans, anxious to prevent the disintegration of the recently revived and still embryonic International, tried to persuade Axelrod not to make good his resignation, arguing that the news from the Mensheviks in Russia was not reliable. But Axelrod could not be swayed. Aside from being assured of the accuracy of his information, he believed that the Western parties had made his position in the International untenable. Since the "authoritative parties . . . have not devoted the necessary energy and perseverance to the organization of the inquiry into [the situation in] Russia," he could not, in good conscience, try to persuade his Menshevik colleagues to take a kindly view of them.[43]

Axelrod may have been relieved at being presented with a pretext for quitting the International. His disillusionment with his Western comrades, as he confessed to Huysmans, had never been so great. Many were now crediting what he considered extremely naïve and biased reports on the situation in Russia. Early in 1920, George Lansbury, a British socialist, visited the country and enthusiastically reported, among other things, that a "real democracy" was being established by the Leninists and that there was no sign of political terror.[44] Axelrod was appalled that "nowhere in the socialist press or in other organs of the organized labor movement were there any expressions of indignation. Unfortunately, this Hottentot morality has, to our general disgrace, deep roots in our ranks."

No sooner had Lansbury returned than the British Labour party sent an official delegation to Russia, and once again Axelrod felt betrayed. True, its report was less romantic and naïve than Lansbury's. But Axelrod noted that at the party congress in 1920 the delegation

42. Axelrod to Huysmans, May 22, July 4, 1920, Axelrod Archive, I.I.S.H.
43. Huysmans to Axelrod, June 30, 1920, *ibid.;* Axelrod to Huysmans, July 4, 1920, *ibid.*
44. On Lansbury's report, see Stephen R. Graubard, *British Labour and the Russian Revolution, 1917–1924* (Cambridge, Mass., 1956), pp. 212–214.

did not even mention the terror in Russia, the oppression of workers, or the absence of freedom of movement and of the press. The deficiencies of these accounts, according to Axelrod, could be traced to the slipshod organization of the trips and careless selection of observers. Western socialists were committing all the blunders he had foreseen.[45]

Axelrod's claim that the International's indifference to his proposal had weakened his influence among the Mensheviks in Russia was an effective debater's point, which he could make in good conscience because he believed it. He soon discovered, however, that his position in the party had been undermined by an altogether different factor. The occasional reports he had received from Moscow in 1918 and 1919, which indicated approval of his activities in the West, gave the appearance of a broader concurrence than had actually existed. Now he realized that he no longer agreed with the leadership of his party about the nature of Bolshevism, the likelihood of a revolution in the West, and, perhaps most startling of all, the relationship between political democracy and socialism.

The modifications in the Mensheviks' attitudes must be seen as a series of tortuous adjustments by them to what they saw as agonizing dilemmas.[46] The inevitable result of these adjustments was a change in doctrine. Not only did the Mensheviks in Russia become somewhat less hostile to Lenin's rule; they even came close to absorbing some of his ideological positions.

This subtle process began shortly after the seizure of power in November 1917. On the one hand, the Mensheviks entertained serious misgivings about Lenin's policies and openly condemned the Bolsheviks for their "utopian" attempts to introduce Communism in a backward society and for having resorted to the use of terror against other socialists. On the other hand, they could not bring themselves actively to oppose the new government for fear of advancing the cause of the counterrevolutionaries, whom they identified as anyone to the right of the Popular Socialists. Moreover, Martov, the predominant Menshevik, maintained that even though the Bolsheviks had relied on nonproletarian groups to attain power, they nevertheless constituted the "bearers

45. Axelrod to Huysmans, July 4, 1920, Axelrod Archive, I.I.S.H. On the report of the British delegation, see Graubard, *British Labour*, pp. 214–217.
46. I am here referring to the dominant group in the Menshevik party in Russia, those who accepted Martov's leadership. There were some right-wing Mensheviks, most notably Potresov, who did not share the party's attitude toward the Bolsheviks.

of the general interest of the revolution" because they were fundamentally a working-class party. The members of a political movement with such impeccable social roots would surely be sensitive to the reasoned arguments of their fellow Marxists.

The upshot of this thinking was that late in 1917 the Mensheviks strongly rejected any military action against the Bolsheviks. The vanquished, Dan explained, might include not only the usurpers of power, but the "Provisional Government and the entire democracy as well." Instead, the Mensheviks proclaimed the policy of "straightening out the revolution" by legal means. After failing in their efforts to form a coalition government of diverse socialist groups, they strove to exert pressure on the Bolsheviks to forgo the use of terror and the program of socialist transformation of the country's economy, which was "unMarxist."

In mid-1918, when the Soviet government was locked in military combat against the counterrevolutionaries and the interventionist armies, the Mensheviks' position seemed all the more justified. They now moved closer to the Bolsheviks by pledging "unqualified support" to the government and calling on their followers to join the Red Army and help in any way possible. They came to regard themselves as a "loyal opposition." Apparently in return for this loyalty, the Bolsheviks legalized the Menshevik party in November 1918. Yet the government persisted in its repression of the party and thus made a mockery of the legalization.

Despite the persecution, throughout 1919 the Mensheviks staunchly followed a dual policy toward Bolshevism, succinctly described by Martov in 1920: "Our tactics may be defined as a struggle against Bolshevism insofar as it is a distortion of socialism and is a terroristic system based on a schism within the proletariat and between the proletariat and the peasantry, but we link this struggle with unconditional support of Bolshevism in its resistance to international imperialism and its internal counterrevolutionary allies." Other Mensheviks, most notably Dan, extended this line of reasoning by offering what amounted to a Marxist rendition of an old theme: "My revolution, right or wrong."[47]

The Mensheviks' dogmatic conception of the theory of dialectical

47. Martov to Axelrod, Jan. 23, 1920, Axelrod Archive, I.I.S.H. See Dan's remarkable statement in *Oborona revoliutsii i sotsial-demokratiia (sbornik)*, ed. Iu. Martov (Moscow, 1920), p. 21.

materialism predisposed them to an even more basic reassessment of the new regime. As time went on, the Bolshevik government's continued existence proved to them that it was a historically necessary phase in the process of attaining socialism. This notion, which had always exerted a strong intellectual and emotional pull on Marxists, was first expounded by Mensheviks in October 1918 when they dropped their demands for recall of the constituent assembly and the introduction of universal suffrage.[48] But it was most explicitly formulated by Martov late in 1919 when he said: "this dictatorship is a fact, and its very duration testifies that under the given correlation of social forces the revolution could not have bypassed it. Moreover, having become a fact, this dictatorship, engendered by the forces of the bourgeois revolution, develops under the banner of socialism and precisely in this form appears on the international arena and naturally becomes the center to which all revolutionary movements in all countries are attracted and which draws upon itself the hatred of all conservative forces."

To buttress his contention that the Soviet experience was a necessary stage, Martov pointed to the similarities between conditions in Western countries late in 1919 and those in Russia in 1917: economic exhaustion, a shortage of workers in the production of consumer goods (many were still in the army), the prevalence in industry of laborers not yet indoctrinated by socialists, and a lack of common interest between soldiers of a disintegrating army and the proletariat.[49] Drawing on these similarities with the Soviet past, Martov suggested that the historical process that had unfolded in his country would repeat itself elsewhere: "In the class struggle entering the phase of civil war there inevitably comes a moment when the vanguard of the revolutionary class, leaning on the consciousness of the masses, whose interests it represents, is forced to realize state power in the form of a dictatorship of the revolutionary minority. Only stupid dogmatism could recoil from this perspective."[50]

It should be noted, however, that the Mensheviks maintained that in two respects their conception of the "dictatorship of the revolutionary minority" diverged from that of the Bolsheviks: the former continued to repudiate terror, and they viewed the dictatorship as a brief "inter-

48. Israel Getzler, *Martov: A Political Biography of a Russian Social Democrat* (Cambridge, Eng., 1967), p. 185.
49. Iu. Martov, "Diktatura i demokratiia," *Za god* (n. p., 1919), pp. 35–38.
50. Iu. Martov, "Konets odnoi dvusmyslennosti," *Sotsial-demokratiia i revoliutsiia. Sbornik dokumentov* (Odessa, 1920), p. 49.

mediate phase" in the "world development toward socialism."[51] Their slogan of early 1920, "through soviets to democracy," demonstrates that they did not equate the Soviet system with democracy, as did the Leninists.[52]

It is also true that in the "April Theses" of 1920 the Mensheviks presented a more nuanced and qualified formulation of the nature of the proletarian dictatorship: "The revolutionary Social Democracy is emphatically against the dictatorship of a minority that contradicts the socialist principle that the liberation of the working class must be the work of the working class itself." Limitations on democracy are "by no means a historically and logically necessary corollary" of the class dictatorship of the proletariat. Such limitations may, however, be imposed in the event of a civil war and would then be a symptom of the dictatorship's weakness. At the same time, the "Theses" stated that should power anywhere in the world fall into the hands of an "active minority of the working class" which "strayed" into the path of "economic utopianism and political terror," the "revolutionary Marxist Social Democracy" should "unconditionally support that minority" against counterrevolution. But the "Theses" strongly urged that the dictatorship be directed only against exploiters and not against working-class groups, as had been done in Russia.[53]

Fear of counterrevolution, inability to view the Bolsheviks as other than misguided spokesmen for the proletariat—these considerations undoubtedly figured prominently in inspiring an ideological shift on the part of the Mensheviks. But there were other factors that seem to have played a role. Throughout 1919 Menshevik influence among the industrial proletariat grew steadily, in large part because of the government's failure to cope with the disastrous economic situation. Martov and his colleagues were probably apprehensive about losing mass support if they adopted wholly negative attitudes toward the Bolshevik experiment and if they failed to advocate a militant political program that assigned preeminence to the working class. In addition, disenchantment with the prospects for the German revolution helped drive the Mensheviks in Russia to the left. Not only did it become increasingly evident that the Germans would not be able to exercise a humanizing

51. *Ibid.; Martov,* "Diktatura i demokratiia," p. 37.
52. Martov to Axelrod, Jan. 23, 1920, Axelrod Archive, I.I.S.H.
53. *Sotsial-demokratiia i revoliutsiia,* pp. 28–32.

influence on the Bolsheviks, as Martov had at one time believed;[54] the events in Germany also raised doubts about the feasibility of attaining socialism by democratic means in any country.

There is yet another intangible, but nonetheless important, factor that must be taken into account: the frame of mind of revolutionary Marxists living in a country where a revolution in the name of the working class had been staged but in which they could not participate. The Mensheviks' mood is poignantly illustrated in a private letter Dan sent Axelrod from Moscow early in 1920. Dan complained that their party's situation was "far from brilliant." Deprived of freedom of the press, assembly, or organization, without funds, "under severe persecution," the Mensheviks were reduced to impotence. Under the circumstances, Dan did not find it surprising that a growing number of his colleagues was being "pushed" into embracing Communism. He assured Axelrod that it was by no means only the "careerist elements" who were defecting; nor were they simply attracted by the "strength of Bolshevism or the brilliance of its outward successes." Above all, they were motivated by a "craving for activity." In the face of this powerful yearning, Dan concluded, it was remarkable that the Menshevik organization had been able to survive at all. He even thought it likely that some good might come from the Menshevik swelling of the Bolshevik ranks because his former comrades might question Leninist policies and thus help create a crisis within the Soviet system.[55] Although Dan's conclusion is debatable, his description of the mood of many Mensheviks in Russia definitely contributes to an understanding of the general drift toward a more sympathetic attitude toward Bolshevism on the part of the movement as a whole.

How the activist ideas of the Mensheviks were affecting their attitude toward the European socialist movement became most evident early in 1920. "We believe," Rafael Abramovich told Friedrich Adler, "that Europe has entered a period of transformation and see no reason to assume that this process will be organic, peaceful, and harmonious, i.e., on the basis of a reconciliation between interested social forces. On the contrary, we think that Europe is facing a fairly long period of grandiose, embittered, and constantly sharpening social conflicts and

54. Ascher, "Russian Marxism," p. 417.
55. Dan to Axelrod, Jan. 31, 1920, Nicolaevsky Collection, Hoover Institution.

convulsions."[56] In the "April Theses" the Menshevik C. C. made a similar point by officially declaring its lack of confidence in the possibility of a peaceful proletarian revolution "within the framework of state institutions of bourgeois society." The "ruling capitalist minority, in control of the military power of the state, will resist the legal transfer of state power into the hands of the working class. Therefore the readiness and ability of the powerless majority forcefully to overthrow the minority holding the reins of power is a necessary condition for the social revolution."

At the time the C. C. released the "Theses," it also announced a new policy toward the International. It rejected the notion of resurrecting the "opportunistic" Second International, which allegedly still supported the wartime strategy of "social peace." The C. C. now claimed that it had agreed to participate in the Bern conference of 1919 "for informational purposes only." But the Mensheviks also refused to join the Communist Third International because it tried to enforce one specific tactic, based entirely on the Soviet model, on all parties and because it assigned hegemony to the Russian party. They deemed these policies "completely utopian and sectarian."

They were therefore left with no choice but to associate themselves with a number of German Independents, French socialists, and several others in forming a new international dedicated to three central propositions: that "the immediate historical task of the era upon which we are entering is the socialist revolution"; that the revolution was to be made by the "working *class*, excluding the necessity of a terroristic dictatorship of a minority"; that the dictatorship of the proletariat may be variously achieved, depending on conditions in different countries.[57] These were the keynotes of the program adopted by the so-called Two and a Half International, founded in February 1921, by the Mensheviks and the left wing of the Bern conference.

Two rather odd premises underlay Menshevik thinking in 1920. First, Martov and his colleagues believed that the proletariat of Central and Western Europe was in a radical mood. But in Germany—which still held the key to revolutionary activity on the Continent—the Majority Socialists, who in 1919 had attracted over five times as many votes as

56. Abramovich to Adler, Jan. 31, 1920, Friedrich and Victor Adler Archive, Verein für Geschichte der Arbeiterbewegung, Vienna.
57. *Sotsial-demokratiia i revoliutsiia*, pp. 27, 30–31, 36–38.

the Independents, unalterably opposed a social revolution. Moreover, in January 1918, when the Soviet government dissolved the constituent assembly, it had dawned on the Majority Socialists that the Russian leaders were really not democrats, and from that moment they had become increasingly critical of Lenin and his policies. The second premise that the Mensheviks had deluded themselves into believing was that a minority dictatorship could avoid terror. They do not seem to have grasped that the Bolshevik practices they found especially repugnant—that is, political repression—had largely resulted from the fact that when Lenin seized power he could only count on the active support of a minority of the population.

Much as the Mensheviks in Russia qualified their ideological shift, to Axelrod and his supporters it appeared as though their comrades had forsaken the fundamentals of the party's creed. Consequently, Axelrod reached a painful conclusion: "From the very beginning Menshevism has had its deepest roots in Georgia. Do you not find," he asked S. D. Shchupak, "that even now it is more solidly entrenched there than in our party?" He confided to his friend that he could no longer identify with the organization to which he had belonged for some seventeen years: "in essence I consider myself free, if I may express myself in this way, from [all] party obligations."[58] Once again, he found himself politically isolated, only this time more hopelessly than ever before.

Comprehending his anguish, his friends in Russia attempted to reassure him. Dan expressed confidence that if the C. C. could only talk to him in person it would quickly convince him of the soundness of its position.[59] Skomorovsky also tried to mollify Axelrod by telling him that the Mensheviks in Russia still considered themselves his students. Very often "we regretted that we were not in touch with you, . . . [for] you could have indicated to us the correct path, [and] with your advice helped us to avert errors." Then, in September 1920, Skomorovsky informed Axelrod that Martov would soon arrive in the West, and he did not doubt that they would quickly reach agreement. An air of optimism pervaded the Menshevik camp, and this, Skomorovsky said, made unity particularly important. "Here we assess the situation as being un-

58. Axelrod to Shchupak, Dec. 24, 1920, Feb. 11, 1921, Nicolaevsky Collection, Hoover Institution.
59. Dan to Axelrod, May 28, 1920, Axelrod Archive, I.I.S.H.

precedentedly favorable for an ideological struggle against Communism."[60] Skomorovsky did not explain his optimism; it would appear that as so often before the Mensheviks had allowed wishful thinking to distort their political judgment.

As soon as Martov arrived in the West he entered into regular correspondence with Axelrod, but gave no sign of intending to reconcile their differences. Indeed, at first Martov seems deliberately to have avoided a personal meeting for fear that it would only result in conflict. Axelrod took umbrage and accused Martov of skirting political questions in his letters. After denying the charge, Martov, in explaining his conduct, confessed that Axelrod's suspicions had been sound: "If I myself did not discuss the content of our differences in [our] correspondence, it was because I believed that before we can fruitfully discuss this, it is necessary for you to hear from us a *factual* account of how and why we changed our policies in Russia." The facts were called for in particular because the differences between them in the "assessments of the phases of the Russian Revolution—as well as certain other questions—are very great." Despite their disagreements, Martov himself as well as the entire C. C. "wished for nothing more than that in the near future you will take a very direct part in party affairs."

He then outlined his view of Axelrod's position, taking pains not to offend him. Most members of the party, he related, had assumed that Axelrod had been familiar with its political line all along and that he had therefore discharged his duties as foreign representative in the spirit of a *"gut disciplinierter Genosse* [well-disciplined comrade]." Now it emerged that he had not been aware that the disagreements between him and the C. C. "derive from different evaluations of the entire historical process that we are experiencing." Under the circumstances, Martov thought "that it is probably best for the cause if for a brief period you do not hold any formal, responsible position in the party." It would only do violence "to your political conscience," an action that Martov would not wish to ask of his friend.[61] Gently but unmistakably,

---

60. Skomorovsky to Axelrod, June 25, Sept. 28, 1920, *ibid.*

61. Martov to Axelrod, Nov. 25, 1920, *ibid.* In suggesting that Axelrod not hold any office in the Menshevik party Martov was really carrying out the wishes of the C. C. In April 1920 the C. C. adopted a resolution that in effect stripped Axelrod of his position as foreign representative because he had for two years been cut off from contact with the movement in Russia. See *Sotsial-demokratiia i revoliutsiia,* p. 60. It is not known when Axelrod learned of the action of the C. C.; he certainly had not

Axelrod was being dislodged from his position of leadership in the Menshevik party. This did not really change anything, for he himself had already declared his independence from the party apparatus.

Early in December 1920 Martov finally visited Axelrod in Switzerland in order to discuss political questions. Neither one changed his position, but they at least clarified the issues that separated them. The visit also tended to reduce the tension between them: thereafter, their relations were cordial, if not as warm as in earlier years. When Martov made plans for the publication of a new journal, *Sotsialisticheskii vestnik*, he assured Axelrod that he would print anything he submitted, "even if in one or another instance it were written in a friendly polemical or critical tone." He also invited Axelrod to join the Menshevik delegation at the conference in Vienna convoked to found the Two and a Half International. He thoughtfully pointed out that such a mandate would not compel Axelrod to violate his conscience, for he would be free to vote his point of view.[62]

Because he did not see the need for another International, Axelrod refused. But he almost regretted his decision when he learned of a new military attack by the Soviet government against Georgia.[63] It occurred to him that it might have been wise to "put to the test" the anti-Communism of the centrists in Vienna by personally appealing to them to protest the invasion of Georgia. And so he did the next best thing: he sent a telegram to Martov urging him to introduce a resolution condemning the action.[64] The question was raised at the conference, and the Mensheviks tried to persuade the delegates to censure the Soviet government. But the feeling was widespread that the evidence was not conclusive. The conference therefore adopted a resolution declaring that if it should indeed be true that powerful Russia, "ruled by a Communist party, wages direct or indirect war against the small neighboring republic of Georgia, then the entire European proletariat would have

---

heard of it in May, when he resigned from the position. There is some evidence to suggest that even in November he still had not been informed of the resolution.

62. Martov to Axelrod, Jan. 30, 1921, Nicolaevsky Collection, Hoover Institution.

63. In May 1918 Georgia had declared its independence from Soviet Russia and for two and a half years was governed by a group of Mensheviks who tried to institute democracy as well as socialism. In February 1921 the Red Army attacked Georgia while the Bolshevik authorities in Moscow denied that their armies had invaded the republic. In less than a month Georgian resistance was crushed. See Richard Pipes, *The Formation of the Soviet Union: Communism and Nationalism 1917–1923* (rev. ed., Cambridge, Mass., 1969), pp. 210–214, 234–241.

64. Axelrod to Woytinsky, Feb. 21, 1921, Nicolaevsky Collection, Hoover Institution.

to voice strong protest; [for the European proletariat] finds it incomprehensible that a conflict between two socialist states should be decided by the same methods that are used by imperialist states."[65]

This tepid and naïve resolution confirmed Axelrod in the correctness of his decision not to attend the conference. Then he received an account of the deliberations from David Dallin, a right-wing member of the Menshevik C. C., which further reinforced his disapproval of the enterprise. Dallin reported that many delegates tended to equate democracy with the Soviet system. This was "bad dogma. It is eclecticism. It is theoretical mishmash." Dallin was even more distressed by the treatment of Kautsky: "He was not included in any delegation. He was not given a consultative vote. They tried not to notice his presence. And he, the teacher of all these 'founders of internationalism,' sat far in the back [of the hall], in the place reserved for guests, and quietly listened while a certain [delegate] Schreider 'exposed' him. A sickening episode."[66] Kautsky had been snubbed because by this time he had denounced the Soviet dictatorship. Had Axelrod attended, he probably also would have been ignored.

Thoroughly disheartened, Axelrod confessed in March 1921 that "I have never [before] endured such moral and spiritual loneliness." In earlier years, when close associates had disregarded his point of view, he had always tried to win them over, generally with success. But he was not confident this time. Though he had made a prodigious effort in the past three years to expose the faults of Bolshevism, by now he was in his seventies, and weak and tired, and the prospect of further exertion dismayed him. Nevertheless, he refused to give up. When, early in 1921, his friend and loyal supporter, Shchupak, confided that he was contemplating a formal rupture with the party, Axelrod advised against it: "However great the influence of Iu. O. [Martov] and however highly we appreciate his talents, nevertheless he is [only] one of the spokesmen —even if very gifted—but not the party [in its entirety]."[67] In this fashion Axelrod let it be known that he intended to try once again to alter the political orientation of Menshevism.

His attempt took the form of publishing a long letter he had written

65. *Protokoll der Internationalen Sozialistischen Konferenz in Wien vom 22. bis 27. Februar 1921* (Vienna, 1921), p. 116.
66. Dallin to Axelrod, Mar. 1, 1921, Axelrod Archive, I.I.S.H. Alexander Schreider was a Left Socialist Revolutionary delegate from Lithuania.
67. Axelrod to N. E. and S. D. Shchupak, Mar. 9, 1921, Nicolaevsky Collection, Hoover Institution; Axelrod to S. D. Shchupak, Mar. 5, 1921, *ibid.*

to Martov a few months earlier criticizing the party's assessment of Bolshevism. Although it had been widely known that he differed with the C. C., the divergencies had never been publicly discussed in detail. By airing his position in *Sotsialisticheskii vestnik*, Axelrod hoped to influence those Menshevik émigrés who still maintained an open mind on the question.

Primarily he set out to refute Martov's contention that the Bolsheviks served a historically progressive role and to disclose the contradictory nature of Martov's attitude toward the new regime. The latter frequently argued—as have historians on occasion[68]—that the Leninists were performing a historical mission comparable to that of the Jacobins in 1793, whom Marxists credited with having introduced a progressive era in France. But if this comparison was valid, Axelrod wrote, then it made no sense to condemn the Bolsheviks for perverting socialism and resorting to terroristic methods. Rather, "revolutionary duty" would seem to dictate that the Mensheviks join the ranks of the party carrying out historically necessary and progressive policies. At the least, their opposition ought to be "cautious, limited, and, of course, benevolent."

But Axelrod found the comparison and its logical consequences absurd, for a careful analysis reveals that Leninism was "a clever parody of the original . . . a skillful imitation of a grandiose, spontaneous event." Axelrod admitted that he had contributed to the terminological confusion by having referred to the Leninists as Jacobins ever since 1903. He had always stressed, however, that his adversaries were a unique breed of political animal.

The Bolsheviks had distorted the Jacobin tradition in various ways. For example, the radicals of 1793 had attained power as a result of an "objective unfolding" of a revolution, which could not be said of their supposed successors of 1917. Furthermore, unlike the Communists, the Jacobins were not a mere faction of revolutionary democracy who seized power by suppressing all other progressive parties.

There is no need to scrutinize Axelrod's interpretation of French history, which is questionable. The important point is that traditionally Jacobinism had been assumed to be a political doctrine that upheld the legitimacy of a small group of individuals acting in the name and in the interest of all the people. In this sense the Bolsheviks were Jacobins, which is what Axelrod had always meant in applying the opprobrious

68. See, e.g., Albert Mathiez, "Le Bolchevisme et le Jacobinisme," *Rivista di Scienza*, XXVII (Jan. 1920), 52–65.

term to his opponents. In the past he had insisted, and this he now repeated, that for Marxists to adopt the Jacobin approach to politics was to betray the Marxist heritage.

Axelrod also took Martov to task for advancing the notion that the Bolshevik government should not be completely repudiated because it enjoyed widespread support among the working class. He doubted the accuracy of the assertion, but even if true it would not invest the Leninist government with legitimacy. After all, in the nineteenth century probably 90 percent of the people were devoted to the Tsar, but this properly did not deter revolutionaries from opposing the autocracy.

Axelrod did make one concession to Martov by granting that it would prove more complicated and risky to combat Communism than tsarism. His reasoning, however, was solely expedient, for he had no doubt that the two systems were equally reprehensible. "Our moral and political right to fight against the Bolsheviks with all means," he declared, "even with weapons in our hands, has been and continues to be axiomatic to me and needs no proof. It follows from the fact that the 'Soviet government' is as incapable, and perhaps even more so, as tsarism was of voluntarily renouncing despotism, and therefore [Communism] . . . just like tsarism, is doomed to be overthrown by force." But as he had pointed out before, only progressives had opposed the old order, whereas reactionaries also opposed Bolshevism. The battle against Lenin could therefore lead to a restoration of counterrevolutionaries and destroy all the political and social gains of 1917. For this reason he focused his strategy on a socialist intervention in Russian affairs, and he called on Martov and the Menshevik party to initiate a new campaign in support of that proposal.

Here Axelrod was not consistent. If he was convinced that Leninist despotism could only be "overthrown by force," then he had obviously given up on the possibility that moral intervention by international socialism might achieve what he hoped for—a return to democracy. It may be that by this time all he really expected was that pressure by Western socialists would impel the Bolsheviks to eliminate some of the more repressive features of their regime. A man as acutely sensitive to human suffering as Axelrod would not have scorned even such a limited accomplishment.[69]

In his rebuttal Martov did not address himself directly to the issues

69. "Tov. P. B. Aksel'rod o bol'shevizme i bor'be s nim," *Sotsialisticheskii vestnik*, no. 6 (Apr. 20, 1921), 3–7, no. 7 (May 4, 1921), 3–5.

raised by Axelrod. He repeated instead the assertions that the Leninists had fulfilled "historically necessary" tasks in carrying out their revolution and that any government that was likely to rise from the ashes of this one would be even worse for Russia: "In the struggle against Bolshevism, when it defends the authentic achievements of the revolution (together with its dictatorship, liable to be abolished) against the counterrevolution, we openly and without reservation take the side of Bolshevism, and do not fear to say to the proletariat: in the face of [P. I.] Wrangel's and Struve's 'democracy' in quotation marks and the 'democracy' of [David] Lloyd George and [Marshal Ferdinand] Foch in quotation marks, you should support the 'Soviet power' in quotation marks and the tyranny—without quotation marks—of Lenin and Trotsky as the lesser evil. The logic of our theoretical position cannot commit us to any other [conclusion]."[70] Martov insisted that in voicing these opinions he was by no means an apologist for the new government.

Axelrod found this reasoning entirely unacceptable. Although he had opposed Lloyd George's policy toward Russia, he certainly would not have considered Lenin's political system superior to that of Britain. Nor could he agree that Russia had to choose between Communism and a counterrevolutionary regime led by a man like Wrangel. He himself had offered another alternative, socialist intervention, and it was Martov's indifference to this possibility (which he had previously favored) that especially grieved Axelrod. This meant, in effect, that rather than collaborate with Social Democrats whom he considered opportunists Martov was prepared to forgo any determined pressure on the Soviet government. In the last analysis, the difference between them turned on the weight each assigned to traditional, liberal democracy. For Axelrod it was of decisive importance; without it, there could be no socialism as he understood the term. Martov was not contemptuous of democracy, but as his comment on Lloyd George suggests, he did not attach nearly as much significance to it as Axelrod.

The Mensheviks who agreed with Axelrod praised his critique of Martov: "If Martov and our other comrades," Tsereteli wrote, "were not under the influence of an unhealthy mood created by the war, this letter would play the same role as your first . . . [article] about Menshevism in *Iskra* [in 1903 and 1904], and it would be the starting point

70. Iu. Martov, "Po povodu pis'ma tov. P. B. Aksel'roda," *ibid.*, no. 8 (May 20, 1921), 3–6.

for a Social Democratic program and the overcoming of Bolshevism."[71] But only a handful of Mensheviks in exile—Woytinsky, Bienstock, Garvi, Shchupak, and a few others—shared Axelrod's views. Martov was by far the dominant figure among the editors of *Sotsialisticheskii vestnik,* and the paper by and large reflected his political attitude. After his death in April 1923 Dan took over as editor in chief, and the paper continued to espouse the position of the Menshevik left.

Although he disagreed with most of the Mensheviks in exile, Axelrod maintained cordial relations with them. In the spring of 1922 he had moved to Berlin, the party's major center in the West, and this made it relatively easy for him to keep informed about Russia and to discuss issues with his friends. The move also eased his personal situation, for he was no longer as lonesome as he had been in Zurich. In the summer of 1922 he underwent a serious bladder operation and thereafter was rarely strong enough to leave his home. Fortunately, he had met a warmhearted Russian woman, E. Landishev, who became his house-keeper and saw to it that he not tax his limited energies.

Whenever he had the strength, he wrote letters—to Tsereteli in France, Kautsky in Vienna, Ingerman in the United States, and occasionally to other socialists whom he entreated to protest Soviet excesses. "Each letter was a political act," Woytinsky recalled. In the summer of 1927 he contemplated writing a major work analyzing anew the defects of Bolshevism and the "conciliatory" attitude of Western Marxists toward Communism. But he could not collect his thoughts for the endeavor, and because of this he "suffered deeply."[72] At all times he was absorbed by the endless debates and political maneuvers of the Mensheviks in exile.

The Mensheviks who lived in Berlin during the 1920's protected themselves from the pain of obscurity by indulging in self-delusion. They were in touch with many Russians who supplied them with detailed and generally accurate accounts about developments in their homeland, and they were better informed than anyone else about the steady consolidation of Bolshevik power and the wave of repression that all but crushed their movement. Yet, for all their knowledge, the émigrés debated the tactics appropriate for their party with a passion

71. Tsereteli to Axelrod, Aug. 9, 1921, Axelrod Archive, **I.I.S.H.**
72. Woytinsky, "Poslednie gody," pp. 12–13.

that suggested they thought their decisions might still affect the course of events in Russia.

In the spring of 1921, at the time of the New Economic Policy, the Soviet government moved to eliminate the Menshevik party altogether. As Leonard Schapiro has argued: "To have left . . . [the Mensheviks] at liberty even with such restricted political freedom as they had enjoyed in 1919 and 1920 would have invited the obvious question why the party, whose policy had hitherto failed, should not yield power to the party whose [economic] policy was now being adopted."[73] Hundreds of Mensheviks, including the entire C. C., were arrested. Many others, reduced to a state of demoralization, offered their services to the government, believing themselves obligated to help rebuild the country. In the election to the Moscow soviet in January 1922 the Mensheviks succeeded in having only one of their number chosen as deputy out of a total of 2,000. At about this time ten of their leaders, including Dan and Nicolaevsky, were allowed to emigrate. By the middle of 1922 Menshevism no longer existed as an organized party in Russia.

Nonetheless, most Mensheviks in Berlin continued to radiate hope. Shortly after his arrival in the West, Dan wrote Axelrod that "I do not believe that the sojourn abroad will be especially long. The contemporary accursed regime is saturated to such a degree from top to bottom with contradictions that it can hardly hold out in its present form for any length of time." The Bolsheviks would either have to move to the right, toward Bonapartism, or to the left, toward democracy. Even if a Bonaparte assumed control, he would be forced to introduce "more or less" liberal measures. "In any case," Dan concluded, "the Bolsheviks will either have to cease controlling the government, or—in one sense or another—stop being 'Communists.' "[74]

Axelrod was far less sanguine than Dan that fundamental changes in the Soviet system would result from internal contradictions. But he blindly continued to believe in the feasibility and efficacy of socialist intervention. In the hope of influencing his European comrades, he agreed to serve as a Menshevik delegate to the Hamburg Congress in 1923, at which the Two and a Half reunited with the remnants of the Second International to form the Socialist and Labor International.

73. Schapiro, *Communist Autocracy*, p. 204.
74. L. O. and F. I. Dan to Axelrod, Feb. 16, 1922, Nicolaevsky Collection, Hoover Institution.

Axelrod had little success in winning converts. The congress passed a resolution calling on the Russian government to end the terror against socialists, but it did not consider the question of a commission of inquiry. This inaction on the part of the Western parties so exasperated Axelrod that he actually derived satisfaction from their setbacks. In October 1924, when the British Labour party fared worse at the polls than expected, he experienced "a feeling very close to *Schadenfreude*, as though the 'defeat' of the Labour government were a historical punishment for it and its organ, the *Daily Herald*, for their stupid (objectively criminal) policies with regard to the Bolsheviks."[75]

In the meantime, the right and left wings among the Mensheviks in exile argued with increasing vehemence about the party's attitude toward the Soviet regime.[76] In the spring of 1925 Garvi complained that there was "growing disaffection and tension" within the Berlin group. He ascribed the "unhealthy situation" not so much to differences of opinion as to the unwillingness of the leaders to allow the minority to publish opinions in the party press that deviated from the official program. "At bottom, this is a continuing heritage of Bolshevik methods, which twenty-five years ago were followed by *Iskra* under Lenin's leadership. Opposition within the party is something impermissible . . . it must always remain silent."[77]

This indictment of Dan and his supporters seems to have been justified. But after a year of bargaining the minority was allowed occasionally to publish its views. Almost invariably, with each new turn of events in Russia, the two factions clashed. Thus, during the struggle for power in 1926, Dan admonished the Mensheviks not to take the position that "both sides stink." Even though they were personally loathsome, Trotsky and G. E. Zinoviev deserved to be supported because they opposed the personal rule that was being established by a man who had hitherto played a secondary role in Russian Marxism, Joseph Stalin. "Objectively . . . in the course of its dialectical evolution the struggle against the dictatorship of Stalin will have to transform itself into a struggle against dictatorship as such and for democracy." Dan even spoke of the possibility of reaching an understanding with Zinoviev and

75. Axelrod to Tsereteli, Oct. 30, 1924, *ibid.*
76. For details on one of these controversies, see Abraham Ascher, "Axelrod and Kautsky," *Slavic Review,* XXVI (Mar. 1967), 109–111.
77. Garvi to Kautsky, May 25, 1925, Kautsky Archive, I.I.S.H.

Trotsky. The right, however, would not make a choice between Stalin and the opposition because they considered the economic and political program of both sides unacceptable. Garvi, one of their spokesmen, contended that Russia could not be industrialized without foreign investments, and "without civil rights and civil order the accumulation of capital in Russia . . . is not possible."[78]

Although Axelrod sympathized more with the position of the rightists than that of Dan, he did not fully agree with either side. He imagined that had he been healthy enough to set forth his views in formal articles or lectures, he would have infuriated all the Mensheviks in Berlin. But it was not only illness that restrained him. He still nursed the belief that someday Menshevism would come to the fore in Russia, and in the interest of this eventuality he wished to preserve party unity.[79]

This is not to say that he expected an early end to the Bolshevik regime. "Everyone who comes from the Bolshevik realm," he wrote in 1926, "is convinced that the dictatorship is still firmly entrenched . . . For the time being, I still dare not dream about revolution."[80] He also rejected Dan's notion that "so amoral a political campaign as was being conducted by Zinoviev, L. B. Kamenev, Trotsky, etc. could serve as the fulcrum for an all-democratic movement against the Bolshevik dictatorship."[81] But he did think that the internecine war, taking place at a time of "hopeless economic and financial crisis," could have an "*indirect* positive significance—in the sense of stimulating, arousing, and aiding the oppositional spirit among the anti-Bolshevik masses and of stimulating among them an aspiration for an active, increasingly systematic struggle against the Bolshevik regime." If the dissension among the leaders continued and became widely known, the socialist opposition would commit an "unpardonable mistake" if it did not exploit the situation by attempting through propaganda to heighten the "revolutionary spirit and organized oppositional activity of the working class and peasantry."

78. Garvi to Kautsky, Sept. 18, 1926, *ibid.*
79. Axelrod to S. M. and J. A. Ingerman, July 20, 1925, Nicolaevsky Collection, Hoover Institution; Axelrod to Ingerman, Dec. 14, 1926, *ibid.*
80. Axelrod to Potresov, Jan. 5, 1926, *ibid.*
81. Axelrod no doubt considered the campaign of Zinoviev, Kamenev, and Trotsky against the tyranny of the party apparatus and in favor of interparty democracy as "amoral" because they themselves had contributed heavily to the emergence of the dictatorial regime.

He was, clearly, still a Marxist and very much a Menshevik. He had not lost faith in the potential of the masses for "independent action." The crucial question, as he saw it, was whether there existed "within the socialist opposition elements and forces capable of transforming this possibility [of mass action] into a real fact." It was for the purpose of seizing upon a major crisis—whenever it might come—that the Mensheviks in exile must maintain themselves as a unified party. "They must prepare themselves, so that at the time of the liquidation of the existing regime they will be in a position to defend the interests of democracy. And this preparation demands of us the application, in essence, of those methods that characterized our party under tsarism." During the "transitional period from Asiatic arbitrariness to European democracy there will open up the possibility for our emigration to return to our native country and begin there the political work approximately comparable to that which is being waged under the political conditions prevailing in [Admiral Miklos] Horthy's realm."

Axelrod supposed that Tsereteli, to whom he addressed these words, was saying to himself: "Well, P. B.'s fantasies have played a trick on him . . . [But] up to now all my pessimistic 'prophecies' have come true, so perhaps this time my not very wonderful but nevertheless relatively optimistic predictions will also come true."[82] His mood in the late 1920's may be compared to his mood in the 1880's: he hoped for radical changes in Russia and had an abiding faith that ultimately they would eventuate, but he dared not expect them in the near future.

Actually, during the last years of his life, Axelrod's moments of guarded optimism were much rarer than his periods of despair and disappointment. He fretted about the "betrayal" of Western socialists and his inability to write more about the causes of the failure of Russian Marxism. He still read avidly, mainly newspapers and occasionally books. But much of the time he was ill and too weak to do anything at all. There were entire weeks during which he could not even write a letter. His neurasthenic attacks recurred regularly, and he never fully recovered from his operation in 1922. He often complained of being a helpless invalid.

It is fortunate that he had many friends who seem almost to have worshiped him. In 1924 Kautsky wrote him about his own seventieth

82. Axelrod to Tsereteli, Aug. 2, Sept. 18, 1926, Nicolaevsky Collection, Hoover Institution; Axelrod to S. M. and J. A. Ingerman, July 20, 1925, *ibid.*

birthday that had just been celebrated and about the preparations for Bernstein's seventy-fifth. "Thus we old people spend our time celebrating each other's 70th and 75th birthdays. Only yours is never observed. You must once and for all decide when you were born. Even if you cannot prove your date, we will believe you, if only so that your 75th will give us the opportunity to prove how much we love you and are devoted to you. I assume that you were born between Ede and me; well, in one or two years we can celebrate your 75th. So hurry up and decide in which year you will want to have been born."[83] Axelrod refused to name a date, but his friends settled on August 25, 1850, and prepared a special issue of *Sotsialisticheskii vestnik* in his honor. With his usual modesty he protested the plans for his birthday, especially after an announcement in the *Arbeiter-Zeitung* implied that he was looking forward to the festivities. "I have never yet celebrated my birthday and am not even certain whether I came into the world in August."[84] Still, he could not but be moved by the generous outpouring of tributes in *Sotsialisticheskii vestnik* from Mensheviks and Marxists throughout Europe.

The high points in his life in Berlin were the frequent visits by Menshevik friends, who consulted him about political issues and paid the closest attention to his health. The Woytinskys visited him every Sunday, and as this became generally known no one else would appear that day. The others took turns so as to provide him with a maximum of diversion.

Wladimir Woytinsky was especially solicitous, and it was largely because of his persistence that Axelrod managed to complete the first of four projected volumes of his memoirs. Woytinsky actually drafted some parts of the book on the basis of oral statements by Axelrod, who then edited them extensively. He also composed sections for subsequent volumes, but most of these were never put in publishable form. Also, whenever he was strong enough, Axelrod related to Woytinsky his "historical analyses of the social and political conditions in old and new Russia," which were to have served as an introduction to a collection of his writings on Bolshevism since 1917.[85]

Axelrod had come to believe that his assessment of Communism since

83. Kautsky to Axelrod, Nov. 14, 1924, Axelrod Archive, I.I.S.H.
84. Axelrod to Luise Kautsky, June 15, 1925, Kautsky Archive, I.I.S.H.
85. Emma Woytinsky to Luise Kautsky, Nov. 14, 1927, *ibid.*

the Revolution of 1917 was his most significant contribution to social-ism, and he was distressed that this was not generally recognized. "Quite often," he wrote Tsereteli in February 1927, "while reflecting about death, I think with bitterness about the fact that no one has a kind word to say either about my letters or my speeches concerning this period." He asked Tsereteli to preserve his manuscripts and printed interviews "on the subject of the tasks and obligations of the International in this historical era."

Much as Axelrod appreciated the warmth extended to him by the Berlin Mensheviks, he nevertheless complained that he felt "relatively isolated among the local public." Apparently, only Tsereteli, who lived in Paris, and a recent young émigré from Russia, Boris Sapir, shared his continuing interest in socialist intervention in Russian affairs. As late as 1927 Tsereteli again tried to persuade the Executive Committee of the Socialist International to implement Axelrod's proposal. Axelrod thanked his colleague "from the bottom of my heart" for his efforts and expressed delight at the news that the International seemed to be moving toward an attempt to send a commission of inquiry to Russia.[86] But late in March 1928, in what must have been one of the last letters he received, he learned from Tsereteli that he had encountered ener-getic opposition to the undertaking and that it did not look as though a delegation would be sent after all.[87] Axelrod's idea never was realized, but in due course more and more Social Democrats and Mensheviks in exile accepted his assessment of the Soviet system.

In the meantime, his health continued to fail. In December 1927 he tried to write a postcard to Kautsky, but could not complete it. "It is so difficult for me to sit on the sofa even for a few minutes."[88] On April 14, 1928, Lydia Dan told Luise Kautsky that "Our poor old man is getting weaker and weaker by the day, and I do not know how many more days the weak flame of his life will still burn."[89] Only two days later, during the night of April 16, he died.

In the country to whose service he had devoted his political career his death received scant notice. Few people knew about his contribu-

86. Axelrod to Tsereteli, Feb. 21, 1927, Nicolaevsky Collection, Hoover Institution.
87. Tsereteli to Axelrod, Mar. 25, 1928, Axelrod Archive, I.I.S.H.
88. Axelrod to Kautsky, Dec. 1927, *ibid.*
89. Lydia Dan to Luise Kautsky, Apr. 14, 1928, Kautsky Archive, I.I.S.H.

tions to Russian Marxism, which allegedly had provided the guiding principles for their government since 1917, and many of those who did were disposed to belittle or discredit him. In its obituary on Axelrod, *Pravda* declared that generally when a prominent figure in the labor movement dies, it is possible to point to some heroic or brilliant period in his life. "About Axelrod this can be said much less than about anyone else." In a brief chronicle of his career, the paper asserted that he had harbored opportunistic tendencies in the 1880's, opposed Economism as a "future Menshevik" in the 1890's, and advocated "armed intervention" in the Soviet Union in 1925. Indeed, he had been an "irreconcilable opportunist" at all stages of the development of the revolutionary movement and Social Democracy. He had, moreover, contributed "nothing valuable to theory."[90] It is ironic that the leading paper in revolutionary Russia did not have a single kind word to say about a man whose commitment to revolution spanned almost six decades. But the cruel treatment of Axelrod's work may also be regarded as a tacit admission that his writings contained ideas too seductive to be broadcast in Russia.

It is also ironic that the Socialist International, which Axelrod had criticized so severely, evaluated his role most accurately: "His willingness to sacrifice himself [for the cause], his self-renunciation, the surrender of his personal life to the life of the party not only had an educational impact on entire generations of Russian socialists, but actually made him into the *conscience of the party.*"[91] The latter epithet is particularly apt, for ever since 1903, when he emerged as an independent leader of his party, his main concern had been to prevent the Mensheviks from forsaking the principles of Marxism as he had conceived of them from the time of his conversion in 1882.

90. *Pravda*, Apr. 18, 1928. A similar obituary appeared in *Izvestiia* of the same date.
91. *Internationale Information*, Apr. 20, 1928.

Epilogue

In a private letter written in September 1917, intended as much as an apology for past criticisms as a compliment to an old friend, Karl Kautsky singled out one of the chief merits of Axelrod's work. Few people, Kautsky declared, understood the "art" of remaining faithful to their convictions while accommodating their behavior to changing conditions. Most men in politics tend either to abandon their principles or to ignore the realities of new circumstances. "You have always known how to avoid both dangers; émigrés are prone to succumb to the latter danger and those who live in their native country, to the former."[1] If the broad span of Axelrod's career is surveyed, one is indeed struck by unmistakable signs of continuity and consistency. His political outlook cannot, however, be characterized as static. On numerous occasions he formulated new tactics or stressed ideas that previously he had only accepted tacitly. But he never strayed from the fundamentals of the position he adopted in 1882, and even as a Marxist he did not deviate from some principles he had professed during the 1870's.

Axelrod's ideological constancy not only makes him unique among the early leaders of Russian Marxism. It also justifies our viewing him as the prototypal Menshevik whose positions on various issues help us to penetrate a movement and ideology that have not been easy to define. As Leopold Haimson recently pointed out, historians have been inclined to exaggerate the "essential coherence and consistency" of both Menshevism and Bolshevism. Scholars have an understandable impulse to assign a logical and almost inexorable pattern to the development of the parties. This kind of approach is all the more alluring because

---

1. Kautsky to Axelrod, Sept. 20, 1917, Nicolaevsky Collection, Hoover Institution.

the protagonists in the intense factional struggles tried to justify their conduct—often long after the battles themselves had lost their significance—by claiming that they had always been motivated by basic convictions and principles. Our study of the oscillations of both Mensheviks and Bolsheviks, however, lends little credence to these claims. In the years 1903–1920 there were too many switches from one faction to another for us now to accept the assertion that the two movements were at all times clearly divided over ideological matters. Professor Haimson correctly contends that the "development of both Bolshevism and Menshevism occurred as the result of a complex process in which the changing character and behavior of each faction profoundly influenced the other; this process unfolded in the setting of changing environments in both Russia and Western Europe, and it encompassed the appearance on the historical stage of at least three political generations, the members of which were characterized in many respects by quite distinctive intellectual and emotional makeups and social backgrounds."[2]

Because of these complexities as well as the many twists and turns of Menshevik policies, it may be appropriate to consider Menshevism as an ideological persuasion rather than as a cohesive doctrine. But it cannot be denied that the movement was a distinct and self-contained political tendency, especially if Axelrod is acknowledged as the major contributor to its evolution. A strong case can be made to support the contention that on broad ideological and tactical questions his role was decisive in shaping the direction and program of the party. On all the issues disputed by the two factions between 1903 and 1914 Axelrod's views became dominant among the Mensheviks. Above all, no matter how much they disagreed with him on specific matters or even temporarily deviated from his line, ultimately the Mensheviks accepted three of his notions that comprised the core of their persuasion.

In the first place, he argued that Social Democracy's primary task in Russia was to create an independent, politically conscious working class. This endeavor, as he put it early in the 1920's, came to be the "essence of Menshevism." But at the same time he maintained—and this was the second aspect of the Menshevik persuasion—that although

2. Leopold Haimson, preface, in Solomon Schwarz, *The Russian Revolution of 1905: The Workers' Movement and the Formation of Bolshevism and Menshevism* (Chicago, 1967), pp. vii–viii.

the proletariat was to "play the role of a vanguard in the bourgeois revolution," it had to realize that in this revolution the working class "must defend the maximum interests of democracy and must not attempt to exceed the limits of capitalist development."[3] The third feature of Axelrod's Menshevism was more elusive and less tangible, but nonetheless important. I am referring to his concern for the moral dimension of politics, which on practical issues was shared by Martov, who, however, in several theoretical works subscribed to the relativist view of ethics. Particularly in his mature years Axelrod rejected the tenet that there existed no universal code of ethical conduct and that therefore any action promoting the socialist cause was inherently moral.

The force of these ideas on Menshevik thinking became most evident in 1917. Although it would be misleading and inaccurate to attribute the party's conduct during that fateful year solely to its dogmatic adherence to these principles, there are few historians who would deny the significance of this factor. Despite all the wrangling over fine theoretical points for over a decade, at the crucial historical moment most Mensheviks did appear to share a general outlook, most of it shaped, or at least strongly influenced, by Axelrod's thinking. Now it is true, as we have indicated, that after the Bolshevik assumption of power, the dominant group of Mensheviks in Russia gradually veered away from the ideas that Axelrod considered vital to the party's creed. But even then the Menshevik leaders did not unequivocally embrace Bolshevism. They continued to call for democratization of the soviets, denounced the "utopian" attempts to introduce socialism in a backward country, and, in condemning the Leninist terror, acknowledged the principle of moral restraint in politics. If official Menshevism after 1919 was not what Axelrod had envisioned, it was even then not completely divorced from his conceptions and unaffected by his influence.

Of all the theoretical problems raised during the long controversy between the Mensheviks and the Bolsheviks probably none is more intractable than the question of which group remained loyal to Marxist teachings. Both parties claimed to be the true interpreters of the creed, and each accused the other of distorting and betraying it. On the surface, it might seem superfluous for the historian to pass judgment on these

3. Axelrod to Georgian comrades, n. d., but early in the 1920's, Axelrod Archive, I.I.S.H.

claims and charges. After all, Marx expected his disciples to adapt his teachings to changing conditions. He never considered his set of ideas a closed system that embodied a ready-made strategy for all conceivable historical contingencies. Consequently, it is legitimate for the historian to devote himself primarily to analyzing the theoretical adjustments of a particular Marxist party and their impact on the party's fortunes.

Yet, the question of consistency should not be altogether avoided, partly because of its meaning to the participants themselves. The charge of having strayed from orthodoxy wounded the Russian party leaders deeply. Moreover, within the movement it was virtually incumbent on both factions to be able to demonstrate theoretical purity, for many activists believed Marxist ideas to be axiomatic. Neither Lenin nor his Menshevik opponents would have dared to acknowledge deviation from orthodoxy even if they thought they had committed it. But this possibility was probably never seriously entertained by any of them: they were true believers convinced of their fidelity to the gospel.

As one of the founders of Russian Marxism, Axelrod was understandably eager to show that he, and not Lenin, had accurately interpreted Marx. He made this attempt most explicitly in 1908 in his only "scholarly" work, a long introduction to the correspondence among Marx, Engels, and F. Sorge. Even if allowance is made for the looseness of many of Marx's formulations and the flexibility of his theoretical system, it must be granted that Axelrod proved his point. To be sure, Marx had not stated unequivocally that Russia must pass through a capitalist phase, and early in the 1880's Engels had supported the Narodovol'tsy's advocacy of terror and an immediate seizure of power. But these opinions preceded the rapid progress of industrialization in Russia and the emergence of a promising labor movement. Now, in 1908—so Axelrod seems to have reasoned—there could be no doubt that he and his colleagues had been right twenty-five years earlier in assuming that the Marxist model of social and political development, devised initially for Western Europe, was also applicable to Russia. And he found his conception of the way the socialist ideal should be realized in Russia indisputably consistent with that of Marx.

He backed his claim with an examination of half a century's worth of statements on tactics made by Marx and Engels. Their foremost concern at all times, he asserted, was to further the dictum he himself had quoted so frequently, that the liberation of the working class must be achieved by the working class itself. They had warned repeatedly against a premature assumption of power by the proletariat. Axelrod placed special weight on advice Marx had offered in September 1850 to the Central Committee of the Communist League, which was then planning an insurrection. Conditions in Germany at that time resembled those in early twentieth-century Russia, according to Axelrod: the bourgeoisie did not yet predominate politically; the contradictions of capitalism had not reached their highest point; vestiges of the feudal order had not been completely eradicated; and, most significantly, there did not yet exist an organized, class-conscious proletariat. Consequently, Marx's warning to the German C. C. was now relevant to the Russian movement: "We tell the workers: 'You have to have the experience of 15, 20, 50 years of civil war [and of a popular movement] not only to change the circumstances but also to [reeducate yourselves and] prepare yourselves for power.'" Axelrod further cited Marx's criticism of those who ignored the "underdeveloped condition of the German proletariat" and used the word "proletariat" in the same cynical way that the democrats used "people . . . as mere phrases."[4] It is surprising that Axelrod did not quote Marx's boast that "We devote ourselves to a party which is precisely far from achieving power," or the contention that "would the proletariat have achieved power, then it would have enacted not proletarian, but petty-bourgeois legislation."[5] The last two points were among Axelrod's most telling arguments against Lenin's elitism and the Bolshevik coup of 1917.

Axelrod slightly doctored Marx's statement of 1850 by adding the bracketed words to the original speech. He also failed to point out that only six months earlier, in March 1850, Marx had urged a Blanquist strategy as well as recourse to terror upon the very same C. C.[6] Nonetheless, Axelrod's argument was valid. Although Marx never expressly repudiated the political strategy he had favored from 1848 until early 1850, during the last three decades of his life he emphasized an entirely different approach, and it was this latter approach that came to dominate the thinking of his followers. The "mature Marx" assigned

4. Pavel Axelrod, introduction, *Pis'ma K. Marksa, Fr. Engel'sa i dr. k F. Zorge* (St. Petersburg, 1908), pp. xxxix–xxxx.
5. For the full quotation, see Shlomo Avineri, *The Social and Political Thought of Karl Marx* (Cambridge, Eng., 1968), pp. 195–196.
6. See Karl Marx and Frederick Engels, *Selected Works* (2 vols., Moscow, 1951), I, 98–108.

increasing importance to certain ideas he had formulated prior to 1848, namely, that the proletariat should not attempt to realize socialism until the necessary socioeconomic conditions prevailed. He further maintained that the use of terror by a revolutionary government was, in the words of one student of Marxism, "an ultimate proof that the aims the revolution wishes to achieve cannot be achieved at present. Terror is less a means towards the realization of a revolutionary aim than a mark of failure."[7]

In addition, it should be noted that the only kind of vanguard Marx was willing to sanction was "one composed of authentic labour leaders."[8] In this connection, it is instructive to recall his conception of the workers' associations, succinctly summarized by Shlomo Avineri: "The association of workers in their meetings and groups is by itself a most revolutionary act, for it changes both reality and the workers themselves . . . Through its organizations the proletariat prepares the conditions for its self-emancipation. Organization and association, even considered apart from their immediate aims, constitute a crucial phase in the liberation of the workers. They change the worker, his way of life, his consciousness of himself and his society."[9]

This passage calls to mind Axelrod's expressions of wonder at the uninhibited participation of the Berlin workers in their party meetings in 1874. For Axelrod as for Marx, the workers' organization was not merely or even primarily a vehicle for attaining power. He conceived of it as an association that would free the masses in a cultural and personal sense, transforming them into independent human beings, conscious of the possibility of a better order and capable of the initiative necessary to attain it. Whether or not political involvement can actually liberate in this manner is beside the point, though there is evidence that it can. The crucial point is that Axelrod believed that it could, an assumption that underlay his views on the organization of the proletariat and at all times separated him from the Bolsheviks. Lenin's main concern was not to convert the workers en masse into participants in the political process, but rather to use a minority of their number to achieve and exercise power while professing to be acting in the interests

7. Avineri, *Social and Political Thought of Karl Marx*, p. 188.
8. George Lichtheim, *Marxism: An Historical and Critical Study* (New York, 1962), p. 128.
9. Avineri, *Social and Political Thought of Karl Marx*, pp. 141–143.

of the entire class. This Jacobin conception of politics had much more in common with the views of the Narodovol'tsy of the 1880's than with the essentials of Marxism as they were understood by most European socialists early in the twentieth century.

If Axelrod's claim to Marxist orthodoxy was more persuasive than Lenin's, the latter had the decisive advantage of offering a program more responsive to the realities of Russian conditions. Contrary to Axelrod's assertions, the Marxism of the European labor movement was not really relevant to the situation in Russia in the late nineteenth and early twentieth centuries. Admittedly, as Axelrod frequently pointed out, there were some parallels between the German states of the 1840's, when Marx first enunciated his ideas, and the tsarist Empire of the 1880's, when the radical movement there began to turn to "scientific socialism." But Axelrod (and his colleagues) exaggerated the parallels. More highly industrialized than Russia and less repressive politically, the German states were also endowed with a larger middle class and better educated and more disciplined lower classes. In any case, Marxism did not begin to evolve into a significant mass movement until the 1870's, by which time the country had undergone important political changes and was rapidly being industrialized. By the 1890's Germany could be termed an industrial state, that is, more than one-half of its population was employed in the industrial sector. It need only be mentioned that as late as 1900 about 3 percent of Russia's population was proletarian to point up one of the vast differences between the two countries.

Although aware of the divergencies, Axelrod nevertheless believed that the tactics of the German Social Democratic party could be transplanted to Russian soil. It was a conviction destined to lead to his greatest disappointments. However many emendations he made in the German model of political activity, and several were certainly ingenious, there were practical obstacles that could not be overcome. The notion that an organized proletariat could strive for bourgeois democracy without falling under middle-class influence seemed theoretically plausible. And it must be granted that when the revolution finally occurred the Russian working class did not serve as "cannon fodder" for the bourgeoisie, as had its German counterpart in 1848 and as Axelrod always feared it would. But at the same time the Russian proletariat did not demonstrate the initiative and restraint Axelrod had hoped for. The working class avoided one pitfall but plunged into another by allowing itself to be dominated by representatives of the radical intelligentsia.

A serious flaw in Axelrod's thinking was his belief that time was on his side. His unshakable faith in the rationality of man led him to expect that in due course the majority of the Russian population could be educated to accept the program that he and his fellow Mensheviks professed. Just as he himself had imparted the gospel to small groups of the intelligentsia, so the latter could pass on the word to ever larger numbers of workers, who in time would be the numerically dominant force in the country.

It was an admirable perspective, firmly rooted in certain traditions of Russian radicalism, but it did not take into account the natural impatience of masses of workers. Was it reasonable to expect the majority of the working class deliberately to place restraints on its political and economic aspirations? If the proletariat could exert as much influence in bringing about the bourgeois revolution as Axelrod assumed, why should it not press for the immediate realization of its maximum program, socialism? Moreover, neither Axelrod nor the Mensheviks in general appreciated the political potential of the peasantry, who constituted the overwhelming majority of the population. It was one of Lenin's most penetrating, though retrospectively obvious, insights that a proletarian party could gain the peasants' support or at least their political neutrality by advocating measures they found attractive. This strategy, one of the keystones of Lenin's bid for power, also entailed deviation from orthodoxy, but, once again, it reflected the virtue of political realism. With modification it has been adopted by Communist movements in backward countries the world over.

Ultimately, the fate of Menshevism exposed the weaknesses, impracticality, and inapplicability of Axelrod's political conception. Perhaps his gravest oversight—and that of orthodox Marxists generally—was that he underestimated the fragility of the state machinery in a backward country. Without the almost total collapse of the Russian state, a Bolshevik victory would have been extremely unlikely. It was precisely in the advanced, highly industrialized countries where Marxism was expected to prevail (most notably in Germany) that radical Marxists could not achieve power, in large measure because the state machinery was too resilient. Yet, in itself this criticism of Axelrod may be too severe. For an event occurred that profoundly affected the course of Russian history but that neither he nor anyone else could have foreseen when the Marxist movement was being organized. That event was the First World War, which produced such extensive dislocation of the country's social, economic, and political fabric that the government's authority was seriously eroded. It is true that in the two years preceding the war Russia witnessed a heightening both of labor militancy and class tensions, and the country seemed to be heading for a new convulsion of major proportions. No one can estimate today how the upheaval might have ended, but it is difficult to conceive that the Bolsheviks could have triumphed without the disintegration of the state engendered by the military conflict.

As a political figure in Russia, Axelrod cannot be judged a success. He realized few of his aims and was unable to prevent his worst apprehensions from coming to pass. In the history of Russian radicalism, however, he occupies an honored place. He took up the cause of the lower classes from which he emerged and fully identified with them throughout his adult life. Although his opinions changed with the passage of time, his commitment to a new social order in which all human beings would be independent subjects rather than objects of capricious authority remained the dominant theme in his political work. This fundamental commitment informed every one of his tactical proposals and endowed him with the stature of leadership in Russian Marxism and, more specifically, in Menshevism.

He was not, superficially, a strong personality in the conventional sense of the term. He did not normally try to dominate colleagues; nor did he have any taste for intraparty intrigue. His influence over young radicals stemmed from his sincerity, modesty, gentleness, and selfless devotion to the cause. He rarely indulged in the self-righteousness, imperiousness, or vindictiveness that afflicted so many leaders of the movement. In his dealings with other people he generally exhibited, especially during his Menshevik period, a compassion that matched the humanity that inspired his political convictions. But by no means can he be characterized as a weak person. In fact, there was in his personality an unusual blend of flexibility and firmness, of pliability and obstinacy. Perhaps his most endearing trait was his refusal to compromise over fundamentals even at the price of following a lonely path within the movement.

Thus, in 1905 he could not be seduced by the possibility of power and strenuously argued against extremist tactics by the proletariat, a position that ultimately was adopted by his faction. Likewise, in 1920 he refused to moderate his hostility to Bolshevism, although this stand led to an ideological rupture with the faction to which he had been devoted for seventeen years. To many Marxists Bolshevism now appeared to be a necessary historical stage or even the wave of the future. But Axelrod had concluded, sooner than most Social Democrats, that not every historical phase necessarily represents moral progress. In sounding this warning Axelrod not only reaffirmed his status as the party's conscience but also as one of its most farsighted thinkers.

Bibliography

PRIMARY SOURCES

Archives

Friedrich and Victor Adler Archive (Verein für Geschichte der Arbeiterbewegung, Vienna).
Archive of Russian and East European History and Culture (Columbia University, New York).
Archive of the Second International (International Institute for Social History, Amsterdam).
Axelrod Archive (International Institute for Social History, Amsterdam).
Kautsky Archive (International Institute for Social History, Amsterdam).
Kleine Korrespondenz (International Institute for Social History, Amsterdam).
Nicolaevsky Collection (Hoover Institution on War, Revolution, and Peace, Stanford University, Stanford, California).
Police Archive at the Schweizerische Landesbibliothek (Bern, Switzerland).

Newspapers and Journals

Arbeiter-Zeitung, Vienna, 1919–1920.
Berner Tagwacht, 1914–1915.
Bote der Russischen Revolution, Stockholm, nos. 1–11, Sept. 15, 1917–Nov. 28, 1917.
Bulletin officiel de la conférence internationale ouvrière et socialiste, 1919.
Chernyi peredel (The Black Repartition), St. Petersburg, 1880–1881.
Golos (The Voice), no. 1; *Nash golos* (Our Voice), nos. 1–5; *Golos*, nos. 6–108; *Nashe slovo* (Our Word), nos. 1–279, Paris, Sept. 1, 1914–Dec. 31, 1915.
Golos sotsialdemokrata (The Voice of the Social Democrat), Paris, 1908–1912.
Iskra (The Spark), Munich-London, Geneva-Vienna, 1900–1905.
Iskra (The Spark), Petrograd, nos. 1–10, 1917.
Izvestiia soveta rabochikh i soldatskikh deputatov (News of the Soviet of Workers' and Soldiers' Deputies), Petrograd, Feb.–Dec. 1917.

Izvestiia zagranichnago sekretariata organizatsionnago komiteta rossiiskoi sotsialdemokraticheskoi rabochei partii (News of the Foreign Secretariat of the Organization Committee of the Russian Social Democratic Workers' Party), nos. 1–10, Geneva, 1915–1917.

La République Russe, Paris, 1919–1920.

Le Populaire, Paris, 1919–1921.

Les Echos de Russie, Stockholm, nos. 1–20/21, 1918.

Narodnaia volia (The People's Will), St. Petersburg, 1879–1885.

Nasha zaria (Our Dawn), St. Petersburg, 1910–1914.

Obshchina (The Commune), Geneva, 1878.

Pour la Russie, Paris, 1921.

Rabochaia gazeta (The Workers' Paper), *Luch* (The Ray), *Zaria* (The Dawn), *Klich* (The Call), *Plamia* (The Flame), *Molniia* (Lightning), *Molot* (The Hammer), *Shchit* (The Shield), *Novyi luch* (The New Ray), St. Petersburg, 1917–1918.

Rabochaia mysl' (The Workers' Thought), St. Petersburg, 1898–1902.

Rabochee delo (The Workers' Cause), Geneva, 1899–1902.

Rabochii (The Worker), St. Petersburg, 1885.

Rabochii internatsional (The Workers' International), Moscow, no. 1, 1919.

Rabotnik (The Worker), Geneva, 1896–1899.

Sotsial-demokrat (The Social Democrat), Geneva, 1888–1892.

Sotsialisticheskii vestnik (Socialist Courier), Berlin-Paris-New York, 1921–1963.

Stimmen aus Russland, Stockholm, 1918.

Vestnik narodnoi voli (The Courier of the People's Will), Geneva, 1883–1886.

Vol'noe slovo (The Free Word), Geneva, 1881–1886.

Zhivaia zhizn' (The Vital Life), St. Petersburg, 1913.

Books, Pamphlets, and Articles

Anan'in, E. A. *Izvospominanii revoliutsionera 1905–1923 g.g.* (Reminiscences of a Revolutionary 1905–1923). New York: Publication of the Inter-University Project on the History of the Menshevik Movement, 1961.

——— [E. Charskii.] "P. B. Aksel'rod ob 'antilikvidatorstve' i ego istoricheskikh korniakh" (P. B. Axelrod on "Antiliquidationism" and Its Historical Roots), *Nasha zaria,* no. 1 (1911), 56–67; no. 3 (1911), 23–30; no. 5 (1911), 20–28. (E. Charskii [Anan'in] is listed as the author of the article, but it is an account of a series of talks given by Axelrod. Axelrod helped prepare the article.)

Aptekman, O. V. *Obshchestvo 'Zemlia i volia' 70-kh gg.: Po lichnym vospominaniia* (The Society 'Land and Freedom' in the '70's: Personal Reminiscences), 2nd ed. Petrograd, 1924.

——— "Zapiski semidesiatnika" (Memoirs of a Seventy-Year Old), *Sovremennyi mir* (Contemporary World), no. 5/6 (1916), 223–236.

Axelrod, Pavel B. "Adler und die russische Sozialdemokratie," *Der Kampf,* V, no. 10 (July 1912), 437–440.

———— [N. D.] "Angliiskie tred-iuniony" (English Trade Unions), *Slovo* (The Word), no. 1 (Jan. 1879), 1–38; no. 2 (Feb. 1879), 57–92.

———— *Bor'ba sotsialisticheskikh i burzhuaznykh tendentsii v russkom revoliutsionnom dvizhenii* (The Struggle between Socialist and Bourgeois Tendencies in the Russian Revolutionary Movement), 2nd ed. St. Petersburg, 1907.

———— "Bor'ba zheleznodorozhnykh rabochikh v Shveitsarii s ikh ekspluatatorami" (The Struggle of the Railway Workers in Switzerland against Their Exploiters), *Rabotnik*, no. 3/4 (1897), 17–46.

———— "Das politische Erwachen der russischen Arbeiter und ihre Maifeier von 1891," *Die Neue Zeit*, X, part 2 (1892), 33–45, 78–84, 109–116.

———— *Die Krise und die Aufgaben der internationalen Sozialdemokratie.* Zurich: Genossenschaftsdruckerei, 1915.

———— "Die Persönlichkeit Trotzkis," in *Die Tragödie Trotzkis*, ed. Grigori Dimitrioff. Berlin: E. Laubsche, 1925, pp. 76–78.

———— "Die politische Rolle und die Taktik der deutschen Sozialdemokratie," *Die Neue Zeit*, XI, part 1 (1893), 492–502, 524–533.

———— "Die revolutionären Kräfte Russlands einst und jetzt," *Die Neue Zeit*, XIII, part 2 (1895), 261–272.

———— *Die Russische Revolution und die sozialistische Internationale: Aus dem literarischen Nachlass von Paul Axelrod*, ed. I. Tsereteli and W. Woytinsky. Jena: Karl Zwing, 1932.

———— "Discours de Paul Axelrod à la conférence de Lucerne," *La République Russe*, no. 15, Nov. 6, 1919.

———— "Doklad predstavitelia org. k-ta. P. B. Aksel'roda na Tsimmerval'dskoi konferentsii" (Address of the Representative of the Organization Committee, P. B. Axelrod, at the Zimmerwald Conference), *Izvestiia zagranichnago sekretariata organizatsionnago komiteta rossiiskoi sotsialdemokraticheskoi rabochei partii*, no. 3, Feb. 5, 1916.

———— *Dve taktiki: Doklad, prochitannyi na s'ezde v Stokgol'me* (Two Tactics: Address Delivered at the Congress in Stockholm). St. Petersburg, 1907.

————, Astrov (I. S. Poves), Iu. O. Martov, A. S. Martynov, and S. Iu. Semkovsky. "Ein Brief an Genosse Tscheidse," *Berner Tagwacht*, Apr. 5, 1917.

———— "Eine nur theilweise auf dem internationalen Arbeiterschutzkongress gehaltene Rede," *Die Neue Zeit*, XVI, part 1 (1897–1898), 45–50.

———— "German Greilikh" (Herman Greulich), *Sotsialisticheskii vestnik*, no. 22, Nov. 30, 1925, 3–9.

———— "German Greilikh" (Herman Greulich), *Zhivoe delo* (The Living Cause), no. 13, Apr. 13, 1912.

———— "Gruppa 'Osvobozhdenie truda'" (The Group "Emancipation of Labor"), *Letopis' marksizma* (Annals of Marxism), VI (1928), 82–112.

———— "Intelligenty i rabochie v nashei partii. Pis'ma k tovarishcham-rabochim. Pis'mo pervoe" (The Intelligentsia and Workers in Our Party. Letters to Comrade-Workers. First Letter), *Iskra*, no. 80, Dec. 15, 1904. (This letter was also published as a Preface in *Rabochii: Rabochie i intelligenty v nashikh organizatsiiakh* (The Worker: Workers and the Intelligentsia in Our Organizations). Geneva, 1904.

———— "Internatsional'nyi kongress sotsialisticheskogo proletariata v Parizh" (The International Congress of the Socialist Proletariat in Paris), *Znamia* (The Banner), II, no. 2, Feb. 8, 1890, 5–6; no. 3, Feb. 15, 1890, 5–6; No. 4, Feb. 22, 1890, 6.

———— "Istochniki raznoglasii mezhdu tak naz. partiitsami i tak naz. likvidatorami" (The Sources of the Differences between the So-called Party People and the So-called Liquidators), *Golos sotsialdemokrata*, III, no. 23 (Nov. 1910).

———— *Istoricheskoe polozhenie i vzaimnoe otnoshenie liberal'noi i sotsialisticheskoi demokratii v Rossii* (The Historical Situation and Reciprocal Relations between Liberals and Social Democrats in Russia). Geneva, 1898.

———— "Istoricheskoi smysl internatsional'nogo chestvovaniia pamiati Bebelia" (The Historical Meaning of the International Celebration in Memory of Bebel), *Nasha zaria*, no. 12 (1913), 3–14.

———— "Itogi mezhdunarodnoi sotsial-demokratii" (The Record of International Social Democracy), *Iskra*, no. 1, Dec. 1900; no. 2, Feb. 1901.

———— "Itogi sotsial'no-demokraticheskoi partii v Germanii" (The Record of the Social Democratic Party in Germany), *Obshchina*, no. 1 (1878), 26–30; no. 2 (1878), 22–25; no. 3/4 (1878), 35–44; no. 6/7 (1878), 33–41; no. 8/9 (1878), 40–49.

———— "Iz besedy s P. B. Aksel'rodom o nashikh raznoglasiiakh" (From Conversations with P. B. Axelrod about Our Differences), *Nashe slovo*, no. 87, May 12, 1915; no. 90, May 16, 1915.

———— "Izvlechenie iz 'Otveta . . .'" (Extracts from the "Response . . ."), *Znamia*, I, no. 15, June 1, 1889, 1–2; no. 16, June 15, 1889, 2.

———— "K. Kautskii i Sovetskaia Rossiia" (K. Kautsky and Soviet Russia), *Sotsialisticheskii vestnik*, no. 21, Nov. 14, 1925, 5–7.

———— "K iubileiu Internatsionala i 70-letiiu K. Kautskogo" (On the Anniversary of the International and the Seventieth Birthday of K. Kautsky), *Sotsialisticheskii vestnik*, no. 21, Nov. 10, 1924, 9–10.

————, P. Lapinskii, and L. [Iu.] Martov. *Kriegs-und Friedensprobleme der Arbeiterklasse. Entwurf eines Manifestes vorgelegt der zweiten Zimmerwalder Konferenz*. Zurich: Genossenschaftsdruckerei, [1916].

———— "Kto fal'sifitsiruet?" (Who Falsifies?), *Iskra*, no. 42, June 15, 1903.

———— *Kto izmenil sotsializmu?* (Who Betrayed Socialism?). New York: Narodopravstvo, 1919.

———— "K voprosu o sotsialisticheskoi interventsii 1920 g." (On the Question of Socialist Intervention, 1920), Nicolaevsky Collection, Hoover Institution.

———— *K voprosu o sovremennykh zadachakh i taktike russkikh sotsialdemokratov* (On the Question of the Contemporary Tasks and Tactics of Russian Social Democrats). Geneva: Union of Russian Social Democrats, 1898.

―――― "K voprosu ob istochnike i znachenii nashikh organizatsionnykh raznoglasii. Iz perepiska s Kautskim" (On the Question of the Sources and Significance of Our Organizational Differences. From the Correspondence with Kautsky), *Iskra*, no. 68, June 15, 1904.

―――― "Le camarade Axelrod nous en expose les tragiques conséquences," *Le Populaire*, Nov. 7, 1921.

―――― "La 'paix immédiate' des Bolchéviks," *Les Echos de Russie*, no. 6/7 (1918).

―――― "L'Enquête socialiste en Russie," *La République Russe*, no. 5, Mar. 1, 1920.

―――― "Les Menchéviks, les Soviets et l'Internationale," *La République Russe*, no. 10, June 1, 1920.

―――― "Les socialistes russes et la paix Bolchévik," *Les Echos de Russie*, no. 8/9 (1918).

―――― "Lettre aux camarades suédois," *La République Russe*, no. 1, Jan. 3, 1920.

―――― "L'opinion de P. Axelrod sur la décision du Labour Party," *La République Russe*, no. 6, Mar. 15, 1920.

―――― "Na ocherednye temy" (On Current Topics), *Nasha zaria*, III, no. 6 (1912), 8–20.

―――― *Narodnaia duma i rabochii s'ezd* (The National Duma and the Workers' Congress). Geneva: Iskra, 1905. (Second edition, which contained new material, was published in St. Petersburg, 1907.)

―――― "Ob'edinenie rossiiskoi sotsialdemokratii i eia zadachi" (The Unification of Russian Social Democracy and Its Tasks), *Iskra*, no. 55, Dec. 15, 1903; no. 57, Jan. 15, 1904.

―――― "Otnoshenie revoliutsionnoi intelligentsii v Rossii k bor'be za politicheskuiu svobodu" (The Attitude of the Revolutionary Intelligentsia in Russia toward the Struggle for Political Freedom), *Znamia*, I, no. 10, Mar. 23, 1889, 1–2; no. 11, Mar. 30, 1889, 1–2; no. 12, Apr. 13, 1889, 1–2; no. 13, May 4, 1889, 2–3; no. 14, May 18, 1889, 1–2.

―――― "P. B. Aksel'rod o bor'be za mir" (P. B. Axelrod on the Struggle for Peace), *Izvestiia soveta rabochikh i soldatskikh deputatov* (Petrograd), no. 60, May 7, 1917.

―――― "P. B. Aksel'rod o taktike s.-d. v russkoi revoliutsii" (P. B. Axelrod on Social Democratic Tactics in the Russian Revolution), *Rabochaia gazeta*, no. 48, May 5, 1917.

―――― "P. B. Aksel'rod o zadachakh sotsialdemokratii" (P. B. Axelrod on the Tasks of Social Democracy), *Tovarishch* (Comrade), no. 153, Dec. 31, 1906–Jan. 13, 1907.

―――― "P. B. Aksel'rod ob edinom fronte" (P. B. Axelrod on the United Front), *Sotsialisticheskii vestnik*, no. 7, Apr. 3, 1922, 5.

——— "P. B. Aksel'rod ob evreiskom rabochem dvizhenii" (P. B. Axelrod on the Jewish Workers' Movement), *Nasha rabochaia gazeta* (Our Workers' Paper), no. 28, June 6, 1914.

——— "Padenie evreiskogo kagala v Shklove" (The Decline of the Jewish Kahal in Shklov), *Mogilevskie gubernskie vedomosti* (The Gazette of the Mogilev Province), no. 59, July 29, 1870.

——— "Pamiati Arona Isakovicha Zundelevicha" (In Memory of Aron Isakovich Zundelevich), *Sotsialisticheskii vestnik*, no. 16, Sept. 16, 1923, 6.

——— "Pamiati Martova" (In Memory of Martov), *Sotsialisticheskii vestnik*, special issue, Apr. 10, 1923, 2–3.

——— "Perekhodnyi moment nashei partii" (The Transitional Moment in Our Party), *Obshchina*, no. 8/9 (1878), 21–33.

——— *Perezhitoe i peredumannoe* (Experiences and Reflections). Berlin: Z. I. Grzhebin, 1923.

——— [Pavel Axelrod.] "Pis'ma o rabochem dvizhenii" (Letters on the Labor Movement) and "Khronika rabochego dvizheniia" (Chronicle of the Labor Movement), *Vol'noe slovo*, Aug. 1881–Apr. 1882.

——— "Pis'mo frantsuzskomu sotsialisticheskomu kongressu" (Letter to the French Socialist Congress), *Izvestiia zagranichnago komiteta rossiiskoi sotsialdemokraticheskoi rabochei partii*, no. 10, Mar. 1, 1917.

——— "Pis'mo P. B. Aksel'roda o bor'be za mir" (P. B. Axelrod's Letter on the Struggle for Peace), *Rabochaia gazeta*, no. 18, Mar. 18, 1917.

——— "Pis'mo v redaktsiiu" (Letter to the Editorial Board), *Nashe slovo*, no. 225, Oct. 27, 1915.

——— *Pis'mo v redaktsiiu 'Rabochago dela'* (Letter to the Editorial Board of 'Rabochee delo'). Geneva: Union of Russian Social Democrats, 1899.

——— "Politicheskaia rol' sotsial'noi demokratii i poslednie vybory v germanskii reikhstag" (The Political Role of Social Democracy and the Last Election to the German Reichstag), *Sotsial-demokrat*, II (1890), 1–42; III (1890), 23–40; IV (1892), 3–45.

——— "Po povodu novogo narodnogo bedstviia" (Apropos of the New National Disaster), *Rabotnik*, no. 5/6 (1899), 159–212.

——— "Po povodu odnoi zametki" (Apropos a Certain Note), *Sotsial-demokrat*, no. 1, Sept. 17, 1906, 1.

——— "Posledniaia izbiratel'naia pobeda avstriiskikh rabochikh" (The Last Electoral Victory of Austrian Labor), *Iskra*, no. 6, July 1901.

——— "Predislovie k kn. Pis'ma K. Marksa, F. Engel'sa i dr. k. F. Zorge i dr." (Preface to the Book: Letters by K. Marx, F. Engels and Others to F. Sorge and Others), in *Pis'ma K. Marksa, F. Engel'sa i dr. k. F. Zorge i dr.*, ed. P. Axelrod. St. Petersburg, 1908.

——— Preface in A. Charasch, *Lenin*, Zurich: O. Füssli, 1920.

——— Preface and Epilogue in [A. Kremer and Iu. Martov,] *Ob agitatsii* (On Agitation). Geneva, 1896.

——— Preface in V. I. Lenin, *Zadachi russkikh sotsial-demokratov* (The Tasks of Russian Social Democrats). Geneva, 1898.

———— Preface in L. [Iu.] Martov, *Krasnoe znamia v Rossii* (The Red Flag in Russia). Geneva: Sotsialdemokrat, 1900.

———— Preface in L. [Iu.] Martov, *Proletarskaia bor'ba v Rossii* (The Proletarian Struggle in Russia). St. Petersburg, 1906.

———— "Prezhde i teper'. (O russkom rabochem dvizhenii)" (In Former Times and Now. [Concerning the Russian Labor Movement]), *Zhivaia zhizn'*, nos. 3, 6, 9, 13, July 13, 17, 20, 25, 1913.

———— *Rabochee dvizhenie i sotsial'naia demokratiia* (The Labor Movement and Social Democracy). Geneva, 1885.

———— "Rabochee dvizhenie v nachale shestidesiatykh godov i teper' " (The Labor Movement in the Early Sixties and Now), *Sotsial-demokrat*, I (1888), 132–188.

———— *Rabochii klass i revoliutsionnoe dvizhenie v Rossii* (The Working Class and the Revolutionary Movement in Russia). St. Petersburg, 1907. (Translation of some of Axelrod's German articles.)

———— "Rech' G. Aleksandrovicha [Axelrod] na sotsialisticheskom kongresse v Khure" (Address by G. Alexandrovich [Axelrod] at the Socialist Congress in Chur), *Vol'noe slovo*, no. 13 (1881), 5–8.

———— "Rumänien," *Jahrbuch für Sozialwissenschaft und Sozialpolitik*, II (1881), 319–327.

———— "Russland," *Jahrbuch für Sozialwissenschaft und Sozialpolitik*, II (1881), 261–306.

———— "Russland und der Krieg," *Berner Tagwacht*, Oct. 26, 27, 1914.

———— "S chego nachat'?" (Where to Begin?), *Izvestiia zagranichnago sekretariata organizatsionnago komiteta rossiiskoi sotsialdemokraticheskoi rabochei partii*, no. 2, June 19, 1915.

———— "Sergei Krawtschinsky," *Arbeiter-Zeitung* (Vienna), no. 8 (1896).

———— "Sotsializm i melkaia burzhuaziia" (Socialism and the Petty Bourgeoisie), *Vestnik narodnoi voli*, I (1884), 159–185; II (1884), 203–214.

———— "Stachka v Shveitsarii i Germanii" (Strikes in Switzerland and Germany), *Rabotnik*, no. 3/4 (1897), 145–159.

———— "The Crisis in the International," *The Socialist Review*, XIII (1916), 234–244.

———— "Tov. P. B. Aksel'rod o bol'shevizme i bor'be s nim" (Comrade P. B. Axelrod on Bolshevism and the Struggle against It), *Sotsialisticheskii vestnik*, no. 6, Apr. 20, 1921, 3–7; no. 7, May 4, 1921, 3–5.

———— "Tseli i sredstva vsemirnoi sotsialdemokratii" (Aims and Methods of World-Wide Social Democracy), *Rabotnik*, no. 1/2 (1896), 1–52.

———— "Uchenie Genri Dzhordzha" (The Teachings of Henry George), *Delo* (The Cause), no. 9 (1883), 50–73. (I was unable to locate the second part of the article, which appeared in *Delo*, no. 10.)

———— "Unsere Aufgabe," *Stimmen aus Russland*, no. 1 (1918), 1–3.

———— "Vil'gelm Libknekht" (Wilhelm Liebknecht), *Iskra*, no. 1, Dec. 1900.

————, Astrov (I. S. Poves), Iu. O. Martov, A. S. Martynov, and S. Iu. Semkovsky. *Vozrozhdenie internatsionala i bor'ba za mir. (Pis'mo k tovarishcham v Rossii*) (The Revival of the International and the Struggle for Peace. [Letter to Comrades in Russia]). Switzerland, 1915.

——— "Vse dlia naroda i posredstvom naroda. (Otvet na pis'mo I. P.)" (Everything for the People by Means of the People. [Response to I. P.'s Letter]), *Vol'noe slovo,* no. 19 (1881), 11–17.

——— "Vybory v germanskii reikhstag i sotsial'no-demokraticheskaia partiia" (The Election to the German Reichstag and the Social Democratic Party), *Rabochii,* no. 2 (1885), 67–76.

——— "Vynuzhdennoe ob'iasnenie" (A Forced Explanation), in *Neobkhodimoe dopolnenie k 'dnevnikam' G. V. Plekhanova* (A Necessary Supplement to G. V. Plekhanov's 'Diary'). Paris: Editors of *Golos sotsialdemokrata,* 1910.

——— "Zadachi rabochei intelligentsii v Rossii" (The Tasks of the Workers' Intelligentsia in Russia), *Sotsialist,* no. 1 (June 1889).

———, Astrov (I. S. Poves), Iu. O. Martov, A. S. Martynov, and S. Iu. Semkovsky. *Zadachi rossiiskago proletariata (pis'mo k tovarishcham v Rossii)* (The Tasks of the Russian Proletariat [Letter to Comrades in Russia]). Geneva, 1915.

Balabanova, Angelica. "Die Zimmerwalder Bewegung 1914–1919," *Archiv für die Geschichte des Sozialismus und der Arbeiterbewegung,* XII (1926), 310–413; XIII (1928), 232–284.

Bernstein, Eduard. *Die Voraussetzungen des Sozialismus und die Aufgaben der Sozialdemokratie.* Stuttgart: J. H. W. Dietz, 1899.

——— "Pavel Aksel'rod, internatsionalist" (Pavel Axelrod, Internationalist), *Sotsialisticheskii vestnik,* no. 15/16, Aug. 18, 1925, 23–25.

"Bol'sheviki na Briussel'skom soveshchanii 1914 g." (The Bolsheviks at the Brussels Conference in 1914), *Istoricheskii arkhiv* (Historical Archive), no. 4 (1959), 9–38.

Bonch-Bruevich, V. D. *Izbrannye sochineniia* (Selected Works), vols. I and II. Moscow, 1959–1961.

Cherevanin, N. [F. A. Lipkin.] *Londonskii s'ezd RSDRP 1907 g.* (The London Congress of the RSDRP 1907). St. Petersburg, 1907.

——— *Organizatsionnyi vopros* (The Organizational Question). Geneva: Russian Social Democratic Workers' Party, 1904.

——— *Proletariat v revoliutsii* (The Proletariat in the Revolution). Moscow, 1907.

Chetvertyi (ob'edinitel'nyi) s'ezd RSDRP: Protokoly (The Fourth [Unification] Congress of the RSDRP: Protocols). Moscow, 1959.

Dan, F. "Bor'ba za legal'nost'" (The Struggle for Legality), *Golos sotsialdemokrata,* III, no. 19/20 (Jan.–Feb. 1910).

——— *Dva goda skitanii (1919–1921)* (Two Years of Wandering [1919–1921]). Berlin: H. S. Hermann, 1922.

———, L. [Iu. O.] Martov, and A. S. Martynov. *Otkrytoe pis'mo P. B. Aksel'rodu i V. I. Zasulich* (Public Letter to P. B. Axelrod and V. I. Zasulich). N. p., 1912.

———— "Paul Axelrod," *Die Gesellschaft,* V (1928), 485–496.

Dan, L. "Okolo redaktsii 'Iskry.' Iz vospominanii" (Around the Editorial Board of "Iskra." Reminiscences), *Protiv techeniia* (Against the Current), II (1954), 57–69.

Deich, L., ed. *Gruppa "Osvobozhdenie truda"* (The Group "Emancipation of Labor"), 6 vols. Moscow, 1923–1928.

———— "O sblizhenii i razryve s narodovol'tsami" (Concerning the Rapprochement and Break with the Narodovol'tsy), *Proletarskaia revoliutsiia,* no. 20 (1923), 5–54.

———— "O vospominaniia P. B. Aksel'roda" (Concerning P. B. Axelrod's Reminiscences), *Proletarskaia revoliutsiia,* no. 22 (1923), 176–201.

———— *Rol' evreev v russkom revoliutsionnom dvizheniem* (The Role of Jews in the Russian Revolutionary Movement), 2nd ed. Moscow, 1925.

Ein Leben für den Sozialismus: Erinnerungen an Karl Kautsky. Hannover: J. H. W. Dietz, 1954.

Ermanskii, O. A. *Iz perezhitogo (1887–1921 g.g.)* (From Experiences [1887–1921]). Moscow, 1927.

Gankin, Olga, and H. H. Fisher, eds. *The Bolsheviks and the World War: The Origins of the Third International.* Stanford: Stanford University Press, 1940.

Garvi, P. A. "Aksel'rod i taktika proletarskoi bor'by" (Axelrod and the Tactics of Proletarian Struggle), *Sotsialisticheskii vestnik,* no. 8/9, May 3, 1928, 9–14.

———— "Episoden der russischen Revolution. Aus den Erinnerungen von Peter Garwy" (Translated by George Garvy), *Archiv für Sozialgeschichte,* V (1965), 443–451.

———— "Iz neopublikovannykh vospominanii" (From Unpublished Memoirs), on deposit at the Inter-University Project on the History of the Menshevik Movement, Columbia University.

———— "P. B. Aksel'rod i men'shevizm" (P. B. Axelrod and Menshevism), *Sotsialisticheskii vestnik,* no. 15/16, Aug. 18, 1925, 10–13.

———— *Vospominaniia: Peterburg—1906* (Reminiscences: St. Petersburg—1906). New York: Publication of the Inter-University Project on the History of the Menshevik Movement, 1961.

———— *Vospominaniia: Peterburg-Odessa-Vena—1912* (Reminiscences: St. Petersburg-Odessa-Vienna—1912). New York: Publication of the Inter-University Project on the History of the Menshevik Movement, 1961.

———— *Vospominaniia sotsialdemokrata: stat'i o zhizni i deiatel'nosti P. A. Garvi* (Reminiscences of a Social Democrat: Articles about the Life and Activities of P. A. Garvi). New York: Privately published by S. Garvy, 1946.

Grigor'ev, Raf. "P. B. Aksel'rod ob internatsionale i voine" (P. B. Axelrod on the International and the War), *Golos,* nos. 86 and 87, Dec. 22, 23, 1914 (Though written by Grigor'ev, the article is based on an interview given by Axelrod, who is quoted extensively.)

Gurevich, G. "Sredi revoliutsionerov v Tsiurikhe" (Among Revolutionaries in Zurich), *Evreiskaia letopis'* (Jewish Annals), IV (1926), 98–103.

Hahlweg, Werner, ed. *Lenins Rückkehr nach Russland. Die deutschen Akten.* Leiden: E. J. Brill, 1957.

Haupt, Georges, ed. *Correspondance entre Lénine et Camille Huysmans 1905– 1914.* The Hague: Mouton, 1963.

———— *Le congrès manqué: l'Internationale à la veille de la première guerre mondiale.* Paris: F. Maspero, 1965.

Iz arkhiva P. B. Aksel'roda, 1881–1896 (From P. B. Axelrod's Archive, 1881– 1896), ed. W. S. Woytinsky, B. I. Nicolaevsky, and L. O. Tsederbaum-Dan. Berlin: Russisches Revolutionsarchiv, 1924.

"K istorii gvozdevshchiny" (On the History of the Gvozdev Movement), *Krasnyi arkhiv* (The Red Archives), no. 67 (1934), 28–92.

"K istorii 'Rabochei gruppy' pri Tsentral'nom voenno-promyshlennom komitete" (On the History of the "Workers' Groups" under the Central Military-Industrial Committee), *Krasnyi arkhiv,* no. 57 (1933), 43–84.

K. Marks, F. Engel's i revoliutsionnaia Rossiia (K. Marx, F. Engels and Revolutionary Russia). Moscow, 1967.

Kautsky, Karl. "Die Differenzen unter den russischen Sozialdemokraten," *Die Neue Zeit,* XXIII, part 2 (1905), 68–79.

———— *Die Internationale und Sowjetrussland.* Berlin: J. H. W. Dietz, 1925.

———— "Paul Axelrod," *Der Kampf,* XXI, no. 5 (May 1928), 185–193.

———— "Was Axelrod uns gab," *Die Gesellschaft,* II (1925), 117–125.

Kommunisticheskaia partiia sovetskogo soiuza v rezoliutsiiakh i resheniiakh s'ezdov, konferentsii i plenumov Ts. K. (The Communist Party of the Soviet Union in Resolutions and Decisions of Congresses, Conferences, and Central Committee Plenary Meetings), 3 vols., 7th ed. Moscow, 1954.

[Kremer, A. and Iu. Martov.] *Ob agitatsii* (On Agitation). Geneva: Union of Russian Social Democrats, 1896.

L. G. [G. D. Leiteizen.] *Rabochii s'ezd ili s'ezd rabochii partii* (A Workers' Congress or a Congress of a Workers' Party). St. Petersburg, 1906.

Lademacher, Horst, ed. *Die Zimmerwalder Bewegung: Protokolle und Korrespondenz,* 2 vols. The Hague: Mouton, 1967.

Larin, Iurii. *Shirokaia rabochaia partiia i rabochii s'ezd* (A Broad Workers' Party and a Workers' Congress). Moscow, 1907.

Lenin, V. I. *Sochineniia* (Works), 30 vols., 3rd ed. Moscow, 1926–1937.

Leninskii sbornik (Lenin Collection), vols. II, III, IV, X. Ed. L. B. Kamenev. Moscow, 1924–1938.

Liadov, M. *Iz zhizni partii v 1903–1907 godakh (vospominaniia)* (From My Life in the Party in the Years 1903–1907 [Reminiscences]). Moscow, 1956.

Lunacharsky, Anatoly. *Revolutionary silhouettes.* Tr. Michael Glenny. London: Penguin Press, 1967.

Luxemburg, Rosa. "Organisationsfragen der russischen Sozialdemokratie," *Die Neue Zeit,* XXII, part 2 (1904), 484–492, 529–535.

Martov, L. [Iu. O.] "Ein Brief an die deutschen Genossen" *Der Sozialist*, IV, no. 52 (1918), 10–12.

———— *Geschichte der russischen Sozialdemokratie: Mit einem Nachtrag von Th. Dan: Die Sozialdemokratie Russlands nach dem Jahre 1918*. Tr. Alexander Stein. Berlin: J. H. W. Dietz, 1926.

————, ed. *Oborona revoliutsii i sotsialdemokratiia*. (*Sbornik*) (In Defense of the Revolution and of Social Democracy. [A Collection]). Moscow, 1920.

———— "Po povodu pis'ma tov. P. B. Aksel'roda" (Apropos a Letter by Comrade P. B. Axelrod), *Sotsialisticheskii vestnik*, no. 8, May 20, 1921, 3–6.

———— *Zapiski sotsial-demokrata* (Memoirs of a Social Democrat). Moscow, 1922.

———— *Spasiteli ili uprazdniteli?* (Saviors or Destroyers?). Paris: Gnatovsky, 1911.

"Materialy k istorii pervogo s'ezda" (Material on the History of the First Congress), *Proletarskaia revoliutsiia* (The Proletarian Revolution), no. 74 (1928), 152–169.

Menders, F. "P. B. Aksel'rod i latviiskaia sots.-demokratiia" (P. B. Axelrod and the Latvian Social Democracy), *Sotsialisticheskii vestnik*, no. 15/16, Aug. 18, 1925, 18–19.

Nicolaevsky, B. I. *Men'sheviki v dni oktiabr'skogo perevorota* (The Mensheviks during the October Revolution). New York: Publication of the Inter-University Project on the History of Menshevism, 1962.

O vserossiiskom rabochem s'ezde. Sbornik statei. (On the All-Russian Workers' Congress. A Collection of Articles). Moscow, 1907.

Otvet redaktsii 'Rabochago dela' na 'pis'mo' P. Aksel'roda i 'Vademecum' G. Plekhanova (Reply of the Editorial Board of 'Rabochee delo' to P. Axelrod's 'Letter' and to G. Plekhanov's 'Vademecum'). Geneva: Union of Russian Social Democrats, 1900.

Perepiska G. V. Plekhanova i P. B. Aksel'roda (Correspondence of G. V. Plekhanov with P. B. Axelrod), 2 vols. Ed. B. I. Nicolaevsky, P. A. Berlin, and W. S. Woytinsky. Moscow, 1925.

"Perepiska G. V. Plekhanova, P. B. Aksel'roda i V. I. Zasulich s L. Iogikhesom (Grozovskim, Tyshkoi), 1891–1892" (Correspondence of G. V. Plekhanov, P. B. Axelrod, and V. I. Zasulich with L. Jogiches [Grozovsky, Tyshka]), *Proletarskaia revoliutsiia*, no. 11/12 (1928), 255–285.

Pervaia obshcherusskaia konferentsiia partiinykh rabotnikov. Otdel'noe prilozhenie k No. 100 'Iskry' (The First All-Russian Conference of Party Workers. Supplement to 'Iskra' no. 100). Geneva, 1905.

Piatyi (Londonskii) s'ezd RSDRP: Protokoly (The Fifth [London] Congress of the RSDRP: Protocols). Moscow, 1963.

Pis'ma P. B. Aksel'roda i Iu. O Martova, 1901–1916 (Letters of P. B. Axelrod and Iu. O. Martov, 1901–1916). Ed. F. Dan, B. I. Nicolaevsky, and L. Tsederbaum-Dan. Berlin: Russisches Revolutionsarchiv, 1924.

Plekhanov, G. V. *Sochineniia* (Works), 24 vols., 2nd ed. Ed. D. Riazanov. Moscow, 1923–1927.

———— *Vademecum dlia redaktsii 'Rabochago dela,' sbornik materialov* (Vademecum for the Editors of 'Rabochee delo,' a Collection of Materials). Geneva, 1900.

Popov, A. [N. Vorob'ev.] "Stranichka vospominaniia o rabote v 'mezhduraionke.' S predisloviem A. Shliapnikova" (A Little Page of Reminiscences about Work in the "Interborough Organization of the United Socialist Democrats." With a preface by A. Shliapnikov), *Proletarskaia revoliutsiia,* no. 22 (1923), 95–111.

Pribyleva-Korba, A. P. *"Narodnaia volia": Vospominaniia o 1870–1880-kh g.g.* ("The Peoples' Will": Recollections of the 1870's and 1880's). Moscow, 1926.

Protokoll der Internationalen Sozialistischen Konferenz in Wien vom 22. bis 27. Februar 1921. Vienna: Verlag der Wiener Volksbuchhandlung, 1921.

Protokoly II-go ocherednogo s'ezda Zagranichnago Ligi Russkoi Revoliutsionnoi Sotsial-demokratii (Protocols of the Second Congress of the Foreign League of Russian Social Democracy). Geneva, 1904.

Renaudel, Pierre. *L'Internationale à Berne. Faits et documents.* Paris: B. Grasset, 1919.

Rusanov, N. S. *Kak my podgotovliali stokgol'mskuiu konferentsiiu: Vospominaniia chlena stokgol'mskoi delegatsii N. S. Rusanova* (How We Prepared the Stockholm Conference: Reminiscences of N. S. Rusanov, Member of the Stockholm Delegation). Archive of Russian and East European History and Culture, Columbia University. N. p., n. d.

Shcheglo, V. A. *O rabochem s'ezde* (On the Workers' Congress). St. Petersburg, 1906.

Shklovskii, G. "Tsimmerval'd" (Zimmerwald), *Proletarskaia revoliutsiia,* no. 44 (1925), 73–106.

Shliapnikov, A. *Kanun semnadtsatogo goda* (On the Eve of the Year Seventeen), part II. 3rd ed. Moscow, 1923.

Shotman, A. "Na vtorom s'ezde partii" (At the Second Party Congress), *Proletarskaia revoliutsiia,* no. 60 (1927), 214–232; no. 77/78 (1928), 62–92.

Sotsial-demokraticheskoe dvizhenie v Rossii. Materialy (The Social Democratic Movement in Russia. Materials). Ed. A. N. Potresov and B. I. Nicolaevsky. Moscow, 1928.

Sotsial-demokratiia i revoliutsiia. Sbornik dokumentov (Social Democracy and Revolution. A Collection of Documents). Odessa, 1920.

Stefanovich, Iakov. "Nashi zadachi v sele" (Our Tasks in the Village), *Obshchina,* no. 8/9 (1878), 33–38.

Steklov, Iu. "V ssylke i v emigratsii (ideinye konflikty)" (In Exile and in Emigration [Ideological Conflicts]), *Proletarskaia revoliutsiia,* no. 17 (1923), 193–250.

Sukhanov, N. *Zapiski o revoliutsii* (Memoirs of the Revolution), 7 vols. Moscow, 1922.

Sukhomlin, V. "Iz epokhi upadka partii 'Nar. volia'" (From the Era of the

Decline of the Party "The People's Will"), *Katorga i ssylka* (Penal Servitude and Exile), no. 25 (1926), 29–48.

Tretii s'ezd RSDRP: Protokoly (The Third Congress of the RSDRP: Protocols). Moscow, 1959.

Trotsky, N. [L.] *Nashi politicheskie zadachi* (Our Political Tasks). Geneva: Russian Social Democratic Workers' Party, 1904.

—— *Vtoroi s'ezd ros. sots.-dem. rabochei partii. Otchet sibirskoi delegatsii* (The Second Congress of the Russian Social Democratic Workers' Party. Report of the Siberian Delegation). Geneva, 1903.

Tsereteli, I. "P. B. Aksel'rod (Cherty dlia kharakteristiki)" (P. B. Axelrod [Outline of His Personality]), *Sotsialisticheskii vestnik*, no. 15/16, Aug. 18, 1925, 16–18.

—— *Vospominaniia o fevral'skoi revoliutsii* (Memoirs of the February Revolution), 2 vols. The Hague: Mouton, 1963.

Unabhängige sozialdemokratische Partei Deutschlands. *Protokoll über die Verhandlungen des ausserordentlichen Parteitages vom 2. bis 6. März 1919.* Berlin: Freiheit, 1919.

Valentinov, Nikolay. *Encounters with Lenin.* Tr. Paul Rosta and Brian Pearce. London: Oxford University Press, 1968.

Victor Adler. Briefwechsel mit August Bebel und Karl Kautsky, sowie mit anderen deutschen Sozialdemokraten. Collected and explained by Friedrich Adler. Vienna: Verlag der Wiener Volksbuchhandlung, 1954.

Volk, S. S., ed. *Revoliutsionnoe narodnichestvo 70-kh godov XIX veka* (Revolutionary Populism in the '70's of the 19th Century), vol. II. Moscow, 1965.

Vserossiiskii rabochii s'ezd. Sbornik statei (The All-Russian Workers' Congress. A Collection of Articles). Moscow, 1907.

Vtoroi s'ezd RSDRP: Protokoly (The Second Congress of the RSDRP: Protocols). Moscow, 1959.

Woytinsky, W. S. "Poslednie gody" (The Last Years), *Sotsialisticheskii vestnik*, no. 8/9, May 3, 1928, 5–13.

Za god: Sbornik statei (For the Last Year: A Collection of Articles). Petrograd, 1919.

SECONDARY SOURCES

Anin, David S. "The February Revolution: Was the Collapse Inevitable?" *Soviet Studies*, XVIII (Apr. 1967), 435–457.

Anweiler, Oskar. *Die Rätebewegung in Russland 1905–1921.* Leiden: E. J. Brill, 1958.

—— "Die russische Revolution von 1905," *Jahrbücher für Geschichte Osteuropas*, III, no. 2, New Ser. (1955), 161–193.

[Aptekman, O. V.] *Pavel Borisovich Aksel'rod: Ego zhizn', literaturnaia i prakticheskaia deiatel'nost'* (Pavel Borisovich Axelrod: His Life, Literary and Practical Activities) Archive of Russian and East European History and Culture, Columbia University. N. p., n. d.

Aronson, G. *Men'shevizm v 1905–1914 g.g. Chast' I: Men'shevizm v 1905 godu* (Menshevism 1905–1914. Part I: Menshevism in 1905). New York: Publication of the Inter-University Project on the History of the Menshevik Project, n. d.

Arsen'ev, Iu. M. *Lenin i sotsial-demokraticheskaia emigratsiia 1900–1904 g. g.* (Lenin and the Social Democratic Emigration, 1900–1904). Moscow, 1971.

Ascher, Abraham. "Axelrod and Kautsky," *Slavic Review,* XXVI (Mar. 1967), 94–112.

———— "Pavel Axelrod: A Conflict between Jewish Loyalty and Revolutionary Dedication," *Russian Review,* XXIV (July 1965), 249–265.

———— "Russian Marxism and the German Revolution, 1917–1920," *Archiv für Sozialgeschichte,* VI/VII (1966/67), 391–439.

————, tr. "The Coming Storm. The Austro-Hungarian Embassy on Russia's Internal Crisis, 1902–06," *Survey: A Journal of Soviet and East European Studies,* no. 53 (Oct. 1964), 148–164.

Avineri, Shlomo. *The Social and Political Thought of Karl Marx.* Cambridge: Cambridge University Press, 1968.

Balabanov, M. *Ot 1905 k 1917. Massovoe rabochee dvizhenie* (From 1905 to 1917. The Mass Labor Movement). Moscow, 1927.

Baron, Samuel H. *Plekhanov: The Father of Russian Marxism.* Stanford: Stanford University Press, 1963.

———— "Plekhanov's Russia: The Impact of the West upon an 'Oriental' Society," *Journal of the History of Ideas,* XIX (June 1958), 388–404.

Belokonskii, I. P. "K istorii zemskogo dvizhenie v Rossii" (On the History of the Zemstvo Movement in Russia), *Istoricheskii sbornik* (Historical Collection). St. Petersburg, 1907, 25–125.

———— *Zemstvo i konstitutsiia* (Zemstvo and Constitution). Moscow, 1910.

Bogucharskii, V. Ia. *Iz istorii politicheskoi bor'by v 70-kh i 80-kh gg. XIX veka: Partiia 'Narodnoi voli'* (From the History of the Political Struggle in the '70's and '80's of the 19th Century: The 'People's Will' Party). Moscow, 1912.

Bourguina, Anna. *Russian Social Democracy. The Menshevik Movement. A Bibliography.* Stanford: Hoover Institution on War, Revolution, and Peace, 1968.

Brachman, Botho. *Russische Sozialdemokraten in Berlin 1895–1914.* Berlin: Akademie-Verlag, 1962.

Braunthal, Julius. *Geschichte der Internationalen,* 2 vols. Hannover: J. H. W. Dietz, 1961–1963.

Brennan, J. F. "The Origins, Development and Failure of Russian Social Democratic Economism, 1886–1903," unpub. diss., University of California, Berkeley, 1963.

Chamberlin, William Henry. *The Russian Revolution 1917–1921,* 2 vols., 5th printing. New York: Macmillan Company, 1960.

Dan, F. *Proiskhozhdenie bol'shevizma* (The Origins of Bolshevism). New York: New Democracy Books, 1946.

DeKay, John. *The Spirit of the International at Berne*. Lucerne: the author, 1919.

Deutscher, Isaac. *The Prophet Armed. Trotsky: 1879–1921*. London: Oxford University Press, 1954.

Donneur, André. *Histoire de l'Union des Partis Socialistes pour l'Action Internationale (1920–1923)*. Sudbury, Ontario: Librarie de l'Université Laurentienne, 1967.

Dvinov, B. *Pervaia mirovaia voina i rossiiskaia sotsialdemokratiia* (The First World War and Russian Social Democracy). New York: Publication of the Inter-University Project on the History of the Menshevik Movement, 1962.

Fainsod, Merle. *International Socialism and the World War*, 2nd printing. New York: Octagon Press, Inc., 1966.

Fenster, P. A. "V. I. Lenin i marksistskii sbornik 'Rabotnik' " (V. I. Lenin and the Marxist Collection "Rabotnik"), *Istoriia SSSR* (History of the USSR), no. 2 (1964), 104–112.

Fischer, Alexander. *Russische Sozialdemokratie und bewaffneter Aufstand im Jahre 1905*. Wiesbaden: Otto Harrassowitz, 1967.

Footman, David. *Red Prelude: A Life of A. I. Zheliabov*, 2nd ed. London: Barrie & Rockliff; Cresset, 1968.

Frankel, Jonathan. "Economism: A Heresy Exploited," *Slavic Review*, XXII (June 1963), 263–284.

——— *Vladimir Akimov on the Dilemmas of Russian Marxism 1895–1903*. Cambridge: Cambridge University Press, 1969.

——— "Volontarisme, Maximalisme: Le Groupe Osvoboždenie Truda 1883–1892," *Cahiers du Monde Russe et Soviétique*, IX (1968), 294–323.

Gay, Peter. *The Dilemma of Democratic Socialism: Eduard Bernstein's Challenge to Marx*. New York: Columbia University Press, 1952.

Getzler, Israel. *Martov: A Political Biography of a Russian Social Democrat*. Cambridge: Cambridge University Press, 1967.

Geyer, Dietrich. "Die russische Parteispaltung im Urteil der deutschen Sozialdemokratie 1903–1905," *International Review of Social History*, III (nos. 2, 3, 1958), 195–219, 418–444.

——— *Lenin in der Russischen Sozialdemokratie. Die Arbeiterbewegung im Zarenreich als Organisationsproblem der revolutionären Intelligenz 1890–1903*. Cologne: Böhlau Verlag, 1962.

Graubard, Stephen R. *British Labour and the Russian Revolution, 1917–1920*. Cambridge, Mass.: Harvard University Press, 1956.

Greenberg, Louis. *The Jews in Russia*, 2 vols. New Haven: Yale University Press, 1944–1951.

Haimson, Leopold. "The Problem of Social Stability in Urban Russia, 1905–1917," *Slavic Review*, XXIII (Dec. 1964), 619–642; XXIV (Mar. 1965), 1–22.

——— *The Russian Marxists and the Origins of Bolshevism*. Cambridge, Mass.: Harvard University Press, 1955.

Herts, Y. Sh., *et al. Di Geshikhte fun Bund*, 3 vols. New York: Verlag Unser Tsait, 1960–1966.

Kantor, R. "Aleksandr III o evreiskikh pogromakh" (Alexander III on the Jewish Pogroms), *Evreiskaia letopis'* (Jewish Annals), I (1923), 149–158.

Katkov, George. *Russia 1917. The February Revolution*. London: Longmans, Green & Co. Ltd., 1967.

Keep, J. L. H. "Russian Social Democracy and the First State Duma," *Slavonic and East European Review*, XXXIV (Dec. 1955), 180–199.

——— *The Rise of Social Democracy in Russia*. Oxford: Oxford University Press, 1963.

Kindersley, Richard. *The First Russian Revisionists. A Study of 'Legal Marxism' in Russia*. Oxford: Oxford University Press, 1962.

Korolev, P. E. "V. I. Lenin i tsimmerval'dskoe ob'edinenie (fevral'–oktiabr' 1917 goda)" (V. I. Lenin and the Unification at Zimmerwald [February–October 1917]), *Voprosy istorii KPSS* (Problems of the History of the Communist Party of the Soviet Union), no. 2 (1960), 139–155.

Krasnyi-Admoni, G. Ia., ed. *Materialy dlia istorii antievreiskikh pogromov v Rossii* (Materials for the History of the Anti-Jewish Pogroms in Russia), vol. II. Petrograd, 1923.

Levin, Alfred. "The Fifth Social Democratic Congress and the Duma," *Journal of Modern History*, XI (Dec. 1939), 484–508.

——— *The Second Duma. A Study of the Social Democratic Party and the Russian Constitutional Experiment*. New Haven: Yale University Press, 1940.

Lichtheim, George. *Marxism. An Historical and Critical Study*. New York: Praeger, 1961.

Lösche, Peter. *Der Bolschewismus im Urteil der Deutschen Sozialdemokratie 1903–1920*. Berlin: Colloquium Verlag, 1967.

Martov, L. [Iu. O.], P. P. Maslov, and A. N. Potresov, eds. *Obshchestvennoe dvizhenie v Rossii v nachale XX-go veka* (The Public Movement in Russia at the Beginning of the Twentieth Century), 4 vols. St. Petersburg, 1909–1914.

Mayer, Arno J. *Political Origins of the New Diplomacy, 1917–1918*. New Haven: Yale University Press, 1959.

——— *Politics and Diplomacy of Peacemaking: Containment and Counterrevolution at Versailles, 1918–1919*. New York: Knopf, 1967.

Menitskii, I. *Revoliutsionnoe dvizhenie voennykh godov, 1914–1917* (The Revolutionary Movement of the War Years, 1914–1917). Moscow, 1925.

Meyer, Alfred G. *Leninism*. Cambridge: Harvard University Press, 1957.

——— *Marxism: The Unity of Theory and Practice*. Cambridge: Harvard University Press, 1954.

Meynell, Hildemarie. "The Stockholm Conference of 1917," *International Review of Social History*, V (nos. 1, 2, 1960), 1–25, 202–225.

Mogilevskii, S. A. *Vosstanovlenie II Internatsionale 1919–1923 g.g.* (The Restoration of the Second International 1919–1923). Leningrad, 1963.

Nettl, J. P. *Rosa Luxemburg,* 2 vols. London: Oxford University Press, 1966.

Nevskii, V., ed. *Istoriko-revoliutsionnyi sbornik* (Historical-Revolutionary Collection), vol. II. Leningrad, 1924.

Nicolaevsky, B. I. Introduction to *A. N. Potresov: Posmertnyi sbornik proizvedenii* (A. N. Potresov: Posthumous Collected Works). Paris: Imprimerie de Navarre, 1937.

[Nicolaevsky,] B. I. "Iz epokhi 'Iskry' i 'Zari' " (From the Era of "Iskra" and "Zaria"), *Katorga i ssylka,* no. 35 (1927), 7–35; no. 36 (1927), 83–100.

N—skii, B. "K istorii II s'ezda RSDRP" (On the History of the Second Congress of the RSDRP), *Katorga i ssylka,* no. 27 (1926), 125–130.

N—skii, B. "K istorii 'partii russkikh sotsialdemokratov' 1884–1886 g." (On the History of the "Party of Russian Social Democrats" 1884–1886), *Katorga i ssylka,* no. 54 (1929), 44–68.

Nicolaevsky, B. I. Lectures delivered at Harvard University during the spring of 1960. On deposit at the Russian Research Center, Harvard University.

N—skii, B. "P. B. Aksel'rod (Osnovnye cherty politicheskoi biografii)" (P. B. Axelrod [Basic Outline of a Political Biography]), *Sotsialisticheskii vestnik,* no. 15/16, Aug. 18, 1925, 3–10.

N—skii, B. "Zhiznennyi put' P. B. Aksel'roda" (The Life of P. B. Axelrod), *Sotsialisticheskii vestnik,* no. 8/9, May 3, 1928, 16–17.

Pipes, Richard. "*Narodnichestvo:* A Semantic Inquiry," *Slavic Review,* XXIII (Sept. 1964), 441–458.

——, ed. *Revolutionary Russia.* Cambridge: Harvard University Press, 1968.

—— "Russian Marxism and Its Populist Background: The Late Nineteenth Century," *Russian Review,* XIX (Oct. 1960), 316–337.

—— *Social Democracy and the St. Petersburg Labor Movement, 1885–1897.* Cambridge: Harvard University Press, 1963.

—— *Struve. Liberal on the Left, 1870–1905.* Cambridge: Harvard University Press, 1970.

—— *The Formation of the Soviet Union. Communism and Nationalism 1917–1923,* rev. ed. Cambridge: Harvard University Press, 1964.

Polevoi, Iu. Z. *Zarozhdenie marksizma v Rossii, 1883–1894 gg.* (The Origins of Marxism in Russia, 1883–1894). Moscow, 1959.

Potresov, A. N. *P. B. Aksel'rod. Sorok piat' let obshchestvennoi deiatel'nosti* (P. B. Axelrod. Forty-five Years of Public Activity). St. Petersburg, 1914.

Radkey, Oliver. *The Agrarian Foes of Bolshevism: Promise and Default of the Russian Socialist Revolutionaries February to October 1917.* New York: Columbia University Press, 1958.

Ruban, N. V. *Oktiabr'skaia revoliutsiia i krakh men'shevizma* (The October Revolution and the Collapse of Menshevism). Moscow, 1968.

Rubel, Maximilien. *Karl Marx: essai de biographie intellectuelle.* Paris: M. Rivière, 1957.

——— K. Marx, F. Engels. Ecrits sur le tsarisme et la Commune russe. Geneva: Droz, 1969.

Schapiro, Leonard. The Communist Party of the Soviet Union. London: Eyre & Spottiswoode, 1960.

——— The Origin of the Communist Autocracy. London: G. Bell and Sons, Ltd., 1955.

——— "The Role of the Jews in the Russian Revolutionary Movement," Slavonic and East European Review, XL (Dec. 1961), 148–167.

Scharlau, Winfried B., and Zbynek A. Zeman. Freibeuter der Revolution. Parvus-Helphand. Eine politische Biographie. Cologne: Verlag Wissenschaft und Politik, 1964.

Schwarz, Solomon M. The Russian Revolution of 1905: The Workers' Movement and the Formation of Bolshevism and Menshevism. Tr. Gertrude Vakar. Chicago: University of Chicago Press, 1967.

Senn, Alfred E. The Russian Revolution in Swizerland 1914–1917. Madison: University of Wisconsin Press, 1971.

Sergievskii, N. "Gruppa 'Osvobozhdenie truda' i marksistskie kruzhki" (The Group "Emancipation of Labor" and Marxist Circles), in Nevskii, ed., Istoriko-revoliutsionnyi sbornik, II, 86–167.

——— "Plekhanov i gruppa Blagoeva" (Plekhanov and the Blagoev Group), Proletarskaia revoliutsiia, no. 79 (1928), 133–151.

Temkin, Ia. G. Lenin i mezhdunarodnaia sotsial-demokratiia 1914–1917 (Lenin and International Social Democracy 1914–1917). Moscow, 1968.

Thun, Alfons. Geschichte der Revolutionären Bewegung in Russland. Leipzig, 1883.

Treadgold, Donald W. Lenin and His Rivals: The Struggle for Russia's Future, 1898–1906. New York: Praeger, 1955.

Tvardovskaia, V. A. Sotsialisticheskaia mysl' Rossii na rubezhe 1870–1880 gg. (Socialist Thought in Russia as the 1870's Gave Way to the 1880's). Moscow, 1969.

Ulam, Adam B. The Bolsheviks. The Intellectual and Political History of the Triumph of Communism in Russia. New York: Macmillan Company, 1965.

——— The Unfinished Revolution. An Essay on the Sources of Influence of Marxism and Communism. New York: Random House, 1960.

Valk, S. "G. G. Romanenko: Iz istorii 'Narodnoi voli' " (G. G. Romanenko: From the History of the "People's Will"), Katorga i ssylka, no. 48 (1928), 36–59.

Vardin, I. Revoliutsiia i men'shevizm (The Revolution and Menshevism). Moscow, 1925.

Venturi, Franco. Roots of Revolution: A History of the Populist and Socialist Movements in Nineteenth Century Russia. Tr. Francis Haskell. New York: Knopf, 1960.

Volk, S. S. Narodnaia volia, 1879–1882 (The People's Will, 1879–1882). Moscow, 1966.

Wade, Rex A. "Argonauts of Peace: The Soviet Delegation to Western Europe in the Summer of 1917," *Slavic Review*, XXVI (Sept. 1967), 453–467.

———— "Irakli Tsereteli and Siberian Zimmerwaldism," *Journal of Modern History*, XXXIX (Dec. 1967), 425–431.

———— *The Russian Search for Peace February–October 1917*. Stanford: Stanford University Press, 1969.

Wildman, Allan K. "Lenin's Battle with *Kustarnichestvo:* The *Iskra* Organization in Russia," *Slavic Review*, XXIII (Sept. 1964), 479–503.

———— *The Making of a Workers' Revolution. Russian Social Democracy, 1891–1903*. Chicago: University of Chicago Press, 1967.

———— "The Russian Intelligentsia in the 1890's," *American Slavic and East European Review*, XIX (Apr. 1960), 157–179.

Wolfe, Bertram D. *Three Who Made a Revolution. A Biographical History*. New York: Dial Press, 1948.

———— *Marxism: One Hundred Years in the Life of a Doctrine*. New York: Dial Press, 1965.

Zaleski, Eugène. *Mouvements Ouvriers et Socialistes (Chronologie et Bibliographie). La Russe*, 2 vols. Paris: Les Editions Ouvrières, 1956.

Index

Abramovich, Rafael, 207, 337, 364
Adler, Friedrich, 351–354, 364
Adler, Victor, 180, 223, 228, 241, 275, 299, 329
Advanced workers, *see* Workers' intelligentsia
Agitation, 102, 119, 127–128, 129–130, 153. *See also Ob agitatsii*
Akimov (Vladimir Makhnovets), 183–184
Alexander II, 52, 69–70, 107
Alexander III, 70
Alexandrovich, G. (Axelrod's pseudonym), 57
Alexinsky, Gregory, 346
Allied Powers, 327, 345, 356
American Federation of Labor, 350
Anan'in, E. A., 217
Anarchism, *see* Bakuninism
Anti-Semitism, 9, 69–78, 339–340
"April Theses" of 1920, 363, 365
Aptekman, O. V., 30–31, 41, 48, 49, 58, 99
Arbeiter-Zeitung, 378
Armand, Inessa, 300
Artel, 19–20, 26
Astrov (I. S. Poves), 311
Auer, Ignaz, 207
August Bloc, 295–297
Austro-German Social Democracy, 343
Avineri, Shlomo, 386
Axelrod, Alexander, 82, 234, 331–332
Axelrod, Baruch, 7–11
Axelrod, Nadezhda, 27–28, 32, 43, 82–83, 172, 232–233
Axelrod, Pavel Borisovich, 1–6; background and childhood, 7–9; education, 9–13, 16–17; character and personality, 11–12, 20, 28, 80–81, 86–87, 90, 98–99, 104–105, 165, 172, 217, 232–233,

381, 389–390; on Jewish question, 13–15, 18, 69–78, 339–340; early reformist zeal, 14–16; became revolutionary, 17–18; first revolutionary activities, 19–23, 29–30; Bakuninist, 22–24, 28, 29, 35–36, 37–41; relations with Bernstein, 25, 54, 56, 83–84, 86–88, 150–151, 318–319, 343; influenced by German Social Democracy, 25–27, 36, 46, 106–107, 136, 387; met Plekhanov, 30–32; as Westernizer, 35, 48, 80–81; writings for *Obshchina*, 35–42; created Southern Union of Russian Workers, 46; active in Chernyi peredel, 47–51; differed with Plekhanov, 51, 148–149, 187, 190, 204, 282–286, 329–330; contributor to *Vol'noe slovo*, 53–54, 65–69; relations with Kautsky, 56, 83–84, 86–88, 208–212, 224–228, 286–288, 295, 318–319, 332–333, 377–378, 381; dispute with Narodnaia volia, 56–63; conversion to Marxism, 64–68, 79–80; moral dimension to politics, 78, 146–149, 290–291, 383; poor health, 82, 86, 104, 172, 271, 289–290, 328, 330, 349, 373, 379; kefir shop, 82–86, 270–271; administrative work for GEL, 89–90, 96; *The Workers' Movement and Social Democracy*, 95–96; friendship with Trotsky, 99, 258–259, 294–296; favored workers' intelligentsia, 101–103, 235–237; editor of *Sotsial-demokrat*, 105–106; doctrine of the hegemony of the proletariat, 111, 134–136, 139, 219; conflict with Jogiches, 111–116; first impressions of Lenin, 119–121, 140; edited *Rabotnik*, 121–122, 124–125, 154; quarrels with youngsters, 122–125, 141–142, 151–156, 159–161, 162–163; opposed Economism,

Russian Research Center Studies

* Out of print.

† Publications of the Harvard Project on the Soviet Social System.
‡ Published jointly with the Center for International Affairs, Harvard University.